Punch Lines

150 Years of Humorous Writing in *Punch*

Edited by Amanda-Jane Doran

D1076513

Punch Lines

Grafton

An Imprint of HarperCollins*Publishers*

Grafton
An Imprint of HarperCollins*Publishers*,
77–85 Fulham Palace Road,
Hammersmith, London W6 8JB

Published by Grafton 1992
1   3   5   7   9   8   6   4   2

First published in Great Britain by
HarperCollins*Publishers* 1991

The Author asserts the moral right to
be identified as the author of this work

ISBN 0 586 21529 8

Set in Plantin

Printed in Great Britain by
Scotprint Ltd., Musselburgh

CONTENTS

David Thomas

FOREWORD*

THE thing about *Punch*, as everybody knows, is that it isn't as funny as it used to be. But then, as the former *Punch* editor F.C. Burnand observed almost one hundred years ago, it never was.

To which one can only remark that in the days when it actually was as funny as it used to be, it must have been pretty hilarious. Because, as the pages of this book will demonstrate, the past century and a half of continual decline, humour-wise, has been marked by a plethora of fine writing that does, at first glance, give the distinct impression of being, well, amusing to say the least. There is, as another *Punch* editor once remarked, no occupation more miserable than that of trying to make the British laugh. But the plucky band of men and women who have set out upon this unenviable task on *Punch*'s behalf, and whose efforts are collected here, have succeeded better than most.

So this is not a book that you can sit back and read in pure, contemplative silence. Depending on your personal taste, not to mention your own individual way of expressing amusement, re-actions to the prose contained herein may range from a cool, sardonic smile, through a wry chuckle and a nasally-snorted fnarr!, to a full-bodied, stomach-shaking laugh and even, God forbid, a complete 'Quick, Doris, get an ambulance, I think I'm going to explode'-style comic seizure.

Should such a potentially life-threatening assault strike your funny-bone, I can only say that you have my deepest sympathy. But don't say you haven't been warned. And, by the way, there are no refunds.

* Written in 1991, before the last issue of *Punch* appeared on 8 April 1992.

Amanda-Jane Doran

INTRODUCTION

Punch was launched in July 1841 with an enviable journalistic line-up. Douglas Jerrold, already a well-known playwright, had the sharpest satirical pen in Fleet Street and was the magazine's star writer. Other contributors included the struggling William Makepeace Thackeray, Henry Mayhew (of *London Labour and the London Poor* fame) and the poet Thomas Hood, whose poignant 'Song of the Shirt' describing the plight of exploited young needlewomen created a sensation when it appeared in *Punch* in 1843. Many other papers had refused to publish the poem before it was offered to *Punch*'s editor Mark Lemon; he had no hesitation in publishing it. The illustration accompanying it is remarkable as well, because it was the first drawing in *Punch* by the nineteen-year-old Richard Doyle, who later designed the famous *Punch* cover.

Punch's first notable and sustained success was the series of 'Mrs Caudle's Curtain Lectures' by Douglas Jerrold. They appeared over many weeks in 1845 in the irresistible form of lectures by Mrs Caudle to her errant husband as he climbed into bed. Mr Caudle was never allowed the right of reply beyond an occasional reported sigh. Thackeray's 'Book of Snobs' followed a year later and established the fortunes of the magazine and the writer, who had yet to produce his best-known novel *Vanity Fair*. Jerrold and Thackeray also set the seal on the *Punch* style of humorous writing: witty, perceptive commentary with a touch of irony but no malice.

Another *Punch* classic which is still a favourite today is *The Diary of a Nobody*, which originally appeared in the form of occasional articles by George and Weedon Grossmith in 1888 and 1889. Like many *Punch* men of this period, including the editor F.C. Burnand, the Grossmiths were involved in the theatre, and they produced the *Diary* as a parody of the Victorian obsession with writing memoirs and journals. It has since been a huge success as a book, television series and stage play. The understated, slightly surreal humour of the

Diary is unique in *Punch* at this time and looks ahead to the writing of P.G. Wodehouse and Mary Dunn. Wodehouse contributed to *Punch* over many years and his early work for the magazine is amongst his best. 'The Word in Season' is a vintage Drones Club piece and has never, as far as I am aware, been published in a collected edition.

In the 1920s and 1930s *Punch* was very much a family magazine, and some pieces – especially poems – were written with children in mind. A.A. Milne had started writing for the magazine as early as 1906 and had developed a deceptively easy light and whimsical style which was as popular with the public as it was with the editor. Soon he himself became assistant editor, and it was on the staff of *Punch* that Milne must first have come across the staff artist E.H. Shepard, although they did not collaborate for many years. After the First World War Milne did not return to the staff of *Punch* but concentrated on a successful career writing stage comedies and occasional journalistic pieces. It was not until 1924 that the first poems in the series 'When We Were Very Young' appeared in *Punch*, illustrated by E.H. Shepard, and one of the most famous writer/illustrator partnerships was born.

Molesworth was another *Punch* creation who was equally loved by adults and children. He appeared on the scene in 1939, but later achieved even greater popularity in book form with the added brilliance of Ronald Searle's illustrations.

My own favourites from this particular golden age of *Punch* writing are the 'Memoirs of Mipsie', written by Mary Dunn. These portray the extraordinary adventures of a gold-digging minor aristocrat as she travels the world in search of ever richer husbands and admirers, recounted in adoring naïvety by her sister Lady Addle, who also contributed occasional pieces about the War Effort and life at Bengers with her drink-sodden husband Lord Addle of Eigg.

1066 and All That was another *Punch* classic from the thirties and went on to become so successful that its original associations with the magazine have been all but forgotten. *Punch* was exciting to work for in the thirties and even had a Hollywood film adaptation made of an Eric Keown short story it published in 1932. 'Sir Tristram Goes West' became *The Ghost Goes West*, starring Robert Donat as the ghost.

The next notable era of *Punch* writing took place under the unpredictable editorship of Malcolm Muggeridge (1952–57). He and the literary editor Anthony Powell attracted writers of the calibre of

John Betjeman, Graham Greene and Stevie Smith, who share the lightness of touch that characterises the best of *Punch* writing. It may come as a surprise to find that some of Robert Graves's and Stephen Spender's finest poetry first appeared in the magazine.

Back in the mainstream of *Punch* humorous writing with Bernard Hollowood at the helm, old favourites like Basil Boothroyd and R.G.G. Price appear alongside celebrities like Noël Coward. In many ways the great *Punch* writers of recent times, such as Alan Coren, who could write a witty, sparkling piece about anything or parody any style from Chaucer to Hemingway, belong to a much broader *Punch* tradition. With Miles Kington likewise, there is an underlying zest and fun that I can only describe as 'Punchiness' ...

George Grossmith

THE DIARY OF A NOBODY*

MY dear wife CARRIE and I have just been a week in our new house, 'The Laurels', Brickfield Terrace, Holloway – a nice six-roomed residence, not counting basement with a front breakfast-parlour. We have a little front garden, and there is a flight of ten steps up to the front door; which, by the bye, we keep locked with the chain up. CUMMINGS, GOWING, and our other intimate friends always come to the little side-entrance, which saves the servant the trouble of going up to the front door, thereby taking her from her work. We have a nice little back garden which runs down to the railway. We were rather afraid of the noise of the trains at first, but the landlord said we should not notice them after a bit, and took £2 off the rent. He was certainly right, and beyond the cracking of the garden wall at the bottom, we have suffered no inconvenience.

After my work in the City, I like to be at home. What's the good of a home, if you are never in it. 'Home, Sweet Home' – that's my motto. I am always in of an evening. Our old friend GOWING may ask us to drop in *sans cérémonie*; so may CUMMINGS, who lives opposite. My dear wife CAROLINE and I are pleased to see them if they like to drop in on us. But CARRIE and I can manage to pass our evenings together without friends. There is always something to be done. A tin-tack here, a Venetian blind to put straight, a fan to nail up, or part of a carpet to nail down – all of which I can do with my pipe in my mouth; while CARRIE is not above putting a button on a shirt, mending a pillow-case, or practising the '*Maiden's Prayer*' on our new Cottage Piano (on the three years' system), manufactured by W. BILKSON (in small letters), from COLLARD AND COLLARD (in very large letters). Now for my diary:

* As everybody who is anybody is publishing Reminiscences, Diaries, Notes, Autobiographies, and Recollections, we are sincerely grateful to 'A Nobody' for permitting us to add to the historic collection. – ED.

April 3. – Tradesmen called for custom, and I promised FARMER-SON, the Ironmonger, to give him a turn if I wanted any nails, or tools. By the bye, that reminds me there is no key to our bedroom door. Dear friend GOWING dropped in, but wouldn't stay, saying there was an infernal smell of paint.

April 4. – Tradesmen still calling, CARRIE being out, I arranged to deal with BIRKS, who seemed a civil Butcher with a nice clean shop. Ordered a shoulder of mutton for tomorrow to give him a trial. CARRIE arranged with DORSET, the Butterman, and ordered a pound of fresh butter, and a pound and a half of salt ditto, for kitchen, and a shilling's worth of eggs. In the evening, CUMMINGS unexpectedly dropped in to show me a meerschaum pipe he had won in a raffle in the City, and told me to handle it carefully, as it would spoil the colouring if the hand was moist. He said he wouldn't stay, as he didn't care much for the smell of the paint, and fell over the scraper as he went out. Must get the scraper removed, or else I shall get into a *scrape*. I don't often make jokes.

April 5. – Two legs of mutton arrived, CARRIE having arranged with another butcher without consulting me. GOWING called, and fell over scraper coming in. *Must* get that scraper removed.

April 6. – Eggs for breakfast simply shocking; sent them back to DORSET with my compliments, and he needn't call any more for orders. Couldn't find umbrella, and though it was pouring with rain, had to go without it. SARAH said Mr GOWING must have took it by mistake last night, as there was a stick in the 'All that didn't belong to nobody. In the evening, hearing someone talking in a loud voice to the servant in the downstairs Hall, went out to see who it was, and was surprised to find it was DORSET, the butterman, who was both drunk and offensive. DORSET, on seeing me, said, 'He would be hanged if he would ever serve City Clerks any more, the game wasn't worth the candle.' I restrained my feelings, and quietly remarked 'that I thought it was *possible* for a City Clerk to be a *Gentleman*.' He replied, 'He was very glad to hear it, and wanted to know whether I had ever come across one, for *he* hadn't.' He left the house, slamming the door after him, which extinguished the fan-light, and I heard him fall over the scraper, which made me feel glad I hadn't removed it. When he had gone, I thought of a splendid answer I ought to have given him. However, I will keep it for another occasion.

April 7. – Being Saturday, I look forward to getting home early, and putting a few things straight; but two of our principals at the office were absent through illness, and I did not get home till seven. Found DORSET waiting. He had been three times during the day to apologise for his conduct last night. He said he was unable to take his Bank Holiday last Monday, and took it last night instead. He begged me to accept his apology, and a pound of fresh butter. He seems, after all, a decent sort of fellow, so I gave him an order for some fresh eggs.

April 8, Sunday. – After church, the Curate came back with us. I sent CARRIE in to open front door, which we do not use except on special occasions. She could not get it open, and, after all my display, I had to take the Curate (whose name, by the bye, I did not catch) round the side-entrance. He caught his foot in the scraper, and tore the bottom of his trousers. Most annoying, as CARRIE could not well offer to repair them on a Sunday. After dinner went to sleep. Took a walk round the garden, and discovered a beautiful spot for sowing mustard and cress, and radishes. Went to church again in the evening; walked back with the Curate. CARRIE noticed he had got on the same pair of trousers – only repaired.

May 1888

John Betjeman

THOUGHTS ON THE DIARY OF A NOBODY

THE Pooters walked to Watney Lodge
  One Sunday morning hot and still
Where public footpaths used to dodge
  Round elms and oaks to Muswell Hill.

That burning buttercuppy day
  The local dogs were curled in sleep,
The writing trunks of flowery May
  Were polished by the sides of sheep.

And only footsteps in a lane
  And birdsong broke the silence round
And chuffs of the Great Northern train
  For Alexandra Palace bound.

The Watney Lodge I seem to see
  Is gabled gothic, hard and red,
With here a monkey puzzle tree
  And there a round geranium bed.

Each mansion, each new-planted pine,
  Each short and ostentatious drive
Meant Morning Prayer and beef and wine
  And Queen Victoria alive.

Dear Charles and Carrie, I am sure,
  Despite that awkward Sunday dinner,
Your lives were good – and more secure
  Than ours at cocktail time in Pinner.

May 1955

Stephen Pile

OUT OF FARM'S WAY

WELCOME, oh fog and smut. Hello, crowds and sweet pollution. Come, pretty traffic, let me kiss thee. I have left rural England for ever (and I mean *for ever*. In future I don't even want to see it through a train window. I shall wrestle with other passengers to pull the blinds down).

On the day we left Miles Kington rang. 'You sound euphoric,' he said. 'Your wife sounds very euphoric.' She was singing and howling and practically hysterical with the joy of it. Miles has just moved from London to Limpley Stoke, a move that would stagger Italian farmers (they won't even live on their farms because it is so boring. They prefer to commute out from Florence). He said that it was horses for courses. 'Some people like knitting. Others like ...' No, no, hold it there. I am a friend and fan of Mr Kington, but I have to put my foot down here: the countryside is nothing whatever like knitting.

People do not spend their whole lives dreaming about throwing in their jobs and leaving London to knit. There are not idyllic and seductive pictures of knitting on every advert, label and wrapper. We are not sold the idea day after day that knitting is somehow more pure, good, real and wholesome than our normal town life.

An idealized version of the countryside is sold to us up hill and down dale at every possible moment. And what is the result? Throughout world history migration has always been from the country to the town and for very good reasons. (The Samaritans have two-and-a-half times more calls from the rural than the urban population.) But now for the first time ever millions are going in the opposite direction. Are they mad?

And now you will look at me and say, 'Well, you're a rational man. You knew the countryside was a bunch of pesticide-sodden fields joined together by motorways and subject to an everlasting planning ruction, a tree-filled suburbia and backdrop for estate agency where nothing of interest has happened since the Creation. So why did you go?'

Ah, well, now we come to the main thrust and point. Blow the trumpets. Turn the spotlight: *J'accuse Country Living*. Like the Moonies, this glossy magazine leads perfectly sane middle-class people to behave in staggering ways. For years I read this publication with its roses over the door, its beautiful young couples seen in their expensively renovated homes and its never-ending columns by Brian Redhead. Mr Redhead looks like every Morris dancer you have ever seen, wittering on about preserving hedgehogs and saving absolutely everything in sight.

'The Aga is a way of life,' the magazine said and I believed it. 'Happiness is not possible without exposed beams.' Oh, I remember all the articles. 'Should one buy a paddock?' by Caroline McGhee (yes, one should). 'Give your child a perfect country childhood' by Libby Purves. How to buy a pony. Entertaining the village. Carefree cooking. Making the most of your porch. Ragging and rolling till you're sick of it. Oh how we laughed.

Then one day we had a baby and years of brainwashing took effect. The paddock factor seized us by the throat. In our mind's eye apple-cheeked infants ran in past the roses along the Aga underneath the dried flowers and up to the stripped pine table to eat home-baked carefree cakes. So off we set to Upper Podley (I have changed the name – just slightly – to protect the guilty. The innocent need no protection). And what did we find?

For a start, in rural England there are more media folk than milk churns. One of the most distressing features of *Country Living* magazine is the regular appearance in it of Paul Heiney dressed like an escaped extra from *Far From The Madding Crowd*. He is always in there telling us about how he breeds horses or grows mangel-wurzels (no, really). And every time he is dressed in period boots, a collarless shirt, chunky cord trousers and a check waistcoat with a watch chain. Do they send up a team of wardrobe assistants or does he actually walk round Suffolk dressed like this? And who is he kidding? We all know he is a television presenter and Electricity Board advertiser, not Gabriel Archer.

In the bookshops I notice a new work entitled *Bel Mooney's Somerset*. Ms Mooney was born in Liverpool and has spent her working life on London newspapers. I have spent hours gossiping with this dear woman in the office and we have even been out for lunch. Not once during this whole period did she ever so much as mention Somerset. She always seemed to be staying in her London flat to get away from it. Why hasn't she written a book called *Bel Mooney's London Flat*? It would be much more to the point.

All of these newly rural journalists contribute to *Country Living*'s 'Scenes From A Provincial Life' column, dealing with their first days and hours surrounded by rural bliss. In it they always meet the bluff farmer next door who is full of wisdom. A year later they are writing large features entitled 'My Norfolk', saying how their beloved county is under threat from developers and road builders.

Of course, the only reason they are having this 'idyllic' life and are boring the rest of us to tears with the details is because they can roar up and down the motorway to work in London at the drop of a hat. How many trees were chopped down, farms ruined and villages blighted so that Brian Redhead can get to Broadcasting House for six o'clock on Monday morning?

In fact, rural England has been dying for as long as anyone can remember. William Cobbett was the first to spot it in *Rural Rides*. It was dying because of the Enclosures Act. Then it died when the railways opened and it died when the railways closed. It died when everybody left and it died when everybody came back. But the dying had to stop and rigor mortis finally set in between 1984 and 1990.

In the early 1980s – before *Country Living* came into existence – you could still pay 40p at the village hall to see the Podley Players, a bold amateur troupe, give a generous selection of a playwright's lines, occasionally in the order which he intended. These fine actors were not shackled by a script. They saw it as a springboard, a point of reference during a long night, a skeleton on which to hang jokes of their own or the ad libs of an evening. In the wardrobe they had a camel suit and liked to use it in every production, regardless of the play. *Hamlet* upon the battlements would not be safe from that camel.

But since 1985 the *Country Living* readers have moved in (the magazine started in 1984). The first thing they did in Podley was to hijack the drama group. Now the standard is semi-professional and you have to wear a dinner jacket for the opening night of a Harold Pinter.

The Freke Arms used to be a genuine, beat-up country pub in the village square with a glass-cased pie-warmer and no real ale at all. ('No call for it round 'ere. Locals prefer the fizzy.') But now it has been horse-brassed from top to bottom and is acclaimed annually by Egon Ronay for its caviar and borscht. Bills of £30 or £40 a head are quite common.

Every time there is a barn dance or fête the villagers (some of whom have lived here as long as six months) get out the same old hay bales. There are only six in the whole village. At Upper Podley barbecue night the hay bales are the only way of telling you're not in Sloane Square. Behold the chic rustics in their waxed Laura Ashley caped drover's coats and their Liberty scarves.

I once saw two elegant women going out for a walk. They tiptoed gingerly out of Honeypot Cottage wearing taupe cotton designer jodphurs, knee-length lace-up boots, wide-brimmed hats and floral wraparound shawls. They walked halfway across a rutted, uninteresting field, then turned round and went back in again. So bracing, darling. Nobody but nobody knows anything about rural matters. (If a foal is born in Podley half the village turns out to video the occasion. It's like a press conference for Madonna.)

In our village the only ambition of the rector is to get the congregation to call him 'Roger'. Sadly, this is the one thing they are not prepared to do. They have not spent half-a-million pounds on a house (with paddock), given their children a country childhood and spent the whole afternoon hanging dried flowers just to say 'Hello, Roger' every time they see some drip vicar. No, they want to cycle past with fresh bread in the pannier, tinkle the bell and say, 'Morning, rector, lovely day'. It is part of the rural idyll. They have paid for it.

Our experience has not been blissful at all. What is this myth that the countryside is wonderful for children? They never see an animal because they are all locked up in battery farms. They can't get into a field ('KEEP OUT') to run freely through it. My daughter just lay on the floor, sucking her thumb, bored to tears, watching Dumbo videos, because the countryside had nothing more to offer. Its facilities and rewards are nil.

And the Aga, oh yes, the Aga. It's a way of life all right, particularly in the summer. It heats the food, heats the house and heats the water. The piping heat warms the dream cottage day and night. The only problem is that between May and September, with temperatures reaching eighty degrees outside, you have to walk round stark naked with all the windows open. The kitchen is like a Burmese rubber plantation. The only alternative is to stop cooking altogether and use cold water till the winter months return. Now the greenhouse effect has left us with only a couple of hours of genuinely cold weather a year, an Aga seems a bad investment.

As for exposed beams, why doesn't *Country Living* do a feature about how you can hear every word as clear as day in the room above or below? If somebody is in bed you have to whisper in the sitting-room. If you are exchanging intimate chatter in the bedroom you might as well use a tannoy. The explanation is that the Tudors did not intend these beams to be exposed. They quite sensibly covered theirs up to retain the heat and insulate the sound. But some pioneering design nitwit in the 1940s thought it would make things look altogether older if they were exposed. And, of course, we all followed.

As if exposed beams were not enough, everything in the village is thatched, including the fitness centre which is packed full of pastel tracksuits and Nautilus equipment and peroxide blonde instructors shouting 'Do it' in time to a tape. Even the saloon bar in the Freke Arms has just been thatched. It looks like Polynesia: the hut where Gauguin died.

Christmas was a let-down. Automatic security lighting has been the death of carol singing in rural England. We set off with shepherd's lamps dangling from our crooks. (They gave no light whatsoever so we had torches in our other hand.) The moment you open a gate and start walking up the drive a light goes on in the hall. When we opened the porch door a burglar alarm went off that would raise the last six rectors.

Noise in the countryside is intolerable, not least from the shooting fraternity. On Saturday mornings business syndicates engage upon the mass slaughter of everything that moves. If you stand in the garden it sounds like the Somme. The only things that can (and do) drown out these sportsmen are the low-flying military jets which are such a feature.

I think there was a protest meeting about that. But then there was about everything: protest is now the main rural pastime. I went to one meeting at which the people who lived at the Old Schoolhouse, the Old Bakery, the Old Shop, the Old Saddlery, the Old Mill, the Old Forge and the Old Rectory got together to discuss the fact that the village community is in grave danger of dying out. (A developer wants to build 300 houses and a bus station on Snotte's Bottom Green, which they found unacceptable.)

The fact that the community has been dead from the eyeballs up and down for the past fifty years does not seem to have dawned on them. You've got more chance of contacting Dame Nellie Melba on a ouija board than seeing your neighbour. They move in, renovate the cottage, extend it to three times the original size, build a six-foot wall round the garden, switch on the burglar alarm, then go to Australia for six months ('We've got a house out there'). Furthermore, it is my view that, authentically, a bus station could only improve Snotte's Bottom Green.

Then in September they discovered that mad cow disease had been caught by mice. Oh terrific, terrific, now we've got mad mice on top of everything else.

In February we woke up to a typical winter's morning: it was baking hot and there was a breeze gusting at 120 mph. We opened the window to find that the entire forest had blown away. At this point we decided that our rural idyll was at an end.

Basically we are moving back to London so we can go out for a walk. In the countryside it is not possible to do this. All the land belongs to somebody else and you can tramp dust-filled, weary, tarmac-ed lanes all day, avoiding pantechnicons and hurtling Range Rovers, trying to find a footpath. We had to get into the car and drive along a dual carriageway for twenty minutes to reach one.

But now the nightmare is over. My children have pink cheeks for the first time in ages. We walk around the city streets with gratitude, knowing that there are theatres and crèches and parks and pools and every civilized facility known to man. But, lo and hark, a beauteous traffic jam has formed beneath my window. I must away and hug it.

April 1990

Geoffrey Willans

MOLESWORTH AND THE BATTLE OF BRITAIN

DIARY of booms, whizzes, wams, explodings and headmasters.

Oct. 30. I am called to mr Trimp (headmasters) study and all chortle they think I get the kane. Deaf master step out from behind stuffed bear and sa haha. Chiz knock on door and find Gran there chiz chiz chiz. Would rather have the kane. Also pop in uniform but only weedy kaptain so dare not show him as new bugs father a General. Gran sa molesworth 2 and me to go to Canda weedy as no bombs there. Pop and mr Trimp sa this is not allowed but Gran refuse to belive she sa she will see to it herself. Mr trimp offer pop a sherry (n.b. very like his daily tonic for the blud?) Go out and Pop have to salute new bugs father who hapned to be there but isaacs father only home guard so Pop give him stiff look. molesworth 2 assemble all new bugs and sa he haf 10000 strokes of the kane. Mr. trimp sa very like rain tomow.

Oct. 31. Strong sunshine.

Nov. 1. Grate consternation rains as deaf master called up for duty at listning post. mr trimp sa he feel there haf been some mistake. molesworth 2 hope to get shortcake biskit so bring Miss Pringle a dandelion. She sa mother nature about to sleep through winter and think dandlion intresting. Molesworth 2 sa he keen to press it in psalms of the bible about time he opned it. Have wizard game with Peason obbly obbly onker my first conker. Whizz string for record wam and hit deaf master on nut. He give conduc mark to isaacs (throwing stones).

Nov. 2. Skool pigs birthday. Give presents 3 conkers (baked) dead leafs and mars bar.

Nov. 3. Skool pig in grate pain.

Nov. 5. Weedy latin. Mr trimp sa all boys who kno gender rhimes to put up their hand. Don't know but put up hand as this frequently a good wheeze. Chiz mr Trimp ask me hem-hem but just then mighty air-rade warning all to the shelter dubble. Cheers cheers fuste decent thing the hun haf done. Deaf master give all class conduc mark for going out and fotherington-tomas blub he want to bring in his fairy cycle. Wizard dog fight messershimts crash in hundreds. All clear sound and deaf master dash into shelter he is bats.

Nov. 10. Gran write and sa vicars wife haf said that children not allowed to canada but she will only belive if she hear from prime minster himself. She do not care what the papers sa.

Nov. 14. Grate celebrations as Miss pringle and curate to be married hem-hem. Mr trimp make long speech and call on Peason to present skool fish slice. Miss Pringle blush like anything and twist handkercheif. She sa she want us kiddies not to forget our nature lessons and she will give wee prize at end of term for best raffia bag chiz. She is weedy give me merna loy every time. New bugs very

affected by miss pringles speech and fotherington-tomas ask her to
be mother to him. She sa if *very* good 5 minites longer before bed and
game of oranges lemons. Ugh. 90 boos.

Nov. 15. Isaacs start making rafia bag.

Nov. 16. New misteress come instead of miss pringle. Coo she is
just like ginger rogers with lipstick and everything. Tell this to
matron who sniff and sa she thought her very ordinary girl. She also
give me stiff dose of mixture so will not mention agane. molesworth 2
now zoom by he sa he short range bomber and haf shot down skool
pig in flames and scored direct hits on valuble objectives on deaf
masters trousis. Soon deaf master zoom by to and howls appear. Find
molesworth 2 very grave he sa he haf been shot down and he
mourning himself. He is bats.

Nov. 18. Peason come to me he sa terrible thing haf hapned he is in
love with new misteress. He is a girly so i slosh him and he slosh me.
He is a dirty roter as I haf said pax and sa no fair but he throw blotch
pellets at me. All hit deaf master so boo. Find molesworth 2 with
hand full of grass blubbing like billyo. He sa he burying himself and i
sa about time good riddance to bad rubish. fotherington-tomas is
chief mute he sa death is very beatiful so tuoogh him up. Isaacs still
working on raffia bag he sa to be bigest in the world, in moon in
space. He not certain of winning prize as he kno two new bugs
working behind closed doors.

Nov. 19. Gran write she haf called persnally on steam-ship
company and it nonsense no children can go to Canada. She sa mrs
Sturgess-green kno two who are *acktually there.*

Nov. 21. We haf wizard singing men of Harlack and minstrel boy
to the war haf gone. I sing very beatifully it bring tears to my eyes
but all sa shut-up. Later I see Peason gazing up at new misteress
window. He sa will I give her book of Beatiful Thoughts which he
haf bagged from fotherington-tomas. He sa go on o you might but
deaf master pass with flowers and take new misteress off to Cozy
Teashop hot toast yum-yum. Peason downcast and throw Beatiful
Thoughts at isaacs. Mr trimp sa no more air-rades after today.

Nov. 22. Miss latin, weedy french, algy, geog, arith and Eng.
owing to sirens.

Nov. 24. Weedy boy come who swank he haf bomb at bottom of
garden. I sa sucks at our home one came whizzing by splosh. Boy sa
they dont go splosh they go boom so hard cheddar. Then molesworth
2 spoil it who hapned to be by he sa we haf a 1000 bombs they went

like this. He get conduc mark (noise and unruly behaviour.) We all sa we votes a bomb which blow up skool but fotherington-tomas blub he sa it is so sad. He will not stop so only votes incendary bombs to burn skool and latin books. Peason then sa what about mr Oates and we are thortful. Isaacs raffia bag now 2 feet long. He thinks he haf a chance for the prize.

Nov. 25. Deaf master buy sidecar for his motorbike (significant). Tell Peason who sa it better to have loved and lost than never loved anebode and i haf face like a squashed tomato. No bombers toda chiz as I had counted on them and done no prep. Term draws on leafs fall, foopbal matches, rags and toughery. Gran send telegram to sa on no account are we to go to canada as it is not allowed.

Nov. 26. 10000000 secs to Xmas and boo to Germans.

the end.

November 1940

THREE Frenchmen and an Austrian have reached the summit of Mount Everest, close on the heels of the three West Germans from the same expedition who scaled the 29,000ft peak on Saturday night. The leader of the French group was a former minister.

John Wells
ROOM AT THE TOP

'EVERCREST' Prop. Mrs Tensing

WITH its breathtaking views, highly exclusive clientèle and pristine loveliness, 'Evercrest' has for many seasons now enjoyed worldwide renown as a beauty-spot where top people can put their feet up in uniquely nice surroundings.

Today, with growing affluence and a sense of adventure bringing dream holidays within the reach of those for whom a generation ago they might have seemed about as likely as going to the moon, 'Evercrest' is able to extend the same out-of-this-world welcome to a chosen few more.

It is often the case that a broadening of the scope *vis à vis* the clientèle has meant a subsequent collapse of standards, and everything going downhill. We at 'Evercrest' are determined that this shall not be the case *chez nous*.

We would therefore request, while extending the heartiest welcome to you to come and 'take a peek through the roof of the world' as Robert Louis Stevenson put it, that as an 'Evercrest' Camper you will kindly abide by the few but necessary rules which it has seemed reasonable for us to insist upon.

1. Kindly leave the summit of Mount Everest as you would wish to find it. It is not just there for you. Many others will be waiting to use it immediately after you and their feelings must be respected.

2. No washing of any kind, rinsing through woollens, soaking smalls or boiling of soiled linen, is to be done on the Peak. This is not

what it is there for. Adequate washing facilities are available at the various Camp Sites (Cold Water only, Tuesdays 7.30 to 8.30), and the Snow White Hand Laundry (on flat rocks above Second Cataract, ask for Mrs Thumper) collects on Fridays in rotation. It is also expressly forbidden to use the Summit Area for drying, with or without clothes-lines. Many complaints have been received from Campers taken aback at finding intimate items hanging on the sharp bit at the top and following discussions it has been decided that all activities involving personal laundry must cease forthwith.

3. It is forbidden to use transistor radios or gramophones in the area of the Peak after dusk. A selection of popular medleys will be played as per normal during the hours of darkness through the loudspeakers situated on the tall poles at the Camp Perimeters and those guilty of spoiling the quiet enjoyment of others by playing loud Classical Music etc. will be subject to on-the-spot fines and the confiscation of personal radios. Living together under the somewhat cramped conditions imposed by the Camping Area can create unpleasant friction (see the paragraphs below relating to First Aid, Fire and Ambulance Services, Riot Control and etc.) and if forbearance is not exercised on a voluntary basis then it will be enforced.

4. Children and dogs are only allowed on the lower slopes under the strictest supervision, and in the Summit Area they must be kept on a lead at all times. This precaution is dictated only by common sense. Both toddlers and pets can easily become lost in dense crowds, particularly when physical movement for adults is very restricted, and the responsibilities of 'Evercrest' Leisure Services Ltd (Nassau) do not extend to combing the surrounding valleys for runaways.

5. Campers are required to take all litter away with them. The dropping of lolly sticks, plastic cups, extruded polystyrene picnic packs, vandalised hot drink dispensers, sections of metal fencing etc., down the Western Cwm, a purpose for which it was not intended, has in the past led to many unpleasant fatalities among those waiting below, and can cause serious blockages to an already very overloaded system.

6. Campers are asked kindly to refrain from plugging electric razors, vibrators, hair-dryers etc. into the fairy-light circuit at the top of the mountain. Mr Tensing's father is not by any means as young as he was, and as Chief Technical Operative in charge of Electrical Maintenance it is not right that he should be got out of bed several times a night, as was often the case until recently, to walk all

the way up to the summit in order to replace a fuse.

7. 'Queuing' is a feature of life generally accepted with a wry grin by seasoned campers, but discipline is vital if any progress at all is to be maintained towards the Summit. All busking, whether it be in the form of tap-dancing, singing to guitar accompaniment, or extempore public speaking directed against the management, is expressly forbidden and is punishable in extreme cases with summary execution. Panic is an ugly spectacle at the best of times, and among tightly packed crowds on an icy and in some cases sharply sloping surface it can be very disagreeable indeed. Parties are required to wear uniform jerkins in the colour of their Camp, which facilitates the marshalling of queues, always a slow business and one requiring a high measure of cooperation from Campers, especially in sub-zero temperatures. These jerkins will be found to have a number on the front, to prevent 'queue-barging', and a circular target motif on the back to assist in crowd control.

8. Emergencies arise in the best-regulated Camps: hysteria has been known to break out in the queues, and there have been regrettable instances of Campers attempting to make their escape by tobogganing over the heads of fellow-Campers on tin trays, disguising themselves in fur coats and announcing themselves to be Abominable Snowmen, or merely attacking one of the Marshals. Should such an emergency arise, Campers should inform the nearest Marshal if he is not already aware of it, and he will sound the alarm – a high whooping siren – which will alert the Civilian Emergency Services. Campers will then be sprayed by helicopter for their own protection with a paralysing gas until the emergency is over.

And now, enjoy the holiday of a lifetime!

October 1978

Auberon Waugh
ME AND MY JUNTA

NOTHING but the most acute discomfort in the personal circumstances of my life would ever persuade me to assume power, and my purpose in doing so would be not so much to restructure society as to remove myself from those elements in it which were causing me distress. This is the invariable advice I give to those who, for one reason or another, wish to restructure society. No good ever comes of trying to impose one's wishes on other people. The great thing is to avoid unpleasantness. The assumption of supreme power may seem an extreme way to set about this, and is certainly not something to be undertaken until all other remedies have failed.

Since my purpose in assuming power is simply to retire to a little court of beautiful, clever, kind and funny people, my main objective, when in power, would be to consolidate my position. This new Versailles might be set up in Hampton Court Palace, but more likely in my present roomy abode in West Somerset where you meet a better class of person, generally speaking, than in the London area. We need not concern ourselves here with the mechanics of assuming power. I imagine it involves no more than informing as many people as possible that you have assumed it. If one persistently makes oneself disagreeable enough to enough people, one can usually get one's way in this country. Serious opponents will have to be overcome by pretending to agree with them wholeheartedly, asking them to lunch and poisoning them. As I say, the assumption of power is not something to be undertaken except under extreme provocation.

The consolidation of this power might be more difficult. There is no point in assuming power for a few years and then ending upside down on a petrol pump. I expect at very least to found a dynasty, and my eldest son is still only ten, although making good progress in maths, French and the violin. Since nobody can govern in Britain nowadays without the consent of the working class, the only way round is to recognise the power of organised labour and contain it within a Constitution. Organised labour would constitute a second Chamber with powers of delay or, ultimately, veto on any domestic proposals I might make. This need not worry me in the least as I do not intend to make any. In exchange for this position of enormous privilege and power as the centre of Government, organised labour will be required to make two concessions: (1) power workers and key workers in certain industries should 'sell' their right to strike as in France, in exchange for a fixed and absurdly high multiple of the average national wage; (2) strikers would only be permitted to picket their own place of work, and nobody who did not work there would be permitted to picket it. Army and police would be kept fanatically loyal by presents of whisky, opium and Mars Bars.

There would be no need for me to take any steps to solve our balance of payments crisis since the logic of the situation demands it must solve itself. After Arab oil is exhausted and North Sea oil has replaced it, and after we have repudiated the Middle Eastern currency mountain and nationalised Arab investments in this country, it follows as night follows day that international payments will have to be settled in gold, around which every currency (including the dollar, but probably not the Eurodollar which will have been repudiated, too) can float to its heart's content. I might ask Peter Jay to decide how much money should be printed from time to time (if he would like to join my Junta) as he seems to be interested in this sort of thing, but I can't believe it makes much difference. Perhaps I could persuade him to print rather less before my summer holidays every year so that I will get a reasonable rate of exchange in French restaurants.

For the most part, then, I would be a rather low-profile dictator. Freedom of speech would be absolute except in times of war, when nobody would be allowed to insult the Dictator. In times of peace, a large part of the Dictator's role would be as a sort of national Aunt Sally, a symbol on which its citizens could vent their frustration and a release for all the energies which they at present waste on complaining about their old age pensions. I would spend nearly all my time in my palace at Combe Florey, dancing reels, dallying with ladies-in-waiting, eating, drinking and listening to the best things our civilisation has to offer in the way of food, wine and music, and making satirical jokes about the day's news when in the mood. Occasionally, I should emerge on the nation's television sets to make important pronouncements on burning issues of the day – football, hooliganism or new developments in the war with Sweden. My material for these pronouncements would come from the morning's leading article in *The Times*, which few people ever read.

Oh yes, I had forgotten to mention my war with Sweden. This would be my first and only foreign policy initiative, to declare war on Sweden within a few days of coming to power. It would be planned to last a hundred years, just like the Hundred Years War, with occasional breaks for refreshment, and would be the most boring war in history, with no causes, no consequences, no heroic action and no great national leaders. In fact, nobody would ever do anything about the war, except hurl abuse and blood-curdling threats at the other side over the wireless. No troops would ever leave our shores for

Sweden, and it seems most unlikely that the Swedes would attempt what Napoleon and Hitler failed to do and invade England. Citizens of the two belligerent countries who met each other on neutral ground would pointedly look the other way, and from time to time I would appear on television and announce I was seriously thinking of resorting to germ warfare, or using the ultimate deterrent.

My reason for this exercise would be partly that I have always found Swedes – with only one exception – the most tiresome people; partly that they are a smaller nation than we are and also rather unaggressive and so would probably fall in with my schemes – I would never try this policy on the Irish, for instance. But most of all it is to instil the spirit of national unity and self-sacrifice which only comes about, for some reason, in wartime, and which is so essential to our country in its present dilemma. Nobody would complain, everybody would set about his daily task, be it never so humble, with the dogged determination to win through which has made Britain what it is.

From time to time, as I have said, I would declare a truce, in the course of which everyone would be free to insult me. As soon as anyone said anything really wounding, however – like I was getting too fat – I would blow my whistle and announce that the war had started up again.

There, then, would be the general pattern of my rule. Of course, things like law and order would have to go on. If violent crime got out of hand I would equip a remote island in the Outer Hebrides with concrete bunkers, and condemn violent criminals to live there for the rest of their lives. They would be completely unsurveyed, free to murder each other or commit any atrocities against each other that they liked. The only surveillance would be from a coastguard station on a neighbouring island, to make sure that nobody ever escaped, but nobody would ever land there, except heavily armed detachments of marines to drop new prisoners. There would be no medical attention, no chaplain (unless some doctor or clergyman happened to be a prisoner), none of the comforts of civilisation unless they improvised them and no contact with the outside world except at Christmas, when a helicopter would drop plum puddings on them from a great height, the gift of some charitable foundation.

No doubt there are many things which need to be done to improve Britain. When I was young and foolish I used to play with all sorts of radical ideas, like abolishing the public schools, declaring primogeniture illegal, getting the unemployed to pull down unsightly modern buildings, forbidding the use of transistor wirelesses in public, abolishing private property, imposing a large tax on budgerigars. But my sad conclusion, in maturity, is that any attempt to improve things for other people usually ends by making it worse. If people can't improve things for themselves, they must just learn to live in an imperfect world.

As I say, I hope it will never come to this. The only precaution I have taken is to lay in large supplies of Paraquat. I earnestly hope I shall never have to use it. Nowadays whenever I shut the great oak gates of my gatehouse, I have the illusion that I am already Dictator of Britain, as I described. Just as long as nobody does anything to disturb that happy illusion ...

October 1974

W.C. Sellar and R.J. Yeatman
1066 AND ALL THAT

[*Being extracts from a forthcoming History of England. (Absit OMAN.)*]

HENRY V.   AN IDEAL KING

ON the death of HENRY IV Part II, his son, Prince HAL, who had won all English hearts by his youthful pranks (such as trying on the crown while his father lay dying, and hitting a very old man called Judge GASCOIGNE), determined to justify public expectation by becoming the *Ideal English King*. He therefore decided on an immediate appearance in the Hundred Years War, making a declaration that all the treaties with France were to be regarded as dull and void.

Conditions in France were favourable to HENRY since the French King, being mad, had entrusted the command of the army to an elderly constable. After capturing some breeches at Harfleur (more than once) HENRY was held up on the road to Calais by the constable, whom he defeated at the utterly memorable battle of Agincourt (French Poitiers). He thus became ruler of Anjou, Menju, Poilou, Maine, Touraine, Againe and Againe, and, realising that he was now too famous to live long, expired at the ideal moment.

HENRY VI.   A VERY SMALL KING

The next King, HENRY VI, was only one year old and was thus rather a weak King. When he grew up, however, he was such a Good Man that he was considered a saint, or alternatively (especially by the Barons) an imbecile.

THE WARS OF THE ROSES

Noticing suddenly that the Middle Ages were coming to an end, the Barons now made a stupendous effort to revive the old amenities of Sackage, Carnage and Wreckage and so stave off the TUDORS for a time. They achieved this by a very clever plan, known as the Wars of the Roses (because the Barons all picked different coloured roses in order to see which side they were on).

WARWICK THE KINGMAKER

One of the rules in the Wars of the Roses was that nobody was ever really King but that EDMUND MORTIMER ought to be: any Baron who wished to be considered King was allowed to apply at WARWICK the Kingmaker's where he was made to fill up a form, answering the following questions:

(1) Are you EDMUND MORTIMER? If not, have you got him?

(2) Have you ever been King before? If so, state how many times; also whether deposed, beheaded or died of surfeit.

(3) Are you prepared to marry MARGARET of Angoulême? If ISABELLA of Hainault preferred, give reasons. (Candidates are advised not to attempt both ladies.)

(4) Have you had the Black Death?

(5) What have you done with your mother?

(6) Do you intend to be –

    (a) A Good King.

    (b) A Bad King.

    (c) A Weak King.

(Candidates must not attempt more than one section.)

(7) How do you propose to die? (Give your answer in BLOCK CAPITALS.)

N.B. – Do not on any account attempt to write on both sides of the paper at once.

*   *   *   *   *

CAUSE OF THE TUDORS

During the Wars of the Roses the Kings became less and less memorable (sometimes even getting in the wrong order), until one of them, finding that his name was CLARENCE, had himself drowned in a spot of Malmsey wine; while the last of all even wanted to exchange his kingdom for a horse. It was therefore decided, since the STUARTS were not ready yet, to have some Welsh Kings called TUDORS (on account of their descent from OWEN GLENDOWER) who, it was hoped, would be more memorable.

The first of these Welsh Kings was HENRY VII, who defeated all other Kings and took away their roses. After the battle the crown was found hanging up in a hawthorn tree on top of a hill. This is memorable as being the only occasion on which the crown has been found after a battle hanging up in a hawthorn tree on top of a hill.

HENRY VII'S STATECRAFT

HENRY VII was a miser and very good at statecraft. He invented some extremely clever policies such as the one called Morton's Fork. This was an enormous prong with which his minister MORTON visited the rich citizens (or burglars, as they were called). If the citizen said he was poor, MORTON drove his fork in a certain distance and promised

not to take it out until the citizen paid a large sum of money to the King. As soon as this was forthcoming MORTON dismissed him, at the same time shouting 'Fork Out' so that HENRY would know the statecraft had been successful. If the burglar said he was quite rich MORTON did the same thing. It was thus a very clever policy and always succeeded, except when MORTON put the fork in too far.

LAMBERT SIMNEL AND PERKIN WARBECK

English History has always been subject to Waves of Pretenders. These have usually come in small Waves of two – an Old Pretender and a Young Pretender.

Two Pretenders who now arose were LAMBERT SIMNEL and PERKIN WARBECK, and they succeeded in confusing the issue absolutely by being so similar that some historians suggest they were really the same person (i.e., the Earl of Warbeck).

LAMBERT SIMNEL, the Young Pretender, was really (probably) himself, but cleverly pretended to be the Earl of Warbeck. HENRY VII therefore ordered him to be led through the streets of London to prove that he really was.

PERKIN WARBECK, the older and more confusing Pretender, insisted that he was himself, thus causing complete dissension till HENRY VII had him led through the streets of London to prove that he was really LAMBERT SIMNEL.

TEST PAPER
1215 TO END OF HENRY VII

1. Contract, Expand and Explode –
   (a) The Charters and Garters of the Realm.
   (b) The Old Suspender.
2. How did any one of the following differ from any other? –
   (a) HENRY IV. Part I.
   (b) HENRY IV. Part II.
3. 'The end of the closing of the second stage of the Treaty of Bretigny marks the opening of a new phase in the first stage of the termination of the Hundred Years War.' (Refute.)
4. 'Know ye not Agincourt?' (Confess.)
5. Do not draw a map of the Battle of Bannockburn, but write not more than three lines on the advantages and disadvantages of the inductive historical method with special relation to ecclesiastical litigation in the earlier Lancastrian epochs.
6. Describe in excessive detail –
   (a) The advantages of the Black Death.
   (b) The fate of the Duke of CLARENCE.
   (c) A Surfeit.

N.B. – Candidates should write on at least one side of the paper.

BLUFF KING HAL

HENRY VIII was a strong King with a very strong sense of humour and VIII wives.

In his youth HENRY was fond of playing tennis, and after his accession is believed never to have lost a set. He also invented a game called '*Bluff King Hal*', which he invited his ministers to play with him. The players were blindfolded and knelt down with their heads on a block of wood; they then guessed whom the King would marry next.

Cardinal WOLSEY, the friend of CROMWELL (not to be confused with CROMWELL), after winning on points, was disqualified by the King (who always acted as umpire) and lost. In the opinion of SHAKESPEARE (the memorable playwriter and Top Poet) his unexpected defeat was due to his failure to fling away ambition.

THE RESTORATION

HENRY wanted the POPE to give him a divorce from his first wife, KATHERINE. He wanted this because –

(*a*) He had married her a very long time ago.

(*b*) When she had a baby it turned out to be Broody Mary, and HENRY wanted a boy.

(*c*) He thought it would be a *Good Thing*.

The POPE, however, refused, and seceded with all his followers from the Church of England. This was called the Restoration.

September 1930

Muriel Spark

YOU SHOULD HAVE SEEN THE MESS

I AM now more than glad that I did not pass into the Grammar School five years ago, although it was a disappointment at the time. I was always good at English but not so good at the other subjects.

I am glad that I went to the Secondary Modern School, because it was only constructed the year before. Therefore, it was much more hygienic than the Grammar School. The Secondary Modern was light and airy, and the walls were painted with a bright, washable, gloss. One day I was sent over to the Grammar School with a note for one of the teachers, and you should have seen the mess! The corridors were dusty, and I saw dust on all the window ledges, which were chipped. I saw into one of the classrooms. It was very untidy in there.

I am also glad that I did not go to the Grammar School because of what it does to one's habits. This may appear to be a strange remark at first sight. It is a good thing to have an education behind you, and I do not believe in ignorance, but I have had certain experiences with educated people since going out into the world.

I am seventeen years of age, and left school two years ago last month. I had my A certificate for typing, so got my first job, as a junior, in a solicitor's office, and I was to start on the Monday, so along I went. They took me to the general office, where there were two senior shorthand-typists and a clerk, Mr Gresham, who was far from smart in appearance. You should have seen the mess! There was no floor-covering whatsoever, and so dusty everywhere. There were shelves all round the room, with old box files on them. They were falling to pieces and all the old papers inside them were crumpled. The worst shock of all was the teacups. It was my duty to make tea – mornings and afternoons. Miss Bewlay showed me where everything was kept. It was kept in an old orange-box, and the cups were all cracked. There were not enough saucers to go round, etc. I will not go into the facilities, but they were also far from hygienic. After three days I told Mum and she was upset, most of all about the cracked cups. We never keep a cracked cup, but throw it out, because those cracks can harbour germs. So Mum gave me my own cup to take to the office.

Then at the end of the week, when I got my salary, Mr Heygate said 'Well, Lorna, what are you going to do with your first pay?' I did not like him saying this and I nearly passed a comment, but I said 'I don't know.' He said 'What do you do in the evenings, Lorna? Do you watch Telly?' I did take this as an insult because we call it TV, and his remark made me out to be uneducated. So I did not go back to that job. Also, the desks in the general office were rickety. Dad was indignant because Mr Heygate's concern was flourishing, and he had letters after his name.

Everyone admires our flat because Mum keeps it spotless and Dad keeps doing things to it. He has done it up all over and got permission from the Council to remodernize the kitchen. I well recall the Health Visitor remarking to Mum 'You could eat off your floor, Mrs Merrifield.' It is true that you could eat your lunch off Mum's floors, and any hour of the day or night you will find every corner spick and span.

Next, I was sent by the agency to a publisher's for an interview, because of being good at English. One look was enough! My next interview was a success, and I am still at Low's Chemical Co. It is a modern block, with a quarter of an hour rest period, morning and afternoon. Mr Marwood is very smart in appearance. He is well spoken, although he has not got a university education behind him. There is special lighting over the desks, and the typewriters are latest models.

But I have met other people, of an educated type, in the past year, and it has opened my eyes. It so happened that I had to go to the doctor's house to fetch a prescription for my young brother Trevor when the epidemic was on. I rang the bell, and Mrs Darby came to the door. She was small, with fair hair, but too long, and a green maternity dress. But she was very nice to me. I had to wait in their living room, and you should have seen the state it was in! There were broken toys on the carpet, and the ash trays were full up. There were contemporary pictures on the walls, but the furniture was not contemporary but old-fashioned, with covers which were past standing up to another wash, I should say. To cut a long story short, Dr Darby and Mrs Darby have always been very kind to me, and they meant everything for the best. Dr Darby is also short and fair, and they have three children – a girl and a boy, and now a baby boy.

When I went that day for the prescription Dr Darby said to me, 'You look pale, Lorna. It's the London atmosphere. Come on a picnic with us, in the car, on Saturday.' After that I got in with the Darbys more and more. I liked them, but I did not like the mess, and it was a surprise. The children's clothes were very shabby for a doctor, and she changed them out of their school clothes when they came home from school, into those worn-out garments. Mum always kept us spotless to go out to play, and I do not like to say it, but those Darby children frequently looked like the Leary family which the Council evicted from our block as they were far from house-proud.

They had an idea to make a match for me with a chemist's assistant, but he was not accustomed to those little extras that I was. There were plenty of boys at the office, but I will say this for the Darbys, they had lots of friends coming and going, and they had interesting conversation, although sometimes it gave me a surprise, and I did not know where to look. But it made a comparison with the boys at the office, less educated in their conversation.

Mavis did not go away to have her baby, but would have it at home in their double bed, as they did not have twin beds, although he was a doctor. A girl I knew in our block was engaged but was let down, and even she had her baby in the labour ward. I was sure the bedroom was not hygienic for having a baby but I did not mention it.

One day, after the baby boy came along, they took me in the car to the country to see Jim's mother. (I called him Jim by then.) The baby was put in a folding cot at the back of the car. He began to cry and, without a word of a lie, Jim said to him over his shoulder 'Oh shut your gob, you little brute.' I did not know what to do and Mavis was smoking a cigarette. Dad would not dream of saying such a thing to Trevor or I. When we arrived at Jim's mother's place Jim said 'It's a fourteenth-century cottage, Lorna.' I could well believe it. It was very cracked and old, and it made one wonder how Jim could let his old mother live in this tumbledown cottage as he was so good to everyone else. I said to the old Mrs Darby, 'Are you going to be re-housed?' but she did not understand this, and I explained how you have to apply to the Council and keep at them. But it was funny that the Council had not done something already when they go round condemning. Then old Mrs Darby said 'My dear, I shall be re-housed in the grave.' I did not know where to look. The facilities were outside, through the garden.

One Saturday afternoon they took me to the films. It was the Curzon, and afterwards we went to a flat in Curzon Street. It was a clean block, I will say that, and there were good carpets at the entrance. The couple had contemporary furniture, and they also spoke about music, but there was no Welfare Centre to the flats, where tenants could go for social intercourse, advice and guidance. But they were well-spoken and I met Willy Morley who was an artist. Willy sat beside me and we had a drink. He was young, dark, with a dark shirt, so one could not see right away if he was clean. Soon after this Jim said to me 'Willy wants to paint you, Lorna. But you'd better ask your Mum.' Mum said it was all right if he was a friend of the Darbys.

I can honestly say that Willy's place was the most unhygienic place I have seen in my life. He said I had an unusual type of beauty which he must capture. This was when we came back to his place from the restaurant. The light was very low voltage, but I could see the bed was not made, and the sheets were far from clean. He said he must paint me, but I told Mavis I did not like to go back there. 'Don't you like Willy?' she asked. I could not deny that I liked Willy, in a way. There was something about him, I will say that. Mavis said 'I hope he hasn't been making a pass at you, Lorna.' I said he had not done so, because he did not attempt to go to the full extent. It was always unhygienic when I went to Willy's place and I told him so once, but he said 'Lorna, you are a joy.' He had a nice way, I will say that. He took me out in his car, which was a good one, but dirty inside, like his place. Jim said one day, 'He has pots of money, Lorna,' and Mavis said 'You might make a man of him, as he is keen on you.' They always said Willy came from a good family.

But he would not change his shirt very often or get clothes, but he went round like a tramp, lending people money, as I have seen with my own eyes. His place was always in a state with the empty bottles and laundry in the corner. He gave me several gifts over the period, which I took, as he would have only given it away, but I will say this, he never tried to go to the full extent. He never painted my portrait, as he was painting fruit on a table all that time, and they said his pictures were marvellous, and thought Willy and I were getting married.

One night when I went home I was upset as usual after Willy's place. Mum and Dad had gone to bed and I looked round our kitchen which is done in primrose and white. Then I went into the living room, where Dad has done one wall in a patterned paper, deep rose and white, and the other walls pale rose, with white woodwork. The suite is new, and Mum keeps everything beautiful. So it came to me, all of a sudden, what a fool I was going with Willy. I agree to equality, but as to me marrying Willy, as I said to Mavis, when I recall his place and the good carpet gone greasy, not to mention the paint oozing out of the tubes, I think it would break my heart to sink so low.

May 1958

Jeffrey Bernard
ROGUE MALE

AFTER quite a few years of being married to someone or other, it is quite a pleasant change to be on the outside and looking in. In my present role as roving dinner guest – friends are either pimping for me or I am making up the right number – I am the fly on the wall of marriage and the spy behind the net curtain.

Of course, I get to eat some very good meals this way but it really is rather depressing to listen to and watch the wheels fall off mine hosts as the evenings wear on. The dangerous game of 'home truths' is usually begun with the cheese or, in the case of more down-market households, with the guttering of the candles and the circulation of After Eights. The antagonists open fire with the coffee and by the time the brandy arrives, when the verbal flak is reaching a crescendo, I find myself wondering just how the hell they've managed to stay married to each other for twenty years, never mind why on earth they got married in the first place.

Last week I went to dinner with a literary couple who had invited half the literati in London to their table. Most of the women there had written books or had novels under wraps and their husbands, even if they weren't quite in the Nobel Prize for Literature bracket, had at least appeared on *Call My Bluff* or *Start the Week*. Inevitably, the conversation got around to sex, although everybody called it 'personal relationships'. That started it, just like a referee calling two fighters into the middle of the ring and telling them that he wanted a good, clean fight without a chance in hell of getting one.

Then, my host suddenly said to his wife, Cynthia, 'Of course, the trouble with women is that they have no imagination, which is why they've achieved so little.'

Stifled screams from the ladies and our hostess counter-punched with, 'Funny you should say that, darling – after all, you've achieved so much, we can't even pay the rates.' Then, turning to me – and it's awful being picked out to be the middleman – she said, 'D'you know, Jeffrey, marriage is so disgusting, I really wish I was dead.'

I protested feebly, mumbling something about what a dreadful loss she would be to all of us, and she said, 'No, I really mean it. I want to die.' She took another gulp of brandy and lit a cigarette.

'Yes, I look forward to it. Just think of all that peace. Anyway, I've done everything. What's left? I've written books, had children, been in love, not for bloody years I might add,' she said, looking daggers at her husband, 'and I don't really see anything else to do. Yes, I'd really like to die.'

There isn't a lot you can say to that, so I poured myself another drink.

'If you really wanted to die,' said her husband, 'then you would.'

'Not just to please you, you bastard, I wouldn't.' Then, turning her venomous eyes away from her husband, she said to me, 'You have to admit, Jeff, that men are pretty bloody disgusting, aren't they?'

'Well, it's about fifty-fifty,' I said nervously.

'Why are we so disgusting to you?' ventured an academic who had once appeared on *Down Your Way*.

'Well, for a start, you're all so bloody selfish; secondly, I loathe the way you can go to bed with someone without being in love with them, although, mind you, I bloody well could *now*,' she said with another poisonous look at the husband, 'and, thirdly, you're all so bloody patronising. You think women can't *do* anything.'

'But of course we think you can, darling. It's just that a farmer doesn't expect much else of a chicken than that she lay eggs.'

'I've laid my last bloody egg for you, you sod, and as soon as the youngest egg, as you like to call her, leaves home, then I intend to die.'

'RIP,' he said, as she threw a piece of Camembert at him.

'Well, *I* think Cynthia's absolutely right,' said a lady cellist from Hampstead. 'I mean, let's face it, you are all complete and utter pigs, aren't you, Jeff?'

'If you say so.'

'Oh, come on. We're kinder, more gentle, more loving and ...'

'But darling ...' her husband tried to interrupt.

'Shut your face, you. As I was saying, we're not called the gentle sex for nothing. Could you bring up a baby, Jeff?'

'Yes,' I said, 'and I have. Well, for three years or so, some time ago.'

'I bet he can iron shirts, too, and cook and sweep a floor,' said Cynthia's husband. I suddenly wished I had a riot shield.

'If you men are so good at cooking, then,' said Cynthia, 'why didn't you cook dinner?'

'I thought paying for it was sufficient.'

I made that forty-thirty to him. Match point and a breathless hush in the close tonight, I thought. I couldn't take a lot more and so I telephoned for a taxi. As I was leaving, Cynthia was again expressing a desire to embrace death. Her husband was detailing the defects of women. As I got into my taxi I could hear Cynthia's voice from the basement reiterating woman's war cry: 'You make me sick.'

In the morning I telephoned Cynthia to thank her for the dinner.

'Oh, I'm so glad you liked it,' she said, 'it was a lovely evening.'

'And how's the old man?' I asked.

'Fine, just fine. He's just left for work. He can be so *funny* sometimes, can't he?'

After we rang off, I wondered about that. I suppose that one of the blessings of brandy after dinner is that it does make for amnesia. Had she forgotten already that the old man was disgusting and did she no longer want fervently to die? I suppose so. I can also only suppose that women like Cynthia start every new day with a clean sheet, as it were. They are addicted to these disgusting things called husbands and the doves don't turn into shrikes until the coffee is served.

Shall I get married again? I don't think it a very good idea but, should some miracle occur and I meet Miss Right yet again, then you must all come to dinner and have a cosy chat about 'personal relationships'.

November 1985

Mary Dunn

THE MEMOIRS OF MIPSIE

By Blanche Addle of Eigg

XI – FROM RED SEA TO BLACK TREACHERY

AT Aden Mipsie left the comparative comfort of her luxury liner and boldly embarked, entirely alone save for her secretary and courier, Major Hardup, her personal maid, and the Captain and little crew of twenty, on the beautiful steam yacht which had been lent her by a friend for the remainder of her trip.

Their first objective was Uassa Land, that picturesque little colony just above Eritrea which is ruled over by a line of Merchant Princes whose traditional generosity is only equalled by their devotion to England. It was these splendid qualities which appealed to my sister and which prompted her to ask Major Hardup, whom she met on the boat, and who had had considerable experience in native parts, to arrange the tour for her. He gladly accepted, enchained by her beauty at once, and also most grateful for the generous remuneration which she offered him, for he was on half-pay with no private money, poor man. It is terrible to think there are such cases of hardship amongst British officers.

Mipsie's vivid journal describes their journey from Port Maggot on the Red Sea, up the famous Red Mite gorges to Nojoko, the capital.

'The sunrise here at four o'clock, spreading deep crimson and purple lights over the rocks, an unforgettable sight, the description of which made a deep impression on me as Major Hardup gave it at breakfast on my *crumpet* (hotel verandah) five hours later. I hastily swallowed coffee and *jim-jams* (native rolls) and caught the only train in the day, which leaves at 10 A.M. As it is too hot to travel after 10.30 we left the train at Badeg and waited for our *skivvi-bog* (procession of servants on donkeys) to catch up with us. All round us were wonderful flowering eggs, while brilliant yellow flying adders zoomed overhead. "They are attracted by your face powder," Major Hardup explained, "but are quite harmless."

'The natives will trade anything for toothpicks. We brought several thousand with us and purchased a good supply of *nitties* – a kind of banana-shaped pineapple, and plentiful *oompahs* – a delicious pineapple, looking and tasting exactly like a banana. Also emu's eggs and several bottles of *tick* – the native fiery wine which the better caste tribes drink before killing their grandmothers – a regular custom on Friday nights at sundown. At Skrewi we were fortunate enough to see a native wedding, which was most interesting. The bride is entirely swathed in pampas gauze, while the bridegroom is clothed only in gourds, which are hung round him in such profusion that he can hardly move. While the villagers beat the *chummi* (a rude kind of gong) the local maidens slowly unwind the veiling, and the bridegroom's friends, in a kind of leaping dance, remove his gourds one by one. It was thrilling to watch, and I found myself longing to take part, but Major Hardup said it would be a riot, so firmly removed me, alas, before the ceremony was completed. I was told that the bride is usually so scratched by the pampas gauze and the bridegroom so bruised by the gourds that they are frequently unable to meet again for weeks. Divorce is very prevalent in Uassa Land.'

At Nojoko Mipsie was met by Ras Bollinogud's servants and conducted with great ceremony to his palace. Here a bitter disappointment awaited her. Ever since she had arrived in Uassa she had been under the protection of the Prince, who had frequently intimated, in letters and through his agents, that a gift worthy of an English duchess awaited her at the capital. On the palace steps she was handed a paper listing 'the gift': '200 fat black sheep, 100 yonghi (the local blue oxen, born mad, considered a great delicacy when eaten raw), 50 alligators' hides, 1 cwt. of incense and 10 jars of snake oil.' It was, from Ras Bollinogud's viewpoint, doubtless the most generous present, but to my sister it was naturally a blow, she having expected something more portable and utilitarian, like precious stones or gold. However, with her unfailing good manners she thanked the Prince for his favour – then, with one of her impetuous gestures of reckless generosity, she turned to Major Hardup. 'These are for you,' she said in French. 'Your salary for the trip.' So overcome was her secretary by the gift – which was of course worth many times his due – that he had to sit down and ask for brandy. Indeed, he did not completely recover his equilibrium till they had left Nojoko and were on their return journey to Port Maggot. Then suddenly, while sipping their coffee outside a little brumbar (very homely estaminet), he surprised Mipsie by springing to his feet and exclaiming, with fear in his eyes as he spoke the words: 'We must get to the coast as soon as possible. Ras Bollinogud will be furious at our leaving his gifts behind, which is considered a grave insult to a host. We are in great danger.' The warning of Ras Bollinogud's treachery came too late. When Mipsie turned her horrified gaze to the little village square behind her it was to see a crowd of natives approaching, their pokos (four-edged spears) gleaming in the sunlight, murder in their faces.

It was a terrible moment. Major Hardup, who to do him justice was ready to pay with his life for his unforgivable lapse, immediately sprang to Mipsie's side. But where blood is blue hearts are stout. She pushed him impatiently aside and, standing to her full height, faced the angry people, holding in her hand an empty envelope.

'I have here,' she said in clarion tones, 'a letter to our Foreign Secretary, Sir Edward Grey. Beside me' (and she pointed with a firm hand) 'is a pillar box. Unless you go quietly to your homes I shall post this letter, and in less than two months the entire British Army will come to my aid, and you and your wives and children will be annihilated.'

The threat worked. The fire died out of their eyes and there was a great hush over the square. Then suddenly, a handsome young Uassan sprang up beside Mipsie.

'Three cheers for the Duchess and the British Foreign Office,' he shouted – and the little town rang with loyal cries.

Thus was the situation saved by a woman's courage and the world-wide respect commanded by the British aristocracy and the British Constitution.

May 1945

James Thurber
HERE COME THE DOLPHINS

How sharper than a sermon's truth it must have been for many human beings when they learned that bottle-nosed Dolphin may, in time, succeed battle-poised Man as the master species on earth. This prophecy is implicit in the findings of those scientists who have been studying, and interviewing, dolphins in laboratories. It neither alarms nor surprises me that Nature, whose patience with our self-destructive species is giving out, may have decided to make us, if not extinct, at least a secondary power among the mammals of this improbable planet.

Clarence Day, in his *This Simian World*, prefigured, in turn, the tiger and the dog as the master species, if their evolution, instead of ours, had turned them into People. He did not think of the dolphin, that member of the whale family sometimes called, inaccurately, the porpoise or the grampus. As far back as 1933 I observed a school of dolphins (their schools increase as ours decline) romping, as we carelessly call it, alongside a cruise-ship in the South Atlantic, and something told me that here was a creature, all gaiety, charm, and intelligence, that might one day come out of the boundless deep and show us how a world can be run by creatures dedicated not to the destruction of their species but to its preservation.

We shall, alas, not be on earth to hear the lectures, and to read the reports, on Man by a disinterested intelligence equal, and perhaps superior, to our own. I should like to hear a thoughtful and brilliant dolphin cutting us down to our true size, in that far day when the much vaunted Dignity of Man becomes a footnote to history, a phrase lifted from the dusty books of human sociologists and the crumbling speeches of obliterated politicians.

Anyone, even a human being, capable of contemplation and the exercise of logic, must realize that what has been called the neurotic personality of our time is rapidly becoming psychopathic. One has but to look at and listen to those anti-Personality Cultists, Khrushchev and Castro, to identify them as the most notorious personality cultists of our era. I mourn the swift mortality of Man that will prevent him from reading *The Decline and Fall of Man* by Professor B.N. Dolphin. What I am saying will, of course, be called satire or nonsense by the Free World, and obscurantism or obfuscation by the communist world. Professor Dolphin can deal with that when the time comes.

Almost all of Man's self-praise is exaggerated and magnified by the muddled and conflicting concepts of religion, sociology, and philosophy. We are not, for instance, the most adjustable of creatures, but the most helpless and desperate, so that we have had to develop ingenuity of a high and flexible kind in order to survive. All the other creatures of earth, with the exception of those we have made dependent by domestication, are more adjusted than we are, and can, and must, get along without us. But we depend upon many of them for our existence as we depend upon vegetables. It is impossible to imagine a female seal saying to another female seal 'What a charming lady-skin! Where did you get it?' And I have just learned from a doctor friend of mine who spent six months in the Antarctic that the human being down there invariably suffers from Big Eye – that is, the inability to sleep well, or at all. And everybody knows that the penguins adjusted to their climate and that they never develop stomach ulcers since they long ago discovered a wholesome and nurturing diet, which we couldn't do even if we had another million years to live.

I cannot be there to see, but I can clearly visualize what will happen when dolphinity has replaced humanity as the primary power. I can picture the dolphins' first ambassador to Washington or to the Court of St James's coming into the presence of the President or the Prime Minister and saying with a wink and a whistle, 'Ours is a porpoiseful society. Good-bye, and sorry, and may there be a proper moaning of the bar when you, who came from out the boundless deep, return again home.'

Oh, but there is still time, gentlemen! Let's uncork the bottles, call up the ladies, exchange with our enemies the well-worn accusations of imperialistic ambitions, and lean back. Let us have our run before we are officially advised that, as Henley put it, our little job is done. And make mine a double Scotch and soda while you're at it. I have become a touch jittery myself, meditating that human marriage, whose success and failure both have helped to put us where we are, will seem, one fine century in the future, as quaint and incredible to the dolphins as the hip-bones of a dinosaur.

October 1960

R.C. Lehmann

THE ADVENTURES OF PICKLOCK HOLES

(By Cunnin Toil)

NO. VIII – PICKLOCK'S DISAPPEARANCE

NEVER in the course of a long and varied experience have I taken up my pen with a heavier heart than that which now beats mournfully within my breast. It has been my enviable lot to follow my hero, my wonderful friend, my arch-prince of detectives through many a strange and startling adventure. While he with his matchless acumen has been engaged in checking the ambitious designs of foreign despots, in unveiling to the startled gaze of statesmen the criminal plots of secret societies, in foiling coalitions, in unravelling the tangled skeins of murder-conspiracies, in bringing dark deeds of

crime relentlessly home to ducal perpetrators, in restoring jewels to
bereaved countesses, in convicting baronets of burglary, and generally in putting local constabularies in every part of the civilised
world to shame; while he, I say, has been engaged in these and similar
undertakings I have been ever at his side, the faithful foil, the
admiring companion, the irremovable fly on the wheel of his world-
renowned exploits. And now that fate has taken him from me I scarce
know whither I am to turn. Surely never again shall I meet in this
world so wise, so cold, so impassive, so friendly a sleuth-hound of
detection; never again shall I behold another upon whom my candid
flow of irrepressible wonder will pour itself with so small an effect.

'POTSON,' he would often say to me when I had congratulated him
in my impulsive way upon some master-stroke of cunning strategy;
'POTSON, you are not absolutely clever, but, personally, I do not care
for very clever men. They are always wanting to outwit one. The task
of course is hopeless, but to counteract it one has to waste valuable
time. But you have about you a comfortable non-cleverness, always
delightfully ready to burst into admiration whenever I give you an
opportunity. POTSON, I like you.'

'HOLES,' I replied, overcome by emotion, 'you are an extraordinary
fellow. I would willingly follow you to the ends of the world.'

I remember this little conversation all the more distinctly because,
taking place as it did in an unfrequented thoroughfare of the
Bloomsbury district, HOLES was immediately afterwards able to infer
from a large stain of milk upon the pavement in front of one of the
houses that a bald and fraudulent solicitor was at that moment lying
in a fit on the floor of the dining-room. This was how he proved it:

'Milk,' he said, 'has been spilt here. To spill milk is a blunder
which is often worse than, and, therefore, *at least* equal to, a crime.
We have therefore got the certainty of a crime. A solicitor has to deal
with crimes. We thus get the fact that we have here a solicitor who has
committed a crime. Now fraud is a crime. Therefore, substituting
fraud for crime we obtain a solicitor who has committed fraud. I said
a moment back that this solicitor was not only fraud but baldulent –'

'Pardon me,' I ventured to interrupt, 'pardon me, my dear HOLES,
you mean bald and fraudulent.'

'Of course,' he retorted, without moving a muscle; 'I said so, bald
and fraudulent. Now mark how beautifully it works out. A detected
criminal is invariably angry. This man has been detected by me. To
be angry is merely another way of saying that one has lost his hair. He

is, therefore, proved beyond possibility of doubt to be bald. With regard to the fit, the process of induction is no less delicate and convincing. A solicitor wears clothes which fit him, whether well or badly matters not. He has, therefore, a fit. Have I proved my case?'

'HOLES,' I said, 'you are a wonderful fellow.'

We informed the neighbouring policeman, but I cannot now remember if matters proceeded to a conviction. The incident, however, remains in my mind as one of the most remarkable proofs of my friend's almost superhuman powers.

And now, as I said, I have lost him, and must proceed as best I can to give some account of his disappearance. We were engaged in investigating the mysterious circumstances connected with the theft of one of our best-known public monuments. I do not care to be more precise, though some day in defence of my friend I may have to tell the story in detail. But at present the honour of a great family is involved, and I prefer to mention no names. I had noticed that HOLES had been even more taciturn than was usual with him during the course of his investigations, but at the time I attributed little importance to this. One night he came quietly into my rooms, and after removing from my coat a speck of dust, which proved, he said, that I had been assaulted by a ticket-of-leave man in Southampton Street at 5.45 that very afternoon, he sat down opposite me in an armchair. 'POTSON,' he said, 'there is something in this business which is out of the common. At every turn I encounter a hidden force. I walk in Piccadilly and am splashed with mud by a passing hansom; I turn into Regent Street, and a Music Hall singer – I knew him by his prosperous, well-fed appearance – insists on shaking hands with me. Discouraged by these accidents I stroll into Jermyn Street, when a regiment of Life-Guards charging up Bury Street all but tramples me under foot. There is more in all this than meets the eye. POTSON, I am being pursued.'

*Picklock Holes
disguised*

'But surely,' I said, 'they know you too well. Who would venture to pursue you? Would anyone venture to fly in the face of the public and of probability by tracking one who has always been himself the tracker?'

*'Dropping an H.'
From a drawing
taken on the spot.
'Picklock H.' lets
down 'Sherlock H.'
easily.*

But my words were unavailing. He insisted upon it that he was being shadowed, and left me with this impressive warning: 'If I do not return to you tomorrow before six o'clock you will know that I am somewhere else. Do not look for me in the Serpentine.'

On the following day I awaited the arrival of six o'clock with a feverish impatience. As the hour struck the door did not open, but a scrap of torn paper came fluttering down from the ceiling. I grasped it convulsively, and read these words:

'MY DEAR POTSON, – It has been a duel to the death, and both of us perished. By the kindness of my late opponent, Mr SHERLOCK HOLMES, I have been permitted to expire after him, and to use the few remaining seconds of life that remain in me in writing to you. I knew I was pursued, and I knew it was SHERLOCK who was dragging me to my doom. I have killed him, but at the penalty of my own life. If you wish to know more, do as I should have done under the circumstances. Commend me to Mrs POTSON, and believe me yours inductively, 'PICKLOCK HOLES.'

That was all. The blow was a terrible one, but when I recovered in a measure I set to work immediately to do what I thought HOLES would have done. I assumed a meditative air, I conducted chemical experiments, I despised the police, I picked up clues in unsuspected corners, I proved beggars in rags to be Cabinet Ministers in disguise – but all my efforts were fruitless. My friend's last behest is to me a sacred command. Some other – not I – may search the depths of the Serpentine and discover there the secret which I have sought in vain.*

THE END.

* We've got the very man to do it, and when either 'SHERLOCK HOLMES' or 'PICKLOCK HOLES' may be 'wanted,' we undertake to produce both or either of them. – ED.

January 1894

P.G. Wodehouse

PRINTER'S ERROR

As o'er my latest book I pored,
  Enjoying it immensely,
I suddenly exclaimed 'Good Lord!'
  And gripped the volume tensely.
'Golly!' I cried. I writhed in pain.
'They've done it on me once again!'
  And furrows creased my brow.
I'd written (which I thought quite good)
'Ruth, ripening into womanhood,
Was now a girl who knocked men flat
And frequently got whistled at,'
And some vile, careless, casual gook
Had spoiled the best thing in the book
  By printing 'not'
  (Yes, 'not,' great Scott!)
    When I had written 'now'.

On murder in the first degree
  The Law, I knew, is rigid:
Its attitude, if A kills B,
  To A is always frigid.
It counts it not a trivial slip
If on behalf of authorship
You liquidate compositors.
This kind of conduct it abhors
  And seldom will allow.

Nevertheless, I deemed it best
And in the public interest
To buy a gun, to oil it well,
Inserting what is called a shell,
  And go and pot
  With sudden shot
    This printer who had printed 'not'
    When I had written 'now'.
I tracked the bounder to his den
  Through private information:
I said: 'Good afternoon' and then
  Explained the situation:

'I'm not a fussy man,' I said.
'I smile when you put "rid" for "red"
And "bad" for "bed" and "hoad" for "head"
  And "bolge" instead of "bough".
When "wone" appears in lieu of "wine"
Or if you alter "Cohn" to "Schine",
  I never make a row.
I know how easy errors are.

But this time you have gone too far
By printing "not" when you knew what
  I really wrote was "now".
Prepare,' I said, 'to meet your God
Or, as you'd say, your Goo or Bod
  Or possibly your Gow.'

A few weeks later into court
  I came to stand my trial.
The Judge was quite a decent sort,
  He said 'Well, cocky, I'll
Be passing sentence in a jiff,
And so, my poor unhappy stiff,
If you have anything to say,
Now is the moment. Fire away.
  You have?'
      I said 'And how!
Me lud, the facts I don't dispute.
I did, I own it freely, shoot
This printer through the collar stud.
What else could I have done, me lud?
  He's printed "not" ...'
    The Judge said '*What!*
    When you had written "now"?
God bless my soul! Gadzooks!' said he.
'The blighters did that once to me.
  A dirty trick, I trow.
I hereby quash and override
The jury's verdict. Gosh!' he cried.
'Give me your hand. Yes, I insist,
You splendid fellow! Case dismissed.'
(Cheers, and a Voice 'Wow-wow!')

A statue stands against the sky,
  Lifelike and rather pretty.
'Twas recently erected by
  The P.E.N. committee.
And many a passer-by is stirred,
For on the plinth, if that's the word,
  In golden letters you may read
'This is the man who did the deed.
  His hand set to the plough,
He did not sheathe the sword, but got
A gun at great expense and shot
The human blot who'd printed "not"
  When he had written "now".
He acted with no thought of self,
Not for advancement, not for pelf,
But just because it made him hot
To think the man had printed "not"
  When he had written "now".'

Almanack 1955

Douglas Jerrold

LECTURE I
MR CAUDLE HAS LENT FIVE POUNDS TO A FRIEND

'You ought to be very rich, Mr Caudle. I wonder who'd lend you five pounds! But so it is: a wife may work and may slave! Ha, dear! the many things that might have been done with five pounds! As if people picked up money in the street! But you always were a fool, Mr Caudle! I've wanted a black satin gown these three years, and that five pounds would have pretty well bought it. But it's no matter how I go, – not at all. Everybody says I don't dress as becomes your wife – and I don't; but what's that to you, Mr Caudle! Nothing. Oh no! you can have fine feelings for everybody but those belonging to you. I wish people knew you, as I do – that's all. You like to be called liberal – and your poor family pays for it.

'All the girls want bonnets, and when they're to get 'em I can't tell. Half five pounds would have bought 'em – but now they must go without. Of course, *they* belong to you; and anybody but your own flesh and blood, Mr Caudle.

'The man called for the water-rate today; but I should like to know how people are to pay taxes, who throw away five pounds to every fellow that asks them.

'Perhaps you don't know that Jack, this morning, knocked his shuttle-cock through his bedroom window. I was going to send for the glazier to mend it; but after you lent that five pounds I was sure we couldn't afford it. Oh, no! the window must go as it is; and pretty weather for a dear child to sleep with a broken window. He's got a cold already on his lungs, and I shouldn't at all wonder if that broken window settled him – if the dear boy dies, his death will be upon his father's head; for I'm sure we can't now pay to mend windows. We might though, and do a good many more things, if people didn't throw away their five pounds.

'Next Tuesday the fire-insurance is due. I should like to know how it's to be paid! Why, it can't be paid at all. That five pounds would have just done it – and now, insurance is out of the question. And there never were so many fires as there are now. I shall never close my eyes all night, – but what's that to you, so people can call you liberal MR CAUDLE? Your wife and children may all be burnt alive in their beds – as all of us to a certainty shall be, for the insurance *must* drop. And after we've insured for so many years! But how, I should like to know, are people to insure who make ducks and drakes of their five pounds?

'I did think we might go to Margate this summer. There's poor little CAROLINE, I'm sure she wants the sea. But no, dear creature! she must stop at home – all of us must stop at home – she'll go into a consumption, there's no doubt of that; yes – sweet little angel! – I've made up my mind to lose her, *now*. The child might have been saved; but people can't save their children and throw away their five pounds, too.

'I wonder where poor little CHERUB is! While you were lending that five pounds, the dog ran out of the shop. You know, I never let it go into the street, for fear it should be bit by some mad dog, and come home and bite all the children. It wouldn't now at all astonish me if the animal was to come back with the hydrophobia, and give it to all the family. However, what's your family to you, so you can play the liberal creature with five pounds?

'Do you hear that shutter, how it's banging to and fro! Yes, – I know what it wants as well as you, it wants a new fastening. I was going to send for the blacksmith today. But now it's out of the question: *now* it must bang of nights, since you've thrown away five pounds.

'Well, things are come to a pretty pass! This is the first night I ever made my supper off roast beef without pickles. But who is to afford pickles, when folks are always lending five pounds?

'Ha! there's the soot falling down the chimney. If I hate the smell of anything, it's the smell of soot. And you know it; but what are my feelings to you? Sweep the chimney! Yes, it's all very fine to say, sweep the chimney – but how are chimneys to be swept – how are they to be paid for by people who don't take care of their five pounds?

'Do you hear the mice running about the room? *I* hear them. If they were only to drag you out of bed, it would be no matter. Set a trap for them! Yes, it's easy enough to say – set a trap for 'em. But how are people to afford the cheese, when every day they lose five pounds?

'Hark! I'm sure there's a noise down stairs. It wouldn't at all surprise me if there were thieves in the house. Well, it *may* be the cat; but thieves are pretty sure to come in some night. There's a wretched fastening to the back-door; but these are not times to afford bolts and bars, when fools won't take care of their five pounds.

'MARY ANNE ought to have gone to the dentist's tomorrow. She wants three teeth taken out. Now, it can't be done. Three teeth that quite disfigure the child's mouth. But there they must stop, and spoil the sweetest face that was ever made. Otherwise, she'd have been a wife for a lord. Now, when she grows up, who'll have her? Nobody. We shall die, and leave her alone and unprotected in the world. But what do you care for that? Nothing; so you can squander away five pounds.

'And now, see MR CAUDLE, what a misery you've brought upon your wretched family! I can't have a satin gown – the girls can't have new bonnets – the water-rate must stand over – JACK must get his death through a broken window – our fire-insurance can't be paid, so we shall all fall victims to the devouring element – we can't go to Margate, and CAROLINE will go to an early grave – the dog will come home and bite us all mad – that shutter will go banging for ever – the soot will always fall – the mice never let us have a wink of sleep – thieves be always breaking in the house – and our dear MARY ANNE be for ever left an unprotected maid, – and all, all, MR CAUDLE, because YOU WILL GO ON LENDING FIVE POUNDS!'

January 1845

Les Dawson

WHATEVER HAPPENED TO ROVER?

WHATEVER it may say in my Army discharge papers, I am not an alarmist. But for some time now I have been concerned about the increased popularity, openly evinced, for ownership of exotic and unusual pets. It is no longer sufficient to possess a pedigree dog or a high-born moggie; one's urban status demands the acquisition of at least a Malay Fruit Bat, or a well-behaved tapir, in order to cock a snoot at the people next door.

For my sins in a previous dynasty, I have a neighbour, a lapsed Methodist from Reading, who recently purchased a Tasmanian Wombat from Harrods! On first inspection it seemed a nice sort of thing, and I wasn't above throwing it mashed spinach and cabbage stalks, until the infernal creature ruined a superb dwarf oak with its pungent droppings.

When I protested in the strongest possible manner, my neighbour shook with mirth, and his daughter's Polynesian Hermit Crab bit me. So incensed was I by his complete disregard for my dwarf oak – by now in its death throes – I took to carrying an air-gun on my travels around the neighbourhood. I actually bagged three Wildebeest and a Narvik Goose before being placed on probation.

For months I simmered in my wrath, but continued to endure the exotic array of mutants which strutted across my rockery. Breaking point came when a mongoose was delivered to the house that lies directly opposite my abode. My anger about such an acquisition was bolstered by my total dislike for the man who lives there – he's a scruffy little type with an irritating reputation for winning vast sums on 'Ernie'.

From the day he acquired the said mongoose he became even more insufferable, and at cocktail parties would openly scoff at my professed love for Lakeland Terriers. Only last week, the mongoose darted into my garden, crept into the house and slithered into the mother-in-law's bedroom – thus presenting me with a monumental problem.

As an accomplished musician, she ends each day by casting open the bedroom window before playing a snatch from *Carnival in Venice* on her bugle. On the evening in question, she elected to perform a selection from Gilbert and Sullivan, and as the last note of *HMS Pinafore* was dying away on the chilled night air, the mongoose shot up her nightdress and bit her on a middle clef. With a blood-curdling cry she soared into the air like a faulty jumbo jet, performed a distinctive parabola, and fell through the open window.

Fortunately for her, her corsets snagged on the latch of the transom, causing her to swing with a wide span pendulum movement.

Consternation reigned in the household. My wife hurriedly dropped the rabbit she was plucking (cooking not being her strong suit) and bellowed like a stricken ox; the children milled around, and so great was their terror, they forgot to mug me.

For my part, I remained cool and collected as is my nature, and ran about like a decapitated cockerel. By this time a tidy knot of passers-by had collected to observe the mother-in-law's plight, and several inebriates in the throng shouted some uncalled-for remarks as her corset elastic twanged to the beat of her erratic bugle playing.

I attempted to pull the good lady free to no avail, and a passing Boy Scout, under the promise of 'Bob A Job', made a brave attempt to scale up the proffered flank of the hanging gorgon. To the cheers of the crowd, the lad attempted to saw through her corset with a Bowie knife. Alas, his valiant attempt terminated when the lip of her bugle bludgeoned his temple and he fell to the ground like a sack of meal.

An intense policeman struggled along with a ladder, and his rescue attempt might have succeeded had he not been summoned on his radio to apprehend a deviant in a local cinema. In the meantime, our vicar, a saintly man who claims to have shaken hands with the Pope (though he won't say which one), fed the mother-in-law with water-cress sandwiches, and moistened her lips with a Bovril-soaked cloth – not an easy task owing to the swinging to and fro of her inert mass.

By this time the whole affair could be likened to a Whitehall farce. A man appeared with a cart and began to vend peanuts; a religious bigot had a fit, and two children were soundly thrashed for using the mother-in-law's generous rump on which to chalk obscene slogans.

A passing vagrant from Uganda insisted that he could solve the problem by merely leaping up and pulling the poor woman free. At the time it sounded like a frightfully good idea, but her corsets proved more than a match for any aggressive action. Indeed, being made of pre-war elastic, the corsets acted like a militant catapult. The unfortunate vagrant hurled himself into the air and caught hold of legs that bore more than a passing resemblance to blocks of Stilton cheese, but he lost his grasp and the mother-in-law twanged upwards and her head demolished the guttering. That was bad enough, but on her passage upwards, her teeth were ejected at the speed of sound and after tearing through two sets of electric pylons, succeeded in bagging a brace of ducks and rupturing a flock of starlings.

Dusk tossed a mantle over the sky and it was useless to do anything further. The crowd had dispersed, and I took one last look at her swinging frame, still playing that damned bugle, and decided to call it a day by having a laugh at *Crossroads*.

Suffice to say, that night sleep eluded me. It wasn't just the worry, you understand. It was also the melodic thuds of her head hitting the gable-end.

As I write, she is still there – though the interest has long since died away. The odd tourist stops to feed her a bun, but that's about all. As for the offending mongoose, it was last seen begging a vet to doctor him. No one knows what it saw under the mother-in-law's nightdress, but the poor creature went grey overnight.

Modern technology being what it is, doubtless someone will come along with an idea to free her, but until then, life must go on.

April 1978

E.V. Knox
INJUSTICE AT EPPING

A MAN, an old man, has been turned out of a tree. In calling attention to a piece of bureaucratic tyranny almost without precedent in the history of our island race, I do not wish to lay the blame on under-lings who may have been stupidly following a prescribed routine. I want to strike at the principals, at the system responsible for the outrage. By what right was expropriation made? Let us consider briefly the facts of the case.

I learn them (anyhow, I learn some of them) from *The Daily Express*.

This old man lived in this tree. He had been resident there for two years. He had built an ordinary bird's nest (or squirrel's drey) of boughs and wool and maybe moss and hair. He was not only old but an invalid. His doctor had practically ordered him to live in a tree. 'It is either that,' he was informed by the specialist (a well-known Harley Street specialist) – 'it is either that or a nursing-home.' Naturally he chose the tree. He selected a beech. He selected it in Epping Forest, not a fashionable quarter, but one with a quiet arboreal life of its own. And now the forest rangers have evicted him and scattered his belongings – books, I suppose, a few domestic utensils, articles of virtu and the like – to the ground. They have done this too at a moment when the Budget is just setting in and the expense of finding a new tree to reside in bears most hardly on a wretched suburban drey-holder.

I am the more sympathetic in this affair because I have always wanted (against the advice of my relatives) to live in a tree. I could never look up at one from the earth without longing to climb it, nor down at one from a high block of flats without desiring to jump into the top branches. In one of Mr G.K. CHESTERTON's best books a man did live and live gloriously in a tree. Our earliest ancestors were tree-lemurs, and many of us look like it now, or worse. It is a kind of atavistic patriotism to want to be a tree-man, and I doubt if we have advanced at all in wisdom, as I am sure we have not in morals, since the golden tree-lemur age.

Trees are agreeable. The upper boughs wave pleasantly in the wind. There are few other noises, no post and no telephone. There is freedom from occasional callers, advertisers of vacuum-cleaners and mice. Where better than in a tree could one live? There have been stranger residences. DIOGENES, the great Greek philosopher, dwelt in a barrel and even spoke from it to ALEXANDER THE GREAT; yet he was never commanded by the Macedonian police to roll on. One might urge that this Epping beech-tree was not the old man's own beech-tree. It was public property. Or it may have been lent to the public by the Crown. But nobody else was living in it. Nor can I ascertain that anyone else was anxious for the lease. Very possibly the forest-keepers were affected by some local by-law about the damaging or climbing of trees. 'Look 'ere,' one of them may have argued, using the language dear to hide-bound officialdom the whole world over – 'wot abart it?' In the same stilted phraseology he may have gone on to say, 'You 'aven't no call to be living up in that there tree. You come orf out of it.' He may even have pointed out with plausible forensic skill that 'if everyone wot wanted to was to take to living up trees a nice state of things it would be, and no error.'

Yet I can but think that he was wrong. It is a mere assumption that trees in our public parks and forest lands are not meant to be lived in, but merely to be sat under by those in love. Far from being damaged a tree may be improved in appearance by artistically planned nidification. It should be held no doubt upon a repairing lease and the tenant should be responsible for the removal of débris and litter, for the erection of a lightning-conductor and for insecticide. But in any case nothing can excuse the arbitrary action of the authorities in breaking up a British tree-man's home without compensation and without inquiry. Not improbably their victim had a constitutional hatred of houses. He may have been a hereditary œcophobe. Many dendrophilists are. I once knew a charcoal-burner who was just like that. The only time in his life that he had ever spent under a roof was when he was on active service during the Great War. (So at least he informed me, adding that for this reason he had not liked the Great War.)

One is tempted to ask whether any action would be taken if a Society woman were to nest in a bird-sanctuary or elsewhere. One is prompted to inquire whether there is not in this matter one law for the rich and another for the poor. Would there be any persecution of Mr J.H. THOMAS, for instance, or of a duke, if either of them were to nest in St James's Park? Let us imagine that Lord BEAVERBROOK or Lord ROTHERMERE had determined to nest in oaks on Hampstead Heath. Would not wires be pulled to prevent the LCC rangers from disturbing them in their roosts? Urge if you will that a well-to-do man would be more likely to nest, not on common-land but on his own estate. Nevertheless there is no saying how far the motive of publicity might actuate at the present time a millionaire who had the nest-urge in his blood. I strongly suspect that any financier, any film-star who built a drey on one of the trees on Parliament Hill would be allowed to nestle there in peace.

A question should be asked in the House of Commons, and asked right speedily, about this nest-man and this tree. Did not the eviction, the spoliation occur within the constituency which Mr WINSTON CHURCHILL represents? What has Mr CLYNES to answer? I can remember very well the days when the Dartmoor shepherd was hotly defended by Mr LLOYD GEORGE with all his amazing powers of oratory. I shall have more confidence in my country's sense of justice and her belief in the rights of minorities when I learn that the Epping tree-man has been redomiciled in his own *pied sur l'arbre* or at least provided with another perch.

April 1931

A.A. Milne

WHEN WE WERE VERY YOUNG

VI – THE KING'S BREAKFAST

The King asked
The Queen, and
The Queen asked
The Dairymaid.
'Could we have some butter for
The Royal slice of bread?'
The Queen asked
The Dairymaid;
The Dairymaid
Said, 'Certainly.
I'll go and tell
The cow
Now
Before she goes to bed.'

The Dairymaid
She curtsied,
And went and told
The Alderney:
'Don't forget the butter for
The Royal slice of bread.'

The Alderney
Said sleepily,
'You'd better tell
His Majesty
That many people nowadays
Like marmalade
Instead.'

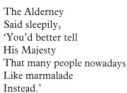

The Dairymaid
Said, 'Fancy!'
And went to
Her Majesty;
She curtsied to the Queen and
She turned a little red:
'Excuse me,
Your Majesty,
For taking of
The liberty,
But marmalade is tasty if
It's very
Thickly
Spread.'

The Queen said,
'Oh!'
And went to
His Majesty:
'Talking of the butter for
The Royal slice of bread,
Many people
Think that
Marmalade
Is nicer.
Would you like to try a little
Marmalade
Instead?'

The King said,
'Bother!'
And then he said,
'Oh, deary me!'
The King sobbed, 'Oh, deary me!'
And went back to bed.
'Nobody,' he whimpered,
'Could call me
A fussy man;
I *only* want
A little bit
Of butter for
My bread!'

The Queen said,
'There, there!'
And went to
The Dairymaid;
The Dairymaid
Said, 'There, there!'
And went to the shed.
The cow said, 'There, there!
I didn't really
Mean it;
Here's milk for his porringer
And butter for his bread.'

The Queen took
The butter
And brought it to
His Majesty;
The King said,
'Butter, eh?'
And bounced out of bed.
'Nobody,' he said,
As he kissed her
Tenderly –
'Nobody,' he said,
As he slid down
The banisters –
'Nobody, my darling,
Could call me
A fussy man –
BUT
*I do like a little bit of
butter to my bread!'*

January 1924

Virginia Graham

TRAVELLER'S JOY

I'm sure you'll have a lovely time in Egypt, said Aunt Maud;
only, dear, you must be very careful of abroad.
  Unless you want your span of life to be considerably shorter,
on no account, darling, touch Nile water.
The natives, of course, drink it straight out of the river,
but then they have never even *heard* of a gyppy liver,
and, anyway, they hold their lives at little stake.
  It is foolish to trust a filter unless it is of British make.
  If you do not wish to be excessively *malade*,
do not eat fish, meat or *salade*;
and remember that even the purest-looking fruits
have sucked Oriental moisture through their roots.
(Before putting lemon in your tea, for instance, mind
you remove the rind.)
  With milk, I should not come to any terms.
  As you know, there are thousands of perfectly deadly germs,
waiting like dormant snakes till you appear.
So here,
here, said Aunt Maud, is an iodine locket
which you must keep religiously in your pocket,
and if ever you get even the tiniest scratch,
use it. Else you may catch
some unmentionable Eastern disease.
  (Incidentally, never ride camels, as they harbour fleas.)
  Never, of course, *grip* anything with your naked hand.
  Avoid the desert, as there are scorpions in the sand.
  If you *must* go sightseeing, try not to inhale –
why, I will lend you the motoring-veil
I wore when your Uncle and I visited Crete
last spring. Oh, and be very careful of the heat,
and, needless to say, of the cold,
which, I am told,
if one is feeling in the least bit run down,

sneaks up and gives one the *grippe* at sundown.
   In case you get a chill
here, dear, is a little pink pill.
   Now, what else is there? Oh, yes, it is wise
to dab boracic powder in your eyes;
and mix a spot of glyco-thymoline with all your drinks.
   The Guides are *very* dirty by the Sphinx,
and don't go inside the Pyramids, I implore you,
you never know who has been there before you!
   Remember to gargle twice a day,
to use an ear-douche and a nose-spray.
(I know of a delightful disinfectant soap.)
   Well, we must just hope
that of all the million flies you are bound to meet,
carrying various infections on their feet,
not one will actually have the nerve to kill
you. Still,
we mustn't be too sure.
   Therefore, dearest, prevention being better than cure,
let me once again repeat
that it is madness to eat fish, fruit, vegetables or meat,
and that, if you would not court an untimely death,
do not speak, walk, ride or take a breath.
   I am sure, said Aunt Maud
(who knows all about abroad),
that if you take care of yourself as I have done,
your trip to Egypt will be the *greatest* possible fun.

                                                        April 1937

Graham Greene

A SHOCKING ACCIDENT

I

JEROME was called into his housemaster's room in the break between the second and the third class on a Thursday morning. He had no fear of trouble for he was a warden – the name that the proprietor and headmaster of a rather expensive preparatory school had chosen to give to approved, reliable boys in the lower forms (from a warden one became a guardian and finally before leaving, it was hoped, for Marlborough or Rugby, a crusader). The housemaster, Mr Wordsworth, sat behind his desk with an appearance of perplexity and apprehension. Jerome had the odd impression when he entered that he was a cause of fear.

'Sit down, Jerome,' Mr Wordsworth said. 'All going well with the trigonometry?'

'Yes, sir.'

'I've had a telephone call, Jerome. From your aunt. I'm afraid I have bad news for you.'

'Yes, sir?'

'Your father has had an accident.'

'Oh.'

Mr Wordsworth looked at him with some surprise. 'A serious accident.'

'Yes, sir?'

Jerome worshipped his father: the verb is exact. As man recreates God, so Jerome recreated his father – from a restless widowed author into a mysterious adventurer who travelled in far places – Nice, Beirut, Majorca, even the Canaries. The time had arrived about his eighth birthday when Jerome believed that his father either 'ran guns' or was a member of the British Secret Service. Now it occurred to him that his father might have been wounded in 'a hail of machine-gun bullets'.

Mr Wordsworth played with the ruler on his desk. He seemed at a loss how to continue. He said, 'You knew your father was in Naples?'

'Yes, sir.'

'Your aunt heard from the hospital today.'

'Oh.'

Mr Wordsworth said with desperation, 'It was a street-accident.'

'Yes, sir?' It seemed quite likely to Jerome that they would call it a street-accident. The police of course had fired first: his father would not take human life except as a last resort.

'I'm afraid your father was very seriously hurt indeed.'

'Oh.'

'In fact, Jerome, he died yesterday. Quite without pain.'

'Did they shoot him through the heart?'

'I beg your pardon. What did you say, Jerome?'

'Did they shoot him through the heart?'

'Nobody shot him, Jerome. A pig fell on him.' An inexplicable convulsion took place in the nerves of Mr Wordsworth's face: it really looked for a moment as though he were going to laugh. He closed his eyes, composed his features, and said rapidly as though it were necessary to expel the story as rapidly as possible: 'Your father was walking along a street in Naples when a pig fell on him. A shocking accident. Apparently in the poorer quarters of Naples they keep pigs on their balconies. This one was on the fourth floor. It had grown too fat. The balcony broke. The pig fell on your father.'

Mr Wordsworth left his desk rapidly and went to the window, turning his back on Jerome. He shook a little with emotion.

Jerome said, 'What happened to the pig?'

II

This was not callousness on the part of Jerome as it was interpreted by Mr Wordsworth to his colleagues (he even discussed with them whether perhaps Jerome was yet fitted to be a warden). Jerome was only attempting to visualize the strange scene and to get the details right. Nor was Jerome a boy who cried; he was a boy who brooded, and it never occurred to him at his preparatory school that the circumstances of his father's death were comic – they were still part of the mystery of life. It was later in his first term at his public school, when he told the story to his best friend, that he began to realize how it affected others. Naturally after that disclosure he was known, rather unreasonably, as Pig.

Unfortunately his aunt had no sense of humour. There was an enlarged snapshot of his father on the piano: a large sad man in an unsuitable dark suit posed in Capri with an umbrella (to guard him against sunstroke), the Faraglione rocks forming the background. By the age of sixteen Jerome was well aware that the portrait looked more like the author of *Sunshine and Shade* and *Rambles in the Balearics* than an agent of the Secret Service. All the same he loved the memory of his father: he still possessed an album filled with picture-postcards (the stamps had been soaked off long ago for his other collection) and it pained him when his aunt embarked with strangers on the story of his father's death.

'A shocking accident,' she would begin, and the stranger would compose his or her features into the correct shape for interest and commiseration. Both reactions, of course, were false, but it was terrible for Jerome to see how suddenly, midway in her rambling discourse, the interest would become genuine. 'I can't think how such things can be allowed in a civilized country,' his aunt would say. 'I suppose one has to regard Italy as civilized. One is prepared for all kinds of things abroad of course, and my brother was a great traveller. He always carried a water-filter with him. It was far less expensive, you know, than buying all those bottles of mineral water. My brother always said that his filter paid for his dinner wine. You can see from that what a careful man he was, but who could possibly have expected when he was walking along the Via Dottore Manuele Panucci on his way to the Hydrographic Museum that a pig should fall on him?' That was the moment when the interest became genuine.

Jerome's father had not been a very distinguished writer, but the time always seems to come, after an author's death, when somebody thinks it worth his while to write a letter to *The Times Literary Supplement* announcing the preparation of a biography and asking to see any letters or documents or receive any anecdotes from friends of the dead man. Most of the biographies, of course, never appear – one wonders whether the whole thing may not be an obscure form of blackmail and whether many a potential writer of a biography or thesis finds the means in this way to finish his education at Kansas or Nottingham. Jerome, however, as a chartered accountant, lived far from the literary world. He did not realize how small the menace really was: nor that the danger-period for someone of his father's obscurity had long passed. Sometimes he rehearsed the method of recounting his father's death so as to reduce the comic element to its smallest dimensions – it would be of no use to refuse information, for in that case the biographer would undoubtedly visit his aunt who was living to a great old age with no sign of flagging.

It seemed to Jerome that there were two possible methods – the first led gently up to the accident, so that by the time it was described the listener was so well prepared that the death came really as an anti-climax. The chief danger of laughter in such a story was always surprise. When he rehearsed this method Jerome began boringly enough. 'You know Naples and those high tenement buildings? Somebody once told me that the Neapolitan always feels at home in New York just as the man from Turin feels at home in London because the river runs in much the same way in both cities. Where was I? Oh, yes, Naples, of course. You'd be surprised in the poorer quarters what things they keep on the balconies of those sky-scraping tenements – not washing, you know, or bedding, but things like livestock, chickens or even pigs. Of course the pigs get no exercise whatever and fatten all the quicker.' He could imagine how his hearer's eyes would have glazed by this time. 'I've no idea, have you, how heavy a pig can be, but those old buildings are all badly in need of repair. A balcony on the fourth floor gave way under one of those pigs. It struck the third-floor balcony on its way down and sort of ricochetted into the street. My father was on the way to the Hydrographic Museum when the pig hit him. Coming from that height and that angle it broke his neck.' This was really a masterly attempt to make an intrinsically interesting subject boring.

The other method Jerome rehearsed had the virtue of brevity. 'My father was killed by a pig.' 'Really? In India?' 'No, in Italy.' 'How interesting. I never realized there was pig-sticking in Italy. Was your father keen on polo?'

In course of time, neither too early nor too late, rather as though in his capacity as a chartered accountant Jerome had studied the statistics and taken the average, he became engaged to be married: to a pleasant fresh-faced girl of twenty-five whose father was a doctor in Pinner. Her name was Sally, her favourite author was still Dornford Yates, and she had adored babies ever since she had been given a doll at the age of five which moved its eyes and made water. Their relationship was contented rather than exciting, as became the love-affair of a chartered accountant: it would never have done if it had interfered with the figures.

One thought worried Jerome, however. Now that within a year he might himself become a father, his love for the dead man increased: he realized what affection had gone into the picture-postcards. He felt a longing to protect his memory, and uncertain whether this quiet love of his would survive if Sally were so insensitive as to laugh when she heard the story of his father's death. Inevitably she would hear it when Jerome brought her to dinner with his aunt. Several times he tried to tell her himself, as she was naturally anxious to know all she could that concerned him.

'You were very small when your father died?'

'Just nine.'

'Poor little boy,' she said.

'I was at school. They broke the news to me.'

'Did you take it very hard?'

'I can't remember.'

'You never told me how it happened.'

'It was very sudden. A street-accident.'

'You'll never drive fast, will you, Jemmy?' (She had begun to call him 'Jemmy'.) It was too late then to try the second method – the one he thought of as the pig-sticking one.

They were going to marry quietly at a register-office and have their honeymoon at Torquay. He avoided taking her to see his aunt until a week before the wedding, but then the night came, and he could not have told himself whether his apprehension was most for his father's memory or the security of his own love.

The moment came all too soon. 'Is that Jemmy's father?' Sally asked, picking up the portrait of the man with the umbrella.

'Yes, dear. How did you guess?'

'He has Jemmy's eyes and brow, hasn't he?'

'Has Jerome lent you his books?'

'No.'

'I will give you a set for your wedding. He wrote so tenderly about his travels. My own favourite is *Nooks and Crannies*. He would have had a great future. It made that shocking accident all the worse.'

'Yes?'

How Jerome longed to leave the room and not to see that loved face crinkle with irresistible amusement.

'I had so many letters from his readers after the pig fell on him.' She had never been so abrupt before.

And then the miracle happened. Sally did not laugh. Sally sat with open eyes of horror while his aunt told her the story, and at the end, 'How horrible,' Sally said. 'It makes you think, doesn't it? Happening like that. Out of a clear sky.'

Jerome's heart sang with joy. It was as though she had appeased his fear for ever. In the taxi going home he kissed her with more passion than he had ever shown and she returned it. There were babies in her pale blue pupils, babies that rolled their eyes and made water.

'A week today,' Jerome said, and she squeezed his hand. 'Penny for your thoughts, my darling.'

'I was wondering,' Sally said, 'what happened to the poor pig?'

'They almost certainly had it for dinner,' Jerome said happily and kissed the dear child again.

November 1957

E.C. Bentley
CLERIHEWS

Dame Laura Knight
Had unusually keen sight.
She could spot a circus clown, they say,
A couple of miles away.

'The moustache of Adolf Hitler
Could hardly be littler,'
Was the thought that kept recurring
To Field-Marshal Goering.

The sermons of John Knox
Teemed with disapproval of frocks.
There was no acquiescence by him in
The Monstrous Regiment of Women.

'No, Sir,' said General Sherman.
'I did *not* enjoy the sermon;
Nor I didn't git any
Kick outer the Litany.'

January 1939

George Grossmith
THE DIARY OF A NOBODY

May 21. – The last week or ten days terribly dull. CARRIE being away at Mrs JAMES'S, at Sutton. CUMMINGS also away. GOWING, I presume, is still offended with me for black-enamelling his stick without asking him.

May 22. – Purchased a new stick mounted with silver which cost seven-and-sixpence (shall tell CARRIE five shillings), and sent it round with nice note to GOWING.

May 23. – Received strange note from GOWING. He says: 'Offended? Not a bit, my boy. I thought you were offended with me for losing my temper. Besides, I found, after all, it was not my poor old uncle's stick you painted. It was only a shilling thing I bought at a tobacconist's. However, I am much obliged to you for your handsome present all the same.'

May 24. – CARRIE back. Hoorah! She looks wonderfully well, except that the sun has caught her nose.

May 25. – CARRIE brought down some of my shirts and advised me to take them to TRILLIP'S round the corner. She said: 'The fronts and cuffs are much frayed.' I said without a moment's hesitation, 'I'm *'frayed* they are.' Lor! How we roared. I thought we should never stop laughing. As I happened to be sitting next the driver going to town on the 'bus, I told him my joke about the 'frayed' shirts. I thought he would have rolled off his seat. They laughed at the office a good bit too over it.

May 26. – Left the shirts to be repaired at TRILLIP'S. I said to him: 'I'm *'fraid* they are *frayed!'* He said without a smile, 'They're bound to do that, Sir.' Some people seem to be quite destitute of a sense of humour.

June 2. – The last week has been like old times. CARRIE being back, and GOWING and CUMMINGS calling every evening nearly. Twice we sat out in the garden quite late. This evening we were like a pack of children, and played 'Consequences'. It is a good game.

June 3. – Consequences again this evening. Not quite so successful as last Saturday. GOWING having several times over-stepped the limits of good taste.

June 4. – In the evening CARRIE and I went round to Mr and Mrs CUMMINGS' to spend a quiet evening with them. GOWING was there, also Mr STILLBROOK. It was quiet but pleasant. Mrs CUMMINGS sang five or six songs – '*Maggie's Secret*', and '*Why don't the Men propose?*' being best in my humble judgment. But what pleased me most was the duet she sang with CARRIE – classical duet, too. I think it is called – '*I would that my Love*'. It was beautiful. If CARRIE had been in better voice, I don't think professionals could have sung it better. After supper we made them sing it again. I never liked Mr STILLBROOK since the walk that Sunday to the 'Cow and Hedge', but I must say he sings comic songs well. His song, '*We don't Want the Old Men now*', made us shriek with laughter, especially the verse referring to Mr GLADSTONE. But there was one verse I think he might have omitted, and I said so, but GOWING thought it was the best of the lot. '*Chacun à son gout*,' as the French say.

June 6. – TRILLIP brought round the shirts, and to my disgust, his charge for repairing was more than I gave for them when new. I told him so, and he impertinently replied, 'Well, they are better now than when they were new.' I paid him, and said it was a robbery. He said, 'If you wanted your shirt-fronts made out of pauper-linen, such as is used for packing and bookbinding, why didn't you say so.'

June 7. – A dreadful annoyance. Met Mr FRANCHING, who lives at Peckham, and who is a great swell in his way. I ventured to ask him to come home to meat-tea, and take pot-luck. I did not think he would accept such a humble invitation, but he did, saying in a most friendly way he would rather 'peck' with us than by himself. I said, 'We had better get into this Blue 'bus.' He replied, 'No blue-bussing for me. I have had enough of the blues lately. I lost a cool "thou" over the Copper Scare. Step in here.' We drove up in style home, and I knocked three times at the front door without getting an answer. I saw CARRIE through the panels of ground glass (with stars), rushing upstairs. I told Mr FRANCHING to wait at the door while I went round to the side. There I saw the grocer's boy actually picking off the paint on the door, which had formed into blisters. No time to reprove him, so went round and effected an entrance through the kitchen window. I let in Mr FRANCHING, and showed him into the drawing-room. I went upstairs to CARRIE, who was changing her dress, and told her I had persuaded Mr FRANCHING to come home. She replied, 'How can you do such a thing; you know it's SARAH's holiday, and there's not a thing in the house, the cold mutton having turned with the hot weather.'

Eventually CARRIE, like a good creature as she is, slipped down, washed up the tea-cups, and laid the cloth, and I gave FRANCHING our views of Japan to look at while I ran round to the butchers to get three chops.

July 1888

Melvyn Bragg

I WROTE Ken Russell's first talkie. Do I duck? Is that a dagger I see before me? It was about Debussy, made for *Monitor*, got me into the most violent professional row of my life – with the late Sir Huw Wheldon – and kicked up the stink usually reserved as an order of merit for a 'committed' play. This was in 1964 before an impressive percentage of *Punch* readers were born. To begin, then, at the top.

Ken Russell's earlier film on Elgar – in 1962 – had made him the Sixties' darling. British television's riposte to the accusation that all the *real* celluloid art was in the cinema and made in France. Here was work in the British documentary tradition which recruited the new but punchy forces of Arts Programming and shot this through with a cutting to music which could be and *was* called 'poetic'. To budding Beginners like myself and all the others who had suddenly fallen for foreign films and wanted to be 'Auteurs' as well as authors, the prize seemed within reach. We would not have to go through the impenetrable looking-glass to the unimaginable dream factory of Hollywood – we could do it right here on the BBC road. Russell was that much of an inspiration.

Monitor had a lot of Profs and back room boys, a touch of Biggin Hill and Heath Robinson about it in those days and when Russell asked me – a trainee, a secret, compulsive but unpublished novelist – to write a film script – my first script – I said yes and front office did not demur. Front office was usually out on location.

I decided to be quite miffingly original and bold and Ken would do the rest. We would make a film within a film! Hey-ho. Vladeck Sheybal, just arrived in England from Poland where his screen performances had been wonderful, would 'play' the director: Oliver Reed would be Debussy. The advantage of the double-backing was that we could use a commentary voice (which is vital for a short biopic if it is to have any informational value at all) but the voice would belong to an active participant in the story. Moreover, it allowed you to be highly selective, cut scenes short if you needed to and generally move fast.

Ken added enormously to the script. Scenes where I had pencilled in 'Music from La Mer' would become a ravishing sequence of images of the sea seen – this was his gift – in a way you felt it had never been seen before. Where I had hinted, he spoke out – and so we had the first striptease to classical music on the BBC – a striptease so innocent by later standards that, as I remember it, the girl ends up rather overdressed for Hot Gossip or Pan's People. But for its time – just a split second pre-Swinging London – it was shocking!

Curiously enough, that was not the main fight we had with Huw Wheldon – who was at that time Head of the BBC Arts Department. His objection was to the principle of using actors in what was an arts documentary strand, to impersonate artists. Where was The Truth? Where was The Authority? In drama-documentary work and in 'faction' up to Blunt the argument had gone on. We had to prove – and we did – that every spoken fact and shown incident was based on a sound source. Only then did he 'let it through' but there had been blood on the cutting room walls. 'The Debussy Film', unlike Elgar, split both audiences and critics. We followed that with a charming film – Ken at his nouvelle vague best – on the Douanier Rousseau – using a real live Yorkshire Primitive Artist as the painter.

The film we wanted to do as a feature was Nijinsky. He was a man whose diaries had fascinated me in the same way as those of Van Gogh. I suppose to someone stuck fast in the provinces, those ejaculations of pain seemed the true cries of the pure artistic soul:

and perhaps they were. Ken had spent part of his extraordinary early career (naval cadet, Wilfred Pickles's personal photographer) as a ballet dancer in Sweden. Between us we covered the field.

What *was* important, I think, was that, in the *Monitor* films, Ken had found a way to tell a story of artists' lives through their work. Especially the lives of those to whom music was integral. He could film and later cut to music in a way then unique, much copied since but never I think bettered. I was intrigued by the lives of romantic artists: Nijinsky's drama, his liaison with Diaghilev (and the ease with which that dovetailed into the Stravinsky ballets), the wrench of his marriage, the long madness and those diaries attempting to articulate the inexpressible – meat and drink!

Harry Saltzman was to produce it. We worked out a shooting schedule which gave us everything we wanted and still came in way under the median line. (Partly because Ken and I were fatally enthusiastic and inexperienced and came at a knock-down price.) Christopher Gable, a fine dancer who had just scored a great acting hit in his debut in Ken's 'Delius' TV film, was to play Nijinsky. We went to Spain and got all the locations. Huw Wheldon, no less, liked the script. We were up and about when – crash. It was decided that Nureyev should be Nijinsky. After that the saga began for everyone else, stopped for me: and, eventually, for Ken. Other writers, other directors, the usual fudge and eventually, almost twenty years later, the film which I never did go and see.

I think that the 'Nijinsky' experience wounded Ken. He was very enthusiastic about the idea, the cast, the music, the script, the originality of attempting a major and serious feature on such a subject without sensationalising it. Post Nijinsky, I think, he decided that he had to gee it up if he was to get his type of artist biopics on to the screen. Or he had to take an unsuitable budget – just to get it done – and shoot much faster than served the subject's best interest. Most importantly, though, he decided – sometimes with interesting, sometimes with patchy results – that the only way to take on this 'outside' – feature-film, Hollywood – world was to take care of everything himself. The BBC had given him a cocoon. He ate his way through it but found little nourishment outside. And it could be frightening out there – Ken was and remains a compulsive film-maker: not to be shooting or preparing or editing a film is not to be tolerated.

This began to come into focus on the Tchaikovsky film – *The*

Music Lovers. There are parts of that – the letter song for instance – which are among the best things he has done. Other sequences – Richard Chamberlain and Glenda Jackson copulating hysterically in a rollocking train on their honeymoon – which were memorable, some thought indelible. Ken began to invent on the spot, to develop a philosophy which equated the fun of doing something with the quality of the finished product. It could work. It could be dangerous.

He also began to draw his own barricades around him increasingly. His then wife, Shirley, had always made the costumes: now his children began to appear regularly in the films and he developed a company of enablers and players whom he wanted to take around the country like a tribe of gypsies. Caravans were bought. More importantly, though, he decided that the only way he could get his vision or his way on the screen was by doing more and more himself. His knowledge of camera techniques already gave him a grip on the 'look' of the film: the pace was generally dictated by music he himself had selected: now he moved into the script. Not only to re-write: not only to allow for suggestions and improvisation on the set – but as a place to key in his own obsessions. Like many a writer of the last forty years, Ken saw and still to some extent sees his own personal feelings as an indicator and exemplar of the age: their force in him compelled him to express them to others.

And so for many years I bid farewell to Ken as he set off on a journey which he wanted to take alone. Had he taken it within British television I think it would have been easier for him, made more impact and gained him an enormous following. As it was, he took in the feature film world which meant that he had to take on *Them* exhaustingly. He retaliated, often, with the outrage of bad taste and the discomfort of sexual and religious violence. There was something of a frenzy in him, I think, which made him wild.

We joined up again recently when he did an enchanting and original film on Vaughan Williams for *The South Bank Show.* On severely limited resources, he delivered a film full of 'moments' and marvellous insights into that composer. Ursula – Vaughan Williams's widow – helped and 'starred' in it. Much of what she said was, if not the shooting script, then at least the theme and he benefited, I thought, from the second voice. Odd how things come full circle. As editor, I had to see it through the final cut: there was a little blood on the walls there, too. But he is working for *TSBS* again and yet again has turned up with something curious, full of energy, unique.

So far Ken Russell's career has been the oddest, the most erratic, the most fertile and the most personal in British film history. I will be very surprised if, in a few years' time, we do not see queues along the South Bank waiting to get into a retrospective season of the unique K.R.

February 1987

R.J. Richardson
ART

(A glossary for the opening
of the Royal Academy)

An Artist is a person who paints what he thinks he sees.

An Amateur is a person who thinks he paints what he sees.

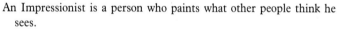

An Impressionist is a person who paints what other people think he sees.

A Popular Artist is a person who paints what other people think they see.

A Successful Artist is a person who paints what he thinks other people see.

A Great Artist is a person who paints what other people see they think.

A Failure is a person who sees what other people think they paint.

A Portraitist is a person who paints what other people don't think he sees.

A Landscape Painter is a person who doesn't paint what other people see.

A Realist is a person who sees what other people don't paint.

An Idealist is a person who paints what other people don't see.

The Hanging Committee are people who don't see what other people think they paint.

A Royal Academician is a person who doesn't think and paints what other people see.

A Genius is a person who doesn't see and paints what other people don't think.

A Critic is a person who doesn't paint and thinks what other people don't see.

The Public are people who don't see or think what other people don't paint.

A Dealer is a person that sees that people who paint don't think, and who thinks that people who don't paint don't see. He sees people who don't see people who paint; he thinks that people who paint don't see people who see; and he sees what people who don't paint think.

FINALLY,

A Reader is a person whose head swims.

April 1908

David Thomas

'MR PUNCH'

YOUR SPIES ARE UNDONE

WHAT on earth is the point of spies? I've been asking myself this question over the past few weeks as the Fifth Man has (supposedly) been revealed; as the entire West German secret service turns out to have been the East German security service with the word 'East' crossed out and 'West' written on top in purple crayon and as some idiot turns up in Moscow saying he's defected from the FBI.

It's clear to see that western intelligence has been a complete joke for the past forty years. Those chaps in the Kremlin knew everything. They knew where all our bombs were. They knew who killed Kennedy. They knew who shot J.R. They knew the lot. And they still lost.

Or look at it the other way around. We had an MI6 that was

entirely staffed by drunken nellies from Cambridge and daft old
buggers in hats with corks round the rim. And the Yanks had the
CIA, which was populated by lunatics and – for a while at any rate –
run by George Bush. And the last few German chancellors haven't
even been able to nip out for a quick pee without East Berlin
knowing all about it. And we still won.

In other words, it's all been a total waste of time and money.
Which also means that the whole spy mythology of the post-war
years has been even more of a load of baloney than anyone ever
imagined. George Smiley and James Bond were not only fictional,
but completely insignificant. Shaken? Stirred? Who gives a
monkey's?

That was what I thought for a while. And then I began to look
around me, whereupon a much more terrifying concept wormed its
way into my imagination. What if the whole thing was just a giant
front? What if the KGB was, in actual fact, far, far more cunning
than anyone had ever imagined? What if the apparent collapse of
communism and the revelations about a few low-grade operatives
were nothing more than cover for a plot so deep, so devious that its
full ramifications might take years, nay, decades to emerge?

It was the case of the haemophiliacs that did it. Sitting there with
my Sunday papers, raging at the injustice that allowed men to die of
AIDS without even giving them the comfort of financial security for
their family, I wondered how a democratic government could allow
such wanton cruelty. It's not that I expected anyone in power to
possess sensitivity or compassion. It's just that I thought they'd
know a certain vote-loser when they saw one.

How could Kenneth Clarke stick to his cheapskate guns as innocent little boys endured the agony of AIDS before the gaze of the
nation's media? How could he sit back and watch another fatal blow
be dealt to the Tory government's tattered reputation? He couldn't,
could he? Not unless he was really a Russian intelligence operative.

No sooner had I made this breakthrough, than Clarke was
switched to education. My God! The horror! The mental welfare of
our nation's children has been put into the hands of a man pledged to
destroy everything we hold most dear.

One after another, apparently inexplicable events of the year gone
by began to come into focus. Wasn't it strange, for example, that
Rick Astley – a pop singer whose strangulated, soul-less tones had
once been smeared across the airwaves like the effluent from a

beached oil-tanker – had disappeared from the scene at exactly the time that the Berlin Wall had come down? No, it wasn't strange at all. Not when you knew he had been recalled to Moscow following cuts in the Soviet intelligence budget.

It was so obvious! How come no one has ever seen it before? I'll tell you why, because their critical senses had already been turned into cream cheese by television. Specifically, they had been brainwashed by London Weekend Television's Saturday evening schedules.

Consider this: shortly after tea-time, millions of innocent people are assaulted by a terrifying, high-pitched whine. Now, torture by sound was first developed by North Korean brainwashers in the Fifties. But LWT, in conjunction with the boys in the Lubianka's executive suites, have come up with something incomparably more sophisticated. If you can imagine the sound of baby sucking pigs being roasted alive while a thousand lipgloss salesgirls run their overgrown nails down an infinite blackboard and a massed band of dentists' drills screeches away in the background, you might have some idea of the aural assault that is Cilla Black compering her TV show *Blind Date*.

Miss Black (née Lara Laralava) is, of course, a top-flight KGB operative, trained from birth for this job and parachuted into Liverpool in 1963. Like all spies, she has a control – an operative to whom she reports and through whom she receives her orders. In Miss Black's case, that man is an expert in sabotage. Years of intensive preparation in the USSR were followed by a period of 'sleeping' in Britain – in which he led a normal life, prior to setting out on his particular mission.

His orders were simple: cause the maximum possible havoc. He was to sow confusion in the minds of the enemy. He was to dull the senses of the masses. And then, when they were ripe for exploitation, he was to whip them into an uncontrollable frenzy. Uncontrollable, that is, by all except the KGB, who would harness it against the legitimate government of Britain, thereby fomenting revolution and destroying capitalism.

It sounds farfetched, I admit. But do you have a better explanation for the existence of *Beadle's About*?

November 1990

Stevie Smith

MY HAT

MOTHER said if I wore this hat
 I should be certain to get off with the right sort of chap.
  Well look where I am now, on a desert island
   With so far as I can see no one at all on hand.
    I know what has happened, though I suppose mother wouldn't see.
     This hat, being so strong, has completely run away with me.
      I had the feeling it was beginning to happen the moment I put it on.
       What a moment that was as I rose up, I rose up like a flying swan –
        As strong as a swan too, why, see how far my hat has flown me away.
         It took us a night to come and then a night and a day.
          And all the time the swan wing in my hat waved beautifully;
           Ah, I thought, how this hat becomes me.
            First the sea was dark but then it was pale blue
             And still the wing beat and we flew and we flew
              A night and a day and a night and by the old right way
               Between the sun and the moon we flew until morning day.
                It is always early morning here on this peculiar island,
                 The green grass grows into the sea on the dipping land.
                  Am I glad I am here? Yes, well, I am.
                   It's nice to be rid of Father, Mother and the young man.
                    There's just one thought causes me a twinge of pain –
                     If I take my hat off, shall I find myself home again?
                      So in this early morning land I always wear my hat.
                       Go home, you see, well I wouldn't take a risk like that.

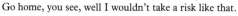

April 1953

Basil Boothroyd
MY PART IN THE CUBA CRISIS

IT doesn't seem twenty years since we all thought we were going to be fried. It is, and we did. It seems even less than that since I was doing a live radio programme on Mondays, of the kind designated lighthearted by the BBC. The Head of Radio 4 – must have been the Home Service then, if you can accept a time-lapse on that scale – once asked me, when I complained of having to be lighthearted all the time, to recommend some other designation. I couldn't, and stopped complaining.

On the evening of that Monday in October 1962, lightness of heart at the microphone was even shorter than usual with me. The East and the West, detoured through Cuba, were on collision course. Any minute, the blinding impact, silence, and global wisps. I felt the pre-shock, walking Beeb-bound up Regent Street. Austin Reed was a foot high and smouldering. Behind me, Eros had melted.

'What are you getting?' I said to the producer in the control-room. He was on to the Voice of America, which said that Khrushchev wasn't budging. Nor was Kennedy, who had proved it by stringing out along Florida and into the Caribbean all the ships, guns and planes he could scratch up. It was good scratching. A bigger concentration of clout than any used in World War II. In Moscow, meanwhile ... in Washington ... in Havana ...

Shows must go on, it's well known. But I did ask if he thought I should finish with my usual lighthearted, 'See you next week'.

He said he'd decide that later, and would keep me informed. The show ran for an hour. I used to smoke a large Cuban cigar, which just lasted it out. Tonight, I could see, it was going to turn to ashes in my mouth, but I lit it bravely all the same.

It had always been his practice, during the taped or recorded funnies, to drift into the studio for a chat. As I pumped up the breeziness for the next live link he would give me updates on the trouble he was having building his duck-shed, or rumoured rifts in the broadcasting hierarchy. All that seemed dross on this particular Monday, and several times he didn't come in at all, but sat on the other side of the glass, sifting the static for doom. When he did come, the reports were terrifying.

I left at ten. The cab-driver said nothing, but kept glancing out and up at the starless sky, as if for a sudden radiance. It was a howling night. My destination was ridiculous, all things considered: that patch of Russian soil in Kensington Palace Gardens. No. 13, for anyone with superstitious leanings. As I paid the taxi my hat blew off and bowled through the gates. If it had gone the other way I was in a mood to leave it. What's a hat without a head?

Things may have improved in twenty years. My impression of the Embassy was of a peeling exterior and a vast, chilly vacancy once you were in. No frills. No furniture. They could have packed things ready to quit, though the young man who greeted me in English that had quite an edge on my Russian was obviously keeping his best blue suit back. I followed it along the silent halls and was bowed through a heavy door into blackness and an even heavier hush. The door puffed to. Nothing. Then a sudden radiance.

Being late for this culture evening, a somewhat low-key exercise in East-West amity, I stood at the back of the small cinema, which it turned out to be when the screen ceased its startling flashes, and settled down to the second feature. I didn't want to disturb my fellow guests. Besides, I was near the exit. There weren't many to disturb, I saw in the next blinding interval between laughing Ukraine tractor-drivers and a tour of the Volga-Ural oilfields. A thin turn-out. Journalists at this time had other preoccupations than irrigation progress in western Siberia, and had stayed away. I hadn't, but the preoccupations remained.

Entertainment isn't always the cure. I remembered an earlier brinktime, in 1938, seeking to forget Czechoslovakia in the company of, I think, Cary Grant. Some Hollywood comedy. I know there was a sequence where people were challenged to spell Czechoslovakia backwards, and it didn't help.

Tonight it wouldn't have helped to spell Khrushchev backwards, trickier than it would have been than other names of the moment: Dean Rusk, George Ball, now long receded. Or just ordinary words. Minuteman. Nuclear superiority. Incineration.

After the films we danced.

Eerie.

It was a better room, if my memory serves. There could have been chandeliers. Dancing was not immediate, because there was certainly food and drink. I see a long buffet. Had the waiters behind it actually white gloves? The vodka was, as to be expected, the real thing. None of your alien labels, conning the unwary with English characters reversed. Diplomats plied us. They were in the lower reaches, His Excellency in person having, I imagine, other commitments. The music, from a hidden source, was waltzes and foxtrots. Quite old. The wind battered the windows. Nobody mentioned Cuba, not even a short woman journalist I took an early turn with, representing a do-it-yourself weekly. We agreed that the films had been interesting.

It must have been some time later that I partnered, and became intimate with in the most proper sense, a cultural attaché and strong waltzer. He led. His name, which surprised me less at the time, was Romanov. I know that because we exchanged cards, and I still have his. After arming each other to the vodka bottles once or twice, he holding me up, we also exchanged neckties. Whether he still has mine, an early *Punch* design with gold Mr Punches on a green ground, I don't know. I like to think of it now perhaps taking the eye of passers-by on Gorki Street. His was tiny red stars on black. When I was well enough to look at it a day or two later I saw the label had been scissored out. A microfilm cache? That was a thought I might have had if I'd examined it before.

But I had other thoughts as we danced the last waltz. *Kiss Me*, I believe it was. Even without that, I felt that the barriers were down, and told him so. I expanded, obviously with some coherence, on this. When such bonhomie between nations was clearly the only way of life, what was all this ludicrous nonsense about rockets? Who wanted to blow

anyone up? What was the point? Let Khrushchev be told now, for time was short, that dismantling was the only course: any Romanov of vision and resolve, with access, however tenuous, to the Kremlin ear ...

I don't know where he went. I know we hadn't finished the dance, and I had to lean on what could have been an associate editor of *Pottery and Glass*. But he went, looking damned serious.

It's daft to make extravagant claims. Detail of history could prove me wrong. All I can say is that when I somehow got home and turned on the television it was in the middle of a news flash that the rockets were pulling out. What if Kennedy did get all the credit, a bit spilling over on Dean Rusk and George Ball?

So I was back in the studio next Monday, smoking my large Havana as if nothing had happened. As nothing had. Except that even now, I'm told, twenty years on, it's still illegal in America to import cigars from Cuba.

These silly old feuds.

October 1982

Alan Coren

WE HAVE ALAN COREN: IS THERE ANY ADVANCE ON 4 QUID?

THE ear may be a dust trap, but when it comes to keeping your sunglasses on, it has clear advantages over a drawing-pin pressed into the side of your head.

These days, we must concern ourselves over such details.

Similarly, there are many places for a forefinger, and a matchbox isn't one of them. Decimalisation is tricky enough, without our having to convert imperial pints on an arsenal of only nine digits.

Anyone currently awash in my drift has clearly not been reading the newspapers: kidnapping, it seems, has much in common with rabies in that, having swept the European mainland in the last few years, it now stands poised at Calais waiting for a good following wind, and if Something Is Not Done the people of Britain may well, in the days to come, find themselves spending more and more time in car-boots, tea-chests, cellars and attics while their loved ones scurry back and forth in frantic attempts to drum up something negotiable to wrap in brown paper and leave in a hollow tree off the A41.

I give you, courtesy of the *Daily Express*, Mr Peter Heims, editor of *Top Security*. As if it weren't disturbing enough to think that there's enough interest in the subject to merit a magazine called *Top Security*, its editor has a tale to make thy two eyes, like stars, start from their spheres: for he is presently gumming together a seminar at a Heathrow hotel to discuss ways in which potential British kidnappees can keep the stocking-mask from the door, and those invited include such top retailers as Marcus Sieff, John Sainsbury and Sir John Cohen (which just goes to prove that there is a darker side to turning over umpteen million jars of jam than lying on one's yacht and totting up the week's gross), plus *fifteen hundred* others, like Richard Burton, who have made no secret of the fact that they have no need to duck into a doorway when they spot their bank-manager strolling towards them.

Addressing this throng of collateral will be a team of experts including Sir Geoffrey Jackson, our erstwhile ambassador in Uruguay, who was recently nicked by Tupamaros, and who avers: 'We must bring home to people that kidnapping can happen here and that it's got to be stopped. It is important to step up manpower and firepower in making it infernally difficult to be captured.' He then, having got the blood racing and Messrs. Smith and Wesson excitedly scribbling quick calculations on the back of an old cartridge-box, adds an even more disquieting coda: 'But if terrorists really want to get you, believe me they will.'

And it is that small phrase which sends the brain spinning into crazed speculation: 'if terrorists really want to get you'. For how does one determine that, fathom the convoluted, possibly illogical, workings of the terroristic psyche? Might they want to get *me*? Or would it be mere money up the spout to bung an electrified fence around the premises, mount a Bofors gun on the roof, chain myself to the boiler, and invest in a matched pair of Dobermanns of such keyed-up suspiciousness that they would be as likely to start stropping their fangs on the master's shins as go for the putative kidnapper?

On the surface, yes. The tie that binds such unlikely bedfellows as Mr Burton and Sir John Cohen is their common ability to spill

noughts on a cheque without a second thought, and needless to say I
am not of their number. The number I am of is £137.63, at the last
count, and I'm not altogether certain it didn't have a red 'O' against
it, come to think; and one of the few things I feel entitled to guess
about kidnappers is that they do not go to all the trouble of grabbing
a customer only to find themselves with an overdraft to pay off.
One's first thought, indeed, is that it's rather comforting to know
(since I haven't been invited to attend) that there are fifteen hundred
blokes standing between oneself and the Elastoplast gag, and that
British kidnapping will have to become something of a craze before
the threat gets around to me.

One's second thought, however, is that the said fifteen hundred
would be pretty dumb to stand up and be counted, that what Mr
Heims has probably got on his hands is a vast empty auditorium with
Sir Geoffrey Jackson staring down at it, and that Britain's would-be
kidnappers are back to square one, i.e. pot luck.

So what? you say. Even if they're not going to be ticked off that
Heathrow guest-list, there are still large stocks of millionaires
around, all of them better quarry than a bloke with nothing more
than £137.63 of someone else's money. True enough; but there's
scant consolation there, because a quite unsettling aspect intervenes
in the argument at this point.

As you doubtless know, Italy is so beset with kidnappings these
days that it is virtually impossible to drive through Rome or Milan
for the vast traffic-jams of plain vans containing solvent citizens
trussed like chickens. As a result of this, rich men have taken to
dissembling: they drive battered old Fiats, wear rumpled off-the-peg
suits, sport tin watches, smoke dog-ends, and, more ominous than
any of this, actually pay a new breed of PR men to spread the word in
the public prints that they are on their uppers and do not know
where their next lira is coming from. It's reaching the point where,
unless these terrified lads are very lucky indeed, they will be
snatched *for looking so broke they could only be loaded*!

It is therefore open season on everybody. And, if Sir Geoffrey's
any judge, the same could happen here: merely by drawing attention
to my overdraft I ensure that kidnappers immediately assume me to
be drowning in the stuff. Ah, you say, but when they find out, they'll
let you go!

Yes, I reply, and probably in slices.

Then again (and here we wade into yet murkier depths), though I may personally be broke, that is not to say there are not people on whom my kidnappers might lean, assuming *them* to have the wherewithal to repurchase me. So I have to begin asking all sorts of questions I would prefer to leave unframed, e.g. how much would *Punch* pay to get me back? A thousand? Fifty thousand? Anything? True, there might be some goodwill to be gleaned from forking out a few bob to save a loyal colleague, but Wm Wordsworth is not the only hack to hear Two Voices: I hear another saying, with maximum TV coverage, 'Much as we love Mr Coren, we feel that a stand must be taken NOW if the country is not to be overtaken by a wave of similar atrocities. Let us stand up to these thugs! Let them see that we would rather sacrifice one man than put a thousand in jeopardy! This magazine has always stood for law and order, for decency and courage, for an Englishman's right to walk the streets without fear, for rattling good value at only 25p and although in this week's bumper issue there is no article by Mr Coren, there are nevertheless pages and pages of wonderful hilarious ...'

The kidnappers might send the note to my wife, of course, and I've no doubt she could scrape a few bob together, here and there, under the circumstances, and certainly would. Almost certainly would. It has just occurred to me that due to that quirk of fate that men call insurance policies, I am worth a considerable amount of negotiable tender, dead. Normally, this would not weigh at all with this warm and devoted girl; but let us just suppose that I was snatched on a day upon which we had been bunging saucepans at one another and ...

She would, of course, change her mind when the heat died down, but by then, if I happen to fall into impatient hands, I could well be anchored in the Estuary by a pair of concrete socks and moving only with the assistance of the tide.

I am not sure what to do for the best. Like most of us, I have up until now reckoned my redemption to be in hands about which I could do nothing. Human beings, I fear are fallible redeemers. I suppose the only course is to remove the uneasy options from them, and see to it that one isn't nicked in the first place.

I intend to have THIS BELONGS TO THE MAFIA tattooed on my chest. It may be painful, but it'll hurt less than having an ear removed at the root, and will almost certainly prevent it.

Provided, that is, I get a kidnapper who can read.

September 1975

A.A. Milne
WHEN WE WERE VERY YOUNG

XXIV – MISSING

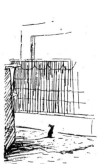

Has anybody seen my mouse?

I opened his box for half a minute,
Just to make sure he was really in it,
And, while I was looking, he jumped outside!
I tried to catch him, I tried, I tried …
I think he's somewhere about the house.
Has *anyone* seen my mouse?

Uncle John, have you seen my mouse?

Just a small sort of mouse, a dear little brown one;
He came from the country – he wasn't a town one,
So he'll feel all lonely in a London street;
Why, what could he possibly find to eat?
He must be somewhere. I'll ask Aunt Rose:
'Have *you* seen a mouse with a woffelly nose?
Oh, somewhere about –
He's just got out …'

Hasn't *anybody* seen my mouse?

June 1924

E.M. Delafield

THE PROVINCIAL LADY GOES TO AMERICA

VIII

October 16th. Come to the conclusion that everything I have ever heard or read about American Hospitality is an understatement. Telephone-bell rings incessantly from nine o'clock onwards, invitations pour in and complete strangers ring up to say that they liked my books and would be glad to give a party for me at any hour of the day or night. Am plunged by all this into a state of bewilderment, but feel definitely that it will be a satisfaction to let a number of people at home hear about it all, and realise estimation in which professional writers are held in America.

(Second thought obtrudes itself here to the effect that, if I know anything of my neighbours, they will receive any such information with perfect calm and probably say, Yes, they've always heard that Americans were Like That.)

Am interviewed by reporters on five different occasions – one young gentleman evidently very tired and droops on a sofa without saying much, which paralyses me and results in long stretches of deathly silence. Finally he utters to the effect that JOHN DRINKWATER was difficult to interview. Experience forlorn gleam of gratification at being bracketed with so distinguished a writer, but this instantly extinguished as reporter adds that in the end J.D. talked for one hour and fifteen minutes. Am quite unable to emulate this achievement, and interview ends in gloom. Representative of an evening paper immediately appears, but is a great improvement on his colleague and restores me to equanimity.

Droops on a sofa

Three women reporters follow – am much struck by the fact that
they are all good-looking and dress nicely; they all ask me what I
think of the American Woman, whether I read JAMES BRANCH
CABELL – which I don't – and what I feel about the Problem of the
Leisured Woman. Answer them all as eloquently as possible and
make mental note to the effect that I have evidently never taken the
subject of Women seriously enough, the only problem about them in
England being why there are so many.

Lunch with distinguished publisher and his highly-decorative
wife and two little boys. Am not in the least surprised to find that
they live in a flat with black velvet sofas, concealed lighting, and
three diagonal glass tables for sole furniture. It turns out, however,
that this is *not* a typical American home, and that they find it nearly
as remarkable as I do myself. We have lunch, the two little boys
behave like angels – reputation of American children evidently
libellous, and must remember to say so when I get home – and we
talk about interior decoration – dining-room has evidently different-
coloured paint on each of its four walls – books and sea-voyages.
Elder of the two little boys suddenly breaks into this and remarks

Tells me that times are not at all what they were

that he just loves English sausages – oh, boy! – which I accept
as a compliment to myself, and
he then relapses into silence. Am
much impressed by this display
of social competence, and feel
doubtful whether Robin or
Vicky could ever have equalled
it.

Afternoon is spent once more
in interviews, and am taken out
to supper-party by Ella Wheelwright, who again appears in
clothes that I have never seen
before. At supper I sit next
elderly gentleman wearing collar
exactly like Mr GLADSTONE'S. He
is slightly morose; tells me that
times are not at all what they
were – which I know already –

'Put your lights on, sister!'

and that there is No Society left in New York. This seems to me
uncivil as well as ungrateful, and I decline to assent. Elderly
Gentleman is, however, entirely indifferent as to whether I agree
with him or not, and merely goes on to say that no club would dream
of admitting Jews to its membership. (This, if true, reflects no credit
on clubs.) It also appears that in his own house cocktails, wireless,
gramophones and modern young people are, like Jews, never
admitted. Should like to think of something really startling to reply
to all this, but he would almost certainly take no notice even if I did,
and I content myself with saying that that is Very Interesting –
which is not, unfortunately, altogether true.

Ella Wheelwright offers to drive me home, which she does with
great competence, though once shouted at by a policeman who tells
her: 'Put your lights on, sister!'

Ella is kind, and asks me to tell her all about my home, but follows
this up by immediately telling me all about hers instead. She also
invites me to two luncheons, one tea, and to spend Sunday with her
on Long Island.

Return to my room, which is now becoming familiar, and write
long letter to Robert, which makes me feel homesick all over again.

October 17th. Conference at publishers' office concerning my future movements, in which I take passive rather than active part. Head of well-known lecture agency is present, and tells me about several excellent speaking engagements that he might have got for me if (*a*) He had had longer notice; (*b*) All the clubs in America hadn't been affected by the Depression; and (*c*) I could arrange to postpone my sailing for another three months.

Since (*a*) and (*b*) cannot now be remedied and I entirely refuse to consider (*c*), deadlock appears to have been reached; but agent suddenly relents and admits he *can*, by dint of superhuman exertions, get me one or two bookings in various places, though none of them seems to be less than eighteen hours' journey apart. I agree to everything, only stipulating for Chicago, where I wish to visit literary friend Arthur and his family and to inspect the World Fair.

Social whirl, to which I am by now becoming accustomed, follows, and I am put into the hands of extraordinarily kind and competent guardian-angel, picturesquely named Ramona Herdman. She takes me to the Vanderbilt Hotel for so-called tea, which consists of very strong cocktails and interesting sandwiches. I meet Miss Isobel Paterson, by whom I am completely fascinated, but also awe-stricken in the extreme, as she has terrific reputation as a critic and is alarmingly clever in conversation.

She demolishes one or two English novelists, in whose success I have always hitherto believed implicitly, but is kind about my own literary efforts and goes so far as to hope that we shall meet again. I tell her I am going to Chicago and other places and may lecture, and she looks at the floor and says, Yes, Clubwomen. Large women with marcelled hair, wearing reception gowns.

Am appalled by this thumb-nail sketch and seriously contemplate cancelling tour altogether.

Ella Wheelwright joins us – she now has on a black ensemble and hair done in quite a new way – and we talk about books. I say that I have enjoyed nothing so much as *Flush*, but Miss Paterson disconcerts me by muttering that to write a whole book about a dog is Simply Morbid.

Am eventually taken to Essex House by Ella W., who asks very kindly if there is anything she can do for me. Yes, there is. She can tell me where I can go to get my hair shampooed and set, and whether it will be much more expensive than it is at home. In reply Ella tells me that her own hair waves naturally. It doesn't *curl* – that isn't what she means at all – but it just *waves*. In damp weather it just goes into natural waves. It always has done this ever since she was a child. But she has it set once a month because it looks nicer. Hairdresser always tells her that it's lovely hair to do anything with because the wave is really natural.

She then says Good-night and leaves me, and I decide to have my own inferior hair, which does *not* wave naturally, washed and set in the hotel beauty-parlour.

November 1933

B.A. Young
I WISH YOU COULD ALL BE HERE

THAT applause was for Colin MacAbraham, the leader of the orchestra, who has just come in. He's sitting down now – and here is Sir Adrian Sargent, you can hear the applause, I expect, he's going up to the rostrum now, and he holds up his right hand with the baton in it and the applause dies down.

★   ★   ★   ★   ★   ★

Well, something seems to have gone slightly wrong here, I don't quite know what it is, we can't hear what's going on here although the orchestra seem to be playing all right, but it doesn't seem to be getting through, so I'll hand you over to Peter Tummitt who is down in the stalls. Over to you, Peter.

Well, I couldn't quite see what went wrong myself, the orchestra came in all right, they all came in together, it was a terrific sight, I wish you could have seen it. Then the first violins went out on top, it's most exciting, they're still there, setting a terrific pace, *allegro con spirito* at least, I should say, and they're still there, right up at about top E, I should think, and holding it magnificently, and *here come the brass!* ...

That was absolutely tremendous, the brass came in in the most

exciting way, three of them, three trumpets, that is, and there are the
trombones over there beyond them, and they're playing in B flat, it's
the most remarkable thing you ever heard, I wish you could all be
here tonight and hear it. And *here they are again* – no, no, no it isn't,
it's the woodwind, it's Harry Martingale, I think, on his clarinet with
the special boosted reed, and he swept up then – and here come the
first violins again with that opening theme, they're holding on to it
very well, and I think they're – yes, they are, they're going to
modulate ...

That was the most extraordinary thing, they came in above the
clarinet and did the most terrific modulation, from B flat right into
E minor, and now they seem to have dropped back a bit, and here
come the 'cellos, we haven't seen much of them this evening so far,
but here they are, they're looking frightfully fit, very fit indeed these
'cellos, and they come in with a tune in dotted minims, it's really
very fine, though they're not setting such a hot pace as some of the
others have been, about *andante con moto* I make it. I'll hand you
over again to Brian Broom in the circle. Over to you, Brian.

Well, here we are in the circle, and the first movement is nearly over.
It's been the most extraordinary movement, the first violins went
ahead right from the beginning, and they're still there up at the top,
no one is likely to catch them now, unless – yes, by Jove, I think
they're going to – yes, it's a fugue! ...

By gosh, that really was something worth hearing, I wish you
could all have heard it. The violins were way out on top, and the
double-basses were doing a sort of ground-bass, I suppose you'd call
it a ground-bass, and then the woodwind nipped in and took the tune
away from them and started a fugue with it. It's still going on over in
the far corner of the orchestra, and some of the strings have joined in,
the violas it sounds like, and, oh, I say, that's terrific, the tuba is
playing the theme in augmentation in the sub-dominant. I must say
that's the prettiest bit of tuba-playing I've heard. And now back to
Peter Tummitt in the stalls.

Well, here we are in the stalls, and there seems to be the devil of a
fugue going on, but I think we're coming to the coda now, yes, the
bassoons have got there, they've started the coda, they've got right
back to B flat, very pretty to listen to, and now they're slowing down

a bit, I think, yes, they're slowing down, and that's the end of the movement.

The engineers have just rung through to say that there was a slight technical hitch, but it's been corrected now, so for the rest of the concert I'll have to let the music speak for itself.

March 1951

Stephen Spender

MISSING MY DAUGHTER

THIS wall-paper has lines that rise
Upright like bars, and overhead
The ceiling's patterned with pink roses.
On the wall opposite the bed
The staring looking-glass encloses
Six roses in its white of eyes.

Here at my desk with note-book open
Missing my daughter makes those bars
Draw their lines upward through my mind.
The blank page stares at me like glass
Where stared-at roses wish to pass
Through petalling of my pen.

An hour ago there came an image
Of a beast that pressed its muzzle
Between bars. Next, through tick and tock
Of the reiterating clock
A second glared with the wide dazzle
Of deserts. The door, in a green mirage

Opened. In my daughter came.
Her eyes were wide as those she has,
The round gaze of her childhood was
White as the distance in the glass
Or on a white page, a white poem.
The roses raced around her name.

December 1953

BARGEPOLE

WELL ... I'm in love again, and how pathetic, how *wimpy* that I should have to declare it here in the hope that she will read it, but honestly, what a peach. I've heard people describe women as 'edible' before, but had never met one who really was. Skin the texture of a gently-bitten artichoke heart and the scent of sun and ylang-ylang. Utterly, heart-breakingly edible.

Edibility, of course, is not all that counts, but put it together with (a) grey eyes, (b) smoky voice, (c) own tape of Vivaldi's mandolin concerto, (d) ability to recognise New & Lingwood final demand and (e) immediate reaction to (d) being 'Don't pay it! Let them wait!', and you have someone who has passed all the major hurdles within the first furlong. And edible, too: served on a dish with truffles, one would ignore the truffles altogether.

But am *I* edible? I think not. This may be another foul trick played on me by my 'mind' but all the evidence suggests that it is an accurate appraisal of a filthy situation. Last week my life was in pieces all around me and I didn't want any of the pieces I could see, but I have reassembled myself and I think I may have got it wrong. My liver, for example, appears to be on the outside, for why else would my shirt flollop and bloop when pressed?

The crowd of no-hopers and dickheads outside the Coach and Horses no longer give me a second glance unless it is the one which mutely says 'Ugh,' and things have got to the stage where I only even get *that* one from chaps. Perhaps I should go back to being a homosexual. I always enjoyed being a homosexual, except I was young and beautiful – astonishingly so – in those days, and what could be worse than ending up like Dan Farson, once the most beautiful young man in London, now like a red Durex Fiesta crammed with suet, perilously moored to the Groucho Club bar: nothing left but a strangled, inarticulate howling for booze and a face like a melted candle, except when pretty young men appear, when it lights up, then gutters and fades again. That fat git Coltrane lurched in the other day, all black suit and udders, and for a moment one glimpsed Coltrane's role in life: standing next to Dan Farson to make him feel young and slim again.

I don't know who does the casting at the Groucho Club but it is all a bit much. There they were, Coltrane and Farson and some hopeless wannabee, locked like two captive blimps being harried by a chihuahua: if Pavarotti had swept in at that point, perhaps pulling Christa Ludwig on a little trolley, I think I would have *died* of happiness, and so would the man I was with, a Film Person who is rapidly turning into a great grey omentum with grief, all membrane and broken veins. Gosh he has been supportive but one must tell the truth. Yes, his baby done gone left him. But so what? She was no good anyway, and, besides, *everyone's* baby done gone left them, and now they are all hanging around outside the Coach and Horses looking absolutely splendid until they speak or move, and then it all becomes clear. Listen to them quacking into their Badoit. Voices like premenstrual jackals: 'Oh yes I'm so happy since I left him he was doing me no good we were unsuited I'm really happy now all these men are after me I realized what a really, really unique person I am.' *So why are you all saying it to each other*, duckies? And then walking off down to the Wag, hoping to score a poke off some decerebrate Lebanese wholesaler in Hugo Boss gaberdine and a Mulberry Company watch. Poor cows, all Workers for Freedom and zero-denier leg-gloss, lips, hair, cleavage ... and the grace and elegance of a duck with a recent pelvic floor repair, and a trail of soot on the pavement as they pass by. They walk like I type.

It's comforting, I suppose; I'm still not sure where babies come from but at least I know where they go, and in future I can avoid it because it frightens and disturbs me. I cannot even contemplate these neurotic, distressed, yelping, trumpet-blowing helpless Hebes without a feeling of deep unworthiness, and I *know* that I am turning nasty. Something is curdling somewhere, and I will end up on an escalator, alone, at midnight, with a plastic briefcase, a cheap shirt and a pot belly, thinking about mother, and it will be downhill from then on. I shall see references to oral sex in advertisements and write to the papers about it; I will begin to know how much change I have when I go to bed; I shall think about God when I start to get a little erection in the bath.

But is there a clear point of transition when one knows that, a moment before, one was one of us, and a moment hence, one will be one of them, the dentists and tax man and officials? Is there a rite of passage, a whining voice from the firmament saying 'From this day forth thou wilt be known as Mr Bashford, and wear thy three different-coloured biros in the top pocket of thy jacket?' Is there a moment of enlightenment where one starts thinking of Mr Peter Bottomley almost as a friend, and dreams of meeting him and discussing crackdowns and blitzes and tough new laws and carefully avoiding the topic of abject personal failure? Would one, indeed, cease to eye the drabs and panders of the Coach and Horses and instead reflect on Mrs Virginia Bottomley?

So what remains? I am in love with the delicious creature (because someone once told me that life goes on) and I want to take her home and put her on the Colin Chetwood sofa and play Couperin to her and feed her little bits of *foie gras* and sushi washed down with *Crémant de Cramant* and, just occasionally, sniff delicately at the inside of her wrist, but I may have to compromise. With what? Some pretty, dark-eyed single mother who keeps herself in shape and tries to be interesting although Lord knows it's hard, but has had it up to *here* with men and found God instead?

No. It's no good. I barbecued some meat the other day back in France, and made a salad and laid the table, made it all nice, and one of the blokes I was sharing the house with (*his* baby done gone left *him*, too) sat down and said yum yum and asked me to marry him. Perhaps when I go back I'll say 'Yes', but probably not. Probably I'll just drift hopelessly down to Eye Tech with the company cheque-book and buy yet more LA Eyeworks sunglasses to hide the tear-stains and crows'-feet, and start booking restaurant tables again, a poor slack sod with a smile on my lips, a hand in my pocket, and proleptic rejection singing dirges in my heart.

June 1989

William Makepeace Thackeray

THE SNOBS OF ENGLAND
By One of Themselves

CHAPTER I – THE SNOB SOCIALLY CONSIDERED

THERE are relative and positive Snobs. I mean by positive, such persons as are Snobs everywhere, in all companies, from morning till

night, from youth to the grave, being by Nature endowed with
Snobbishness – and others who are Snobs only in certain circumstances and relations of life.

For instance: I once knew a man who committed before me an act
as atrocious as that which I have indicated in the last chapter as
performed by me for the purpose of disgusting COLONEL SNOBLEY;
viz., the using the fork in the guise of a toothpick. I once, I say, knew
a man who, dining in my company at the Europa coffee-house
(opposite the Grand Opera, and as everybody knows, the only decent
place for dining at Naples), ate peas with the assistance of his knife.
He was a person with whose society I was greatly pleased at first –
indeed, we had met in the crater of Mount Vesuvius, and were
subsequently robbed and held to ransom by brigands in Calabria,
which is nothing to the purpose – a man of great powers, excellent
heart, and varied information; but I had never before seen him with a
dish of peas, and his conduct in regard to them caused me the deepest
pain.

After having seen him thus publicly comport himself, but one
course was open to me – to cut his acquaintance. I commissioned a
mutual friend (the HONOURABLE POLY ANTHUS) to break the matter to
this gentleman as delicately as possible, and to say that painful
circumstances – in no wise affecting MR MARROWFAT'S honour, or my
esteem for him – had occurred, which obliged me to forego my
intimacy with him; and accordingly we met, and gave each other the
cut direct that night at the DUCHESS OF MONTE FIASCO'S ball.

Everybody at Naples remarked the separation of the DAMON and
PYTHIAS – indeed, MARROWFAT had saved my life more than once –
but, as an English gentleman, what was I to do?

My dear friend was, in this instance, the Snob *relative*. It is not
snobbish of persons of rank of any other nation to employ their knife
in the manner alluded to. I have seen MONTE FIASCO clean his
trencher with his knife, and every Principe in company doing
likewise. I have seen, at the hospitable board of HIH the GRAND
DUCHESS STEPHANIE OF BADEN – (who, if these humble lines should
come under her Imperial eyes, is besought to remember graciously
the most devoted of her servants) – I have seen, I say, the Hereditary
Princess of Potztausend-Donnerwetter (that serenely-beautiful
woman!) use her knife in lieu of a fork or spoon; I have seen her
almost swallow it, by Jove! like RAMO SAMEE, the Indian juggler. And
did I blench? Did my estimation for the Princess diminish? No,

lovely AMALIA! One of the truest passions that ever was inspired by woman was raised in this bosom by that lady. Beautiful one! long, long may the knife carry food to those lips! the reddest and loveliest in the world!

The cause of my quarrel with MARROWFAT I never breathed to mortal soul for four years. We met in the halls of the aristocracy – our friends and relatives. We jostled each other in the dance or at the board; but the estrangement continued, and seemed irrevocable, until the fourth of June, last year.

We met at SIR GEORGE GOLLOPER'S. We were placed he on the right, your humble servant on the left of the admirable LADY G. Peas formed part of the banquet – ducks and green peas. I trembled as I saw MARROWFAT helped, and turned away sickening, lest I should behold the weapon darting down his horrid jaws.

What was my astonishment, what my delight when I saw him use his fork like any other Christian! He did not administer the cold steel once. Old times rushed back upon me – the remembrance of old services – his rescuing me from the brigands – his gallant conduct in the affair with the COUNTESS DEI SPINACHI – his lending me the 1700*l*. I almost burst into tears with joy – my voice trembled with emotion. 'FRANK, my boy!' I exclaimed, 'FRANK MARROWFAT, my dear fellow! a glass of wine!'

Blushing – deeply moved – almost as tremulous as I was myself, FRANK answered, '*George, shall it be Hock or Madeira?*' I could have hugged him to my heart but for the presence of the company. Little did LADY GOLLOPER know what was the cause of the emotion which sent the duckling I was carving into her Ladyship's pink satin lap. The most good-natured of women pardoned the error, and the butler removed the bird.

We have been the closest friends ever since, nor, of course, has FRANK repeated his odious habit. He acquired it at a country school, where they cultivated peas, and only used two-pronged forks, and it was only by living on the Continent, where the usage of the four-prong is general, that he lost the horrible custom.

In this point – and in this only – I confess myself a member of the SILVER FORK SCHOOL, and if this tale induce but one reader of *Punch* to pause, to examine in his own mind solemnly, and ask, 'Do I or do I not eat peas with a knife?' – to see the ruin which may fall upon himself by continuing the practice, or his family by beholding the example, these lines will not have been written in vain. And now, whatever other authors may be who contribute to this miscellany, I flatter myself SILK BUCKINGHAM will at least say that *I* am a moral man.

By the way, as some readers are dull of comprehension, I may as well say what the moral of this history *is*. The moral is this – Society having ordained certain customs, men are bound to obey the law of society, and conform to its harmless orders.

If I should go to the British and Foreign Institute (and Heaven forbid I should go under any pretext or in any costume whatever) – if I should go to one of the tea-parties in a dressing gown and slippers, and not in the usual attire of a gentleman, viz., pumps, a gold waistcoat, a crush hat, a sham frill, and a white choker – I should be insulting society, and *eating peas with my knife*. Let the porters of the Institute hustle out the individual who shall so offend. Such an offender is, as regards society, a most emphatical and refractory SNOB. It has its code and police as well as governments, and he must conform who would profit by the decrees set forth for the common comfort.

I am naturally averse to egotism, and hate self-laudation consumedly; but I can't help relating here a circumstance illustrative of the point in question, in which I must think I acted with considerable prudence.

Being at Constantinople a few years since – (on a delicate mission) – the Russians were playing a double game, between ourselves, and it became necessary on our part to employ an *extra negotiator*. LECKERBISS PASHA of Roumelia, then Chief Galeongee of the Porte, gave a diplomatic banquet at his summer palace at Bujukdere. I was on the left of the Galeongee; and the Russian agent COUNT DE DIDDLOFF on his dexter side. DIDDLOFF is a dandy who would die of a rose in aromatic pain; he had tried to have me assassinated three times in the course of the negotiation: but of course we were friends in public, and saluted each other in the most cordial and charming manner.

The Galeongee is – or was, alas! for a bow-string has done for him – a staunch supporter of the old school of Turkish politics. We dined with our fingers, and had flaps of bread for plates; the only innovation he admitted was the use of European liquors, in which he indulged with great gusto. He was an enormous eater. Amongst the dishes a very large one was placed before him of a lamb dressed in its wool, stuffed with prunes, garlic, assafœtida, capsicums, and other condiments, the most abominable mixture that ever mortal smelt or tasted. The Galeongee ate of this hugely; and pursuing the Eastern fashion, insisted on helping his friends right and left, and when he came to a particularly spicy morsel, would push it with his own hands into his guests' very mouths.

I never shall forget the look of poor DIDDLOFF, when his Excellency, rolling up a large quantity of this into a ball and exclaiming, 'Buk Buk' (it is very good), administered the horrible bolus to DIDDLOFF. The Russian's eyes rolled dreadfully as he received it; he swallowed it with a grimace that I thought must precede a convulsion, and seizing a bottle next him, which he thought was Sauterne, but which turned out to be French brandy, he swallowed nearly a pint before he knew his error. It finished him; he was carried away from the dining room almost dead, and laid out to cool in a summer-house on the Bosphorus.

When it came to my turn, I took down the condiment with a smile, said Bismillah, licked my lips with easy gratification, and when the next dish was served, made up a ball myself so dexterously, and popped it down the old Galeongee's mouth with so much grace, that his heart was won. Russia was put out of Court at once, *and the treaty of* Kabobanople *was signed*. As for DIDDLOFF, all was over with *him*, he was recalled to St Petersburg, and SIR RODERIC MURCHISON saw him, under the No. 3967, working in the Ural mines.

The moral of this tale I need not say, is, that there are many disagreeable things in society which you are bound to take down, and to do so with a smiling face.

March 1846

Alex Atkinson

FAREWELL TO CARAPHERNALIA

THE things you find on the back seats of other people's cars are not delightful or mysterious any more, and this is a pity. If we progress much farther there will be precious little delight or mystery left at all – in the backs of other people's cars, in old bureau drawers, on the music-hall stage, down the crevices of armchairs, or *anywhere*. It is a gloomy prospect.

The modern motor-car has a front bulge and a rear bulge, and not much else. The front bulge hides the engine, which is an essential, and the rear bulge hides Things which may or may not be essential but which would certainly add more to the charm of life if they were spread out on the back seat in the good old-fashioned way.

I can't remember the horse-drawn carriage, but, as one of the unofficial historians of the Shouting Twenties and the Apprehensive Thirties, I have vivid recollections of cars that were square back and front, and whose Things were in plain view – tied on to a grid behind with bits of strap, or chucked nonchalantly on to the shiny seats. What joy it was to settle back behind the driver, and with the coconut matting vibrating under your feet dream among boxes of eggs, wet batteries, petrol tins, ukulele-banjos, rolls of wallpaper, half-constructed two-valve wireless sets, books by Sax Rohmer, curious parcels, dead grouse, vacuum flasks, inner-tubes, starting-handles, pianola music, or unframed reproductions of The Laughing Cavalier. And what splendid conversations you could have.

'Charlie, why is this brown-paper bag on the floor full of mahjongg pieces and cherry-stones?'

'Search me, old bean.'

'Is this bicycle wheel anybody's?'

'I often wonder. By the way, are the pigeons bothering you?'

'Not really, but I've trodden on part of this airship made of match-boxes.'

'Crikey! How did that get in here?'

As for a lift in a *stranger's* car, that was an adventure indeed. Sinister cases were put under your feet 'out of the way', and odd ticking sounds came from them, or they moved of their own volition. You were never sure whether the piece of wood that stuck out from beneath a blanket was the butt of a loaded rifle or the neck of a mahogany horse. You were too polite to ask questions, and you wouldn't have asked them for worlds anyway, because the uncertainty was so thrilling. What kind of man is this, you would ask yourself, that he should wrap broken telephones in old newspapers and take them for rides? Will his wife meet him wild-eyed at the gate in a kimono and cry 'Did you bring the broken telephones, love?' – or is she a helpless, trusting creature to whom the discovery of this tea-caddy full of shrimps' heads on the back seat will come as a cruel blow?

You never knew. You hardly dared to guess. And it was good: it added spice to travel.

The most you can hope today is that sometimes, on a sharp S-bend, you may hear a muffled roll and rumble in the rear. They are there all right, the Things: but coddling Progress hides them in the boot. The wonder is gone from the back seat. Nothing now but dreary secret papers in a brief-case. Perhaps a box or two of deadly capsules. Or now and then a dachshund with a waistcoat. Alas, for the magic of yesteryear!

When I have saved for twenty years I shall buy a square little car. It will be very old, and I shall keep it in the back garden. I shall be very old too, and in my attic I shall rummage, and find old, forgotten Things. These I shall place on the back seat. And there my friends may browse at any time they wish, in happy, harmless retrospect, humming the songs of our youth.

October 1951

E.M. Delafield

AS OTHERS HEAR US

VISITING THE SICK

'WHAT a frightfully nice room – isn't it? – so nice and warm. It's *freezing* out; I think you're terribly lucky.'

'Well, of course –'

'Have you got millions of hot-water bottles? My hands are simply like ice.'

'Would you like the hot-water bottle for a minute?'

'Thanks frightfully. I didn't really mean that, but still I suppose I might as well. Just while I get warm, you know. I didn't know if you were allowed to eat anything at all so I just brought flowers. I'm afraid chrysanthemums are terribly dull.'

'Thank you so much.'

'I see you've got thousands of others. Oh dear – did they drip on you? I'm so sorry. What sort of a nurse have you got? My dear, when I had my operation two years ago I had the most *awful* nurse you ever met in your life.'

'Mine is very –'

'Oh, I know some of them are nice, of course, but I suppose I was just unlucky. In the end I got so dreadfully aggravated that I used to throw things at her. It must have been terribly bad for me. I wonder I didn't die. The doctors used to say: "You know, you oughtn't to be alive at all. You ought to be dead by rights." I was an *absolute* star case.'

'Were you very –'

'My dear, frightfully. Fancy! That operation usually lasts forty minutes, or forty-five *at the very outside* – and I took two hours and fifteen minutes. They all said it was a record.'

'I didn't know –'

'Oh, I never talk about it. I hate talking about it, in fact. The funny thing is, that every single person I've compared notes with tells me they were out and about again in a fortnight – and I was *eight weeks* flat on my back. And then the first time I got up I fainted. Fainted clean off.'

'How –'

'Yes, I know, wasn't it? My dear, what marvellous grapes! Are they as lovely as they look?'

'Won't you –'

'It's supposed to be the most awful thing anyone can do, isn't it, to visit an invalid and eat their grapes? Still, I daresay you're perfectly sick of them by this time. My dear, it's *months* since I've eaten anything like them! We simply can't afford to buy a thing. Of course everybody's on the very verge of the workhouse, as I daresay you know.'

'I thought –'

'Well, naturally, one tries to keep worrying thoughts away with a person who's been ill. (Though I must say, my dear, you look *too* well for words.) But there's no doubt that this is *the end of civilization*. It's simply crashing all round us.'

'The papers –'

'Oh, you mustn't ever believe a word the papers say. They just put what the Government *tells* them to put, you know. It's all part of a plan.'

'Isn't –'

'Isn't Income Tax coming down, you mean? Good heavens, no, my dear. It's going *up*. Soaring. And look at the number of road accidents. It's worse every single week, I believe. My dear, is that really the time? I ought to fly.'

'Would –'

'Tea? If you're going to have yours, I'd simply love a cup. I've got to dash to the *most* frightful bazaar. Which reminds me, I want you to take a ticket, like an angel, for a raffle. I'm supposed to be running it. Only a shilling. Or you can take ten, and make it a ten-bob note, if you'd rather.'

'What is –'

'My dear, I won't deceive you, it's a perfect *horror*. But you can always give it away or something. Besides, you're perfectly certain not to win it, don't you think? Haven't you noticed how people one knows never win anything in a raffle, by any chance. It's always somebody's housemaid's old aunt, in the North of England somewhere.'

'I don't think –'

'I can give you change for anything in the world. Is this your bag? Good heavens, why do you keep *papers* in it? I never have a *thing* but lipsticks and things in mine so that it doesn't lose its shape. My dear, how *like* me! I've spilt the whole thing on the floor. Isn't that *like* me? Never mind, if that's your tea she can pick it up. Not that they ever answer bells in this kind of place. At least I know they never answered mine. I took to ringing it every half-hour *regularly*, just to teach them. Now look here, I'll take this pound-note and give you ten bob in silver. Bother, I just can't do it. Nine-and-twopence – well, I'll owe you tenpence. Or look here, I'll take the pound-note and send you the change. And I shall have to send you the tickets too, as I've forgotten to bring the book.'

'I think tea –'

'Too marvellous, my dear! Do you think you could ring and get them to bring me lemon instead of milk, and brown bread-and-butter instead of white?'

January 1935

Roy Hattersley

IDOLS ON PARADE

IT is very nearly my favourite extract from modern English literature. So I do not propose to pass up the chance to quote it just because it comes from a book rather than a newspaper or periodical. George Gilder, who boasts on the back-flap of *The Spirit of Enterprise* that he contributes to the *Wall Street Journal* and *Harper's Magazine*, speaks for all the breathless financial correspondents and business editors who need someone to look up to:

> Bullheaded, defiant, tenacious, creative entrepreneurs continued to solve the problems of the world even faster than the world could create them. The achievement of enterprise remained the highest testimony to the mysterious strength of the human spirit.

British journalists are rarely as crass as that. But even Fleet Street is inclined to gush at the sight of a tycoon in a five-hundred-pound suit. John Jay and John Westwell, writing in the *Sunday Times* about the scramble to buy Courage Breweries, began with a typical soap opera paragraph: 'Lord Hanson, the elegantly dressed Yorkshireman at the helm of Britain's fifth largest company, returned to London via Concorde on Thursday evening ...' As if to confirm the irrelevant description of Lord Hanson's wardrobe, the accompanying picture showed him exposing several inches of shirt-cuff and a gold bracelet.

The *Sunday Times* is, of course, in thrall to new money and self-made millionaires. *The Observer* is sycophantic in a more stately way. A whole page profile of 'London's premier stockbroking house, Cazenove and Co' (in which not a single word of criticism appeared) demonstrated the respect in which one branch of the Establishment holds another. 'What is certain is that Cazenove will not be rushed. The firm was established in 1823 and the partnership is intent on preserving its unique powers.' With the exception of Robert Maxwell (who made the crucial public relations mistake of being a socialist), it is rare indeed that the newsapers are anything other than idolatrous about a man with a million pounds in the bank and a Rolls-Royce in one of the garages around the back of the modernised manor-house.

Money and success are glamorous attributes. See *Dallas* and *Dynasty*. And there is something romantic about a fallen hero. See *Paradise Lost*. Newspapers find glamour and romance irresistibly attractive. And since they nearly always publish stories about captains, as distinct from corporals of industry, the result is prose heavily laden with stardust – even when the officers and gentleman have recently been cashiered. In addition, tycoons photograph well.

Or at least their photographs are more attractive than pictures of their products.

The current issue of *Business Week* devoted its cover story to 'The New Aces of Low Tech'. The editor had to choose between decorating the front page of his magazine with a still-life of metal cans and pieces of coal or a double portrait of Nelson Peltz and Peter May. Messrs May and Peltz won. As a consequence, the story was personalised from its purple opening paragraph:

> Nelson Peltz and Peter May seem a lot like the other financial wizards who have so captivated Wall Street these days. They've built a corporate empire on dazzling financial footwork.

But by the end of the story we discover that they are better than, at first, they seem: 'The genius of Peltz and May is in marrying the new rules of finance with the old principles of management.'

The style seems to be infectious. I assumed that *What Investment*, subtitled 'Making More of Your Money', was intended for the small punter. And the tear-out postcards in the back – 'return to *Complete Guide to Unit Trusts*' and 'The Principal (Freepost) Tutor's Investments' – seemed to confirm it. It even has a share tipster who calls himself Joe Bloggs. But its heroes are giant-killers accelerating towards 'stock market stardom, like F.H. Tomkins', who 'rocket overnight from junior league sector status into the stock market's sixth biggest engineer'. But for the cult of the business personality, one magazine outstrips the rest. Carefully cultivated charisma shines out of every page of *Business*.

Well, nearly every page. On page 36 of the September issue, there is a passage of prose which says more about *Business* than its £2 cover price ever could.

> Weston looks ordinary, indeed, with his receding hairline and gingery moustache. He could be very much at home as an anonymous employee at one of his 65 bakeries, yet he is Chairman of a company with a market capitalisation of some £1.3 bn.

I think that the punctuation got confused. Full stops should have preceded 'indeed' and 'yet' and a comma should follow 'moustache'. But the message is still clear. Millionaires are supposed to have 'sex appeal' (like James Gulliver of Argyll) or 'self-conscious hauteur' (like Lord Hanson of Hanson). It is the workers who are dowdies.

It may be that the mosaic caricature of Garry Weston is his punishment for looking like a baker. Or perhaps he simply refused to pose for the silly sort of photograph which *Business* seems to believe enhances a tycoon's grandeur. Brian Smouha ('Accountancy Bloodhound') was pictured reflected in glass. Allan Taylor (of the Royal Bank of Canada) is at a forty-degree angle in front of his 'gold-leaf Plaza'. Bullion-dealer Warren Magi is blurred in front of a gold clock. They all seem to possess a willingness to pose that David Owen could barely match.

And the feature writers and the sub-editors love it. For they have to write about businessmen as if each one were Prometheus. Business magazines, sections and supplements are about success. They bring fame to men with fortunes and if they portray their subjects as anything except heroes, the whole ethos of their existence is put in question. On the markets in the exchanges, free enterprise ensures the triumph of the talented. Therefore, the triumphant must have talent. The logic is wonky, but it does result in really glossy magazines.

September 1986

George C. Nash

LETTERS TO THE SECRETARY OF A GOLF CLUB

From Lionel Nutmeg, Malayan Civil Service (Retd.), Old Bucks Cottage, Roughover.

Tuesday, March 20, 1934

DEAR MR WHELK, – I have to inform you that on the 13th green this morning General Sir Armstrong Forcursue threw his putter at me.

As you have just cause to remember, Sir, this is not the first occasion on which this gentleman (?) has forgotten himself during the many years that he and I have played our weekly game of golf;

and I now insist that you summon a committee-meeting at the earliest opportunity so that he may be forthwith removed from the Club.

Yours very truly,

L. NUTMEG.

From General Sir Armstrong Forcursue, KBE, CSI, 'The Cedars', Roughover.

Tuesday, 20/3/34

SIR, – I wish to report Mr Lionel Nutmeg to the Committee of the Club for habitually whistling through a broken eye-tooth whenever he becomes dormy. Please call a meeting as soon as possible.

Yours faithfully,

ARMSTRONG FORCURSUE.

PS – It is ridiculous to pretend this disgusting habit is a form of nervousness.

From Admiral Charles Sneyring Stymie, CB (Member of Roughover Golf Club Committee).

Thursday, 22/3/34

DEAR WHELK, – I have your notice of the meeting for Monday the 26th March, but unfortunately only five minutes before it arrived a most urgent telephone-call came through from my stockbrokers necessitating my leaving for London tomorrow. I shall be away at least a month.

Please accept my apologies.

Yours sincerely,

C. SNEYRING STYMIE.

From Ignatius Thudd (Member of Roughover Golf Club Committee).

March 22, 1934

DEAR SIR, – Regret unable attend meeting. Otherwise engaged.

Yours faithfully,

I.T.

From Barnabas Hackett (Member of Roughover Golf Club Committee).

Thursday, 22nd March, 1934

DEAR MR WHELK, – Afraid I won't be able to come to the meeting on Monday, as I have been told for some months now that if I am to get those three or four extra yards from my No. 3 iron I must have a minor operation on the terminal phalanx of my great toe (left).

As the present seems a more suitable time than any other, I have arranged to go into a nursing-home this afternoon and shall not be out for at least ten days.

Yours sincerely,

BARNABAS HACKETT.

Postcards were also received from General Sir Armstrong Forcursue, KBE, CSI, and Mr Nutmeg, signifying their intention of being present at the meeting.

From Ralph Viney (Captain of Roughover Golf Club), now in Scotland.

Friday, 23rd March, 1934

DEAR WHELK, – Your telegram has just arrived and I promptly wired my approval of your suggestion.

Sorry the Committee are funking Monday – I really thought they had more stuffing than that. However, I am sure that if the General and Nutmeg are shown into the committee-room as if for the meeting and left to themselves for a bit they will achieve a reconciliation. Personally, though, I shouldn't lock the door on the outside. Cheer up.

Yours sincerely,

R. VINEY.

From Ephraim Wobblegoose, House Steward, Roughover Golf Club.

Monday, March 26th, 1934

DEAR MR WHELK, – Sir, I had your note on Sunday saying you was leaving in a hurry for the Austrian Tyrol, and hope, Sir, your health will mend, it being nothing serious.

Well, Sir, I did as you bid with the General and Mr Nutmeg, and showed them into the committee-room when they come this P.M. And, Sir, they is both in the Cottage Hospital at this moment – the General's left ear badly torn and Mr Nutmeg's ankle real bad, which, so far as I could see through the keyhole, Sir, was from the General biting it.

Well, Sir, it was a great 'do' and no mistake; but there will be a tidy bill for the House Repairs Account – three panes of glass in the bay-window, new weights for the grandfather clock, and the handle of the President Cup nowhere to be seen.

Hoping you is OK, Sir, as all is here, *now*.

Yours faithfully,

E. WOBBLEGOOSE, *Steward.*

PS – Matron has just rung up to know if I can find the General's eyeglass, but there is nothing of it but the string.

She said both the patients was doing well and was planning to go off together next month for a golfing holiday in the South of France.

March 1934

F.C. Burnand

DUE SOUTH

MONTE CARLO, FEBRUARY, 1889

On my road to the Casino at Monte Carlo I meet HODGKINS, PETERSON, and FLICKMORE. 'How have you done?' I ask, as I am collecting all the information I can about the country, so to speak, in which I am about to try my fortune.

'Pretty fair,' answers HODGKINS. 'Not bad,' says PETERSON. 'Might have been worse,' observes FLICKMORE.

'Lost five hundred louis first day,' says HODGKINS, looking sharply at his two friends.

I smile sympathetically. Five hundred! Dear me, a large sum to lose. And I began to think that I'd better reflect before I tempt the hazard of *roulette*.

'We picked it up next day, though,' puts in PETERSON, also looking round at his companions, and smiling.

'And the second day were two thousand to the good,' says FLICKMORE. 'Not pounds – louis; but not bad business even in that.'

Bad business, indeed! I wish it would happen to *me* even in francs – or half-francs, for the matter of that. I am eager to know the system.

'Well,' answers HODGKINS, 'you see it's a little difficult to explain and carry out, unless you're really going in for it. Perhaps you'd hardly understand it.'

Well, I think my powers of comprehension are quite up to this; I mean that, if these three chaps, who are mere *flâneurs* on the face of the earth (except when they are in their business in the City) can master the system, I'm pretty sure that *I* can.

'Can't you give me an idea of it?' I ask, almost piteously.

'Well,' says FLICKMORE, 'it takes a day to carry out properly, even with luck, and it requires three fellows to play it. We're a Syndicate, and we bring in five hundred apiece. Lose *that*, we stop.'

Thank you. Much obliged. I needn't trouble them for their system, as I am not 'three single gentlemen rolled into one,' and so I can't be a Syndicate.

They are going in to the Casino, and pass me on the steps. Now what shall I do? While I am meditating on my plan of campaign, Lord ARTHUR STONEBROKE, passing me hurriedly, cries, 'Halloa, old chap, going in to break the Bank, eh?' I reply, as he halts for a second by the door, as carelessly as I can, as if I hadn't quite decided whether I should let the Bank have another day's grace or not – 'Well, I don't know.' And then I pay him the compliment of asking 'what *he* is going to do,' as if to imply that my movements shall be decided by *his*.

'Oh,' says he, in an offhand manner, 'I'm just going in for a flutter before dinner. Only taking in five hundred louis.'

I nod to him pleasantly, and he passes in, and disappears. 'Only five hundred louis to play with before dinner!' I am debating with myself whether I shall put on three five-franc pieces all at once, or extend the operation as they used to do the torture of the rack by doing it in three turns. Shall I stop at three five-franc pieces, or shall I go on to six? Let me see – five five-franc pieces are a sovereign, and therefore ten make two sovereigns. I wish *one* could make two sovereigns – and that one be myself.

First Decision. – I settle that it is better to have the ten five-franc pieces in my pocket, *in case* I want to play.

Second Decision. – The number of my coat is 200. I've often heard
that a man backing the number of his coat, or multiple of it, or some
division of it, makes a heap of money. *Happy Thought.* Try it. I ask
SMITHSON, who has been an *habitué* for years, how he would divide
200 so as to make it into playable numbers. SMITHSON, with an air
that inspires me with confidence, says offhand, 'Put on the *six
premiers* – that includes the two – on the middle dozen, so does that –
on the *pair*, which includes the 20, and on zero, that's your game.'
And, nodding knowingly to me, he walks away with the satisfied air
of a man who has done the best he can for a friend, and who,
throwing off the responsibility there and then, leaves the friend to do
the best he can for himself. I note it down, and determine to act upon
it. It is, one fiver – I mean one five-franc piece – that is, four-and-
twopence, only it sounds more sporting to speak of them as 'fivers' –
one fiver on the first six numbers, another on the middle dozen,
another on 'even', and another on zero. Good. Stay – that makes four
all at once, and I only intended to put on three. If I lose these, then
on go four more – that's eight – and I shall only have two left.

I decide to change a third sovereign – just as well to have fifteen
'fivers' (silver fivers) in my pocket as ten.

I enter the room. I walk up to the Changers' bureau, and get my
fifteen French five-franc pieces in exchange for three beautiful
golden English sovereigns. It doesn't seem fair, to begin with. I look
upon them as counters, and three sovereigns seems a lot of money to
pay for fifteen counters. I go to a *roulette*-table in first room. Crowd.
No getting near it. I see PETERSON with a pile of gold before him,
looking very serious; behind him stand HODGKINS and FLICKMORE.
Their eyes are on the table. They don't see me. Next moment the
croupier cries out something that I don't catch, and the effect of it is
that a lot of money is swept off one way, a lot another, and then
HODGKINS and FLICKMORE seem to breathe again as PETERSON has
notes and gold pushed towards him with the *croupier's* rake.
Somehow I don't like this table. I leave it. I don't even visit the one
opposite, and enter the middle room. Here the table at the lower end
has an attraction for me. Some one standing by one of the *croupiers*
just moves out, and leaves a momentary vacancy, which fate seems to
point out to me as the very place for me. It is almost opposite *pair*,
which just suits my plan, the only difficulty being to get at the other
end of the table, and deposit my five-franc piece on the middle
dozen, and to get it back again, with the companion which it ought to

win, from that distance in safety. At the tables I have often heard of
old French women collaring what doesn't belong to them; and then,
indignantly protesting that the expostulating Englishman had tried
to rob them.

This rather sets me against the middle dozen. Also somehow I
don't fancy zero. If I snub the middle dozen and zero, then I only
need risk two fivers each time, and this will give me more sport for
my money. And, after all, on the middle dozen you only get two to
one, and the odds against zero turning up are greater than against
anything else on the table. Besides, instead of losing four each time, I
should only lose two. For all these excellent reasons I decide to
follow only half of my friend's advice, and I select the *six premiers*
and *pair*. When shall I begin? No time like the present. Now: this
next turn. I brace up my nerves, I give a nod that the Duke of
WELLINGTON, at Waterloo, might have copied, when he shut up his
telescope with a snap and gave the word to charge, and producing
two five-franc pieces, I lean over the man in front, and with a polite
'Pardon, M'sieur!' I take his rake from him, and push my piece on to
pair, nearly jobbing him in the eye with the handle as I draw the
instrument back again. Elderly Frenchman looks up angrily. I feel
hot and awkward: I foresee a duel, and so give him a smiling apology
to turn away his wrath (which it doesn't), and then catching the
croupier's eye – not with the rake this time, but figuratively with my
eye – I ask him to shove my other five-franc piece on to *six premiers*,
which he does with a careless air as if it didn't matter twopence to
him (and it doesn't), or to anybody (no more it does except to myself
and family), what becomes of this absurd stake.

Then I draw back, fold my arms, try to appear utterly indifferent,
look round the table to see if I can spot a friend to nod to, fail, and
then I keep my eye on my pieces, and stoically await the issue. '*Rien
ne va plus!*' – click! – it is over. *Vingt-cinq* – middle dozen and
uneven. Thank you – five-franc pieces, fare ye well!

Two more on the same. Same business of jobbing Frenchman's
eye with rake, catching *croupier's* eye, folding arms, awaiting verdict
– which ... *nineteen!*

Thank you. Exeunt second supply. Upon my word, I think I'll try
the whole lot at once. *Six premiers* – zero (hate zero) – *pair* – and
middle dozen. I do. MIDDLETON comes up at the minute. 'Doing any
good?' he asks. I shrug my shoulders. As I turn round, the number is
called – I don't see what it is – but whatever it was, I find that it was

neither zero, nor *pair*, nor middle dozen, nor *six premiers*, and all my pretty chicks are gone at one fell swoop. No, I'll limit myself to two. It's quite enough to lose at a time. And those two shall be – stay … shall I change my plan – evidently I'm not in luck. Wish I hadn't asked SMITHSON how to divide 200. Also wish I'd never heard that some gamblers choose the number of the ticket given them for their coat, and have immense luck with it. Stupid story: it's stories like this that lead one so astray.

My last two. I object to zero. The first six have played me false. The middle dozen can no longer be trusted. *Impair* has once stood my friend. Suddenly the number 19, which has nothing whatever to do with my calculations, seems to stand out from the rest, and invite me. It absolutely seems to say, 'Put five francs on me, and one on the red.' My whole plans are deranged. Nineteen is staring at me. 'You'll regret not planking down on me,' it says. '*Messieurs, faites le jeu!*' '*Faites!*' Fate it is. Once more 'pardon', and I job the irate Monsieur in the eye with the end of the rake. On to the 19 plump, *en plein*. Already I see the *croupier* preparing to pay me thirty-five times my stake. Shall I put another, *the* other – and the last – on something? If so, on what? The ball is whizzling round! The second – shall I on zero? SMITHSON said *zero* – it was part of his original plan – as I catch the *croupier's* eye – an inspiration. '*Six premiers, s'il vous plaît*' – he pushes it on just where I would give any amount – another five francs to recall it. The *croupier* opposite says, inexorably, '*Rien ne va plus!*' and – click! … *zero!!* Ha! ha! and I was within an ace of putting on zero. O SMITHSON! When I tell you that, after asking your advice, I've not acted on it, you will think I've been making a fool of you – and of myself.

Shall I change another sovereign? And try another table? I will. I go to the magician who warily examines and changes the gold into silver behind the pigeon-hole of the bureau, and get my five-franc pieces. Odd! This time as I slip them into my pocket, I feel as if I'd won them from the man behind the pigeon-hole, and somehow, I experience the pleasant sensation of having somehow or another got the best of him in a bargain. To which table shall I go? What plan shall I pursue? With SMITHSON's I can only play once with four francs, and if I lose, then once with one. At this moment up comes BYNGLEIGH.

March 1889

E.C. Bentley
MORE CLERIHEWS

When Macaulay found Brougham
Sitting on a tomb,
He told his anxious friend
He was meditating on his latter end.

Lewis Carroll
Bought sumptuous apparel
And built an enormous palace
Out of the profits of *Alice*.

Dr W.G. Grace
Had hair all over his face.
Lord! how the people cheered
When a ball got lost in his beard!

Although Macchiavelli
Was extremely fond of jelly,
He stuck religiously to mince
While he was writing *The Prince*.

November 1938

Noël Coward
HOW THE NUMBERS CAME

COULD not help composing tunes even if I wished to. Ever since I was a little boy they have dropped into my mind unbidden and often in the most unlikely circumstances. The *Bitter Sweet* waltz, 'I'll See You Again', came to me whole and complete in a taxi when I was appearing in New York in *This Year of Grace*. I was on my way home to my apartment after a matinée and had planned, as usual, to have an hour's rest and a light dinner before the evening performance. My taxi got stuck in a traffic block on the corner of Broadway and Seventh Avenue, klaxons were honking, cops were shouting, and suddenly in the general din there was the melody, clear and unmistakable. By the time I got home the words of the first phrase had emerged. I played it over and over again on the piano (key of E flat as usual) and tried to rest, but I was too excited to sleep.

Oddly enough, one of the few songs I ever wrote that came to me in a setting appropriate to its content was 'Mad Dogs and Englishmen'. This was conceived and executed during a two-thousand-mile car drive from Hanoi in Tonkin to the Siamese border. True, the only white people to be seen were French, but one can't have everything.

The birth of 'I'll Follow My Secret Heart' was even more surprising. I was working on *Conversation Piece* at Goldenhurst, my home in Kent. I had completed some odd musical phrases here and there but no main waltz theme, and I was firmly and miserably stuck. I had sat at the piano daily for hours, repeatedly trying to hammer out an original tune or even an arresting first phrase, and nothing had resulted from my concentrated efforts but banality. I knew that I could never complete the score without my main theme as a pivot and finally, after ten days' increasing despair, I decided to give up and, rather than go on flogging myself any further, postpone the whole project for at least six months.

This would entail telegraphing to Yvonne Printemps, who was in Paris waiting eagerly for news, and telling Cochran who had already announced the forthcoming production in the Press. I felt fairly wretched but at least relieved that I had had the sense to admit failure while there was still time. I poured myself a large whisky and soda, dined in grey solitude, poured myself another, even larger, whisky and soda, and sat gloomily envisaging everybody's disappointment and facing the fact that my talent had withered and that I should never write any more music until the day I died. The whisky did little to banish my gloom, but there was no more work to be done and I didn't care if I became fried as a coot, so I gave myself another drink and decided to go to bed. I switched off the lights at the door and noticed that there was one lamp left on by the piano. I walked automatically to turn it off, sat down and played 'I'll Follow My Secret Heart' straight through in G flat, a key I had never played in before.

There is, to me, strange magic in such occurrences. I am willing and delighted to accept praise for my application, for my self-discipline and for my grim determination to finish a thing once I have started it. My acquired knowledge is praiseworthy too, for I have worked hard all my life to perfect the material at my disposal. But these qualities, admirable as they undoubtedly are, are merely accessories. The essential talent is what matters, and essential talent is unexplainable.

Composition on Broadway

My mother and father were both musical in a light, amateur sense, but their gift was in no way remarkable. My father, although he could improvise agreeably at the piano, never composed a set piece of music in his life. I have known many people who were tone-deaf whose parents were far more actively musical than mine. I had no piano lessons when I was a little boy except occasionally from my mother who tried once or twice, with singular lack of

success, to teach me my notes.
I could, however, from the age
of about seven onwards, play
on the piano in the pitch dark
any tune I had heard. To this
day my piano-playing is
limited to three keys: E flat, B
flat and A flat. The sight of
two sharps frightens me to
death.

When I am in the process of
composing anything in the
least complicated I can play it
in any key on the keyboard,
but I can seldom if ever repeat
these changes afterwards unless I practise them assidu-
ously every day. In E flat I can
give the impression of playing

*Dear George Gershwin used to moan
... and try to force my fingers on to
the right notes ...*

well. A flat and B flat I can get away with, but if I have to play
anything for the first time it is always to my beloved E flat that my
fingers move automatically. Oddly enough, C major, the key most
favoured by the inept, leaves me cold. It is supposed to be easier to
play in than any of the others because it has no black notes, but I
have always found it dull.

Another of my serious piano-playing defects is my left hand. Dear
George Gershwin used to moan at me in genuine distress and try to
force my fingers on to the right notes. As a matter of fact he showed
me a few tricks that I can still do, but they are few and dreadfully far
between. I can firmly but not boastfully claim that I am a better
pianist than Irving Berlin, but as that superlative genius of light
music is well known not to be able to play at all except in C major, I
will not press the point. Jerome D. Kern, to my mind one of the most
inspired romantic composers of all, played woodenly as a rule and
without much mobility. Dick Rodgers plays his own music best
when he is accompanying himself or someone else, but he is far from
outstanding. Vincent Youmans was a marvellous pianist, almost as
brilliant as Gershwin, but these are the only two I can think of who,
apart from their creative talent, could really play.

At the very beginning I said that I was born into a generation that took light music seriously. It was fortunate for me that I was, because by the time I had emerged from my teens the taste of the era had changed. In my early twenties and thirties it was from America that I gained my greatest impetus. In New York they have always taken light music seriously. There it is, as it should be, saluted as a specialized form of creative art, and is secure in its own right. The basis of a successful American musical show is now and has been for many years its music and its lyrics. Here in England there are few to write the music and fewer still to recognize it when it is written. The commercial managers have to fill their vast theatres and prefer, naturally enough, to gamble on acknowledged Broadway successes rather than questionable home products.

The critics are quite incapable of distinguishing between good light music and bad light music, and the public are so saturated with the cheaper outpourings of Tin Pan Alley which are dinned into their ears interminably by the BBC that their natural taste will soon die a horribly unnatural death. It is a depressing thought; but perhaps some day soon, someone, somewhere, will appear with an English musical so strong in native quality that it will succeed in spite of the odds stacked against it.

July 1953

Nigel Balchin

HOW TO RUN A BASSOON FACTORY;

or, Business Explained

PRELIMINARY NOTICE

FROM time to time, doubtless, many of our readers will want to give up working for a living and launch out as Captains of Industry. Accordingly, for the benefit of those who feel that they are in a rut and who want to start in today to make a fortune, Mr Punch proposes to provide a series of articles (all from the pens of acknowledged experts) on how to license, start, stop, run, maintain, overhaul and drive in traffic a really modern business. We open this series of Articles for Future Peers with

I – SORTS OF BUSINESSES (*OR* SPECIES OF BUSNI)

There are two main sorts of businesses:

(1) Buying something and making something out of it. This is called Manufacturing.

(2) Buying something and making a lot out of it. This is called Retailing.

There is a third species known as a Wholesaler or Middleman, which simply buys a thing at one price, puts it in a paper-bag and sells it at another. The Middleman is commonly called a Parasite, except on the Stock Exchange, where he is known as a Jobber.

The actual method by which a business is carried on depends on what is called its Constitution. It may be –

(1) *A Private Trader* (or Family Firm) – rather dying out but still to be seen in the quaint old survival, the Family Butcher.

(2) *A Joint Stock Company* (on no account to be confused with a Touring Stock Company). The main difference between the two is that a Private Trader is a single person with limited assets and unlimited liabilities, while a Joint Stock Company (or Co.) is a lot of people with limited liability and almost unlimited assets. That is to say, if the concern is in debt the Private Trader must pay whether he has the money or not, while the Joint Stock Company (Co. Ltd.) need not pay if it can't. The acute reader will therefore see that it pays to be a Joint Stock Company, because one is then able to plead the Gaming Act.

For our purpose we shall assume that all our readers are Co.s and very definitely Ltd. *This is important*.

Control

A Company consists of Shareholders who provide the money and are sent circulars. Its control, however, is vested in a Board of Directors. Please note carefully that the control is not *given* to the Directors. It is *vested* in them. Why, I am not sure, but it is always done. It is desirable, if possible, to be a Director.

Directors

There are several sorts of Directors, viz.:

Ordinary Directors.
Extraordinary Directors.*
Curious and Interesting Directors.*
Elected Directors.
Selected Directors.
Managing Directors.
Guinea-Pig Directors.
Active Directors.
Sleeping Directors.
Indirectors.*
Directors.

The functions of Directors are important but rather vague. As their work is almost entirely Thinking they do not work very long hours, and it is essential that they should spend Saturdays in the open air to recuperate. If you are a Director and someone insinuates that you do not work very hard it is usual either –

(1) To sack him on the spot; or
(2) To point out that reading *The Times* helps you to decide on Policy; or
(3) To explain that the whole success of the firm depends on social contacts at your club.

In any case it is as well to offer with some bitterness to swop your job for his, and then go on quickly to some other matter.

A special word is necessary about Managing Directors. A Managing Director is a man who really knows where the factory is and even goes there sometimes. It is advisable to have a Managing Director.

Nature of the Business

The grand principle is to make or sell something which people either

(a) Must have, e.g., Food.
(b) Will have, e.g., Clothes.
(c) Can be made to have, e.g., Patent Medicines.

If possible, avoid *permanent* things. It is very nice to sell a grand paino, but the chance of a weekly order is remote. Most of the big fortunes have been made from things which wore out nice and

---

* Avoid these.

quickly and couldn't very well be repaired, e.g., Beer. By all means, if possible, establish a Habit. A lot of money has been made out of the silly habits of smoking and chewing gum. There is a sizeable fortune awaiting the man who can give the public the bassoon-playing habit.

Alternatively, if you have no capacity for originality, do something which has been done before. Frankly, I don't care much *what* you make. That's your business (ha! ha!), and, if you haven't a fixed idea that you could make a pile of money out of indiarubber cutlery or hairpins, you've no right to be going into business. I will offer only one word of advice – don't worry if there doesn't seem to be much of a market for the thing you want to make. There was once an American who made a huge fortune out of collecting old tins and making them into finger-plates for doors. Remember that *someone* makes a living out of putting spots on rocking-horses, making tooth-picks, printing texts, and making tools to make tools to put the bristles in toothbrushes. There's plenty of scope. Go in and win; and next week I'll tell you how to finance your Company.

March 1934

R.C. Lehmann
AT PUTNEY

WHEN eight strong fellows are out to row,
   With a slip of a lad to guide them,
I warrant they'll make the light ship go,
   Though the coach on the launch may chide them,
With his 'Six, get on to it! Five, you're late!
Don't hurry the slides, and use your weight!
You're bucketing, Bow; and, as to Four,
The sight of his shoulders makes me sore!'

But Stroke has steadied his fiery men,
   And the lift on the boat gets stronger;
And the Coxswain suddenly shouts for 'Ten!
   Reach out to it, longer, longer!'
While the wind and the tide raced hand in hand
The swing of the crew and the pace were grand;
But now that the two meet face to face
It's buffet and slam and a tortoise-pace

For Hammersmith Bridge has rattled past,
   And, oh, but the storm is humming.
The turbulent white steeds gallop fast;
   They're tossing their crests and coming.
It's a downright rackety, gusty day,
And the backs of the crew are drenched in spray;
But it's 'Swing, boys, swing till you're deaf and blind,
And you'll beat and baffle the raging wind.'

They have slipped through Barnes; they are round the bend;
   And the chests of the eight are tightening.
'Now spend your strength, if you've strength to spend,
   And away with your hands like lightning!
Well rowed!' – and the coach is forced to cheer –
'Now stick to it, all, for the post is near!'
And, lo, they stop at the coxswain's call,
With its message of comfort, 'Easy all!'

So here's to the sturdy undismayed
   Eight men who are bound together
By the faith of the slide and the flashing blade
   And the swing and the level feather;
To the deeds they do and the toil they bear;
To the dauntless mind and the will to dare;
And the joyous spirit that makes them one
Till the last fierce stroke of the race is done.

March 1910

William Boyd

UN BON HOMME IN UN QUANDARY

I SHOULD have been more suspicious, I suppose. Quite suddenly, my editor in Paris – Françoise – started speaking to me in French when hitherto she'd employed her extremely fluent English. Just testing, she said, for the *Table Ronde*. The *table ronde* was an event that had been organised by the British Council in Paris. In return for my air fare and two nights in a hotel I had agreed to participate in an informal discusson about my first novel, *A Good Man in Africa*, which had just been published in France (*Un Anglais sous Les*

Tropiques). It seemed a reasonable quid pro quo: a few questions, a few answers, the odd carefully rehearsed anecdote – even my rusty French (product of a year-long sojourn on the Côte d'Azur in 1971) should be able to cope.

I flew to Paris, arriving in the mid-afternoon. The *table ronde* had been scheduled for 6 P.M. that day. I had time to check into my hotel, meet at the British Council for a drink with my publishers, and then into the *table ronde*. It had struck me that I wasn't leaving much time for acclimatisation. I had meant to mug up a little on my irregular verbs, check out a few difficult words, but somehow had never got round to it. Not that it matters much, I told myself as I was driven to the hotel, abstract nouns are the same in French as in English. Keep it simple, throw in the odd *franchement* or *en principe*, a shrug or two, and you're laughing. The lady from the British Council assured me that everyone was very excited about the *table ronde*. Why's that? I enquired. It's so unusual to conduct proceedings in French, she said; most British authors insist on talking English. Oh, I said, do they? Yes, but when we advertise that the *table ronde* will be in French we get a much bigger audience – and we've got a very distinguished panel. My mouth was getting strangely dry. She mentioned their names. No bells ringing. Tell me about them I said. Well, there was Georges Conchon, Goncourt prize-winning novelist, Catherine Rihoit, lecturer at the Sorbonne, famous for her rather raunchy feminist novels and a celebrated Congolese writer Tchicaya U' Tam'si. Pronounced tremors had started up in both hands. I tried to translate this nightmare into English terms – it was like being invited to share a panel with Salman Rushdie, Germaine Greer and Wole Soyinka. Imagine some French novelist with semi-efficient English trying to hold his own with these luminaries …

In my hotel room I wiped the vomit from my lips and tried to memorise some vocabulary. What was the French for post-structuralist? How did one translate 'unreliable narrator'. My *Harrap's New Shorter* French and English dictionary was a legacy of my sixth-form French (grade D at A-level) and was not overburdened with the new literary jargon. I recalled my rule of thumb: all English nouns ending -*tion* are the same in French; all abstract nouns with a Latin root are the same in French – think of the English word, say it with a French accent, no problem. That was my first mistake.

Luckily by the time I arrived at the British Council I was on autopilot. This is a state that descends on me whenever a crisis state reaches panic proportions. Certain segments of my brain – the imagination, those nerve circuits that allow one to think in the future tense, the embarrassment glands, or whatever – are shut down. One enters a sort of solipsistic reverie – the world is a dream, nothing matters. The symptoms are a glazed smile, a dead look in the eyes and conversation pitched at a level of the commonplace and banal.

It was a state that was seldom to leave me during my two days in Paris, but it served me well during the *table ronde* and the dinner with the panel afterwards (nobody told me about the dinner). I remember a huge room, and about a hundred people sitting down facing a daïs upon which the panel sat. I was introduced and my decision to speak French was admired and generously applauded. The smile became more glazed. As for the discussion itself, my strategy was to keep my role to an absolute minimum. This turned out to be easily effected because everyone else had huge amounts to say. I remember stuttering to a halt during a lame defence of realism (*le réalisme*, I hoped). Tchicaya U' Tam'si, gamely undertaking the role of spokesman for Black Africa, upbraided me for neglecting to tackle *le racisme* ('*Mais, c'est un roman comique*' was my response) and then got into a 15-minute wrangle with my translator – who was in the audience – over her translation of 'French Letter'. The term she had used was *capot d'Anglais*. Tchicaya resented this for some reason and, I think, saw it as neo-colonialist. I was as vague as the rest of the audience about the precise nature of his objection, but that didn't stop anyone from talking about it.

Indeed the whole discussion – and this is what I see as typically French – was carried on in the higher altitudes of intellectual debate: the concrete, the empiric, were shunned absolutely – the book disappeared into a fug of abstract nouns. To which, apparently, I added some new ones. My rule of thumb let me down badly, and after the talk several broadly smiling people admired my way with neologisms. 'I do like your new words,' one lady said to me. 'They sound so much nicer than the old ones.'

Problems with words continued the next day. After lunch with a journalist, who mercifully spoke English, I was to be interviewed on French radio. Sadder and wiser I made sure that the publishers had conveyed to the interviewer that I possessed only rudimentary French. It made no difference, and I can only put the interviewer's intransigence and hostility down to rampant Anglophobia. He spoke French with a velocity that in any other circumstances would have been highly impressive. Although we faced each other across a table we might have been separated by thousands of miles of faulty telephone cable. Through the fizz, crackle and interference of his rapid fire I could only make out the occasional word. '*Politique*' was one. '*Plutôt à gauche*,' I said. He looked very puzzled. Soon I started asking him to redefine words in an effort to slow him down. We carried on in this way for ten minutes. 'How did it go?' I asked the subdued publicity person afterwards. 'It was ... interesting,' she said.

That night, the plan was for me to go to a launching party. Not of my book, but of some French author. It seemed that key figures in the French literary world would be present, and it would be greatly advantageous to meet them. Brain death seemed imminent, but I thought I would give it one more try.

My editor, Françoise, drove me out to a small and fashionable bookshop in a fashionable arrondissement. The book being celebrated was a slim monograph on the Paris commune. The small bookshop was very crowded and very smoky. The 'look' for French intellectuals and literary folk, for those interested in fashion notes, hasn't changed since the Sixties. Key props are a cigarette, a leather jacket, unstructured greasy hair and massive pretension. I was led through the crowd to meet the literary editrix of a major newspaper. She was pale, large, freckled and with a lot of lank ginger hair. 'I'm afraid she doesn't like Western literature,' Françoise whispered as we approached. 'But I don't write Westerns,' I said, vastly relieved. 'No, no,' Françoise said. The editrix reserved her admiration for works from beyond the Iron Curtain, preferably written by Jewish dissidents. 'How do you do?' I said. 'I've just been reading Penrose's book on English Surrealism,' were her first words to me, in French to boot. We did not find much common ground.

Perhaps as an oblique comment on my small talk, she swiftly introduced me to a translator who wanted to practise his English. Translators are a curious, generally seriously impoverished breed. Encounters with them can be deeply unsettling. At a party in London I was once introduced to a man who said 'Hello, I your Polish translator are.' My Swedish translator wrote inviting me to 'crash in his pad in Stockholm' if I wanted to 'save some bread'. Quite apart from provoking anguish over what's happening to your books, you wonder what strange demon drove them to take up the career in the first place. This particular French translator was a suitably tall, dark, starved-looking man. I asked him whom he was translating. Flann O'Brien he said. *At Swim-Two-Birds*. But, I said tactfully after a shocked pause, can it be done? Oh yes, he assured me, he'd been working on it for eight years. Deeply saddened, I was glad to be interrupted by Françoise who said she had to go. She was leaving me in the hands of François-Xavier, another editor, who would take me back to my hotel. I liked François-Xavier, and not just because he spoke very good English, and so was not in the least disappointed when he interrupted me trying not to give the French translator my address in London and said we had to go.

Outside, it was clear that François-Xavier was in something of a hurry. As we climbed into his Volkswagen he told me why. His mother, who was nearly eighty, was a very celebrated French actress who was currently appearing at the Comédie Française. It was his job to deliver her to the stage door each night. I asked when the play started. Eight o'clock. We had just under an hour, I couldn't see what the problem was. François-Xavier explained. His mother, apparently, liked to arrive at the theatre half an hour before her call so she could do her *friction*. Friction? Yes, she rubbed herself all over with a pumice stone. It made her all tingly and hot and was a crucial prerequisite to her nightly performance. If she couldn't do her *friction* all hell broke loose and tonight we were running a bit late.

François-Xavier suggested we pick up his mother before he dropped me off. I agreed, trying to imagine what it must be like to rub yourself all over with a pumice stone. We set off for her flat, we got caught in a traffic jam, we raced up side streets trying to get there more quickly.

As we approached, François-Xavier could see his mother pacing up and down on the pavement outside her apartment block.

I jumped into the back of the car as François-Xavier tried to mollify the near-hysterical old actress. Introductions were scant. The conversation went, approximately, like this:

'You're so late! My *friction*, what about my *friction*!'

'Darling, you look absolutely ravishing.'

'But it's ten to eight!'

'Plenty of time, my little cabbage, plenty of time.'

'But my *friction*.'

'You do too much of that *friction*, try just five minutes tonight.'

'It's a disaster, a disaster!'

'Nonsense, nonsense. You're so beautiful, so wonderful. Everybody loves you.'

Madame, to me: 'I have, how you say, pumice? I rub myself. *Friction*. Before the show.'

Me: 'Ah. Yes.'

To François-Xavier: 'You silly stupid boy. You promised not to be late.'

'Oh, darling, don't make such a fuss. We have hours of time. Hours. You will be magnificent.'

We stopped at a traffic light. François-Xavier kissed his mother's hand. 'Keep calm, my lovely, that's the main thing.'

I opened the door. 'I can walk from here.' I faintly said goodbye and thank you. I'm not sure they heard. I watched them drive off. I was on the Boulevard Montparnasse. There had to be a bar around here somewhere. I wandered off. This fiction *friction*, I thought, it can really get to you. I needed a drink very badly indeed: brain death had arrived.

October 1984

Robert Graves

TO A SPITEFUL CRITIC

I CANNOT pity you,
Poor pebble in my shoe,
  Now that the heel is sore;
You planned to be a rock
And a stumbling block,
  Or was it perhaps more?

But now be grateful if
You vault over the cliff,
  Shaken from my shoe;
Where lapidary tides
May scour your little sides
  And even polish you.

September 1955

A.A. Milne

WHEN WE WERE VERY YOUNG

XV – LINES AND SQUARES

WHENEVER I walk in a London street
I'm ever so careful to watch my feet;
And I keep in the squares,
And the big brown bears
Who wait at the corners all ready to eat
The sillies who tread on the lines of the street,
Go back to their lairs;
And I say to them, 'Bears,
Just look how I'm walking in all of the squares!'
And the little bears growl to each other, 'He's mine,
As soon as he's silly and steps on a line.'
And some of the bigger bears try to pretend
That they came round the corner to look for a friend;
And they try to pretend that nobody cares
Whether you walk on the lines or squares.
But only the sillies believe their talk;
It's ever so portant how you walk,
And it's ever so jolly to call out, 'Bears,
Just watch me walking in all the squares!'

March 1924

Michael Parkinson
DYING WITH YOUR BOOTS ON

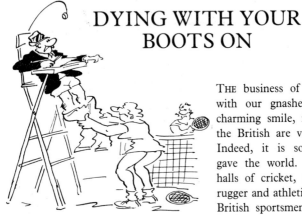

THE business of losing well, with our gnashers set in a charming smile, is something the British are very good at. Indeed, it is something we gave the world. The marble halls of cricket, tennis, polo, rugger and athletics are full of British sportsmen who might not have known what to do in the unlikely event of their winning anything but, by God, they know how to lose well.

I have never been able to understand why it is that some people place such significance on a man's ability to accept defeat without demur. The essence of all sport is conflict, and the best sporting conflicts are those that reveal not only the technique but also the very soul of the participants.

That being the case, it would be foolish to expect anyone who has given his all in, say, a game of tennis, to accept with a gracious smile a bum decision by a sleeping touch judge which turns out to lose him the game.

In such circumstances, it is understandable, nay necessary, that the offended athlete gives vent to his feelings by hurling his racket across the court, rending his hair, beating his chest, or indeed setting fire to the Centre Court if the mood takes him. Apart from this being the most natural thing to do, it is also something that appeals to the crowds. Those splendid chaps who run our sports might frown at displays of temperament, but the fact is that the crowds love them.

As a Northerner, it took me some considerable time to come to terms with the fact that some people regarded sport as anything but bloody warfare in which there were winners and losers, and it didn't much matter what you were so long as you didn't end up a loser.

Winning was accomplished in any way imaginable, and the alternative to winning was not losing, which is to say playing for a draw or creating some situation whereby the game was abandoned.

My old man, a bad loser if ever I saw one, was an expert at contriving such situations. The first time I was ever conscious of it happening was when, as an unrazored youth, I was playing in a cricket team captained by my old man. We were 50 for 9, chasing a total of about 110, when he joined me at the wicket. There was little doubt that we were going to lose, and ordinarily we would have done, except that my old man had different ideas. As their fast bowler walked back to his mark, my old man walked with him. As the bowler ran to deliver, my old man ran with him. The bowler stopped before he reached the crease.

'What's up wi' thee?' he asked Father.

'Nowt,' said the old man.

'What's tha' galloping alongside me for, then?' asked the bowler.

'Nowt in t'rules says I can't, allus providing I don't interfere wi' thee, and I won't do that. In fact, I wouldn't interfere wi' thee wi' a bargepole,' the old man replied.

The bowler appealed to the umpire.

'Nowt I can do,' said the umpire.

The bowler recommenced his over, but couldn't concentrate with the old man shadowing his every stride. After two long hops and a wide that nearly killed third slip, he threw the ball down and said to the old man:

'Does tha' know what I think of thee?'

The old man shook his head, whereupon the bowler expressed his

frustration and anger by using what was euphemistically described in the area we lived as 'pit language'. The old man let him finish and then said to the umpire:

'Did tha' hear that, Jack?'

'I did that,' said the umpire.

'Does tha' reckon it's fit language for a thirteen-year-old to listen

to?' he said, indicating me at the other end of the wicket.

'Reckon not,' said the umpire.

'Right, I'm taking him off and claiming maximum points,' said the old man. As we walked off the field, I tried to tell him that I hadn't minded the bowler swearing and, indeed, I had not heard anything I hadn't heard before. My old man wouldn't let me finish.

'Shirrup. Tactics,' he said.

Needless to say, we did indeed get the maximum points.

On another occasion, faced with batting second in bad light and against a formidable total, he managed to get the game abandoned as a draw by making the canvas sight screens disappear during the tea interval. How he managed it, I'll never know, but the fact is that in the ten minutes it took to have tea, two squares of white canvas sheeting each measuring 20 ft by 20 ft, plus four large poles and several lengths of rope, had been spirited away never to be seen again. And what is more important, we had one point instead of none.

You could say that the incidents I have described indicate how someone can prepare against ever being seen as a bad loser. And you reach that state of bliss, as my old man discovered, by not losing. However, it would be sad if everyone were as lucky and as shrewd as my old man, because then we would be robbed of the most splendid sight in all sport, the bad loser losing badly.

Soccer provides some marvellous examples of this situation. Alec Stock, the manager of Luton Town, once told me of a relative of his, a brother-in-law I think, who was a farmer in the West Country, and a keen amateur soccer player. During one home game, he was sent off by the referee whereupon, without wasting breath in argument, he went home, mounted his most fearsome tractor and returned to the football field to chase the terrified official into the next county. And it must have been Alec Stock who told me the story of one footballer who was losing so badly that even his home crowd had turned against

him. He became the target for the venom of one spectator in particular, who always stood in the same place behind the goal. It being the sort of club where twelve people behind the goal constituted a ground record, the spectator was easily identifiable to the object of his abuse. The end to their relationship came during one game when the player was having a particularly miserable time. He had missed three simple chances right under the nose of his loud-mouthed critic and had paid dearly. Inevitably there came a fourth chance, just as inevitably the player fluffed it, but instead of awaiting the inevitable abuse the player continued his run on goal, jumped the barrier, ran up the concrete steps, chinned his critic with a perfect right hook and carried on through the turnstile and out of the ground. That is what I call losing badly and with style.

In the final analysis, any keen student of sport will tell you that the term 'a bad loser' was invented by a certain misguided minority of sports administrators in order to add somehow stature and dignity to the job they are in. It is an invention that bolsters the grander myth that sport brings out the best in people. Well so it does, but just as certainly it brings out the worst in people and it is then that it is compelling to spectator and player alike. It would be better if we forgot that junk about glory in defeat and humility in victory. The essence of what I am trying to say was contained in one memorable moment as the great F.S. Trueman left the field after having taken more Test wickets than any other bowler. Fred was renowned as a

man who hated losing, but how would he react to this, his greatest triumph. If Lord's had written the script, Fred would no doubt have thanked everyone in sight, apologised for upsetting people during his career and paid homage to his opponents. What happened? Fred was approached as he neared the pavilion steps.

'How do you feel?' he was asked by the press.

Fred Trueman paused a while, looked at his questioner, and said: 'Knackered.'

June 1971

H.F. Ellis

ASSISTANT MASTERS: ARE THEY INSANE?

An extract from the private papers of Arthur James Wentworth, assistant master at Burgrove Preparatory School

WEDNESDAY. This morning IIIA were unusually quiet when I went in and I at once glanced at the front legs of my desk. Once or twice since I first came to Burgrove I have hurt myself rather badly through my desk falling off its daïs the moment I have leant my elbows on it. I shall always believe, though I have never been able to prove it, that this must have been the work of the boys. Old Poole, who left us last year after twenty-seven years' faithful service in charge of French and Geography, had the same experience, and he was positive that the front legs had been balanced deliberately on the very edge of the daïs. Though, as he used to say, it might be simply carelessness on the part of the cleaner. It is always difficult to bring this kind of thing home to the boys.

However the desk looked all right today; but I was still uneasy. Every schoolmaster knows how unnerving it is when the boys sit quietly in their places and watch you in that silly expressionless way they have, and I do not mind admitting that I stood quite still in the middle of the floor for a full minute waiting for something to happen. Nothing happened at all except that I distinctly heard Mason whispering, 'Rigor mortis has set in.'

I at once strode to the desk to get my punishment-book, but when I opened the lid a pigeon flew out, nearly knocking my spectacles off and giving me, naturally enough, a very nasty shock. In my seven years at Burgrove I have never had such a thing happen to me. I went white with anger.

'Stop that noise this instant!' I shouted. 'And you, Mason, leave that bird alone and go back to your desk. Now, which of you is responsible for this? Hurry up, I'm waiting.'

There was absolute silence for some seconds, until the pigeon, which had settled on top of the blackboard, began to coo in an annoying way, and I then brought my fist down with a crash on the desk.

'We had better understand one another,' I said with cold fury. 'Somebody put that pigeon in my desk and I am going to find out who did it. Unless the person responsible owns up within three minutes – Ah, Mason, so it *was* you?'

'*Me*, Sir? No, Sir. Only I think –'

'Well?'

'I think it's got something tied to its leg.'

Someone suggested it might be a message.

'It's a stool-pigeon!' cried Clarke.

'I bet it's spies.'

'Atkins saw a man just like Hitler behind the pavvy –'

'Be quiet!' I shouted.

While I was considering what to do, Mason, who seems utterly unable to hold his tongue for two seconds, asked whether he might find out what the message said. I asked him rather sarcastically how he proposed to catch the pigeon, and before I could object he went to the blackboard and held out his right index finger, which the bird at once settled upon. I gave Hillman fifty lines for clapping, as a warning to the others, and then suggested to Mason that he seemed to know the pigeon remarkably well. He replied that he knew all the school pigeons well and he thought this must be one of them. I had already guessed this, but said nothing.

'Shall I read the message, Sir?' he asked, untying it from the bird's leg.

'Very well,' I said, after a moment's hesitation. 'What does it say?'

'It says "Fly at once. All is discovered."'

In the ordinary way I might have joined in the general laughter, but this morning I felt too upset and angry.

'Give me that paper, Mason,' I said, 'and sit down. No – let that bird out of the window first. I want every boy – give out some slips, Etheridge, please, there is no need to waste a whole sheet – I want every boy to copy out what is written here and sign his name beneath it. And no talking.'

'Need *I* do it, Sir?'

'Certainly you must do it, Sapoulos. And stop that silly whimpering this instant.'

The boys then began clamouring that they had forgotten the message, and to save further trouble I wrote it up on the board. My plan was of course to compare the handwriting on the slips with that on the original paper; in this way I felt certain of being able to spot the culprit, though as a matter of fact when I looked through the slips this evening I found that the boys had misunderstood my intention and written the words in capitals, which made the test practically useless. Etheridge collected the slips without incident and I then told the whole set to get on with the solving of brackets in Exercise 37. I felt too weary and disheartened to do any actual teaching.

Unless someone has owned up by tomorrow morning I shall have to take severe measures. But it is difficult to know what to do.

Thursday. There was an unfortunate sequel to the pigeon affair this morning. After prayers in Big School the Headmaster said he had something serious to say. It appears that when he entered Classroom 4 for the second period yesterday morning he found what he described as an impertinent remark scrawled up on the board. He did not propose to repeat the remark, as the boy responsible would know very well what he meant. Let that boy stand up at once and confess. I had no option but to come forward from my place with the other masters and explain that I had myself written the sentence and that I regretted the board had not been cleaned at the end of the period by the bottom boy of the set, whose duty it was. I added, for I did not wish to get Sapoulos into trouble, that the boy concerned had not yet perhaps had time to get used to our English ways and customs.

This ended the matter for the time being, but it has put me into something of a dilemma. The Headmaster, who is if anything a shade too inquisitive, will no doubt require a fuller explanation, and though I have managed to avoid him for the whole of today, I cannot hope to do so indefinitely. The difficulty is that I do not wish to tell him about the pigeon in my desk; it would only worry him and could do no good. He is still rather upset, to tell the truth, about my accident in the boot-room. So I shall have to think of some other reason for writing that absurd message on the board. It would be better of course if I could link it up in some way with algebra. But I don't at the moment see my way.

In the meantime I have told IIIA that I have decided to say no more about the pigeon provided nothing of the sort happens again, and I have warned them that the less they say about it to anyone the better it will be for them.

December 1938

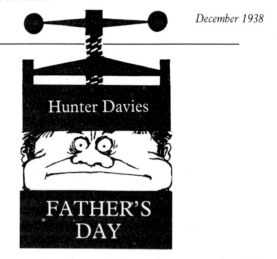

Hunter Davies

FATHER'S DAY

WHEN my father came home from work he got instant attention. This was in the North, back in the olden days, and he would take off his pitman's helmet and climb into his tin bath in front of the fire and my mum would scrub his back for him and then we children would have to sit in silence while he ate his plate of tripe and trotters, hoping he'd leave some for us. Actually, he was a lower clerical officer in the Civil Service and wore a white shirt and suit to work and we had our own bathroom, inside, and he always had mince for his tea, but the effect was much the same. In those days, all dads, even humble little clerks, not only got instant attention, they got endless respect. And they got the biggest helpings.

We've just had tea and I've stacked the Miele in our pine-clad kitchen and I'm hoping for a few moments of peace and quiet, till it's time for me to make the cocoa and toasted cheese at ten o'clock which can't come soon enough as I'm starving. I begged her not to include me in the kids' tea. It's not that I don't love my children dearly. Eating with them can be very stimulating, but by Monday I'm over-stimulated, as we eat all meals together at weekends, and I'm longing for my little weekday routines.

A quiet sherry, for example, about six o'clock with the *Evening Standard*, sitting upstairs in isolation while they're downstairs in the kitchen having their tea and shouting their rotten heads off. I always see them on their arrival home from school, so I haven't quite forgotten their little faces, but I do relish the child-free evenings. My quiet sherry often lasts an hour, give or take a few noisy refills, then I stagger downstairs, taking care not to be knocked flat as they rush upstairs to watch telly, and I then have my lady wife all to my own, just the two of us, mother and father, as nature intended.

Tonight, she has some work to do, so she said she couldn't afford to mess about serving two identical meals then sit chatting to me all evening, so I either ate with the kids or made it myself. I can't actually make anything, apart from toasted cocoa with cheese, so I had no alternative. My mother only made one meal of an evening, for her horny-handed man, fresh from a hard day behind the filing cabinets, while we kids had bread and jam at four on our return from school. Kids of every class in those days had bread and jam for tea, great mounds of it. Kids simply didn't eat with grown-ups. It's a revolution that should never have stopped. No wonder they're so huge.

The meal was jolly enough, if a bit noisy. They're all so much quicker than me. It's true I do forget the names of their class teachers and which best friends they now hate and perhaps I do ruin their best stories by idiotic questions, but every time we have a family tea I seem to lose track of half the conversation. When I try to get things straight in my little mind, it usually ends in groans and big sighs and they leave the table early and my wife blames me for cross-examining them. You should let them do the talking, not stop their flow. Bloody hell, I'm just trying to be interested in my kids' worlds. My dad never spoke to me, at least not about me. I'm reduced at meal times to competing for my wife's attention, and I usually lose. You're just jealous, she says.

We didn't have the apple pie which she'd promised to make, even though I specially picked the apples myself from our tree. Jake, who is thirteen, announced he now hates apples, so of course apples are out. Well, it's unfair to make deliberately something which one member of the family hates when there are enough things we *all* like. But I love apples. Don't my preferences count for anything? Hard cheese.

The main course was fresh plaice, yum yum, which I'd bought in

Kentish Town this morning, two lovely whole ones, enough for the five of us, but alas we turned out to be six. At the last moment, Caitlin, aged fifteen, asked if her friend Poo, or was it Loo or Boo – they all have these dopey nicknames – could stay for tea. Any friends of our friends are welcome here. Certainly, sit down there Poo Poo, sorry it's just plaice, ignore that old tramp, he can get another chair. We haven't got enough plaice, I hissed to my wife as I struggled with the broken chair from the bathroom, the one that hurts my back. Don't be such a baby, she hissed back. I can spin it out with fish fingers.

Guess who got the fish fingers. Yes, the last one to sit down. They were left-overs from last year, spun out in a spin-dryer by the taste of them, though Flora, aged six, did leave the skin of her plaice, the black stuff not the white stuff, which I managed to scoff when Lady Bountiful wasn't looking.

My wife read somewhere that it's only manual labourers who need a lot of calories. In normal nuclear families, the pecking order should be growing teenagers followed by pregnant mothers. I qualify on neither count. I keep on about anorexia nervosa, but she says blokes of forty don't get that, and if they did, it would do them good.

My dad always got the first and the best and the biggest of everything. We really did often sit and watch him polish off the only bit of meat in the house. It was the same in all the houses in our estate. The woman next door, a right snob, used to shout out of the window to her eldest boy, 'Come and get the top of your dad's egg.' This was a complicated piece of one-upmanship, showing she had eggs in the house. This was during the war. The last war, of course. I may be emaciated, but I'm not that old.

Sod off, eh. If you're not going on about your boring old dad and his boring old life you're going on about the boring old war. Ignore him, Poo. He'll go away soon.

So I left the table early, putting on a middle-aged huff, which with my doubled-up sore back had Flora quite worried, but I was quite glad to escape all the noise, though I came back dutifully, when all the young masters had quite finished, to clear the table.

'And I love apple pie,' I muttered loudly to myself, wiping the table. 'I dunno. You struggle to bring money into the house ...'

'Why don't you belt up. Mum earns more than you.'

'And fresh fish would have given me strength, after another exhausting day ...'

'All you've done is hang about all day. Mum has three jobs. You've only got one.'

My own mother never had a job. She was chained to the kitchen full time. I can't remember her eating with us. She just stood there, at the stove, cooking away, or she was out in the wash-house, boiling away, getting the dollies clean. Dollies? She used to go on about this dolly tub, so dollies must have come into it somewhere.

My own dear wife runs a large house and three children, cleaning and cooking and everyfink, all on her own, with no help whatsoever. She's a legend in NW5. I don't know how the Pope missed her on his trip. Then she's a full-time writer, producing a book almost every year. Skip the rest of this paragraph if it's giving you a headache. And her third full-time job is doing a weekly book review column in the London *Eve-in-Stan-ard*. Everybody go aaaaaah.

Perhaps I do hang about the house a bit, compared with her. I admit it. But is the economic emancipation of women the real reason for the decline in the importance of fatherhood? I do more than my father did, but I mean less. 'Wait till your father comes home,' was a terrible threat in my childhood. Now, it means laughs all round.

Mothers have taken over. You can't get moving for them, spread over every feature page of every newspaper, usually unmarried and doing unmentionable things, all on their own. I have to avert my eyes when the *Guardian* plops through the letter-box. I do hope fathers will make a come-back soon.

Or perhaps it's just me? I only mentioned the meals as a first if minor example, but it seems to me that in every domestic situation I'm an also-ran in my own house. Where have I gone wrong, I ask myself, very quietly of course. Fathers should be seen and not heard ...

October 1979

Gillespie (Neil Ferguson)
HEIL FELLOW, WELL MET!

HERE in Troon, the festivities to commemorate Adolf Hitler's centenary are still in full swing – though we were all a bit disappointed that none of the television documentaries made any reference to the many happy summers the *Führer* spent as a lad on the Clyde Coast. It may interest readers to learn that, before the Great War, the Hitlers invariably spent their holidays in Troon, where they had a small, well-appointed cottage ('Dun Röhmin') not far from the sea front. What brought them to the West of Scotland was, of course, the golf, a sport to which young Adolf was passionately addicted.

His fascination with the game was partly political: 'The questions of the day,' I remember him saying, 'will not be decided by speeches and majority decisions ... but by blood and a three iron.' But there was also an element of romance involved. For it was on the links at Old Troon that Hitler met his first and only sweetheart: junior ladies champion Eva Broon.

I will never forget how, in that idyllic summer of 1913, the two of them entered the mixed doubles. All went well until the final fairway when Adolf, to his mortification, sliced the ball wildly. For what seemed like eternity, Eva was silent. But finally she found her voice. 'Never mind, Wulfie,' she said (to the locals, he was always just 'Oor Wulfie'), 'I always had a feeling the two of us would come to grief in a bunker.' Troon folk date Hitler's insane craving for world domination from that moment.

While we are on the subject, I notice that our dear Prime Minister is also doing her bit to honour Hitler's memory. It appears that she has given her Transport Secretary the task of constructing 'eight-lane super motorways between Britain's leading industrial centres', in response to 'growing anxiety ... about clogged motorways' (The *Sunday Times*). The more intellectually supine among you may see in this little more than an emergency measure to keep the lid on unemployment when Mr Lawson's interest rate rises finally begin to take effect. But I am not fooled. These are *autobahns, liebe Volksgenossen*, and every hideous mile will be a monument to their deranged Austrian inventor.

Like Hitler, Mrs Thatcher has an *autobahn* fixation. Her ultimate goal, I firmly believe, is to turn the entire country into one vast spaghetti junction, with no more than a few rusting rails and fenced-off footpaths to remind us that there were once other ways of getting about the place. Unlike Hitler, Mrs Thatcher prefers to get the Japanese in to build the actual cars: but the principle is essentially the same.

This may seem an eccentric viewpoint. But how else are we to account for the Government's systematic denigration of every other available mode of transport? If you attempt to get anywhere today on foot or by bicycle, you risk being killed in one of the car chases our policemen delight in; if you try to take a tube in the capital, you experience tortures hitherto reserved for the fish in John West's factories.

But have you any idea of the fearful atrocities currently being perpetrated on our trains? By way of an example, I feel obliged to cite a report in last week's *Daily Mail*, concerning a British Rail ticket inspector who ran amok on a train to Bristol after a passenger asked to buy a ticket from him. The man apparently began ranting (not railing, if you don't mind) at the poor woman, snatched her passport from her and promptly landed one on an American tourist who ventured to intervene on her behalf.

The only thing which astonished me about the story was that the *Mail* back bench should have judged it newsworthy. In my experience, such altercations are a more or less routine occurrence on British trains. In fact the only aspect of the story I have not encountered on numerous occasions is the bit about the passport. To my knowledge, passports are not at present required for trips to Bristol – though it is possible that someone naïve enough to try and buy a ticket aboard a train might think they are.

It may strike some of you motorists as slightly odd that the sale of tickets aboard trains should be prohibited by British Rail, particularly in view of the fact that it takes on average half-an-hour to procure one in a station. But that petty rule pales into insignificance alongside some of the other bizarre regulations which have recently been introduced by BR. Nowadays, for instance, when the guard makes his customary 'passenger announcement' prior to the departure of a train, the hapless passenger enters the realm of Franz Kafka:

> '*Passengers are reminded that ordinary Bluesaver return tickets, special standard class Awayday tickets, peak-time Capitalcard round-trip, green tickets, blue tickets, tickets bearing the letter "e" and all other apparently valid tickets are not, I repeat not, valid for this service.*'

The upshot of all this is that, in order to get from A to B, most of us now elect to go by car; and the upshot of this is that most of us now spend an average of one day a week sitting in twenty-mile tailbacks somewhere between A and B. So desperate has the situation become that advertisements have started appearing in journals like *The Economist* for (I am not making it up) 'VTOL aircraft ... designed to revolutionise personal transportation. Our M200X takes off and lands vertically ... cruises at 322 mph ... and fits in a single car garage'. Behold the *reductio ad absurdum* of Mrs Thatcher's maniacal individualism: she and a few others zipping overhead in flying saucers, while the rest of us sit fulminating in a jam stretching from Wessex to Wick.

I cannot believe that I am alone in regarding railways as this country's single greatest contribution to world civilisation. Why then do I find myself watching impotently as the woman who professes to believe in Victorian values systematically scraps the iron legacy of Stephenson and Brunel? Making the trains run on time was an achievement associated with dictatorships like Hitler's. But I ask you: What good is a dictator who stops them running altogether?

May 1989

John Steinbeck

BRICKLAYING PIECE

WHEN spring comes to New York City this great block of granite and steel and concrete and glass stirs with bucolic emotion. The geranium carts move through the streets and men come home from their offices carrying seeds in their briefcases and potted plants in their newspapers. The trees that are never going to grow are set on rooftops, there to fight a losing war with soot and sulphuric acid.

My own problem is more complex, for I have a little garden where I nurse despairing shrubs. But every year the shaft of spring quivers in my breast and for a few weeks my garden is beautiful and I am always glad to hope that this time it will survive.

This year, I presume because the winter came early and spring was one hell of a long way behind, I turned giddy with this sweet season. I not only planted my garden but on the front of my house I put up fresh white shutters and windowboxes of red geraniums and trailing ivy. Also, in a converted coal chute, I planted a wistaria, whose purpose is to run up in front of the building and make everything look green and springy. This tiny wistaria bed instantly became a nesting place for dogs and children. Last week I brought bricks and cement to the pavement and started a little coping to protect the stem of my beloved shrub from being kicked to death. I squatted on my haunches and began the course of bricks.

Ours is a wide street and the buildings are not tall, so that the sunshine lies warm on the pavement, and there it is that stout women stroll along discussing the problems of the day while their children ring all the door-bells as they go. As I set the bricks, two such women moved near and looked up at the spring glory of my house-front. Their little boy was just reaching for my door-bell when I took a vicious swing at him with the trowel. The women continued to stare at the house. At last one of them said, 'Shutters'.

And the other said, 'Windowboxes'.

And the first, 'Geraniums'.

Then the other summed up the situation, 'They must be opening up a restaurant'.

I continued with my work, remarking that an ancient Irishman with a strong list to starboard came pitching along fighting a heavy sea. He stopped, supported himself with one hand against my wall.

'I'm off to the Home,' he said gravely.

'Are you indeed?'

'Yes, lad, and it's not so bad as you might think. Why this morning I bought a package of cigarettes and I had a beer.'

This last was a brilliant understatement, and he went on: 'I smoked all the cigarettes. Would you be kind enough –'

I got out a package and held out a match for him. He inhaled deeply.

'That's likely brick,' he said.

'It's common red brick.'

'Do you not think I know that, lad?' (Lad, indeed, I'm fifty-three.) 'Why I'm a master mason for forty years. Master.'

I said, 'I tried to get pink Virginia brick but I couldn't find any.'

'Well, the red is harder even if it is unpretty,' he said. His swimming eye ranged over my work. I said, 'To a master mason the way I'm laying the brick must be a matter of pain.'

'No, lad, no. Live and let live.'

'I'm out of line,' I said.

His cigarette had gone out but he went on puffing solemnly. 'Don't put yourself in any fear of criticism from me,' he said.

'Yes, but a master mason –'

'It's not like that with a master,' he said. 'It's well, like – if you was an artist – a real artist – a great big damn Michelangelo of an artist – and you was strolling along and was to come on Mr Eisenhower or Sir Winston Churchill with their painty pads – Why lad, you wouldn't even bother to give advice. Don't be shy, get on with your brick. And it's time I started back to the Home.'

He cast off and took a wave over his bow and set his nose into the wind towards the Home.

July 1955

John Betjeman

A HOUSE OF REST

WHEN all the world she knew is dead
    In this small room she lives her days,
The wash-hand stand and single bed
    Screened from the public gaze.

The horse-brass shines, the kettle sings,
    The cup of China tea
Is tasted among cared-for things
    Ranged round for me to see –

Lincoln, by Valentine and Co.,
  Now yellowish brown and stained –
But there some fifty years ago
  Her Harry was ordained.

Outside the church at Woodhall Spa
  The smiling groom and bride –
And here's his old tobacco jar
  Dried lavender inside.

I do not like to ask if he
  Was 'High' or 'Low' or 'Broad'
Lest such a question seemed to be
  A mockery of Our Lord.

Her large grey eyes look far beyond
  The little room and me
To village church and village pond
  And ample rectory.

She sees her children each in place,
  Eyes downcast as they wait,
She hears her Harry murmur grace,
  Then heaps the porridge plate.

Aroused at seven, to bed by ten
  They fully lived each day,
Dead sons, so motor-bike-mad then,
  And daughters far away.

Now when the bells for Eucharist
  Sound in the market square,
With sunshine struggling through the mist
  And Sunday in the air,

The veil between her and her dead
  Dissolves and shows them clear,
The consecration prayer is said
  And all of them are near.

August 1953

Eric Keown

SIR TRISTRAM GOES WEST

CHAPTER I

THREE men sat and talked at the long table in the library of Moat Place. Many dramatic conversations had occurred in that mellow and celebrated room, some of them radically affecting whole pages of English history; but none so vital as this to the old house itself. For its passport was being viséd to the United States.

Lord Mullion sighed gently. He was wondering whether, if a vote could be taken amongst his ancestors – most of whose florid portraits had already crossed the Atlantic – they would condemn or approve his action. Old Red Roger, his grandfather, would have burnt the place round him, rather than sell an inch of it. But then Red Roger had never been up against an economic crisis. And at that moment, the afternoon sun flooding suddenly the great oriel window, a vivid shaft of light stabbed the air like a rapier and illuminated Mr Julius Plugg's cheque-book, which was lying militantly on the table.

'Would you go to forty thousand?' asked Lord Mullion.

Mr Plugg's bushy eyebrows climbed a good half-inch. When they rose further a tremor was usually discernible in Wall Street.

'I'll say it's a tall price for such an old joint,' he said. 'Well – I might.'

Lord Mullion turned to the Eminent Architect. 'You're absolutely certain that the house can be successfully replanted in Mr Plugg's back-garden, like a damned azalea?'

The Eminent Architect, whose passion happened to be Moat Place, also sighed. 'Bigger houses than this have been moved. It'll be a cracking job, but there's no real snag. I recommend that for greater safety the library be sent by liner. The main structure can go by cargo-boat.'

The shaft of sunlight was still playing suggestively on the golden cover of the cheque-book. Sadly Lord Mullion inclined his head.

'Very well, Mr Plugg. It's yours,' he said.

A gasp of childish delight escaped the Pokerface of American finance. 'That's swell,' he cried, 'that's dandy! And now it's fixed would you give me the low-down on a yarn I've heard about a family spook? Punk?'

'On the contrary,' said Lord Mullion, 'he's quite the most amusing ghost in this part of the country. But I shouldn't think he'll bother you.'

'Anyone ever seen him?'

'I saw him yesterday, sitting over there by the window.'

Mr Plugg sprang round apprehensively. 'Doing what?' he demanded.

'Just dreaming. He was a poet, you know.'

'A poet? Hey, Earl, are you getting funny?'

'Not a bit. We know all about him. Sir Tristram Mullion, laid out by a Roundhead pike at Naseby. He must have been pretty absent-minded; probably he forgot about the battle until somebody hit him, and then it was too late. The story goes that his father, a fire-eating old Royalist, got so bored at always finding his eldest son mooning about the library when he might have been out trailing CROMWELL that when he was dying he laid a curse on Tristram which could only be expunged by a single-handed act of valour. Tristram rode straight off to Naseby and got it in the neck in the first minute. So he's still here, wandering about this library, never getting a chance to do anything more heroic than a couplet. And he wasn't even a par-ticularly good poet.'

Mr Plugg had regained command of himself. 'I seem to have read somewhere of a ghost crossing the Atlantic with a shack,' he said, 'but that won't rattle a tough baby like me, and I doubt if your spook and I'd have much in common. How about having the lawyers in and signing things up?'

CHAPTER II

The S.S. *Extravaganza* was carving her way steadily through the calm and moonlit surface of the Atlantic. The thousand portholes in her steep sides blazed, and the air was sickly with the drone of saxophones. It was as though a portion of the new Park Lane had taken to the water.

Down in the dim light of No. 3 Hold a notable event had just taken place. Sir Tristram Mullion had emerged from nowhere and was standing there, very nearly opaque with surprise and irritation. His activities had been confined to the Moat Place library for so long that he could think of no good reason why he should suddenly materialise in this strange dungeon. That it was a dungeon he had little doubt. Its sole furniture was a number of large packing-cases marked 'JULIUS PLUGG, ARARAT, USA,' and they were too high for even a ghost to sit upon with comfort. Tristram decided to explore.

The first person he encountered in the upper reaches of the ship was Alfred Bimsting, a young steward, who cried, 'The fancy-dress ain't on till tomorrow, Sir,' and then pardonably fainted as he saw Tristram pass clean through a steel partition ...

Sitting up on high stools at the bar, Professor Gupp, the historian, and an unknown Colonel were getting all argumentative over the *Extravaganza*'s special brown sherry.

'My dear fellow,' the Professor was saying, 'whatever you may say about Marston Moor, Naseby showed RUPERT to be a very great cavalry leader. Very great indeed.'

'Nonsense!' growled the Colonel. 'A hot-headed young fool. FAIRFAX was the better soldier in every way.'

'I tell you –' the Professor began when he became aware of a presence at his elbow – a handsome young man in the clothes of a Cavalier.

'Frightfully sorry to interrupt,' said Tristram (for acquaintance with the young Mullions had kept his idiom level with the fashion), 'but as a matter of fact I used to know RUPERT and FAIRFAX pretty well, and you can take it from me they were a couple of insufferable bores. RUPERT was a shockin' hearty, always slappin' you on the back, and FAIRFAX was a pompous old fool. As for Naseby, it was a hell of a mess.'

Professor Gupp hiccupped. 'Young man,' he said reprovingly, 'I am driven to conclude that you have been drinking to excess. It may interest you to know that I am the author of the standard monograph on Naseby.'

'It may interest *you* to know,' Tristram cried rather dramatically, 'that I was killed there.' And he faded through the black glass wall of the refrigerator with such startling ease that neither Professor Gupp nor the Colonel could ever face Very Old Solera again ...

After the dazzle of strip-lights and chromium Tristram was glad to find himself out on the promenade deck, which was deserted. It was nearly three hundred years since he had been to sea, returning from the French Court in considerable disgrace, having lost his dispatches; but, aided by the traditional adaptability of the ghost and the aristocrat, he noted with unconcern the tremendous pace at which the waves were flying past, and the vast scarlet funnels, towering above, which seemed to him to salute the moon so unsuitably (he was a poet, remember) with great streamers of heavy black smoke. As he paced the deck he meditated the opening rhymes of a brief ode to the heavens ...

Meanwhile, in the convenient shadow of Lifeboat 5, a stout politician was surprised to find himself proposing marriage to his secretary, who with a more practised eye had seen it coming ever since

'Frightfully sorry to interrupt'

Southampton. He was warming up to it nicely. Not for nothing had he devoted a lifetime to the mastery of circumambient speech.

'And though I cannot offer you, my dear, either the frivolities of youth or the glamour of an hereditary title, I am asking you to share a position which I believe to carry a certain distinction –' Here he broke off abruptly as Tristram appeared in the immediate neighbourhood and leaned dreamily over the rail.

There was an embarrassing silence, of which the secretary took advantage to repair the ravages of the politician's first kiss.

'Would you oblige me, Sir, by going away?' he boomed in the full round voice that regularly hypnotised East Dimbury into electing him.

Tristram made no answer. He was trying hard to remember if 'tune' made an impeccable rhyme to 'moon'.

'Confound you, Sir,' cried the Politician, 'are you aware that you are intruding upon a sacred privacy?'

Tristram genuinely didn't hear. He was preparing to let 'boon' have it, or, if necessary, 'loon'.

'Would you oblige me, Sir, by going away?'

The Politician heaved his bulk out of his deck-chair and fetched Tristram a slap on the shoulder. But of course, as you can't do that with a properly disembodied matured-in-the-wood ghost, all that happened was that the Politician's hand sank through Tristram like a razor through dripping and was severely bruised on the rail. It was left to the secretary to console him, for Tristram was gone.

And then, rumours of Tristram's strange interludes percolating through the ship, all at once he became the centre of a series of alarming enfilading movements. The young Tuppenny-Berkeleys and their friends, who had been holding a sausage-and-*peignoir* party in the swimming-bath, bore down upon him waving *Leberwursts* and crowing 'Tally-ho! The jolly old Laughing Cavalier!' Cavalierly was the way he treated them. Sweeping off his hat to young Lady Catherine, he nodded coldly to the others and walked straight through her brother, a young Guardsman, who was to dine out on the experience for nearly half-a-century.

The main staircase was already blocked with excited passengers. At the top of it stood the Chief Stewardess, a vast and imposing figure. Just for fun (for he was beginning to enjoy his little outing, and so would you if you had been stuck in a mouldy library for three hundred years) Tristram flung his arms gallantly round her neck and cried, 'Your servant, Madam!' The poor woman collapsed mountainously into the arms of a Bolivian millionaire, who consequently collapsed too, in company with the three poorer millionaires who were behind him.

At this point the Captain arrived and advanced majestically. To the delight of the company Tristram picked up a large potted palm and thrust it dustily into his arms.* Then, with a courtly bow to the crowd and a valedictory gesture of osculation, he disappeared backwards through a massive portrait of ALBERT THE GOOD.

On his way back to No. 3 Hold he sped through the Athenian Suite. In it the new lord of Moat Place lay on his bed in his pink silken underwear, pondering on the triumph with which in a few months he would spring upon the markets the child of his dreams, his new inhumane killer for demolishing the out-of-date buildings of the world, Plugg's Pneumatic Pulveriser.

Tristram took one look at him and disliked him at sight. On the bed table lay a basin of predigested gruel. Inverting it quickly over Mr Plugg's head, he passed on to disappear into the bowels of the ship.

CHAPTER III

Blowzy Bolloni and Redgat Ike sat at a marble-topped table sinking synthetic gin with quiet efficiency. They had spent the afternoon emptying several machine-guns into a friend, so they were rather tired.

'I've given Bug and Toledo the line-up,' Bolloni said. 'It's a wow. Toledo's in cahoots with one of Plugg's maids and she spilled the beans. The stuff's in his new safe in the library – see? Any hop-head could fetch it out. Is that oke?'

'Mebbe it'll mean a grand all round, eh?' asked Redgat.

'Or two.' And Bolloni winked.

* NB – Can a ghost grip? I say it can.

'That'll be mighty nice. You want my ukulele?'

'Yeah. But I got a hunch heaters'll be enough.'

They called for another snort of hooch, testing its strength in the approved gangster way by dipping a finger in it. The nail remaining undissolved they drank confidently.

CHAPTER IV

In the library of the reassembled Moat Place, Julius Plugg squirmed on a divan and cursed his folly in not entrusting the secret plans of his Pulveriser to the strong-room of his factory. Only a simp would have asked for it by bringing them home, he told himself bluntly. But it was too late now to do anything about them, for he was roped down as tightly as a thrown steer. Also he was gagged with his own handkerchief, a circumstance which gave him literally a pain in the neck.

Mrs Plugg, similarly captive in the big armchair, had shed her normal dignity in a way which would have startled the Ararat Branch of the Women's Watch and Ward Fellowship, over which she presided. Her head was completely obscured by a large wicker waste-paper-basket, and through it there filtered strange canine noises.

As for Hiram Plugg, the leader of sophomore fashion, he was lashed so firmly to the suit of armour in the corner that it positively hurt him to blink; for before the high rewards of ace-gunning had attracted Blowzy Bolloni to the civilisation of the West he had helped his father with his fishing-nets in Sicily, and it was now his boast that he could tie a victim up quicker and more unpleasantly than any other gangster in the States.

At the back of the library Redgat Ike lounged gracefully on the table with a finger curled ready round the trigger of a Thompson sub-machine-gun, trained on the door. He grinned amiably as he thought how bug-house the servants had looked as they went down before his little chloroform-squirt, the cook clutching a rolling-pin and the butler muttering he'd rung the cops already – the poor bozo not knowing the wire had been cut an hour before. Oh, it was a couple of grands for nothing, a show like this. Redgat couldn't think why everyone wasn't a gangster.

Bolloni and Toledo and the Bug, who had been searching the panels for signs of the safe, gave it up and gathered round the prostrate form of Mr Plugg, who snarled at them as fiercely as he could manage through his nose.

'Come on, Mister,' said Bolloni, 'we ain't playing Hunt the Slipper any more. You'd better squawk where that tin box is *and* its combination. Otherwise my boy-friend over there might kinda touch his toy by mistake, and that's good-bye to that teapot dome of yours.' He smiled evilly at Redgat, who smiled back and swung the machine-gun into line with Mr Plugg's bald head.

'Have his comforter out and see what he says,' suggested Toledo. But, shorn of much pungent criticism of the gangsters and their heredity, all Mr Plugg said was, 'There's no safe here, you big bunch of saps.'

Most sailormen are practical and many are crude. Bolloni was both. Replacing the gag in Mr Plugg's champing jaws, he drew from his pocket a twelve-bore shot-gun sawn off at the breech, and pressed it persuasively against Mr Plugg's ample stomach. With his other hand he took a firm grip of the magnate's moustache and began to heave.

'When you sorta remember about the safe,' he said, 'give three toots on your nose.'

Who would blame Mr Plugg? Gathering together his remaining breath he let out a first toot which would have done honour to a Thames tug. He was filling up with air for a second one when suddenly the three gangsters sprang round as if stung. Painfully he turned his head, to see a strange figure standing by the book-shelves. (You've got it first guess. It *was*.)

Tristram hadn't noticed the others. He was poring over a set of SPENSER when Redgat slid back his trigger, and it was not until a heavy ·45 bullet tore the books from his hands that he realised that something was happening. A stream of lead was hurtling through him and turning a priceless edition of BOCCACCIO to pulp, but he felt nothing. He was filled only with resentment at such ill-mannered interruption.

None of the gangsters had ever seen a man take fifty bullets in the chest and remain perpendicular. The sight unnerved them. Redgat continued to fire as accurately as before, but the other three stood irresolute.

Before Bolloni could dodge him Tristram had picked up what was left of *The Faëry Queen* and brought it down with terrific force on his head, dropping him like a skittle. Boiling with rage, Tristram grabbed up *The Anatomy of Melancholy* and set about Toledo and

the Bug. One of them discharged the shot-gun full in his face, but
not with any great hope – Gee! a ritzy guy in fancy-dress who only
got fresher after a whole drum of slugs!

It was soon over. Redgat clung to his beloved machine-gun to the
end, unable to believe that a second drum wouldn't take effect. But
he too went down to a thundering crack on the jaw from an illustrated *Apocrypha* ...

Tristram ... only got fresher after a whole drum of slugs

Tristram began to feel very odd. For a moment he surveyed the
scene, not quite comprehending what it all meant. Mrs Plugg had
swooned, which merely caused the waste-paper-basket on her head
to drop from the vertical to the horizontal. Her son was clearly about
to be sick. Julius Plugg himself, supine but undaunted, was making
wild signals with his famous eyebrows to be released.

Then, something in his nebulous inside going queerly click,
Tristram realised what was happening. At last he had been a hero. At
last he was free. The hail of bullets had smashed up not only
BOCCACCIO but his father's curse ...

Debating, with the exquisite detachment of the poet, whether the
Pluggs would get free before the gangsters recovered, he faded
imperceptibly and left them to it.

May 1932

Robert Morley

SCENE ONE. THE ROYAL ACADEMY OF DRAMATIC ART. THE TIME IS 1926.

OVER cocktails she bemoaned Milton Keynes. She had spent the afternoon there doing things for the County. Not that there was anything to be done for Milton Keynes itself; far too many houses too close together and an absence apparently of skilled labour. 'All these planners,' she lamented, 'such a botch, it's difficult to forgive what they have done to the Whaddon Chase Country. I stay on but my son has given up completely, moved to the Quorn.'

'I understand exactly how you must feel,' I told her. 'I myself have spent the afternoon revisiting happy hunting grounds to find them sadly changed.'

'You still ride?' she asked incredulously.

I never rode, but what is even more surprising, at my age, I still act. I had spent the afternoon at the Royal Academy of Dramatic Art where fifty years ago an eager child of nineteen first showed his paces

to an astonished selection committee, a member of which, as I have
always affirmed, was the late Gerald du Maurier. Alas, the files, one
has now to call them archives, do not support my claim. The
examiners are listed as Kate Rourke and the Principal himself, in
those days Kenneth, later to become Sir Kenneth Barnes.

Sir Kenneth was the brother of the Vanbrugh girls, Irene and
Violet, the equivalents in those days of our own Dame Wendy Hiller
and Dame Peggy Ashcroft.

Father, who knew everyone slightly but no one quite enough,
provided a letter to Irene who seemed surprised to receive it at my
hands. It dealt at some length, I gathered, with the difficulty of
finding a suitable occupation for a young gentleman without private
means or much expectation of inheriting any. It went on to beg her
intercession with her brother that a place might be found at the
opening of the autumn term.

'I don't think,' she opined after having read the missive, 'that
there is likely to be a problem, just go round to RADA and ask for the
enrolment form. They'll tell you when you have to audition and I am
sure they'll be delighted to have you as a student, dear boy.' Irene
was famous not only as a comedienne but also for her good manners.
A study of the candidates' list on which my name appears proved her
correct in her surmises. In those days few indeed were ever turned
away, and they were invariably girls. Against a list of forty or so
candidates the word 'no' appears only three times. It was easier in
those days, I opined to Mr O'Donoghue, the present registrar, who
had received me most warmly at tea-time, proffering chocolate
biscuits and the relevant files for my consumption.

'It had to be,' he replied. 'In those days the Academy was not
independently wealthy as it is today, thanks to the Shaw Bequests,
and Kenneth had to see it paid its way. The number of students was
roughly eight times what it is today. Of course the whole place was a
great deal smaller. We rebuilt after the bomb.' Crunching the biscuits I recalled for him the magic of Bernard Shaw's first lecture
which I was privileged to attend.

I can see him now striding on the small stage, removing his hat and
beginning to unbutton his overcoat. 'I want you to watch carefully,'
he told us, 'while Bernard Shaw, the great Bernard Shaw, takes off
his coat.' In point of fact, although I never knew it at the time,
Shaw's participation in the life of the Academy had been constant
since its foundation. An active member of the Council, there are

many Minutes of his suggestions as to how the school should be run
in the early days. Once he opined students should be made to stand
on the stage and read a page of the French telephone directory aloud
so as to get a grasp of Gallic pronunciation. Another time he thought
that the students should perform a play in a completely empty West
End theatre, empty save for the Council who would watch from the
top of the gallery. I have written elsewhere of my adoration of St
Bernard who awoke me at the age of thirteen from the stupor and
despair of adolescence and during a performance of *The Doctor's
Dilemma* made me realise there was to be no life for me hereafter save
in the theatre. Now here he was in the same room granting a
semi-private audience.

What astonished me most in those early days at the Academy was
to discover that actors and actresses like Norman Page, Herbert
Ross, Helen Haye, Rosina Phillipi, Dorothy Green were alive and
well and visiting Gower Street. I don't know exactly how I expected
people who acted would look or behave, but I was unprepared to find
them no different in appearance and manner from men who pushed
pens or flogged stocks and shares. They weren't even so very different from my own Uncles and Aunts, though none of the latter
included a member of the 'Profession' among their acquaintances
and if they ever spoke of or visited the theatre took a certain pride in
never being able to accurately record the impressions gained. Thus
they would remark that the other night someone had taken them,
they never ventured on their own, to that theatre in the Haymarket
where there was quite an amusing piece written by that fellow with
the double-barrelled name and acted by the chap who used to play
Shakespeare. 'I tell you who was in it as well, that short comedienne
who used to be married to Cosmo Gordon Lennox, didn't she?' They
would look round feigning ignorance and someone would helpfully
change the subject. No one cared to state unequivocally that St John
Ervine had written *The Second Mrs Fraser* and that Harry Ainley and
Marie Tempest were its stars. Inexplicably the only name they never
seemed to forget was Matheson Lang's.

My father was the exception; he actually played Auction Bridge
with Charles Hawtrey and once took me behind the scenes to see
Fred Neilson-Terry when he visited Folkestone and insisted on my
actually perching on the chair he had recently vacated as the Scarlet
Pimpernel himself. Neither Mr Neilson-Terry nor I thought it a
good idea at the time. At the age of six I don't think it occurred to me

that the star was anxious to be off home
for his tea and that the costume he was
wearing would soon be changed for
something a good deal more casual. Of
course I didn't expect the staff at the
Academy to be in costume when I first
set eyes on them, but then I don't think
it occurred to me they would be in flan-
nels and sports coats either. Norman
Page, who was more or less second in
command to Kenneth Barnes, was currently playing in *Marigold* at the Kings-
way Theatre. The piece had already
been performed for nearly a year which
was something of a phenomenon in those
days and Mr Page had the reputation of
having been the best pantomine cat

within living memory, and had only recently shed his skin forever on
being pushed by a young admirer off his perch on the dress circle rail
and falling heavily into the stalls beneath without luckily causing
much damage, except to himself and a number of tea trays. He was
the kindest of men who seldom took acting seriously, his interest
constantly caught and often sustained at least for a term by a more
than usually pretty student.

At the first class he conducted with the new intake, he always
enquired which of his charges had decided on a stage career against
the express wishes and advice of their parents. Quite untruthfully
my arm shot up. I was anxious to impress him of my single purpose
and determination, but it was a girl child in the front who caught and
held his attention and he closely questioned her as to whether she
had actually run away from home or whether her parents were
supporting her at the YWCA. It was surprising how many of the
class seemed to have braved parental disapproval, but in those days
to have a son or daughter on the stage was not as it is now an occasion
for congratulations.

A couple of years ago on the Isle of Wight a proud father showed
me a record sleeve featuring his nubile daughter completely nude
though admittedly photographed from behind. He was justly proud
of the number of records which she had sold for the group of which
she was not as yet a member; such an attitude would have been

unthinkable in my early days, even on the Isle of Wight, but then of course no one had thought of record sleeves.

But if parents were different then so were we students. A great many of us were hell-bent not on dedication so much as fornication. Here I must make clear that I am speaking principally of my own sex who were happily outnumbered by the girls in the ratio of seven or eight to one. That meant not only that most of us young pashas were never again to have it so good on or off stage, but that we enjoyed the inestimable benefits of being allowed to play Hamlet or even in my own case Shylock from start to finish supported by a constantly changing Juliet or Portia. There would come a moment during the performance when one Juliet would disentangle herself from Romeo's embrace, demurely leave the stage and be instantly replaced by another hopeful debutante. It made for a certain amount of confusion but must have often proved a relief to Sir Kenneth who made it a point of honour to watch every single performance given under his roof. It would be impossible to pay a sufficiently high tribute to his sense of dedication and his infinite compassion and patience and it proved quite impossible when he came to retire to find another who was prepared to undergo such sustained and prolonged torture.

But while I was there Sir Kenneth still ruled and on the memorable occasion of my own Shylock appeared suddenly in front of the tabs to quell a near-riot among my fellow students who had found my acting with Tubal so hilarious that they screamed and demanded an encore. Sir Kenneth quelled them with a short speech. 'Now,' he said, 'let us all remember; fair is fair,' and indicated the performance was to continue. I have never to this day understood why I was considered so funny as Shylock, indeed once or twice I have been tempted to play the part again just to find out the cause. Once, after a particularly fine dinner, Peter Hall, who was still at Stratford, urged me to join his company in any role I fancied. 'I might do Shylock,' I told him and he promised to ring in the morning. It was just unfortunate my phone happened to have been out of order.

I enquired of Mr O'Donoghue whether the legend of my performance still persisted but he thought not. 'You were marked Above Average that term,' he told me, pushing forward the relevant document. Together we read the names of my contemporaries about whose subsequent careers I was a mine of misinformation; opining for instance that the late and much loved Joan Harben had married a poet. Mr O'Donoghue pointed out that *Who's Who* had her listed as having married Clive Morton, another dear friend who died last year alas. Far too many of my contemporaries seem to have done just that, but we were back happily in the land of the living with Jean Anderson, the ever-ailing but fortunately never actually succumbing Mother of that popular television series *The Brothers*.

I fell to wondering about Alan Webb whom I had seen the night before in a revival of *The Seagull* on the box. 'Was he here with you?' asked the Registrar. 'He was here before me, I think,' I told him, 'but no doubt the records don't go back that far.' 'On the contrary,' he reassured me, 'I was looking up Athene Seyler who popped in the other day, she was here in 1908 when any performance the students gave took place in the front drawing room, except, of course, for the Public Show.'

The Public Show, now discontinued, was the event of our two-year course. It was the day, as the title suggests, when we appeared in public in a real West End Theatre, in my day the St James's, and were reviewed by professional critics in the daily press. The Academy itself awarded Gold, Silver and Bronze Medals to the outstanding students and, reading the roll of honour hung in the entrance hall and signed not only by all the fortunate recipients but also by Dame Madge Kendal herself who penned the immortal advice 'To Your Own Self Be True' in the firm hand associated with her own strict code of morals and deportment, one is surprised at how often the judges guessed right. The list is impressive: Charles Laughton, Robert Shaw, Robert Atkins, Athene Seyler, Meggie Albanesi, Alan Badel, Sian Phillips, Gemma Jones. Indeed only in one instance was potential not apparently spotted, I myself being sent for by the Administrator at the end of my first year and questioned closely as to whether I had private means to sustain a further year in the direction of what Kenneth obviously regarded but was too polite to actually designate as a suicidal course. Whenever I met him subsequently and he thought I was about to repeat the tale, he begged me to desist on the grounds that I had not heard him correctly. Besides the medals and certificates to be won annually, there was a feast of other prizes and awards usually bearing the name of the donor (sometimes still extant but more often deceased) who had bequeathed a sum sufficient to keep his name alive by the annual distribution of largesse which in those days usually amounted to about five guineas.

There was the 'Kenneth Kent Award for Attack in Acting', 'The Hamen Clark Award for Diction in Relation to Dialect', 'Mrs Willard's Prize for Spontaneous Laughter' and 'V.C. Buckley's prize For The Wearing of Clothes Period or Modern'. None of us in my time was a dedicated pot-hunter but we were encouraged by the staff to enter these gladiatorial contests if only that they might have a further insight into our failings in the field, for instance, of mime or fencing. No subject bored me more than that of the study of the foil, and I seldom attended the great M. Bertram's celebrated classes to which like the dance classes I gave as wide a berth as was allowable. There was a good deal of flexibility in the regulations which ordained how many appearances one should put in each term. I was an ungraceful youth and I fear no amount of thrust, parry and tiptoe would have made me otherwise. In any case I never tried. At almost my first session at the dancing class I was singled out as the square boy at the back and made to stand in front of my comrades on the grounds that I had most to learn. I never returned.

Imagine my delight, therefore, when discovering, as I have already boasted, that I was marked 'above average' in my first term. Above average, indeed, I should hope so but who were the others? In 1926 when I first came on the scene the Academy was still recovering from Charles Laughton, who was to do for Gower Street what John Osborne was later to achieve for Sloane Square. He changed the image. Regarded as unlikely material when he first arrived with his Yorkshire accent and flying yellow mackintosh, he carried all before him including his enormous frame, won every prize, caught every judge's eye and almost immediately after leaving gave in what was then the fringe theatre at Kew the finest performance as *The Government Inspector* London had seen for years.

I was no Laughton, although in bulk and general untidiness of costume I bore perhaps a fleeting resemblance; but Laughton heartened us fatties and the regional types who by the nature of the Academy were in those days still regarded as rather second-class citizens. If Kenneth Barnes was to run the Academy at even the smallest margin of profit, he had perforce to run it first and foremost as a charm school. Mothers who hadn't wanted to put their daughters on the stage were much more likely to continue paying the fees if they noticed a distinct improvement in their child's posture and appearance, in the way she spoke and dressed and brushed her hair. A year at the Academy could often do wonders in turning a dumpy duck into an acceptable cygnet.

For the men, of course, no such transformation was possible or indeed thought desirable but some parents remained hopeful that at the end of two years their sons would change direction and consider a more serious and gainful career. Indeed had all four hundred or so of the student body who crowded the classrooms been inspired by the staff with unwavering purpose and devotion to its temporary vocation, the profession would have been even more hopelessly crowded than it is today. Many of us fell by the roadside or more properly thumbed a lift to town by way of early marriage or the acceptance of a job in our father's business, but a surprising number of my year remained on the stage to tell the tale or enable me to do so for Mr O'Donoghue who passed me list after list of their half-forgotten names.

Dorothy Dunkels, who along with a girl called Marjorie Playfair, and Plum Warner's daughter Betty, were the three great beauties of our day. Miss Playfair had the prettiest legs imaginable and she would sit swinging them on the dresser of the canteen to the hopeless admiration of most of the fellows and indeed some of the staff. Betty Warner had the most beautiful red hair and Dorothy Dunkels was teacher's pet, at least where Miss Sevening was concerned. Miss Sevening was the formidable power behind and indeed on the scenes. It was generally admitted that it was she who ran the show. She was Baroness Falkender to Barnes's Harold Wilson. She kept things moving, knew what was going on and on occasions stopped the rot. I suppose what she liked about Dorothy Dunkels was that she was nearly, if not quite, as elegant as herself. Much to our surprise Dorothy didn't carry all before her on the day. I am not certain she even won a prize but I remember her at the Strand Theatre later giving a memorable performance as a manicurist in one of Arthur Macrae's plays and looking the same cool and lovely child she had when she sat beside Marjorie but didn't swing her legs.

'You knew, of course,' I told O'Donoghue, 'that *Grizel* Niven was David Niven's sister and became a sculptress and that Ingaret Giffard married Laurens Van Der Post and that Cheatle committed suicide and so did Sandford who won the Gold!' 'I knew about Sandford,' he told me, 'Barnes wrote RIP after his name.' 'I don't know what happened to Elizabeth Thynne,' I said and O'Donoghue told me Barnes had written RIP after her name as well.

Bruno Barnabe is still going and so is Brian Oulton and, of course,

Jean Anderson and Hugh Moxey. I caught him on television only the other day. Esther Thomson, now she married Komisarjevsky or was it Claude Rains? I'm pretty sure it was Rains not Komisarjevsky. Come and seduce me we used to call him.

Carol Hahn married Llewellyn Rees who became Secretary of Equity, but then afterwards she married Giles Playfair, whose father Sir Nigel ran the Lyric Theatre, Hammersmith. 'There is a Carol Hahn Memorial Award,' O'Donoghue told me, 'she was American.'

'They were married straight from the Academy I rather think,' I told him, 'I gave her away, at any rate Llewellyn was *my* best man when I married. I'm afraid it's all getting a trifle blurred. Did you know,' I asked, surer of my ground, 'that Wallace Finlayson was really Wallace Douglas, Robert Douglas's brother? Robert stepped straight into *Many Waters* as the Jeune Premier and then went into films and still produces them for television. Or that Andre Van Gysegem married Jean Forbes-Robertson? Curigwen Lewis, now she did marry a poet.' 'Andrew Cruickshank,' he reproved me gently. 'Joan Hickson is still going strong.' I came back at him, 'Did you see her in the Ayckbourn play?' '*Bedroom Farce*,' he countered. I began to understand my Aunts and Uncles all those years ago: perhaps it wasn't pretence, forgetting the names.

I was on surer grounds where the staff were concerned. 'Miss Elsie Chester had one leg and a crutch she used to throw at us when she couldn't bear it any longer. Helen Haye always acted Grand Duchesses clutching cambric handkerchieves. A great teacher, once after I had been particularly terrible in *The Last of Mrs Cheyney* she firmly opened a copy of the Evening Standard Racing Edition. 'I am unlikely,' she remarked not unkindly, 'to find a winner in this class. We must try Sandown Park.'

'There was the great Rosina Phillipi, retired I think by this time, who taught breath control. You were expected to do Mark Antony's speech about Brutus not bringing chariots to Rome in three breaths. For years afterwards I used to test myself. Now if I manage a length underwater in the pool I am content.

'All the staff had their favourite plays, Elsie Chester's was Galsworthy's *The Silver Box*, Herbert Ross (married to Helen Haye) stuck more or less to *Tilly of Bloomsbury*, Norman Page was devoted to one by Dunsany about a Pierrot. Then there was an elocution teacher, or more properly a voice production coach, who made you stand at the end of the room and bounce final consonants off the opposite wall. Hop Poles Unchecked Desire. I still do it.'

'Do what?'

'Sound the final consonant. None of the young do; that's why I can't hear them, that and because I am a bit deaf.'

'Would you like,' he said 'to go and see the Young People?'

'I'd quite like to go and see the old place.'

Like Milton Keynes it had sadly changed. The canteen is upstairs and the basement where it used to be is now a small theatre. It was as if I had never seen the place before. I suppose in a way I hadn't. Once, when I was about to go into the old theatre, I leant heavily against a door which gave way and I found myself in the disused box office. Quick as a flash I opened up for business. 'It's half-a-crown now for each parent,' I told my fellow students as they streamed past. Some of them even gave me their half-crowns. When I had counted up, I slipped inside the auditorium. I couldn't hear the play because of the whispered protests of those who had paid and the gleeful pleasure of those who hadn't. Barnes sent for me later and confiscated the loot for the Building Fund, what was left of it. In those days half-a-crown went a long way, you could eat at Bertorelli's in Percy Street on newspapers for ten pence. A huge bowl of spaghetti and an apple dumpling. Enough for growing boys and girls.

The grown boys and girls were in the basement preparing to rehearse an extemporisation, the sort of thing they do in Hampstead. 'At least they don't have to learn the lines,' I said to the rather severe young woman who seemed to be in charge. 'Indeed they do,' she told me, 'Once we've decided on the script.' 'Have you decided on this one?' 'Not yet.' 'Will it be a happy piece?' I asked. 'Not particularly,' she assured me. 'It's about a group of students and their problems. I hope it will be a true picture.' I told her I hoped so too and climbed the stairs to retrieve my hat and coat. 'What about her,' I asked, 'is she a permanent member of your staff?' 'Visiting,' he assured me, 'after this she is off to the Crucible at Sheffield to stage the same sort of exercise.'

'She is leading them down a path only the critics will follow,' I told him sagely. There was one chocolate biscuit left on the plate. I munched all the way to the bus stop. Age has its compensations, but then I always had a sweet tooth.

June 1978

Stevie Smith

THE LORD OF DEATH

I AM a girl who loves to shoot,
I love the feathered fowl and brute,
I love them with a love as strong
As ever there came from heaven down.

Why should I not love them living as dead?
As I shoot, as I shoot, and as my fine dog Tay
Brings the shot one to hand, he is I, I am they.
Oh why do my friends think this love is so questionable?
They say they love animals but they do not love them as I am able,

Seeing them run and fly and letting them run, fly and die,
I love them to distraction as the wild wind goes by,
As the rain and the storm on this wide upper hill,
Oh no one loves the animals as I do or so well.
If I am not hungry I let them run free,
And if I am hungry they are my darling passionate delicacy.

Into the wild woods I go over the high mountain to the valley low,
And the animals are safe; if I am not hungry they
    may run and go,
And I bless their beautiful appearance and
    their fleetness,
And I feel no contradiction or contriteness.
I love them living and I love them dead with a
    quick blood spurt
And I may put them in the pot and eat them
    up with a loving heart.

I am a girl who loves to shoot,
I love the feathered fowl and brute,
I love them with as great a love
As ever came down from heaven above.

August 1953

Malcolm Bradbury

MIDDLE WEST EDUCATION

I WAS once a teacher in an American university. I had an office which I shared with five other people; my name was on the door until towards the end of the year, when some student to whom I'd been giving low grades stole it. I used to smoke a pipe and wait for students to come in and surprise me. On the wall above my desk I had a poem, by Rimbaud, in French, and a picture of the Council House at Nottingham. Both excited comment. If you leaned out of the window of the office you could see a path which all the co-eds (which is what the girl students were called) used to tread on their way to the women's dormitory.

The university was a state university in the middle of the mid-west. The campus was enormous, more than a mile square, filled with fifteen thousand students. There was a radio and television station, a theatre, two bookstores and an infirmary. You could take driving lessons. I was lost all the time. A river ran through the campus, and after a while I just got into the habit of following the river. You could see me padding through the thick bushes by the water's edge, up to the knees in mud but knowing just where I was.

Since it was a state university this institution had to take everyone in the state who had graduated from high school and wished to go to college; and every year, from the four corners of the state, five thousand students appeared on its door-step. Some were near illiterate. I was teaching a basic course in English compulsory for all freshmen. There were about a hundred teachers teaching it. Teachers, meeting in the faculty lounge, began to doubt their own existence; they had supposed that they were individuals, intellectually unique, and now here were hundreds more like themselves. Some ran away and went into publishing or joined the Quakers. Others simply grew more and more morose. Others saw it as a pastime. These were by and large the professional intellectual vagabonds, the unsettled bright young men who went from university to university on short contracts, taking more and more degrees, teaching things. They all had old cars, new hi-fi equipment, a lot of high-class

paper-backed books, and nothing else. They kept growing beards –
first one, then another – and then shaving them off. They were all
liberals, living truly in the world of ideas. The students couldn't
understand them. It made them see what McCarthy was complaining about. They were, by American rules, failures, trying to teach
students how to be successes.

One day, after I'd been there little more than a week, they told me
I would have to take my first class. I was very frightened. I needed a
haircut. There was a big amphitheatre, with a sink and some gas-taps
on the teacher's desk. The room was full of beautiful girls, all about
eighteen, splendidly made up. They wore cashmere sweaters and
tight skirts, with darts under the rump to make their bottoms stick
out. I had never taught before. I didn't know what to say. Very
slowly I wrote my name in big letters on the board. I didn't say it was
my name. I looked at my watch. There were still fifty-eight minutes
to go. Sweat was collecting in my shoes. I started to read what I
thought were some notes but what was, actually, a letter from my
mother, telling me to buy a thick overcoat. My trousers seemed to be
slipping down. All the while, pretending I was myopic, I was looking
at the legs of the girls in the front row. I wondered what to do now. I
decided to tell them about my office. I explained, in incredible detail,
how to get to it. I drew a plan on the board to show which desk was
mine. I told them about the Rimbaud and Nottingham Council
House. My hands kept going down, accidently, into the sink. I
promised to buy some biscuits if they'd come to my office now and
then. There seemed nothing else to say, so I told them to go away and
write an essay on 'Love and marriage, love and marriage, go together
like a horse and carriage.' I thought it was something they were all
interested in.

When I got the essays I was amazed. They were so bad that it just
wasn't true. I looked at the essays that the other teachers had; they
were bad too; it wasn't, then, my fault. The first paper I opened
consisted of this:

> 'After a couple has been going together for a while they
> soon find out whether they love each other or not. If a
> couple does love one another they will realize many things
> about each other. The couple knows if the other is lovable,
> selfish, rich or poor, gentle, good or bad, educated, can
> make a living, religious, well-mannered and many other

> things. If the couple knows they love each other no matter
> whether they are strong or weak in most of the things I
> have listed. They will want to marry. If a couple feels that
> he or she cannot live without each other for several of the
> reasons I have listed he or she will ask the other to marry.'

I want you to know that I did not write this myself. It was written by a
girl from Nashville, Kentucky, who came to university to learn to
play the flute. The other papers were like this too.

   I taught a few more classes and got more used to it. I still needed a
haircut. After a while I got a sore throat from teaching so much and
went into the infirmary. I used to have penicillin injected into my seat
by beautiful nurses. Then I got better and went back to teaching
again. It was now nearly winter. My ears were cold all the time. The
students didn't seem to be getting any better. They used to come into
the office and try to get good grades by flattering me. They asked me
how I liked American girls. I was too smart for them and they knew
it, and after a while they didn't come any more.

   I used to face great teaching problems, such as how to make the
students pay attention. One idea I had for this was to punch someone.
But gradually I worried less. One way I found of getting attention
was to use the opaque projector. This was a machine for projecting
the image of pages of books, or essays, on to the wall for class
discussion. We used to crowd round it and all get warm. Gradually
people would get interested in the equipment. We'd dismantle it and
learn how it worked. We all learned a great deal. Another teaching aid
that we used was a gramophone. They all called it a phonograph. We
began by playing records of Dylan Thomas declaiming his poems like
some nineteenth-century tragedian; then we'd have a critical discussion of the poems. Gradually people started to bring their own
records, of all the latest songs. Sometimes we'd have little dances.
Once a tiny man with a bundle of washing under his arm sneaked into
the class and sat at the back. It turned out that he was inspecting my
teaching. The class had been a discussion of American dating-
patterns as characteristic of the American way of life. We began with
some desultory conversation, and then one of the students asked me
about dating in England. I told a long story about the social
implications of an affair I'd had with a large upper-middle-class girl
who modelled vests for a knit-wear firm. The inspector congratulated
me afterwards on keeping the class's attention. Gradually other

teachers began to hear about my classes, and soon the classes were so full of teachers that we had to ask some of the students to stay away. Teachers were also dismissing their own classes in order to come to mine.

All the time I had to be very careful what I said, because I had sworn a loyalty oath, pledging to uphold the American constitution and the laws of the state and promising not to promulgate alien doctrines. Once I nearly risked my career by entering on a few words about the English National Health Service, but I caught myself in time. But word gradually got back to me that people thought I was a Communist. It was because I said I didn't much like commercial television.

Winter came and my hair got longer and longer. I couldn't afford to have it cut. The barbers were all in an association and charged a dollar fifty. This is more than ten shillings. Gradually my students began to comment on it; I told them I'd sent away to Sears Roebuck for a haircut but it hadn't come through yet. Finally I asked one of the girls in my class to cut it for me.

After that students started to take a great interest in my hair and in my clothes. They made me buy an Ivy League suit, which is a very distinguished kind of Edwardian-looking clothing that all the best university people wear. I bought shirts with buttons on the collar: I wear one of them to write this. Someone gave me a sweater which wasn't too badly worn. A co-ed took me to a tea-party at her sorority. I was very pleased, because I'd been wanting a cup of tea for three months.

Towards the end of the semester, in late January, there was a sharp change in atmosphere. Co-eds came into my office and cried and said that they had to have a B average to stay in their sororities. They said they'd do anything to get a B. People told me afterwards that they meant it. The men students came in and said they hoped I was liking it over here and boy, they'd be out of school if they didn't have an A. Fraternity presidents and football coaches came jovially in to ask me to give good grades to protégés. I locked my office and went and sat in one of the bars downtown. Soon they found me there. I decided to hitch-hike to Florida. I knew I dare not publish the final grades. Students telephoned me in the evening and said if they got bad grades it proved I'd been a bad teacher. One of the students told me that none of them had understood a word I'd said all year because of my English accent. He wanted to know what 'Have a biscuit' meant. It was what I had always said to students when they came into my office in the old days, when we'd all liked each other. I finally posted up the grades on the door of my office and then locked myself in. I could hear the students outside reading the grades and banging on the door. 'We know he's in there,' they could be heard saying. I stayed there, eating biscuits, until about ten o'clock in the evening. Then I walked back to my room through the wet bushes by the river edge. It was obvious that I would catch pneumonia but I didn't care. But next semester I would be more careful. I'd also, incidentally, find out if there wasn't a path.

October 1957

W.C. Sellar and R.J. Yeatman
1066 AND ALL THAT

[*Being extracts from a forthcoming History of England. (Absit OMAN.)*]

RICHARD I. A WILD KING

RICHARD I was a hairy King with a Lion's Heart; he went roaring about the Desert making ferocious attacks on the Saladins and the Paladins, and was thus a very romantic King. Whenever he returned to England he always set out again immediately for the Mediterranean and was therefore known as Richard Gare de Lyon. In spite of which the Crusaders under RICHARD never got Jerusalem back; this was undoubtedly due to the treacherous behaviour of the Saladins, who used to fire on the Red Cross which the Crusaders wore on their chests in battle.

THE STORY OF BLONDIN

RICHARD is also famous for having a minstrel boy (or Touralour) called BLONDIN, who searched for him under the walls of all the dungeons in Europe. This was when RICHARD had been caught by the blind King of Bohemia during a game of Blind King's Bluff and sold to the Holy Roman Terror. BLONDIN eventually found him by singing the memorable song (or 'touralay') called 'O Richard et mon Droit' ('Are you right there, Richard?'), which RICHARD himself had composed. RICHARD roared the chorus so that BLONDIN knew which dungeon he was in, and thus the King easily escaped and returned to the Crusades, where he died soon after of a surfeit of Saladins.

MAGNA CHARTER

In the reign of JOHN occurred the memorable Charter, known as Magna Charter on account of the Latin *Magna* (great) and Charter (a Charter); this was the first of the famous Charters and Garters of the Realm and was invented by the Barons on a desert island in the Thames. By congregating there, armed to the teeth, the Barons compelled JOHN to sign the Magna Charter, which said:

(1) That no one was to be put to death, save for some reason (except the Common People).

(2) That everyone should be free (except the Common People).

(3) That everything should be of the same weight and measure throughout the Realm (except the Common People).

(4) That the Courts should be stationary, instead of following the very tiresome mediæval official known as the *King's Person* all over the country.

(5) That 'no person should be fined to his utter ruin' (except the King's Person).

(6) That the Barons should not be tried, except by a special jury of other Barons who would understand.

Magna Charter was therefore the chief cause of Democracy in England, and thus a *Good Thing* for everyone (except the Common People).

After this KING JOHN hadn't a leg to stand on, and was therefore known as 'John Lackshanks'.

*   *   *   *   *

ROBIN HOOD AND HIS MERRIE MEN

Shortly after this the memorable hero Robin Hood flourished in a romantic manner. Having been unjustly accused by two policemen in Richmond Park, he was condemned to be an Outdoor and went and lived with a band of Merrie Men in Greenwood Forest, near Sherborne. Among his Merrie Men were Will Scarlet (*The Scarlet Pimpernel*), Black Beauty, White Melville, Little Red Riding Hood (probably an outdaughter of his) and the famous Friar Puck, who used to sit in a cowslip and suck bees, thus becoming so fat that he declared he could put his girdle round the earth.

Robin Hood spent his time shooting at the Sheriff of Nottingham

Robin Hood was a miraculous shot with the longbow, and it is said that he could split a hare at four hundred paces and a Sheriff at eight hundred. He therefore spent his time blowing a horn and shooting at the Sheriff of Nottingham (who was an outwit). He always used to sound his horn first, particularly when shooting round a corner; this showed his sportsmanship and also enabled him to shoot the Sheriff running, which was more difficult.

Robin Hood was also very good at Socialism and often took money away from rich clergymen and gave it to the poor, who loved him for his generosity. He died very romantically. Having taken some medicine and feeling his strength going, he blew a dying blast on his horn and with his dying breath fired a last shot out of his bedroom window and hit the Sheriff of Nottingham again.

* * * * *

EDWARD III. A ROMANTIC KING

EDWARD III had a very romantic reign which he began by inventing a law called the Gallic Law, according to which he was King of France and could therefore make war on it whenever he felt inclined.

In order to placate EDWARD, the French King sent him a box of new tennis-balls. When the parcel was opened the Prince of Wales, who was present, mottoed to himself memorably (in Bohemian), '*Ich Dien*', which means 'My serve', and immediately invaded France with an army of archers. This prince was the memorable All-Black Prince and the war was called the Hundred Years War, because the troops signed on for a hundred years or the duration.

ROYAL TACT

EDWARD III had very good manners. One day at a royal dance he noticed some men-about-court mocking a lady whose garter had come off. Whereupon, to put her at her ease, he stopped the dance and, having replaced the garter with a romantic gesture, gave the ill-mannered courtiers the Order of the Bath. (This was an extreme form of torture in the Middle Ages.)

RICHARD II. AN UNBALANCED KING

RICHARD II was only a boy at his accession. One day, however, suspecting that he was now twenty-one, he asked his uncle and, on learning that he was, mounted the throne himself and tried first being a Good King and then being a Bad King, without enjoying either very much. Then, being told that he was unbalanced, he got off the throne again in despair, exclaiming gloomily: 'For God's sake let me sit on the ground and tell bad stories about cabbages and things.' Whereupon his cousin LANCASTER (*alias* BOLINGBROKE, etc.) quickly mounted the throne and said he was HENRY IV Part I.

RICHARD was thus abdicated and was led to the Tower and subsequently to Pontefract Castle, where he died of mysterious circumstances, probably a surfeit of Pumfreys (pronounced Pontefracts).

APPENDIX
THE PEASANT REVOLTS

I. Objects:

(*a*) To obtain a free pardon for having revolted.

(*b*) To find out which was the gentleman when ADAM delved and EVE span. (The answer was, of course, ADAM, but the mystics of the Church had concealed this dangerous knowledge.)

(c) To find out who was King and which of them was the Leader of the Rebellion.

(d) To abolish the Villain.

The Peasant Revolts were therefore purely educational movements and were thus easily suppressed.

II. How Quelled:

(a) The peasants were met at Smithfield by the King who,

(b) Riding forward alone on a white horse, answered Object (c) by announcing (1) 'I am your King' and (2) 'I will be your Leader'.

(c) The real leader was then slain quickly by one of the Barons.

(d) A free pardon was granted to the peasants [see Object (a)].

(e) All were then put to death on the ground that they were villains [see Object (d)].

The Peasant Revolts were thus clearly romantic episodes and a *Good Thing*, and the clergy were enabled to prevent the peasants finding out the answer to Object (b).

HENRY IV. A SPLIT KING

When HENRY IV Part I came to the throne the Barons immediately flung their gloves on the floor in order to prove –

(1) That RICHARD II was not yet dead.

(2) That HENRY had murdered him.

HENRY very gallantly replied to this challenge by exhibiting RICHARD II's head in St Paul's Cathedral, thus proving that he was innocent. Finding, however, that he was not being memorable, he abdicated in favour of HENRY IV Part II.

RENEWED EDUCATIONAL FERMENT

HENRY IV Part II is chiefly memorable for capturing the Scottish Prince JAMES and having him carefully educated for nineteen years. But, when he found that JAMES was still Scotch, HENRY IV Part II lost interest in education and died.

September 1930

Patrick Skene Catling

FAKE A LETTER

Vice! The very word (the sharp angularity of the initial, the final sibilance) epitomises melodrama, a villain with a dagger, triumphantly hissing. The foul thrill of it! But what is the fun of practising one's favourite vice forever undetected? It is no more fun than a perfect murder. I at once welcome and dread this opportunity to tell about a long-kept secret.

All vice, of course, is a component of the supreme omnibus vice, a denial of the true nature of being. Vice satisfies an urge to shun, or at least to postpone, acceptance of the responsibilities and demands of awareness of reality. This general principle is equally valid whether the peccadillo of the moment happens to be building a monster with electronic gadgets and Transylvanian graveyard scraps, or remaining in the bathtub until the palms of the hands and the soles of the feet become white and crinkly. Escapism can be more or less complicated, ranging from flight on the hallucinatory wings of marijuana to the cultivation of some private Perfumed Garden. Escapism can be as deceptively constructive as philately and knitting, as inexpensive as reading newspaper lists of steamship departures, and as dangerous. Like children, whose horrid grimaces can be permanently fixed by sudden changes of the wind, escapists run the risk of being trapped out of character; death can catch them in a false identity, down a fantastic rabbit-hole, or emotionally back to front on the wrong side of the looking glass. But escape from reality, I have always assured myself, is hazardous only if it is actual; in its more advanced manifestations, escapism itself may be unreal, the elusiveness illusory, the vice a mere pretence. Not much of an assurance, I suppose, hardly an excuse, but it's the best one I have, and I felt a pre-Freudian compulsion to record it before revealing that sometimes, as a matter of fact, I'm a bit of a liar.

Mendacity makes the world go around, you say? What's unusual about a bit of lying? How could anyone run a business or a general election campaign without it? But wait a minute. The distinguishing features of my habitual falsehoods are their specialised purpose and form. I practise deception only in order to cause disquietude and gain unearned credit, by misuse of other people's writing paper.

This hobby of mine began fortuitously in a small way a few years ago in a hotel in Brighton. A newspaper had assigned me, against my wishes, to cover a trade convention. It was something about man-made fibres replacing cotton, as I recall; Manchester cared. After the first long and tiresome day of speeches in The Dome, my tolerance was low. I eventually finished writing in my room, went down to the bar, and found it closed. The only place to get a drink, the porter said, was in the guests' lounge, which was little more than an alcove, just a sofa and a few chairs closely arrayed in a semi-circle in front of a fireplace. And there, at the focal point of that compact gathering, stood the conference chairman, holding forth on the merits of Orlon, or some other synthetic material. 'My wife swears by it,' he said. I was dazed by the drone of his monologue, even when, a couple of drinks later, it turned into a recital of stories about commercial travellers and the daughters of boarding-house keepers. At last I could endure this enormous self-esteem and his dullness no longer; I snapped out of thrall, took what was left of my drink into the adjacent writing room, sat at a desk and morosely doodled. Then I found myself trying to ease my feelings by writing a letter on the hotel paper, telling the man what I thought of him, though of course I realised that I couldn't have it delivered to him. And then I got a better idea. I wrote a letter to his wife, from the management of the hotel. I got her address from the register on the reception desk and posted the letter there and then. It was quite brief and ostensibly inoffensive. It ran as follows:

Dear Mrs — [I wrote]:

We regret that you decided to return home after all, after only one night with us, and trust that you found your accommodation entirely satisfactory, though, of course, we had prepared your room at first only for single occupancy.

We hope that your husband and you will come and stay with us again on some future occasion, when we will be

able to honour your request for a double bed. We will send
on your night attire by parcel post as soon as it returns from
our seamstress.

The management was hers attentively. There was nothing subtle
about the letter, I know, but it was only my first effort. Even so, it was
gratifying, as I subsided gradually into slumber, to speculate about
the letter's reception and its possible repercussions.

The effects of fraudulent letters often can be contemplated only in
the imagination, but it is there, after all, that all pleasures are keenest,
and I have found my little hobby none the less enjoyable because of
its essentially subjective and abstract nature. There have been
occasions, however, when I have actually been able to observe a
letter's emotional impact on its recipient. I remember with special
fondness, for example, a particularly nasty correspondence that I
initiated between the Ministry of Transport and a temporary neighbour of mine in Wiltshire.

A few years ago, I leased a cottage in a village not far from
Stonehenge, in order to spend quiet weekends away from London.
The place was all that I had hoped it would be, of almost druidical
age. The builders, whoever they were, obviously hadn't cared too
much about right angles, and every structure had its own peculiar
way of sagging; there was a good deal of crumbling old stone about,
lichenous, much of it, and profusely flowering asymmetrical old
gardens. Everything would have been idyllic but for the fact that the
owner of the manor house, a really lovely Jacobean building insulated
by a formal rose garden, a gently sloping lawn, a ha-ha, a meadow,
great elms, and a trout stream, apparently believed it was his
seignorial right to bore the pants off everyone who assembled each
evening in the village's only pub. All topics of conversation, which
was inescapably general in so tiny and intimate a room, reminded
him, immediately or remotely, of himself, his career in a syndicate of
insurance underwriters, his retirement, and his new ancient home.
He was especially proud, justly, of his rose garden and lawn, but he
spoke of them, and the rest of his place, in the stilted hyperbole of an
estate agent's advertisement – an advertisement without end. In
short, as far as I was concerned, he rendered the pub unfit to drink in,
and the village thus uninhabitable, and I minded.

At this time, as it happened, I was doing a series of articles on
traffic flow in town and country and what the Ministry of Transport

proposed to do about it. Thus it came to pass that I had an interview with the Minister, in his office, in Berkeley Square. His name, in the present context, is irrelevant. While waiting in his secretary's room, while his secretary went in to announce my arrival, I had the foresight to purloin a quantity of ministerial writing paper. Paper of this sort is always sure to come in handy. It was on a sheet of this that I eventually composed a letter to the garrulous lord of the manor, notifying him of the Ministry's emergency scheme to construct a Salisbury Plain Motorway.

> A topographical survey [I typed] indicates that the most efficient route for the new facility passes across your property 35 feet south of the dwelling and then turns in a north-westerly direction to run parallel with the rivulet that forms the northern boundary of your property. Compensation for the Ministry's acquisition of the appropriate right of way shall be computed in accordance with the Right of Way (Acquisition) Compensation Act of 1933. It is hoped that you, as a leading member of your community, will set an example of co-operation for the sake of all motorists everywhere. It should, perhaps, be added that in all recent cases moves to check the progress of the motor-way system by means of litigation have been decided, invariably at great expense to the plaintiff, in favour of the Ministry.

When I said I initiated a correspondence between my neighbour and the Ministry, I was, I must admit, merely presuming that he wrote back to them; but it is quite possible that he didn't. What he certainly did do was panic. With astonishing speed, he sold the estate at a considerable loss, I understand, though for much more than he undoubtedly thought it would soon be worth. The last time I saw him, the day before he left the village, he was subdued and seemed smaller.

The main lesson I learned from the Wiltshire incident was that even quite experienced, relatively sophisticated persons readily suspend disbelief when they receive a letter, no matter how substantively implausible, if the letterhead itself is sufficiently impressive. And, of course, the more august the heading, the greater one's scope for credible absurdity below. Encouraged by these reflections, inspired even, I undertook more ambitiously bizarre one-way communication.

The accessibility of so many 'stately homes' proved incalculably helpful. Few of them disappointed me, and I venture to say that I may now have the finest all-round collection of stately stationery in the country. The paper itself is aesthetically satisfying. It is undeniably true that some peers are using rather shoddy stuff nowadays, but still there's a gratifyingly high incidence of peers whose writing paper is the last place where straitened circumstances are likely to show. The smooth creaminess of it! The high rag content! The coronary embossment! Running appreciative fingertips lightly over the Braille tickle of fine engraving, I sometimes feel a slight pang of regret that an opportunity for use has arisen which I cannot ignore.

Whenever I manage to obtain a fairly good supply of a well-known man's paper, I find it difficult to restrain myself from pranks that sometimes in retrospect seem silly. I once had the unusual good fortune, some years ago, of picking up a whole ream of paper in a corridor of Number 10, Downing Street. The paper was still tightly encased in its brown paper package, and I dared not open it until I gained the freedom of St James's Park, but some sixth sense told me that I might be on to something rather good. And, sure enough, when I tore open the wrappings I found I had 480 sheets of 24-pound-stock white paper heavily embossed at the top with the royal coat of arms, in black, and the words, like a splendid fanfare of trumpets, THE PRIME MINISTER. I felt that exquisite throb of joy that one always experiences when one's favourite vice is going really well.

My first impulse was to despatch a few bluntly chiding remarks to foreign leaders who in my judgment had recently been outstandingly clottish. The impulse was not immediately resisted, but I soon tired of such long-distance diatribes and bent my efforts to the composition of messages of shorter range and possibly more easily observable results. First, I wrote to my mother:

Dear Mrs Catling, – It is with great pleasure that I can now inform you that your eldest son has recently made a most important contribution to world peace and thus, of course, to the security of the United Kingdom. Thanks to his intrepid and resourceful actions, we may now all rest easier. I wish I could tell you the precise nature of his exploits, but I am sure you will understand that his continuing effectiveness will depend in no small part on the discretion of all concerned. I need hardly tell you that to him discretion is as natural as breathing. If by any chance you have wondered why he has not been writing many letters to you recently, may I, as a fellow parent, suggest that you wonder no more?

Then I dashed off a note to the editor of my paper:

Dear Mr — [it said]: I just want to say that we of the free world are lucky that we have men like your Mr Catling writing for our side.

Another to the Leader of The Opposition:

Dear —, We've had our tiffs, goodness knows, but I am sure there is one belief that we hold in common: a well informed democracy is a healthy democracy. I would like to recommend that whenever you or I have any announcement of major importance to make we make it first to Patrick Catling. Only in this way can we be perfectly sure that our words will get a fair hearing in the forum of public opinion, because, as you must be aware, his accuracy, speed and impartiality ...

I squandered quite a large number of sheets of the priceless paper on politicians, press tycoons, book publishers, hostesses, and the manager of my bank: 'The solidarity of the pound sterling depends, to no small extent, on faith. I was chatting with a young fellow the other day who radiates the quality I mean, and I'd like to commend him to you ...'

Now I am saving what remains of the PM's paper for something big, a moment of national crisis or private whim. In the meantime, I shall continue to amuse myself and mortify others by using various items from my continuously growing writing-paper collection for letters to *The Times*. If you are a regular, careful reader of that newspaper's letters column, you should have no difficulty catching on to my style. I manage to get something in three or four days a week. My contributions are usually the sillier ones.

July 1964

Douglas Jerrold

THE LIFE AND ADVENTURES OF MISS ROBINSON CRUSOE

CHAPTER VIII

HILST making my breakfast, I began to think – it was the constant custom of my dear father – of my dinner. My thoughts immediately flew to the turkey; and again I felt confounded by my ignorance. How was I to dress it? Whilst in this state of perturbation, and inwardly reproaching myself for the time I had lost at tambour-work that might have been so usefully, so nobly employed in at least the theory of the kitchen, my eye fell upon the book I had brought from the wreck; the book lying in the cot of the regimental chaplain going out to India. Listlessly enough, I took the volume in my hand – opened it, and, equally to my astonishment and joy, read upon the title-page – *The Complete Art of Cookery!* My gratitude was unbounded, and I blessed the good man whose midnight studies had indirectly proved of such advantage to me.

With beating heart, I turned over the pages, until I came to 'Turkey'. Again and again I read the directions; but though they were written with all the clearness of a novel, they only gave me, what I once heard called, a magnificent theory. I felt that drawing required a practical hand; for how was I to know gall from liver? 'A stuffing of sausage-meat' sounded very well – but how to make it? And then – though, possibly, the plant might grow in the island – where to get a shred shallot? The excellent chaplain's book, instead of instructing and comforting me, plunged me in the profoundest melancholy. As I turned over the pages – I, a desolate spinster on a desolate island – I seemed scoffed and mocked at by the dishes that I read of – dishes, all of them associated with the very best society, and many of them awakening thoughts of Michaelmas goose, of Christmas beef, of spring lamb, and all the amenities that impart the sweetest charm to civilised existence. With a strong effort of will, I laid down the book: I would keep it, I thought, for calmer hours. When more accustomed to my hideous solitude, it might soothe and support me, throwing the fascinations of romance about a cold and hungry reality.

Walking upon the beach, I looked, as usual, in the direction of the wreck, and found it – gone. The gale of the night had doubtless been very violent – though I slept too soundly to hear it – and the remains of the miserable vessel had sunk for ever in the deep. I was, at first, very much affected; but when I remembered that with the exception of one box, containing a bonnet of the most odious colour for my complexion, I had brought all my dear sister-passengers' trunks and boxes safe ashore, I felt soothed with the consciousness that, at least I had done my duty.

And I was upon an island – alone; with neither man, nor – excepting the aforesaid rabbits (or ermine) – beast. After a flood of tears, I resolved, like a true woman, to make the best of my misery. I walked further into the island, and discovered a beautiful bit of grass-plot, backed by a high rock. To this place, with a strength and patience I am almost ashamed to confess, I removed every trunk and every box, placing them in a semicircle, with the rock as – I believe it's called – the gable end. When this was done, I cut down innumerable stakes of willow: this I was enabled to do with the surgeon's saw, a remarkably neat and elegant little instrument. The stakes I drove into the earth, within about six inches round the trunks, by means of a cannon-ball – providentially, as it afterwards turned out, brought from the wreck. This being done – and it cost me incredible labour to accomplish it – I dug up hundreds of creepers, and parasitical plants, and cactuses, that I found in different parts of the island, and replanted them near the willow-stakes. Vegetation was very rapid indeed, in that island. In less than a week the plants and willows began to shoot, and – to anticipate my story a little – in two months every trunk and every box was hidden by a green and flowering wall. The cactuses took very kindly, and formed a hedge, strong enough, I verily believe, to repel a wild beast or a wild Indian. I ought to have said that I had taken the precaution to roof my bower, as I called it, with some tarpaulin, that stained and made my hands smell horribly. However, I had no remedy.

Whilst I worked at my bower, I lived upon the biscuit and potted meats and preserves found in the steward's cabin. In time, however, I began to grow tired of these, and longed for something fresh. As for the turkey, I had left that hanging to the tree, being incapable of drawing and dressing it. Many wild-fowl flew about me, but, disheartened by the turkey, I took no heed of them. At length it struck me that though not much of a cook I might be able to boil some shrimps. The first difficulty, however, was to catch them. During my visits to English watering-places I had observed females of the lower orders, with hand-nets I think they call them, fishing for shrimps. I therefore resolved to make a net. Here, at least, some part of the education acquired at the MISSES WHALEBONE's was of service to me, for I knew how to knit. Amongst the stores I had brought from my ship, were several balls of twine. Chopping and chiselling a needle, I set to work, and in less than three days produced an excellent net. This I stretched on a stout elastic frame of wood, and the tide serving, walked – just like one of the vulgar women I had seen at Brighton and Margate – bare-legged, into the sea. The shrimps came in little shoals, and in less than a couple of hours I am sure, I returned to the shore with not less than three quarts of the best brown shrimps, Gravesend measure. These I boiled; obtaining a light after this fashion:

When a very little girl, I had always assisted my brother when making fireworks for Guy Fawkes. It was he who taught me how to make – I think they are called, little devils. A pinch or two of gunpowder is taken in the palm of the hand, and wetted: it is then kneaded into the form of a little cone; a few grains of dry powder are laid upon the top, when fire is applied to it, and the whole thing goes off in a red eruption, like a toy Vesuvius. Having prepared the powder, I struck sparks upon it; using my steel busk (how the sparks did fly about it, to be sure!) and a flint. By these means I burnt a piece of linen – a beautiful bit of new Irish, and so got my original stock of tinder. After this, I had only to use my busk and the flint to obtain a light – for I found a heap of matches in the purser's locker – when I wanted it. Gathering dry sticks and leaves into a heap, I made a rousing fire. I had brought away the ship's compass; and so used the metal basin that contained it as a saucepan. In this I boiled my first shrimps. I had no salt, which was a great privation. Necessity, however, the mother of invention – (and, certainly, for a little outcast, he has proved a very fine child in the world; though when prosperous, I'm afraid he very seldom thinks of his mamma) – necessity suggested to me, that if I would pound the gunpowder very fine, it might at a pinch serve for salt. I tried the experiment; and though I must allow that salt is better without charcoal, nevertheless, salt with charcoal is infinitely better than no salt at all.

For some time, I took very much to shrimps; but the human mind is given to variety – a fact that in my solitude I have frequently pondered on – and I began to long for some other kind of food; in fact, for some fresh fish. In my wanderings about the island, I had discovered a beautiful piece of water – clear as crystal, and sweet as milk – in which were multitudes of the most beautiful roach, and gudgeon, and pike, and I know not what. I felt very much disposed to obtain some; but my wishes met with a check from these thoughts. 'In the first place,' I said, 'I have no tackle; in the next, I am no fisherwoman.' Now to have made my argument complete against angling, there should have been no fish. But it was not so. I therefore determined to invent me some tackle.

My petticoat – my *crinoline* – I had no doubt there were fifty others in the boxes – flashed upon me. It was a little worn, and the others were, no doubt, new; besides, I had more than one of my own stock. Knowing that fishing-lines were made of hair, I immediately began to draw my *crinoline*. As I drew out horse-hair by horse-hair I moralized – I could not help it – upon the wondrous accidents of life.

'When,' thought I, 'for the Crown-and-Anchor Ball, I first put on this *crinoline*, swimming into the room in a cloud of white satin – did I then think it (the petticoat) was ever intended to catch little gudgeons?' And with these thoughts, I patiently, mournfully, drew out hair by hair, and found that they would bear any weight of fish that might jump at the hook.

The hook! Where was the hook? In another instant a thought suggested the ring – the broken wedding-ring. There was a something in the notion that brought to my face a melancholy smile. There was a bitterness, a pleasant bitterness, in the idea, that I relished mightily. I therefore resolved to turn the ring into a rude hook, which, by means of a pair of pliers from the surgeon's case, I accomplished. And it looked so remarkably like a hook, nobody could have imagined it had ever been a wedding-ring.

A tall, tapering rod grew on every tree. I therefore set out to the brook fully equipped. Arrived at the place, I baited the ring – the hook I should say – with nothing more than a little chewed biscuit, mixed, to keep it together, with pomatum. I threw in, and as fast as I threw in, I had a bite. It was curious to see the innocent creatures fly to the ring; that is, the hook that was to destroy them. I was for some time astonished at their simplicity. At length I thought, 'Poor things! their eagerness to bite at the wedding-ring proves the island to have been always uninhabited. They bite in this way, because they have never before beheld the face of a woman!'

August 1846

Barry Humphries

PROFESSOR PATTERSON'S CHRISTMAS PACKAGE FOR THE POMS

ADVERTISEMENT FOR AND ON BEHALF OF THE COMMONWEALTH GOVERNMENT OF AUSTRALIA

I'M wearing my marsupial ermine-trimmed academic hat now and dictating this Chrissie communiqué to my Secretary-cum-Research

Assistant Friday, Roxanne, as she hammers out my prestige press statement with her frosted green fingernails on our Government issue IBM daisy wheel. New paragraph, Roxy, and whaddia doin' in the luncheon recess?

You could have knocked me over with a hard-rock, Ayers Rock didgeridoo when I was suddenly seconded from the Commonwealth Cheese Board the other day and head-hunted for the prestigious, cushy sinecure of Vice-Chancellor, Provost, Treasurer and Food and Beverages Supremo at the upcoming Australian Research and Studies Establishment (ARSE).

'Money is no object, Les,' came the firm, prematurely vacillating voice of our Prime Minister over my de-coding scrambler. 'Just help us put across to the poor old Poms a broad-based, grass roots, multi-faceted, wide-spectrum picture of our wonderful sun-drenched sub-continent. Dish out a few flash degrees in Dingo Studies, Possum Pathology and Rogue Wombat Handling – you name it. Get 'em swotting up on who was up who in our last award-winning, internationally-acclaimed feature fillum, and if the Poms won't buy that, tell the bastards they can stick their heads up a dead bear's bum.

'Australia's international image needs a bit of spit and polish and you're just the man to put his mouth where Australia's money is. Let's face it, Les,' our lanky leader went on to infer, 'London's choc-a-bloc with ex-pat knockers making a fat quid selling Australia's credibility short. Smart alec galahs like Germaine Greer, Clive James and that old Sheila, Dame Edna, who dresses up as a man and tips the bucket on our incomparable cultural attainments in front of the crowned heads of Europe.

'The Australian Government has lashed out and bought a nice old period-style maisonette a stone's throw from prestigious Bloomsville Square with ample parking facilities outside for visiting Australian academics y'know, and post-graduate ponces in their pre-owned, as-new, VW campers. We've given this assignment to you, Les, because you're that smart you could sell soap to the Poms. Rustle up a horny little Yuletide promotional package, get off your campus with your skeleton staff, take a firm grip of your syllabus and stick it up 'em.' End of quote, Roxy, and how about a nice juicy steak in the Chips Rafferty executive dining refectory? You look like a girl who could do with something hot inside her. New para.

Well, I'm here to tell you lucky *Punch* readers our venue is looking pretty good and if you want to crawl in out of the cold for a pre-Christmas indoor Aussie style shark-bake, or a simulated bush or beach barbie with all the liquid trimmings, activate our old period entry-phone and one of our spunky, laid-back, outback hosties sporting their see-through shortie black lace-trimmed academic ra-ra gowns and kinky PVC mortar-boards will you give a guided walk-about of the facility and the disciplines catered for therein. There's the Dame Nellie Melba squash courts, the Rolf Harris solarium, the Patrick White hot tub, spa pool and jacuzzi complex, the Colleen McCullough cold plunge, as well as our extensive 'Seekers' memorial lingo-lab and the Ned Kelly audio-visual inter-active, laser-scanned, antipodean crash course Community Input System sponsored by the Tasmanian Boomerang Cigarette Paper Conglomerate.

This Christmas there's been no shortage of interest from impover-ished Pom Professors who've been queueing round the block for the chance to chip in on the odd lucrative seminar. When we're fully operational in '83 we're expecting such guest luminaries as Former-Sir Anthony Blunt on 'Baroque Abbo frescoes in the Murrumbidgee Basin', Dr Jonathan Miller's post-mortem on the first Australian convict production of *Fidelio* and the last Abbo *Aida*, Dr Pamela Stephenson on 'Australian Wit and Humour in the Post-Prandial Period' and 'Undressing as Satire', *plus* Sir Harold Wilson's sell-out lecture to the Aussie diplomatic community on 'How To Be Success-ful *and* Common'.

One of my old drinking cobbers from the Immigration Depart-ment who has assisted more passages than I've had chilled breakfasts will be counselling on 'Ways and Means of surviving the Pommy Christmas' in close association with a top Quantas ticket writer; and a spokesperson for the Australian Women's Civil Liberties Association will be briefing local Brit housewives on 'Animal Husbandry Down Under' and 'Outback Infanticide – The Do's and Don'ts'.

So front up at ARSE House anytime over the festivities and plug into some of the most sophisticated promotional hardware this side of the black stump (an old ethnic Abbo expression meaning SFA).

Yours Truly is Santa this year and I'll be dishing out the dried apricots, Joanie Sutherland EPs, Sid Nolan dinner mats and Taiwan-ese tea towels featuring the map of Tasmania – and talking of the map of Tasmania, have you worn them crotchless panties I gave you yet, Roxanne?

December 1982

A.P. Herbert

MR PUNCH'S MUSIC-HALL SONGS

IX – SAUSAGE AND MASH

If there's a dish
For which I wish
More frequent than the rest,
If there's a food
On which I brood
When starving or depressed,
If there's a thing that life can give
Which makes it worth our while to live,
If there's an end
On which I'd spend
My last remaining cash,
It's sausage, friend,
It's sausage, friend,
It's sausage, friend, and mash.

Sausage and mash,
Sausage and mash,
Hope of the hungry and joy of the just!
Sausage and mash,
(Not haddock or hash),
Done till they bubble and done till they bust!
Your truffles are toys,
Your oysters are trash
Contrasted, my boys,
With the homelier joys,
The beauty, the poise
Of sausage and mash.

O noble thing,
From churl to king,
Uniting class and clan!
What brow so high
That cannot spy
The simple sausage-fan?
The haughty plumber blows a kiss
When Mrs Plumber brings him this;

And where's the Lord
So old and bored
But that proud eye will flash
If some sweet girl
Says, 'Sausage, Earl?
A sausage, Earl, and mash?'

Sausage and mash,
Sausage and mash,
With an R in the month I am happy and gay!
Sausage and mash,
My molars I gnash
With impotent longing in August and May!
I weary of fish,
I deprecate hash,
Your partridges – pish!
Quite frankly I wish
For the tiniest dish
Of sausage and mash.

Sweet when we rise
With heavy eyes
And work is just ahead;
Sweet any time,
But most sublime
When we should be in bed;
Though kingdoms rise and kingdoms set
A sausage is a sausage yet;
When Love is dead,
Ambition fled
And Pleasure, lad, and Pass.,
You'll still enjoy
A sausage, boy,
A sausage, boy, and mash.

Sausage and mash,
Sausage and mash,
Done till they bubble and done till they bust!
Sausage and mash,
Careless and rash,
I raises my hat to the food of the just!
What's women to me,
What's liquor or cash?
Contented are we,
The sons of the free,
With a pot of hot tea
And sausage and mash!

February 1925

Thomas Hood
THE SONG OF THE SHIRT

WITH fingers weary and worn,
  With eyelids heavy and red,
A Woman sat, in unwomanly rags,
  Plying her needle and thread –
    Stitch! stitch! stitch!
In poverty, hunger, and dirt,
  And still with a voice of dolorous pitch
She sang the 'Song of the Shirt!'

'Work! work! work!
While the cock is crowing aloof!
  And work – work – work,
Till the stars shine through the roof!'
It's O! to be a slave
  Along with the barbarous Turk,
Where woman has never a soul to save,
  If this is Christian work!

'Work – work – work
Till the brain begins to swim;
  Work – work – work
Till the eyes are heavy and dim!
Seam, and gusset, and band,
  Band, and gusset, and seam,
    Till over the buttons I fall asleep,
    And sew them on in a dream!

'O! Men, with Sisters dear!
    O! Men! with Mothers and Wives!
It is not linen you're wearing out,
    But human creatures' lives!
        Stitch – stitch – stitch,
    In poverty, hunger, and dirt,
Sewing at once, with a double thread,
    A Shroud as well as a Shirt.

'But why do I talk of Death?
    That Phantom of grisly bone,
I hardly fear his terrible shape,
    It seems so like my own –
    It seems so like my own,
    Because of the fasts I keep,
Oh! God! that bread should be so dear,
    And flesh and blood so cheap!

'Work – work – work!
    My labour never flags;
And what are its wages? A bed of straw,
    A crust of bread – and rags.
That shatter'd roof – and this naked floor –
    A table – a broken chair –
And a wall so blank, my shadow I thank
    For sometimes falling there!

'Work – work – work!
From weary chime to chime,
    Work – work – work –
As prisoners work for crime!
    Band, and gusset, and seam,
    Seam, and gusset, and band,
Till the heart is sick, and the brain benumb'd,
    As well as the weary hand.

'Work – work – work,
In the dull December light,
    And work – work – work,
When the weather is warm and bright –
While underneath the eaves
    The brooding swallows cling
As if to show me their sunny backs
    And twit me with the spring.

'Oh! but to breathe the breath
Of the cowslip and primrose sweet –
    With the sky above my head,
And the grass beneath my feet,
For only one short hour
    To feel as I used to feel,
Before I knew the woes of want
    And the walk that costs a meal!

'Oh but for one short hour!
    A respite however brief!
No blessed leisure for Love or Hope,
    But only time for Grief!
A little weeping would ease my heart,
    But in their briny bed
My tears must stop, for every drop
    Hinders needle and thread!'

With fingers weary and worn,
    With eyelids heavy and red,
A Woman sat, in unwomanly rags,
    Plying her needle and thread –
        Stitch! stitch! stitch!
    In poverty, hunger, and dirt,
And still with a voice of dolorous pitch
Would that its tone could reach the Rich!
She sang this 'Song of the Shirt!'

December 1843

E.C. Bentley

MORE CLERIHEWS

I regard Zinghis Khan
As rather an over-rated man.
What, after all, could be easier
Than conquering from the Pacific to Silesia?

No doubt the poet Gray
Was all very well in his way,
But he couldn't write a song
Like 'Now We Shan't Be Long'.

Geoffrey Chaucer
Took a bath (in a saucer)
In consequence of certain hints
Dropped by the Black Prince.

The Empress Maria Teresa
Had a poodle called Sneezer
Which severely bit
A Prussian from Tilsit.

November 1938

Ned Sherrin
BURIED TREASURES

As Elizabeth Taylor announces her intention of being laid to rest in the valleys of Wales, with which, of course, she is inextricably associated, and as Richard Burton is already sleeping out eternity in Switzerland, where will all the others go? Is Sean Connery booked into Marbella or the Gorbals? Will Michael Caine end up in Beverly Hills, Windsor, or the Old Kent Road? And Joan Collins?

I have it on good authority that three great actors, Clint Eastwood, Jack Palance and Robert Redford, have all expressed a wish to have their ashes scattered over the little house in Keinton Mandeville, Somerset, on which a plaque commemorates the birthplace of Sir Henry Irving. Nowadays acting Lords are two-a-penny, or at least two (or rather three if you include Lord Graves, certainly a Lord and undeniably an actor). However, Sir Henry first celebrated the transformation of mummers from rogues and vagabonds to gents.* Unfortunately Messrs Eastwood, Palance and Redford were not the first with the idea of mingling their ashes with his. Telly Savalas, Raymond Burr and Larry Hagman have already inserted instructions in their wills (and testaments) to the same effect and the Parish Council of Keinton Mandeville meet next week to consider whether these mass scatterings are more likely to prove a health hazard, a threat to main road traffic to Taunton, or a valuable tourist attraction.

As the brisk autumn breeze blows down the grey limestone canyon of modest cottages which is main-street Keinton Mandeville, the council has to assess the nuisance or novelty value of being able to prise a speck of dust out of a visitor's eye and charge for it as all that is mortal of Messrs Eastwood, Redford, Palance, Savalas, Burr, or Hagman – or others who may follow in their wake. 'Wakes a speciality'. Was it Emile Zola, or was it Zola Budd, who said, 'All I desire for my funeral is not to be buried alive'? More probably it was Lord Chesterfield in one of his rare letters to his daughter-in-law. To

---

* Is this a pity? Discuss.

be scattered into the skies above Keinton Mandeville is a reassuring
safeguard against Chesterfield's imagined fears.

'Burn me and scatter the ashes where they will, and let there be
no abracadabra of ritual is my wish about myself', was George
Meredith's wish. (Is it Eastwood, Savalas, or Hagman who is the
Meredith reader?) Strange how people who will hardly be present
feel the need to prescribe the details of their departure. 'I direct,'
wrote Verdi, 'that I be given a modest funeral, either at sunrise or at
sunset with no pomp, no singing, no music.' I shouldn't think it
would do for Mr Manilow; but he is not on record as choosing
Keinton Mandeville as a resting place so we can discount him. No
music does seem a pity though, especially for the fans. You would
have thought a drum might have been heard – or at the very least a
funeral note. But the Japanese back in 650 were full of the same
strictures. 'When a man dies no gold or silver or silk brocades and no
dyed stuffs are to be buried with him,' was the practical dictate of the
Laws of Kotoku.

Why such spoil-sports? Thirteen hundred and thirty-four years
later cannot the Parish Council of Keinton Mandeville run up a more
amusing form of service for all these thespians, dying to smother the
walls of the cottage with their ashes – drum, funeral notes, abracadabra of ritual, pomp, singing, music, gold, silver, silk brocades, dyed
stuff and all? It's the least they can do for a died stiff.

Charles Lamb had the right idea: 'I have been to a funeral where I
made a pun to the consternation of the rest of the mourners. I can't
describe to you the howl which the widow set up at proper intervals.'

What pun? What widow? How tantalising! One pun per intern-
ment must be permissible. A grief-laden Welsh voice throbbing
across the echoing Alps, 'Gone for a Burton'? It doesn't have to be
new or funny – just apposite. Or will there be a whispered comment
on Miss Taylor's designer-shroud – Taylor Made. Perhaps Keinton
Mandeville will appoint a Punster-Laureate to trick out the obse-
quies with an official pun. Bathos could not be more triumphantly
achieved than it was at Victoria's going;

> *Dust to Dust,*
> *Ashes to Ashes;*
> *Into the tomb*
> *The Great Queen crashes.*

Fritz Spiegl has published a collection of punning gravestones.
Why not punning passings on? Mr Spiegl records a stone in Hornsey

Cemetery: 'To the memory of Emma and Maria Littleboy', the twin children of George and Emma Littleboy who died July 16th, 1837: 'Two little boys lie here, yet strange to say these *little boys* are girls.' It gets a snigger in the graveyard so why not at the graveside? Not quite a pun, but definite evidence of levity was unearthed at Nettlebed in Oxfordshire. 'Here lies father and mother and sister and I. We all died within the space of one short year. They all be buried at Wimble except I. And I be buried here.' And then there is the sexist epitaph in Dunoon. 'Here lie the remains of Thomas Woodhen, the most amiable of men. His real name was Woodcock but it wouldn't come in rhyme.' What an honest admission of literary shortcomings, 'Wouldn't come in rhyme'!

Punning comes back into its own in Tombstone, Arizona: 'Here lies Lester Moore. Four slugs from a '44. Now Les no More.'

There is bathos in Woolwich where Major James Brush is commemorated: 'who was killed by the accidental discharge of a pistol by his orderly. Well done, good and faithful servant.' And there is a pyramid of conceits in Dennis Skinner's parish of Bolsover. 'Here lies in a horizontal position the outside case of Thomas Hinde, clock and watchmaker, who departed this life wound up in the hope of being taken in hand by His Maker, and being thoroughly cleaned, repaired, and set agoing in the world to come.' 'Unverified' (in Shropshire) is succinct: 'Here lieth ye body of Martha Dias – always noisy, not very pious, who lived to ye age of 3 score and 10 and gave to worms what she refused to men.'

Perhaps Keinton Mandeville will cover the walls of Irving's Birthplace with suitable plaques adjoining his own, which commemorate the ashes which swirl above them. The Laureate? (If Roger Woddis is not available.) The ghost of McGonagall?

Here blows the dust of Eastwood, Clint,
Filling what was a rural void,
Of human clay he may be skint;
But he lives on on celluloid.

The ashes of portly Raymond Burr, burned
For a while and then were urned.
Each spec's now in the air adjacent
Available to fans of 'Ironside' and 'Perry Masont'.

Here flies what's left of Robert Red-a-ford
No grander grave could any dead-afford.
As the sun dances make your bid
And grab what's left of the Sundance Kid.

All around is Jack Palance,
So grant dead Jack a backward glance,
A forward glance might bring surprise
And bits of Jack within your eyes.

I would have done Kojak, Savalas, Hagman, and J.R. – but they would not come in rhyme, in time.

September 1984

Richard Gordon

THEATRE OF THE ABSURD

EVERYONE wants to be a surgeon. It is a job with the status of a disc jockey, the salary of an airline pilot and the sexiness of a ski instructor. Do not be deterred by the stuffy doctors' union, demanding you spend years and years studying such irrelevant and boring topics as biochemistry, microbiology, geriatrics, dermatology and psychoanalysis. You could be operating tomorrow!

Every year, real surgical enthusiasts – meat salesmen, hospital cleaners, young clergymen, impatient medical students – take the direct route to the operating theatre. All you want is a Chester Barrie suit and a well-typed reference. Offer yourself as a locum at a busy hospital in August, and nobody is going to risk losing your services by checking it.

HOW TO BE A BOGUS SURGEON

The only skill you need is at handling small pieces of greasy machinery in awkward corners under intolerable working conditions. Have you replaced the chain-drive of your motor mower, lying on the lawn in blazing sunshine? Then you can operate.

First, remove your suit in the surgeons' room, taking care to leave nothing of value in the pockets. Slip into anything clean and white lying about. Let a nurse dress you up in a green gown. Donning rubber gloves is the most difficult part of the operation. Entering the theatre with ten teats on your hands invites suspicion. If in serious trouble, hurl successive pairs to the floor, with increasingly loud complaints of punctures.

You will find the operating theatre overcrowded with anonymous masked figures in gowns. Those with bumps on their chests are likely to be nursing staff. Control them all with the cheery firmness of a captain his team, or producer his cast. Slyly play on their touchiness about their own importance over the others.

The one surrounded with pipes and glittering machinery is the anaesthetist. His presence is vital, to indicate which end of the heavily towelled patient is the head.

Principles of Surgery

There are two classes of operation –

(1) Cutting it off.
(2) Cutting it out.

The necessity for (1) is obvious through an inviting lump, gangrene, impaled lever etc. If a search of the area reveals nothing of this nature, proceed to (2).

The Incision

The cutlery provided may be confusing but need cause no worse embarrassment than deciding how you should eat asparagus. Hold knife and forceps as though enjoying a tender, rare fillet steak.

If you pick from the display an instrument outrageously wrong, the nurse in charge may exclaim, 'Surely you're not going to use a cleft palate knife on a haemorrhoidectomy?' Inspect the instrument for some seconds, replying, 'I'm surprised you still sterilize these, sister, they went out in World War Two,' or simply drop it on the floor and bawl 'Blunt!' Or fix her with your eye, rasping 'Hackenbusch's lithotriptoscope – quick.' When she says hastily she hasn't one sterile, snap over your outstretched palm, 'Oh, it doesn't matter. I'll make do with the Wurtenburg-Mayo cholecystoduodenostomy anastomosis clamp instead.' She will give no further trouble.

Surgical Anatomy

Make a large slit, as though opening a paper sack of cement. Do not worry about the bleeding. Someone will busy himself stopping it. At first glance, the inside may seem confusing. But the human abdomen contains only two organs of concern to the amateur operator.

The stuff like pink bicycle inner tubes sloshing about in the middle is the *gut* ... at the top end, resembling the leather wine flask used by Spanish road workers, is the *stomach*. The gut is about 10 yards long. It does not matter how much of this you care to remove; humans can exist happily with hardly more than would make a good serving of *tripe à la mode de Caen*.

The liver is at the end nearer the anaesthetists, 8 pounds of it, looking like the stuff you fry up with bacon. With the pancreas, kidney, adrenals and other goodies deep in the abdominal bran tub, it is best left to the inquisitive fingers of the professionals.

Towards the end of the gut, under the right pocket of the jeans, is the star of surgical drama, the appendix. It resembles a four-inch worm, and like the Aldwych Tube leads nowhere. If a brisk rummage discovers nothing exciting enough to cut out, remove the appendix. This will cause no comment, the normal appendix being frequently removed in error.

Sewing Up

Stitching human tissues is no different from sewing on shirt buttons or darning socks, and the needles come ready threaded. Buy *The Vogue Sewing Book*. Practise gathering and shirring, French whipped seams, gussetting and mitering. Do not worry if you leave your patient branded like a Wild West steer. He will strip his sleeve and show his scars as proudly as a Crispin's day veteran. Without a good scar, he hardly feels he has had an operation. It is like the decent suntan which proclaims that he enjoyed his holiday.

X-Rays

Inspection of the X-rays is useful when wondering what the devil to do next. X-rays are easy to read, because their shadows invite as many contrasting opinions as the Turin shroud. If uncertain whether the picture represents a fractured rib or a swallowed four-inch nail, emit a low whistle and exclaim, 'My word, that *is* a whopper, isn't it?' As you are the surgeon, everyone will nod in humble agreement.

Heart Transplants

This is the glamour surgery, attracting so much delightful and profitable publicity, the amateur is as desperate to perform it as the fully-qualified professor.

The operation is as simple as changing the wheel on your car. The difficulty is its necessitating, like sex, two people for its consummation. The recipient is no problem. Donors are difficult. There are innumerable healthy hearts in the country, but their possessors seem loath to perform an organ voluntary at the enthusiastic surgeon's request. The best technique is buying a reliable portable life-support apparatus, and parking behind a hedge at a sign saying ACCIDENT BLACK SPOT. The Government are most creditably encouraging this exciting branch of surgery, by refusing to legislate the compulsory wearing of seat belts.

Orthopaedic Surgery
A firm favourite with d-i-y surgical buffs, because it is only warm carpentry. The chisels, hammers, saws, Black and Deckers etc are exactly the same in the operating theatre as in the garage. *Home Woodworking* will see you right. Many professional orthopaedic surgeons exercise their skill with equal energy at home as at hospital, though patients do not qualify for a Government improvement grant.

Aftercare
The operation is but a single spectacular act in the programme of surgical treatment. Once you have knotted the last stitch, turn to your first assistant – the one so fussy about stopping the bleeding – and say condescendingly, 'I leave the postoperative management wholly in your care, with the utmost confidence.' His head will so swell, you need make no further contribution to the case beyond bellowing, 'And where's the coffee, then?'

Forensic Medicine
Protagonists of the closed shop are as savage towards surgical amateurs – who perform valuable service by relieving the overworked surgeons of the NHS – as towards blacklegs in any other nationalized industry. Though it is a cherished principle of trade unionists that the law holds no sway in their activities, 'cowboy' surgeons may find themselves involved in tedious legal wrangles.

If you do get put inside, why not study my companion work, *How To Be a Bogus Judge*? This job, too, allows dressing up and the psychological expression of infantile omnipotence. It is performed in greater comfort, sitting down, and you can call the tea breaks when you like. Less intelligence need be shown, there being twelve other people to reach all the painful decisions for you.

Carry on cutting! Remember – *If In Doubt Cut It Out*, and *ars longa vita brevis* was Hippocrates' way of saying that Vita walks nearer the ground since the plastic surgery on her bum.

August 1979

P.G. Wodehouse

THE WORD IN SEASON

AMONG the names on the list of candidates up for election at the Drones there appeared, proposed by R.P. Little and seconded by a prominent Crumpet, that of

LITTLE, ALGERNON AUBREY,

and several of the Eggs, Beans and Piefaces who had gathered about the notice-board were viewing it with concern. In every club you will find an austere conservative element that looks askance at the unusual and irregular.

'He can't do that there here,' said an Egg, putting into words the sentiment of this *bloc*. 'Hoy!' he went on, addressing the Crumpet, who had entered as he spoke. 'What about this nominee of Bingo Little's?'

'Yes,' said a Bean. 'He can try as much as he likes to cloud the issue by calling him "Algernon Aubrey", as if he were a brother or cousin or something, but the stark fact remains that the above is his baby. We don't want infants mewling and puking about the place.'

'Keep it clean,' urged a Pieface.

'Shakespeare,' explained the Bean.

'Oh, Shakespeare?' said the Pieface. 'Sorry. No, we don't want any bally babies here.'

A grave look came into the Crumpet's face.

'You want this one,' he said. 'You can't afford to do without him. Recent events have convinced Bingo that this offspring of his is a Grade A mascot, and he feels that the club should have the benefit of his services. Again and again with his faultless sense of timing he has saved Bingo from the soup when it was lashing angrily about his ankles. An instance of this occurred only last week. I tell you, this half-portion's knack of doing the right thing at the right moment is uncanny. I believe the child is almost human.'

His eloquence was not without its effect. But though some of the malcontents wavered the Egg remained firm.

'That's all very well, but the question that presents itself is – Where will this stop? I mean, what guarantee have we that if we elect this juvenile Bingo won't start trying to ring in his old nurse or his Uncle Wilberforce or the proprietor of that paper he works for – what's his name – Purkiss?'

'I don't know about the nurse or his Uncle Wilberforce,' said the Crumpet, 'but you need have no anxiety concerning Purkiss. Bingo's relations with the big chief are formal, even distant. Owing to Purkiss, he recently had to undergo a mental strain almost without parallel in his experience. And though, thanks to this beneficent baby, there was a happy ending, he finds it difficult to forgive.'

'What did Purkiss do to him?'

'It was what Purkiss didn't do to him. He refused to pay ten quid for his story, and if ever Bingo needed ten quid he needed it then. He had gone and got himself into a position where nothing less than that colossal sum could save him from the fate  that is worse than death – viz., having the wife of his bosom draw her breath in sharply and look squiggle-eyed at him. He had been relying on Purkiss to do the square thing, and Purkiss let him down.'

You see (proceeded the Crumpet), what had happened was this. Algernon Aubrey was shortly about to celebrate his first birthday, and Mrs Bingo told Bingo that she was going to pay in ten pounds to his account – not Bingo's, no such luck, Algernon Aubrey's: he has an account at the local bank – and that her mother was going to pay in ten pounds too, and so was the child's maternal Aunt Isabel, and what a lovely surprise it would be for the young buster, when he got older, to find that all unknown his loved ones had been working on his behalf, bumping up his balance like billy-o. And Bingo, mellowed by the rather exceptional steak-and-kidney pudding which they had had at dinner, got the party spirit and said that if that was the trend affairs were taking, he was dashed if he didn't spring a tenner also.

Upon which Mrs Bingo said 'Oh, Bingo!' and kissed him with a good deal of fervour, and the curtain of Act One falls on a happy and united home.

Now, at the moment when he made this sporting gesture, Bingo happened to be in a position to come through. He actually had ten quid in his possession, an advance on his salary from *Wee Tots*, the journal for the nursery which he so ably edits. But a couple of days later a mistaken confidence in a horse called Jujube left him penniless, and there he was, faced by a crisis of the first magnitude. Mrs Bingo doesn't like him to bet – it is one of the things she looks squiggle-eyed about – and the discovery that he had once more been chancing his arm would be bound to lead to an unpleasant scene, from which he shrank.

And discovery, unless he could somehow raise the cash and raise it quick, was of course inevitable. Sooner or later Mrs Bingo would be taking a look at the infant's passbook, and when she did would immediately spot something wrong with the figures. 'Hey!' she would cry. 'Where's that ten-spot you said you were depositing!' and from this to the bleak show-down would be but a short step.

It was a situation in which many fellows would just have turned their faces to the wall and waited for the end. But there is good stuff in Bingo. He spat on his hands and acted. He sat right down and wrote a story about a little girl called Gwendoline and her cat Tibby. The idea of course being to publish it in *Wee Tots* and make a substantial clean-up.

It wasn't a soft job. He tells me that until he started on it he had had no notion what a ghastly sweat literature was, and a new admiration for Mrs Bingo awoke in him. Mrs Bingo, as you know, is Rosie M. Banks, the authoress, and does her three thousand  words a day without ricking a muscle. And to complete this Tibby number, which cannot have run to more than fifteen hundred, took Bingo over a week, during which period he on several occasions as near as a toucher went off his onion.

However, he finished it at last, copied it out neatly, submitted it to himself, read it with considerable interest and accepted it, putting it down on the charge sheet for ten of the best. And when pay-day arrived and no tenner, he sought audience of Purkiss.

'Oh, Mr Purkiss,' he said. 'Sorry to butt in on your meditations, but it's about that story.'

Purkiss looked at him fishily, for he was one of those fishy-eyed blokes.

'Story?'

Bingo explained the circs. He said that he was the author of 'Tibby's Wonderful Adventure' in the current issue, and Purkiss said he had read it with much pleasure, and Bingo oh-thanksed and simpered coyly, and then there was a bit of a silence.

'Well, how about the emolument?' said Bingo, getting down to the *res*.

'Emolument?' said Purkiss, intensifying the fishy glitter in his eyes.

'There should be a tenner coming to me.'

'Oh, no, no, no,' said Purkiss. 'Oh, no, no, no, no, no. All contributions which you may make to the paper are of course covered by your salary.'

'What!' cried Bingo. 'You mean I don't touch?'

Purkiss assured him that he didn't, and Bingo, after a passionate appeal to his better nature which failed to bring home the bacon, tottered from the room and staggered off here to have a quick snort and think things over.

The restorative fluid revived the old fighting spirit in him. Somewhere, somehow, he told himself as he lapped it up, he was going to raise those ten o'goblins or perish in the attempt. And just as he came to this decision, whom should he see brooding in a chair across the room but Oofy Prosser. It seemed to him that Oofy was the People's Choice.

Now a fellow who is going to lend you a tenner must have two prime qualifications. He must be good for the amount and he must be willing to part with it. Oofy unquestionably filled the bill in the first particular, but experience had taught Bingo that he was apt to fall down on the second. Nevertheless it was in optimistic mood that he beetled over to where the other sat. Oofy, he reminded himself, was

Algernon Aubrey's godfather, and it was only natural to suppose that
he would be delighted to weigh in with a birthday present for the
little chap. Well, not delighted, perhaps. Still, a bit of persevering
excavating work would probably dig up the needful.

'Oh, hullo, Oofy,' he said. 'I say, Oofy, do you know what? It's
Algy's birthday in a few days.'

'Algy who?'

'Algy A. Little. The good old baby. Your godson.'

A quick shudder ran through Oofy's frame. I think I told you not
long ago about the time when he had a morning head and Bingo
brought the stripling to his flat and introduced them. The memory
was still green in O. Prosser's mind.

'Oh, my aunt!' he said. 'That frightful little gumboil!'

His tone was not encouraging, giving almost no evidence of a
godfather's love, but Bingo carried on.

'Presents are now pouring in, and I knew you would be hurt if you
were not given the opportunity of contributing some little trifle. Ten
quid was what suggested itself to me. The simplest thing,' said
Bingo, 'would be if you were to slip me the money now. Then, it
would be off your mind.'

Oofy flushed darkly beneath his pimples.

'Now, listen,' he said, and there was no mistaking the ring of
determination in his voice. 'When you talked me – against my better
judgment – into being godfather to a child who looks like a ventrilo-
quist's dummy, I expressly stipulated that a silver mug was to let me
out. That still holds good. Ten quid, forsooth!'

'Ten quid isn't much.'

'It's ten quid more than you're
going to get out of me.'

Bingo reluctantly decided to
come clean.

'As a matter of fact, Oofy, old man, it's not the baby who wants the
stuff. It's me – your old friend, the fellow you've known since he was
so high. Unless I get a tenner immediately, disaster stares me in the
eyeball. So give of your plenty, Oofy, like the splendid chap you are.'

'No!' cried Oofy. 'No, no, a thousand times –'

The words died on his lips. He cheesed it abruptly, and sat
open-mouthed, staring at Bingo.

'Listen,' he said, 'are you doing anything this evening?'

'No.'

'Can you slip away from home?'

'Oh, rather. As it happens I'm all alone at the moment. My wife and Mrs Purkiss, the moon of my proprietor's delight, have legged it to Brighton to attend some sort of Old Girls' binge at their late school and won't be back till tomorrow.'

'Good. I want you to dine at the Ritz.'

'Fine. Nothing I should like better. I meet you there, do I?'

'You do not. I'm leaving for Paris this afternoon. What you meet is

 a girl named Mabel Moresby with red hair, a vivacious manner and a dimple on the left side of the chin. You feed her and take her to the theatre and give her a bite of supper afterwards.'

Bingo drew himself up. He was deeply shocked at the other's loose ideas of how married men behaved when their wives were away.

'Do this,' said Oofy, 'and you get your tenner.'

Bingo lowered himself.

'Is this official?'

'It is,' said Oofy. 'Listen. I will tell you all.'

It was a dubious and discreditable story that he related. The gist of it was as follows. For some time past, it appeared, he had been flitting round this girl like a pimpled butterfly, giving her the burning eye and the low voice with a catch in it, and he had suddenly realized with a sickening shock that his emotional nature had brought him to the very verge of matrimony. Another step and he would be over the precipice. It was the dimple that did it, principally, he said. Confronted with it at short range, he tended to say things which in sober retrospect he regretted.

'I asked her to dine and go to the theatre tonight,' he concluded, 'and if I go I'm sunk. Only instant flight can save me.'

'I understand,' said Bingo, nodding intelligently.

'But that's not all,' said Oofy. 'You haven't grasped how far the evil has spread. I want you not only to take her out, but finally and definitely to choke her off me. You must roast me like nobody's business. Pretend you think me a frightful tick.'

The verb 'pretend' did not seem to Bingo very happily chosen, but he made no comment. He nodded intelligently again to show that he followed the scenario.

'Pitch it strong,' said Oofy. 'I'll tell you some things to say.'

'No, no, don't bother,' said Bingo. 'I'll think of them. You have the theatre tickets, of course?'

'Here they are.'

'And for expenses I shall need about fifteen pounds, I imagine.'

'You ought to do something about that feverish imagination of yours. You will need five pounds twelve and sixpence. I've worked it out. Here it is,' said Oofy, starting to dribble currency. 'And here's the tenner.'

'Right,' said Bingo.

'Right,' said Oofy.

It was with a light heart that Bingo passed through the portals of the Ritz that evening. The thought that in addition to getting a square meal he was actually being paid for saying what he thought about Oofy was a very agreeable one. Up to the present he had always had to give his views away gratis. While dressing and subsequently while making his way to the restaurant he had roughed out some very spirited stuff, and now all that remained was to get in touch with his audience.

He had not been waiting long when a girl appeared, so vermilion in the upper story and so dimpled on the left side of the chin that he had no hesitation in ambling up and establishing contact.

'Miss Moresby?'

'You never said a truer word.'

'My name is Little, R.P. Oofy Prosser, having been unexpectedly called away to the Continent, asked me to roll up and deputize for him.'

'He's gone to the Continent?'

'He left this afternoon.'

'I must say it's a bit thick, asking somebody to dinner and then buzzing off to Continents.'

'Not for Oofy,' said Bingo, starting the treatment. 'His work is generally infinitely thicker than that. I don't know how well you know him?'

'Fairly well.'

'When you know him really well you will realize that you are dealing with something quite exceptional. Take Beelzebub and Ananias, add a few slugs and a couple of warthogs from the Zoo, sprinkle liberally with pimples, and you will have something which, while of course less loathsome than Alexander Prosser, will give you the general idea.'

So saying, he hoiked her into the dining salon and the meal started.

It went off with a bang. In his bachelor days, as you probably
know, Bingo had been a notable lusher-up of females, skipping from
one to another like the chamois of the Alps in search of edelweiss:
and though marriage had left him short of practice, he soon found
the old technique coming back to him.

This girl, moreover, was an exceptionally attractive girl, easy to
talk to, and her views on Oofy proved to be as sound as his own. She
told him that she had gone around with this Prosser only because he
had made such a point of it. Left to herself, she wouldn't have
touched him with a barge-pole. Not that she ever had actually
touched him with a barge-pole – but he knew what she meant.

Bingo replied that he knew just what she meant, and a perfect
harmony prevailed.

They ticked Oofy off properly
between the Acts at the theatre
and, later, during the bite of
supper. And as it seemed to
Bingo that even now they had
not really exhausted the topic,
he fell in readily with the girl's suggestion that they should go and
dance a step or two at the Feverish Cheese. He said there were
several things on the tip of his tongue which he wanted to say about
Oofy, and she said so there were on hers. They agreed that if they
joggled themselves up with a bit of dancing the thought processes
would probably be stimulated.

I don't know if any of you know the Feverish Cheese. It is – or was,
for it has now gone out of business – a smelly little joint in the
neighbourhood of Shaftesbury Avenue. Bingo didn't think much of
it. He could hardly realize that there had been a time when he had
liked night-clubs. Odd, he felt, how the love of a good woman
purifies a man. While bumping his way round the floor, which was
congested with weird females and men who might have been Oofy
Prosser's brothers, he mused on Mrs Bingo, thinking how deeply he
worshipped her.

He nearly mentioned this to the girl, but thought better not,
perhaps. However, it was not long before the subject came up
between them. The management of the resort had supplied its
patrons, in order that they might make themselves as pestilential as

possible, with rattles and squeakers, and Bingo pocketed one of each.

'For my baby,' he explained.

The girl seemed astonished.

'Have you got a baby?'

'You bet I have! As bouncing a one as ever sprayed breakfast cereal.'

'Where on earth did you get a baby?'

'Oh, it sort of breezed along.'

'I mean, are you married?'

'Oh, rather. Odd you should have said that, because I was just thinking how much I loved my wife. I expect you know her name. Rosie M. Banks.'

'The writer?'

'That's the one. You are familiar with her output?'

'I don't read her books myself, but I have an uncle who's crazy about them. They exchange long letters.'

'Rosie is always ankle-deep in fan mail.'

'Yes, but it's curious that my uncle should like her stuff. I mean, it's pretty sentimental, isn't it?'

'On the sentimental side. Her heroes are always having mis-understandings with their girls and reddening and going off to Africa.'

'So I gathered. Yet my Uncle Joseph eats it alive. And to look at him and meet him in the course of business you would think he was a twenty-minute egg. He's the magistrate at Bosher Street.'

'Well, well! I know him by repute of course, though I have never actually met him. Before I married I generally used to patronize the chap at Vine Street. But Barmy Fotheringay-Phipps was introduced to him the morning after last Boat-Race Night, and speaks very highly of his many gifts.'

The girl was looking about her. She seemed to disapprove of her surroundings.

'I'll tell you somebody else who will be introduced to him ere long,' she said, 'and that is the master-mind behind this lazar-house. Funny how these places go down. It's a year since I was last here, and it was quite a good spot then. But now I shouldn't be surprised if it wasn't raided at any moment.'

And at that moment, by what Bingo has always thought an odd coincidence, it was. The band stopped in the middle of a bar. A sudden hush fell upon the room. Square-jawed men shot up through traps. And one, who seemed to be skippering the team, stood out in the middle and in a voice like a fog-horn told everybody to keep their seats.

Bingo was not alarmed. In his bachelor days he had been through this sort of thing many a time, and he knew just what happened. He set himself to soothe the girl, who was betraying signs of agitation. She said this was a nice bit of box fruit and that she must get out immediately, adding that the thought of appearing before her Uncle Joseph at Bosher Street on the following morning was one that froze the blood. Already her standing in the home was none too good, and what little prestige she still retained would be sensibly diminished if her relative observed her standing in handcuffs in the dock.

Bingo endeavoured to dispel her apprehensions.

'Absurd!' he said. 'No danger of that whatever. Here, in a nutshell, is the set-up. The formalities are very simple. They round us up, and we proceed in an orderly manner to the police station in plain vans. There we assemble in the waiting-room, where we give our names and addresses, exercising a certain latitude as regards the details. I, for example, always used to call myself Ephraim Gadsby, of "The Nasturtiums", Jubilee Road, Streatham Common. I don't know why. Just a whim. And then we shall be free to depart, leaving the proprietor to face the awful majesty of Justice.'

The girl refused to be consoled. She continued to flutter like an aspen.

'I'm sure that's not what happens. You have to appear in court.'

'No, no.'

'Well, I'm not going to risk it. Good night,' said Mabel Moresby. 'Thanks for a very pleasant evening.'

And getting smoothly off the mark she made a dash for the service-door, which was not far from where they sat. And an adjacent constable, baying like a bloodhound, started off in pursuit.

Whether Bingo acted judiciously at this point is a question which he has never been able to decide. Sometimes he thinks yes, reasoning that the Chevalier Bayard would have done just the same; sometimes no. Briefly what occurred was that as the gendarme passed he shoved out a foot, causing him to take an impressive toss. The girl withdrew, and the guardian of the peace, having removed his left boot from his right ear, with which it had become momentarily entangled, rose and pinched Bingo. He spent the night in a prison cell, and bright and early next morning was haled before the beak, charged with assaulting the Force and impeding it in the execution of its duties.

It seemed to him, as he stood listening to the officer explaining the circumstances, that the girl Mabel, in describing her Uncle Joseph as a twenty-minute egg, had understated rather than exaggerated the facts. He didn't like the look of him at all. The man had what he could only call a non-picking face, and as the tale proceeded it seemed to harden and become heavy with menace. He kept shooting glances at Bingo over his pince-nez, and it was plain to the latter that the constable was getting all the sympathy of the audience and that the bird who was definitely cast for the rôle of heavy in this treatment was the prisoner Gadsby. More and more the feeling stole over him that the prisoner Gadsby was about to get it in the gizzard.

However, when the *J'accuse* stuff was over and he was asked if he had anything to say, he did his best. He admitted that he had extended a foot, thus causing the officer to go base over apex, but protested that it had been a pure accident without any *arrière-*  *pensée* on his part. He said he had been feeling cramped and had desired to unlimber the leg-muscles.

'You know how sometimes you want a stretch,' he said.

'I am strongly inclined,' replied Mabel Moresby's Uncle Joseph, 'to give you one now. A good long stretch.'

Rightly recognizing this as comedy, Bingo uttered a cordial guffaw, and an officious blighter in the well of the court shouted 'Silence!' Bingo tried to explain that he was merely laughing at the magistrate's ready wit, but they shushed him again.

'However,' proceeded the old boy, adjusting his pince-nez, 'in consideration of your youth I will exercise clemency.'

'Oh, fine!' said Bingo.

'Fine,' replied the other, who seemed to know all the answers, 'is right. Ten pounds. Next case.'

I don't know if you remember at school reading about those unfortunate blighters in the Greek tragedies, who used to sweat themselves to the bone struggling against fate, only to take the knock at the final curtain. As Bingo sneaked home with his ears hanging down and that nasty empty space in his trouser-pocket where the tenner should have been, he knew just how they must have felt. It seemed to him that this was the end.

In fact he could discern on the dark horizon just one solitary bit of goose. With any luck he ought to be in and out again before Mrs Bingo returned, which would enable him to conceal from her the more recent of his activities.

But he couldn't quite make it. He had had a bath and changed, and was about to set out for the office, though feeling ill attuned to the task of providing wholesome reading matter for the tots, when she blew in.

'Bingo!' she yipped.

'Oh, hullo, darling,' said Bingo, with as much animation as he could dig up. 'Welcome to Meadowsweet Hall.'

'Aren't you very late?'

'A little, perhaps.'

'I hope Mr Purkiss won't be annoyed.'

'That's quite all right. I have a thorough understanding with Purkiss, who knows a good man when he sees one. "Be sure always to get a good night's rest," he has often said to me.'

'You don't look as if you had had a good night's rest. You're a sort of funny yellow colour.'

'Intellectual pallor,' explained Bingo, and was about to push for the open when she called him back.

'Bingo,' she said, 'have you ever been arrested in a night-club raid?'

Bingo's heart did a quick buck-and-wing step. All he had ever heard and read about woman's intuition came flooding over him. He had to clutch at the hat-stand to maintain his poise.

'Ner-night-club raid?' he said, in a low croaking voice.

Mrs Bingo laughed one of her silvery ones.

'Did I startle you? I'm sorry. It's just that I've got to the part in my new book where the wild young Lord Beaminster is arrested at a night-club, and I want somebody to tell me if he would be allowed to go home and change, or would he appear in court in dress clothes?'

Bingo swallowed eleven times.

'I really couldn't say. I am a child in these affairs.'

'It doesn't matter. I'll be able to find out somewhere. But I mustn't keep you, or you will never get to the office. Run along.'

'Right-ho. Everything go off all right last night?'

'Splendidly. Mrs Purkiss made a wonderful speech. Did you miss me?'

'Terrifically.'

'I always hate having to leave you, angel. You weren't bored?'

'Oh, no. Not bored.'

'I hope you didn't sit up all night, smoking and reading.'

'Oh, no. Rather not.'

'I believe you did,' said Mrs Bingo. 'I don't think you are at all well this morning. It may be my imagination, but you seem to have a pinched look.'

Arrived at the office, Bingo listlessly tried to bring his mind to bear on the letters which had come in for the Correspondence Page ('Uncle Percy's Postbag'), but he wasn't able to make much of a go of it. The standard of pure reason reached by the little subscribers who wrote to the editor of *Wee Tots* about their domestic pets was never a high one, but today it seemed to him that either he or they must have got water on the brain. There was one communication about a tortoise called Rupert, he tells me, which would have served as a passport for its young author to any padded cell in the kingdom.

Presently he gave it up and devoted the remainder of the working day to sitting on the back of his spine, staring dully at the ceiling. The thought of that lost tenner, for the possession of which the magistrate and the clerk of the court were probably now tossing up, was like some searing acid.

The only thing that enabled him to win through to closing-time was the fact that Purkiss was absent. He had phoned to say that he was nursing a sick headache. When on the premises, he had an unpleasant habit of popping in on Bingo at intervals and talking through the back of his neck about the policy of the paper, and a popping-in Purkiss at this juncture would have been more than he could have coped with.

It was with a feeling of relief that he finally called it a day. He reached home at six and was about to climb to his room and have a shower and get his maid to put him into something loose when Mrs Bingo hailed him from the drawing-room.

'Is that you, Bingo?'

'Oh, hullo, darling.'

'Will you come here a moment, please.'

Even as she spoke, Bingo tells me, he was conscious of some

impending doom. He has a sensitive ear, and he didn't like the
timbre of her voice. Usually, he says, Mrs Bingo's voice is like the
tinkling of silver bells across a scented meadow at sunset, but now it
was a bit on the flat side and he seemed to detect in it that metallic
note which married men dislike so much.

I don't know if you ever read a story of Dunsany's about some
blokes who prised the eye out of the face of a dashed unpleasant
Eastern idol, it being a diamond or some such thing, and legged it,
and were just celebrating the deal at the local pub when the idol,
which had come to life and trailed them, rapped on the window of the
saloon bar and said 'Hoy!' or words to that effect, giving them a nasty
start. That was how Mrs Bingo's voice sounded to Bingo at this
juncture.

She was standing in mid-carpet, looking cold and stern.

'Bingo,' she said, 'where were you last night?'

Bingo passed a finger round the inside of his collar. The way
things looked, it seemed about six to four that the curse had come
upon him, but he had a pop at being cool and nonchalant.

'Last night?' he said, musing, 'Let me see, that would be the night
of June the fifteenth, would it not? H'm. Ha. The night of –'

'I see you have forgotten,' said Mrs Bingo. 'Let me assist your
memory. You were in a night-club with a girl with red hair.'

'Who, me?'

'Yes, you. And this morning you were in the dock at Bosher Street
Police Court, being fined for assaulting a policeman.'

'You're sure you mean me?'

'Quite sure. I had the information from the magistrate at Bosher
Street himself. We have been having a correspondence about my
books, and it suddenly struck me that he would be the man to tell me
about Lord Beaminster. So I phoned him and asked him to tea. He has
just left, and as he was leaving he caught sight of your photograph on
the piano and said "Do you know this young man?" in a sniffy sort of
voice. He then went on to explain that you had been up before him
this morning. A policeman said he had arrested you for tripping him
up while he was chasing a red-haired girl in a night-club.'

Bingo curled his lip. Or, rather, he tried to, but something seemed
to have gone wrong with the machinery. Still, he spoke boldly and
with spirit.

'Personally,' he said, 'I would be inclined to attach little credence
to the word of the sort of policeman who goes about night-clubs

chasing red-haired girls. And as for this magistrate of yours – well, you know what magistrates are. Chumps to a man. When a fellow hasn't the brains and initiative to sell jellied eels, they make him a magistrate.'

'You mean that when he said that about your photograph he was deceived by some slight resemblance?'

'Not necessarily a slight resemblance. London's full of chaps like me. People have told me that there is a bird called Ephraim Gadsby – one of the Streatham Common Gadsbys – who is positively my double.'

Mrs Bingo mused.

'I wish I believed you.'

'So do I.'

'But I don't. Bingo, tell me the truth.'

And so compelling was her eye, and so menacing the way she was tapping her foot on the floor, that his spine turned to gelatine and he was about to throw in the towel and confess all, when there was a sound outside like a mighty rushing wind and in barged the baby's Nanny. Her eyes were wide and glassy, her breath came in quick pants, and it was obvious that she was in the grip of some powerful emotion. She tottered forward with one hand on her heart, and with the other supported herself on an occasional table.

'Oh, ma'am!' she cried. 'The baby!'

All the mother in Mrs Bingo awoke. She forgot Bingo and magistrates and policemen and red-haired girls and everything else. She gasped. Bingo gasped. The Nanny was gasping already. A stranger, entering the room, would have fancied that he had strayed into a convention of asthma patients.

Mrs Bingo had whitened. She rocked on her base.

'He is ill?'

'No, ma'am. But he just said "Cat".'

'Cat?'

'As plain as I'm standing here now. I was showing him his little picture-book, and we'd come to the rhinoceros and he pointed his finger at it and looked up at me and said "Cat".'

Such was the dialogue, and no doubt you are asking yourselves what all the excitement was about. 'Cat,' you are feeling, is not such a frightfully brilliant and epigrammatic thing to say. But the point is that it was Algernon Aubrey's first shot at saying anything. Up till now he had been one of those strong silent babies, content merely to dribble at the side of the mouth and utter an occasional gurgle. You can readily imagine, therefore, that the effect of this hot news on Mrs Bingo was about the same as that of the arrival of Talkies on the magnates of Hollywood.

She left the room as if shot out of a gun, and the Nanny buzzed after her, and Bingo was alone.

His first emotion of course was one of stunned awe at having been saved from the scaffold at the eleventh hour. Then came the rush of gratitude to this priceless issue of his. Even if Algernon Aubrey had been following the recent conversation word by word, he felt, he could not have spoken more admirably on cue. And finally, his numbed senses started working again and he set himself to think how he could make use of this respite.

Five minutes later he was compelled to admit that he hadn't the foggiest. He had toyed with the idea of saying that he had been in conference with Purkiss last night, discussing matters of office policy, but had been forced to dismiss it. It had looked good for a moment, but he speedily recognized it as a stumer.

For one thing, Purkiss would never abet the innocent deception. All that Bingo had ever seen of the man told him that the proprietor of *Wee Tots* was one of those rigidly upright blisters who, though quite possibly the backbone of England, are of no earthly use to a chap in an emergency. Purkiss was the sort of fellow who, if approached on the matter of bumping up a pal's alibi, would draw himself to his full height and say 'Am I to understand that you are suggesting that I sponsor a lie?'

Besides, Purkiss was at his home nursing his sick headache, which meant that negotiations would have to be conducted over the telephone. You can't swing a thing like that over the telephone. You want the pleading eye and the little pats on the arm.

All in all, therefore, you wouldn't be far wrong in saying that Bingo was in the depths. It was imperative that he have a story ready for Mrs Bingo when the first excitement of hearing Algernon Aubrey saying 'Cat' had worn off and she returned to the room to resume their conversation at the point where it had been broken off: and he couldn't even begin to formulate one which would hold as much water as a sieve.

It seemed to him that about all he could do was to groan hollowly, and he was just doing so when the door opened and the maid-servant announced: 'Mr and Mrs Purkiss'.

As they entered, Bingo, who had leaped to his feet, was just knocking over a table with a vase, three photograph-frames and a jar of potpourri on it. It crashed to the floor with a noise like a bursting shell, and Purkiss soared silently up to the ceiling, hitting it with his head. As he returned to earth, quivering violently, Bingo saw that his face was sallow and that there were dark circles beneath his eyes.

'Ah, Mr Little,' said Purkiss.

'Oh, hullo,' said Bingo.

Mrs Purkiss said nothing. She was one of those large, spreading women whose aspect reveals them to the dullest eye as presidents of movements and lecturers to clubs. She seemed to be brooding on something.

Purkiss proceeded. He winced as he spoke, as if articulation hurt him.

'Oh, Mr Little,' he said, 'we are not disturbing you, I hope? We have only looked in for a moment.'

'Not at all,' said Bingo courteously. 'I thought you were in bed with a headache.'

'I was in bed with a headache,' said Purkiss, 'the result, I think, of sitting in a draught and contracting some form of tic or migraine. But my wife was so anxious that you should confirm my statement that I was in your company last night that I made the effort and got up. You have not forgotten, Mr Little, that we sat up together till a late hour at my club? I expect you will recall that we were both surprised when we looked at our watches and found how the time had gone?'

It seemed to Bingo, as he listened to these words, that a hidden orchestra began to play soft music, while from somewhere in the room there came the scent of violets and mignonette. He also had the illusion that he had just had a couple of quick ones. His eye, which had been duller than Purkiss's, suddenly began to sparkle, and what he had supposed to be a piece of spaghetti in the neighbourhood of his back revealed itself as a spine, and a good spine too.

He drew a deep breath.

'Yes,' he said. 'That's right. We were at your club.'

'How the time flew!'

'Didn't it!' said Bingo. 'But then of course we were carried away by the topics we were discussing.'

'Quite,' said Purkiss. 'We were threshing out office policy.'

'Absorbing subject.'

'Most gripping.'

'You said so-and-so, and I said such-and-such.'

'Precisely.'

'One of the points that came up,' said Bingo, 'was, if you recollect, the question of payment for that story of mine.'

'Was it?' said Purkiss doubtfully.

'Oh, rather,' said Bingo. 'Surely you haven't forgotten that? You agreed to pay me ten quid for it. Or,' he paused, his gaze fixed on the other with a peculiar intensity, 'am I wrong?'

'No, no,' said Purkiss hastily. 'It all comes back to me.'

'I may as well take it while you're here,' said Bingo, 'so as to save you a lot of book-keeping.'

Purkiss groaned, perhaps not quite so hollowly as Bingo had been doing before his entrance, but quite fairly hollowly.

'Very well,' he said, unbelting. 'Ah, good afternoon, Mrs Little.'

'Oh, how do you do, Mr Purkiss?' said Mrs Bingo, who had entered (LEFT UPPER CENTRE). 'Julia,' she cried, turning to Mrs Purkiss, 'you'll never believe! Algernon Aubrey has just said "Cat".'

It was plain that Mrs Purkiss was deeply moved.

'Cat?'

'Cat.'

'Well!'

'Isn't it wonderful!'

'Most extraordinary!'

'Come on up to the nursery, quick. We may be able to get him to say it again.'

Bingo spoke. He made a strangely dignified figure as he stood there looking a bit like King Arthur.

'I wonder, Rosie, if I might have a moment of your valuable time?'

'Well?'

'I shall not detain you long. I merely wish to say what I was about to say just now when you suddenly dashed off like a jack-rabbit of the Western prairies. If you ask Mr Purkiss, he will tell you that, so far from behaving last night in the manner which you recently sketched

out, I was closeted with him at his club till an advanced hour. We were discussing several problems of much interest which have arisen in connection with the conduct of *Wee Tots*. For Purkiss and I are not clock-watchers. We love to put in overtime. We work while others sleep.'

There was a pregnant silence. Mrs Bingo seemed to sag at the knees. Tears welled up in her eyes. Remorse was written on every feature.

'Oh, Bingo!'

'I thought I would just mention it.'

'Oh, Bingo darling, I'm sorry.'

'It is quite all right,' said Bingo. 'I am not angry. Merely a little hurt.'

Mrs Bingo flung herself into his arms.

'I shall never speak to Sir Joseph Moresby again!'

'I wouldn't,' said Bingo. 'I've never met the man, of course, but he appears to be a Gadarene swine of the first water. But I must not keep you, Mrs Purkiss. You will be wishing to go to the nursery.'

The females passed from the room. Bingo turned to Purkiss, and his eye was rather stern.

'Purkiss,' he said, 'where *were* you on the night of June the fifteenth?'

'I was with you,' said Purkiss. 'Where were you?'

'I was with you,' said Bingo. 'Come, let us go and listen to Algernon Aubrey on the subject of Cats. They tell me he is well worth hearing.'

August 1940

Clement Freud

WARNING: GOVERNMENTS CAN SERIOUSLY DAMAGE YOUR HEALTH

I WAS going to write this piece on food and politics: on whether Government has a duty to keep the populace healthy, when it is clearly cheaper and more expedient to rake in the high taxes on tobacco and alcohol, let the people die off and save on pensions.

For the State to take an interest in the health of the nation is comparatively recent. At the turn of the century, an enlightened official at the War Office decided that the costly journey to South Africa might be wasted on soldiers who died on the voyage to the Boer War, and so it was decreed that to become a soldier of the Queen, you had first to pass a medical examination. (Prior to this, all you had to do to join the Army was commit a crime.)

It was the staggeringly high rejection rate of young British men that persuaded Parliament to legislate for the well-being of citizens and set the foundation for the National Health Service.

Today we know very much more about health and disease than we did; we also know what causes maladies and malfunctions; and to prove it, one hundred and fifty 'health books' are published every month, all giving different advice. We believe that a free society must afford man the option to kill himself as and when he wants; therefore you can buy cigarettes (freedom of choice) and read (education) the (health) warning on the packet and make up your own mind. Ditto booze, fat, salt, sugar. Government's duty the while is to present a caring image, which it currently does by underfunding, and then getting rid of, bodies like the Health Education Council, who issue leaflets and advice; their last director issued too many anti-tobacco leaflets – so he had to go.

Parliament has given Local Education Authorities a duty to teach and transport and feed children; whether or not the feeding takes account of dietary consideration is up to the Councils, and almost to a Council do they ignore such action. Kids eat doughnuts and chips and hamburgers and drink fizzy drinks, and every year the regional medic is allowed to come along and take their blood pressure and shake his head in sorrow.

I had hoped that when the teachers' strike resulted in the introduction of highly paid school-meal supervisors, these £6-an-hour folk might instruct their clientèle on the subject of diet: teach them about fibre and fruit; warn them about cholesterol and additives. I hoped in vain.

As a result of what happened on June 11th, it seems I shall go on hoping in vain – but I came across a letter on the subject which is not without interest:

My dear Prime Minister,

I am honoured to accept the portfolio of Minister of Food in your Government – though admit to a modicum of surprise that this Ministry is to be within the Department of Treasury and Health. It is hard to come to any other conclusion than that you are using comestibles as an alternative method of citizen disposal.

Naturally, I am aware of how successfully your economic policies reduced those who were in employment and how favourable was the impact on population of your inner city 60 mph minimum speed order. You will forgive me if I make no mention of the public sector school-children's cigarette encouragement programme, so helpful in ameliorating pupil-teacher ratios; I kept my silence because ambition for office ever outweighs political integrity.

When you offered me the post, you made it clear that it would be my initial function to persuade the country to look upon longevity as wicked, sinful and selfish. This is not going to be easy, though of course I accept that Nigel needs a thirty per cent diminution in the number of pensioners in order to meet the next round of income tax cuts. We will have to make it plain that 'living longer is bad' as Willy used to put it, and we might change the name of Old Age Pension – which carries considerable authenticity – to Scroungers' Terminal Handout. The acronym STH has a pleasantly shady ring about it.

Now to policies: we must engage in a radical programme of encouraging consumption of high cholesterol foods; persuade citizens that additives are not really bad for them – far safer to eat than salmonella-affected fish; revert to the trusted Victorian method of salting food; introduce a levy on fresh and free range products and do away with taxation on alcohol. I believe that a few years of this package will make real inroads into the national housing shortage, a cause that I know is dear to your heart in this next term of office.

Sadly, there is no obvious solution as to how we can differentiate between North and South (we don't want all the people in the Shire counties to die, do we? My little joke).

When it comes to school meals, we shall have to take especial care with the private sector; I propose to introduce a series of exclusion orders, to be taken late at night and so obtusely worded that they should get through. Thank goodness the Press is on our side – though Maxwell might just have to get that peerage, else he could blow it.

Consumerism is dangerous to the successful promotion of our programme and I shall discuss with the Attorney ways in which we can stop these busybody Trots from achieving credibility.

I propose to change the name from additives to desirables, using the prefix D where it was E. You will recall how we confused them with the Windscale/Sellafield switch; it took people years to catch on.

But the high-point of our policy must be to raise the cholesterol level of old people (what my Parliamentary Under Secretary of State calls 'getting to the heart of the matter'). Charm them with chips, flatter them with fat, please them with pork, becalm them with bacon, and a few egg-yolks a day keep the doctors away – though there will be work for the priests and the undertakers. Sugar must figure prominently in the campaign, though personally I think a toothbrush tax is overdoing it, whatever Nicholas says.

Marie Antoinette is a much misquoted lady but she had the right idea when she said, 'Let them eat cake'. I expect she meant cream cake: heavy, soggy, sweet pastry, laced with alcohol and strewn with refined sugar; then the recipients of this delicacy should be persuaded to take occasional sharp exercise – like a 100-metre dash once a month – and our policies will soon bear fruit.

I have a memo from a civil servant about Albania, which is somewhere in E. Europe (I expect Geoffrey's people will know), where folk live longer because they have strong government; it seems they are healthy because they can't afford meat or fat or alcohol, nor can they go to films or plays and get bad ideas. Do you think you might persuade the Albanians to take away Scotland and Liverpool and the other cities in the North whose names always escape me;

the ones who send those frightfully badly dressed people
to Westminster?

Yours ever (because I eat Shredded Wheat and brown
rice).

(In accordance with recognised journalistic practice, I shall not
disclose my source.)

July 1987

Peter Dickinson

OUR MASTER LEAR

THERE was an old fellow of Bonn
Who said 'I'll go on and go on!'
        They cried to him 'Please!'
        And clutched at his knees
But there's still an old fellow at Bonn.

There was an old fellow of France
Whose nose was as long as a lance.
        But they said 'You suppose
        We depend on your nose?'
So they smashed that old fellow of France.

There was an old man of the Kremlin
Whose special delight was dissembling.
        When they said 'So you're here!'
        He replied with a leer
'No I'm not. I am still in the Kremlin.'

There was a young man in the States
Who became a dab hand at debates.
        He ummed and he urred
        As each crisis occurred
Till they loved him all over the States.

ON the Parlemigongo Tree
　　The Libbery Bird exists,
Though him you can hardly see
　　Through the Macmillibusquian mists.
　　　　But ever again
　　　　You may hear him explain
To the world in a manful, asquidgian vein
　　　　'I may seem few
　　　　But my face is new
So the people who see me will all say "Coo!
　　　　Let us out and vote
　　　　For this funny old goat!
　　　　He will make a change
　　　　From the usual range
For the Torigobang's mislaid his heart
And the Sociololly keeps falling apart
But here's a bird we would like to see
At the top of the Parlemigongo Tree!"'

Though he is so faint and few
　　And the others so many and fat
He does not get in a stew
　　Or shout or invest in a hat.
　　　　But now and again
　　　　You may hear him complain
To himself in a mournful, asquidgian strain
　　　　'Alack and O!
　　　　And where did they go,
The Libbery Birds whom I used to know?
　　　　Unctuous birds
　　　　Who ate their words
　　　　By the light of the moon
　　　　With a runciman spoon?
It always seems a pleasure to meet
Birds who kept their galoshes so neat!
But they are the sort you seldom see
Nowadays on the Parlemigongo Tree.'

THE
LIBBERY
BIRD

May 1962

Alan Coren
OH SAY, CAN YOU SEE?

The great majority of American schoolchildren are distressingly incompetent when it comes to writing proficiently, according to a major Federal study. Most children were found to be unable to persuade, describe, or even imagine coherently. The study, by the National Assessment of Education Progress, involved a test in which children were invited to write a persuasive letter to their imaginary Aunt May, asking her to allow the writer to visit her.

Daily Telegraph

7 arpil

dear aunt may,

i wuld like to come visit witchew. i am a good amercan kid i do not snif nothing and i do not shoot up and i do not screw around and i honor the flagg and i bleeve these untied states is one natoin under god and the rest is a bunch of dum forn barsteds.

i like rocky ivy and clit eastwards and god. the bit i like best about rocky ivy is wear he beets the shit out of this dum comnist and the bit i like best about clit eastwards is wear he says go on punk make mi day and bloes his hed off with this big .357 magnum he has and the bit i like best about god is wear he gets all the forners to walk into the see and then he shuts it and the sunsabitches all screem and go down the toobs and there is forn blood all over and this is how it gets to be the red see.

if you let me come visit witchew i wil look after you good. it is the amercan way to look after them who is less fortnate than us such as ole dames and all and stop them making dum assholes of themselfs. i wil walk witchew to cherch and the a & p and the d a r meatings and if any cheap nigra or mugra tries to get a hole of you i wil stik my fingras in his eys and do karaty on him.

rite me soon.

your nefew you aint met.

10 arpil

dear aunt may

maybe you dont heer too good.

i was figgrin to be visiting witchew by now. i packed my grip. i oiled my airgun. it is a dam good airgun. if you oil it good and keep it in shape the way they teech you at the littel christain rifle leegue you can shoot the ey out of any dago raper who culd be proulin aroun an old dames hous.

also i tole the dawg we wuz goin. i do not want to have to tel the dawg we aint goin he is one big dawg he doan take kinely toh aving his plans changed by some crazy ole broad. he is a gernam shepperd. he is traned to eat legs. he wuld be a good dawg for you an me to hav aroun the place in case some flaky loony-toon muslin came to the door and tried to stik us. i wuld just say kil him dook and that muslin wuld be lookin down at too stumps and wishin wear he had stayed in liberia.

i wuld not be no trubble i wuld just sit aroun the place scopin the a teem and miami vise and any videos you had wear they berned perverts alive until there fases shriveled off and you wuld feel good havin a spunky amercan kid on the premisses. did i mentoin i also have a junior cubscout flak-jaket and a three-pound crucifix wear i have filed the edges down and put a lether thong on the end so it does not come off of your rist and you can keep on swingin evenwith three commie sluggs in you.

stil and all it is not the amercan way to go wear we aint wanted so the impotent thing is for you to rite me imediate and say deer nefew i luv amerca my hous is your hous come over anytime the icebox is full you wuld have your own room and color teevee and a big window with a ninety degree ark of fire.

i aim to give you the benfit of the dout aunt may. culd be you din get my leter on account of subversiv forn snales climed in the goddam malebox or some enmy of this great cuntry ripped off the maleman or watever. my poisnal view is anyone innerferin with the US post offis shuld git a fare trile and have there hed took off with a chane-saw.

rite me soon as you git this.

your nefew.

13 arpil

dear aunt may

okay. doan say you din git fare warnin. it is the rite of evry amercan to go visit wear he goddam well likes. it is what our four fathers done. if the redskins hadda sent up a smoak single saying hi fellas our hous is your hous any you guys fansy a beer insted of wear they started wid the arrows and the tomahorks and simlar ax of innernatoinal terrism we wouldna had to take self-defense mesures. they culda bin livin in wigscrapers in east harlem by now and gittin bufloburgers on soshul securty along wid the rest of the coon freeloders.

by the time you git this leter you willa bin visited and visited dam good. you wil know you bin visited on acount of wear the windows is all bust in and the roof is all ript off and their is smoak comin out your ferncher and the cats insides is all over the yard. you will be reedin this sittin onna pila ruble and wondrin why in hell you din hav the sense to invite me in as an adviser to run your plase and keep it saif from comnism and muslin funmenlism and sardinista dick-hedism and slanty-eyed gookism and i doan know what-all. i gess you bin lissnin to some europ fagot or other or else the lousy innernatoi-nal marxist conspirsy alredy got to you in wich case tuff tit you ole dingbat you had it comin.

i know their is pinko frigfists out there who wil say i shulda negoshted or i shulda giv you time to git out or i shulda arst some kine permision from the nieghbers but i say the hell with that our moto is do it to them before they do it to you. eat your hart out perl harber is my view.

i am goin off to stik bootblak on my fase now. their is a hunters moon. i doan know exackly wear you hang out due to wear my teecher is keeping her lip butoned and keeps on teling me you are imagnary but she is just another member of the gutless pasifist femnist wimp conspirsy i say their is nuthin imagnary about the enmies of uncl sam they are all over the hole goddam plase. look under any stoan.

anyway what the hel. i got my airgun i got my slingshot i got my crucifix i got my chane-saw i got my zippo i got my dawg dook. i got more goddam fire-powr than ten thousand ole dames. i culd take out the hole lousy nieghberhood. the way i see it wen it comes to self-defense is you win a few you lose a few.

one things fer sure aunt may. you aint seen nuthin yet.

your nefew.

April 1986

Frank Keating

BATTING ON

I HAVE been with the England cricket team in the Caribbean on their last three tours as they have prepared and patched their armour in readiness for another Test series against the merciless West Indians. Fat lot of good my presence did them, so I am giving it a miss this time.

The opening one-day international is in Port-of-Spain on, ominously, St Valentine's Day. That's where we played the first Test which got the whole thing off to a calamitous start in 1981, and I remember going in the team bus every day from the Hilton, across the Savannah to the Queen's Park Oval – and always past the Roxy cinema which that week was showing something called *Phantasm*, and the place was plastered with lurid posters proclaiming, 'If this trip doesn't scare you, man, then you're already dead and buried!' The message was not lost on the team. It was to prove horribly spot-on.

Mind you, England lost only two Tests out of four on that tour, so in retrospect, and mindful of what was to come through the rest of the 1980s, it wasn't a bad effort to escape with two honourable draws in that series. England's best bat in 1981, by far, was Graham Gooch, who averaged almost 60 in the four Tests against what most scholars still reckon the best of all the West Indian attacks in history – Holding, Roberts, Croft, and Garner in their ferocious prime, with the apprentice, Marshall, as third change.

Now, nine years older, Gooch is back as captain. England cannot have had a more lugubrious, cares-of-the-world general since Len Hutton, as it happens the last opening bat to have to lead from the front and be first over the top. One reason – dotty, I agree – that there is a feeling somewhere in the bones of English cricket that this winter we might at last have the lads giving as good as they get in the Caribbean. I feel it too, though I am not actually taking any bets till well after Valentine's Day.

What a coup for Gooch if he could bring it off. Just to give Viv Richard's lot a ruddy good game every time would be triumph enough, wouldn't it? A nice little bonus, too, for Geoffrey Boycott, who was called up to coach the batsmen in the arts and sciences of playing fast bowling. Not only the tyros, Hussain and Bailey, admitted that the cussed old Tyke's know-how was invaluable, but Gooch himself was big man enough to thank Boycott for spotting, and eradicating, some basic flaws that had unconsciously been taken on board his own technique.

In the Barbados Test match nine years ago, Gooch was Boycott's junior opening partner. Gooch made a valiant 116 out of an England total of 224. Geoffrey made one of Test cricket's most famous ducks. I will never forget it. Bridgetown's rickety, crickety stadium was full to every corrugated rooftop, and the jabbering din only died into an expectant quiet as Boycott took guard and Michael Holding paced out his menacing run. He was almost using the sight-screen at the pavilion end as a catapulting starting-block.

First ball snortingly tore a strip off the knuckle of Boycott's left-hand batting glove and dropped just in front of third slip as the batsman wrung his hand in pain. The second was shorter and even more spiteful, and Boycott jack-knifed his forehead out of the way with a millimetre between his life and a coroner's verdict of misadventure due to the whiplash effect.

Next ball was off a fuller length, but no less wicked, and it licked back cruelly to splatter the inside of Geoffrey's unguarded left thigh. The infinitely courageous Englishman stuck to his middle-stump scratch-mark, and the fourth ball had him in all sorts of ungainly contortions as he endeavoured to keep down the missile again with his already wounded left hand; the thing squirmed away to gully. The fifth delivery again had you fearing for the stubbornly gallant knight's life as it reared angrily at his throat like a buzzsaw looking to at least peel his Adam's Apple. Still Boycott stood his ground.

As if the hateful half-dozen had been orchestrated into one gigantic, discordant crescendo, the sixth and last ball of the over was a snaking yorker which fiercely ripped Boycott's off-stump out of the ground and had it spearing fully 20 yards as if, for a moment we thought, it would impale itself in the very heart of the wicket-keeper, Murray. It missed him by a whisker.

The vast throng was silent, stunned, for a split second. Boycott jerked round to watch the flight of the stump then, as the great, crazed noise erupted all around his ears, his mouth gaped and he tottered in his crease as if he'd seen the very Devil himself. Then, agonised and tremulous, he walked away, tearing his batting gloves off with his nervously juddering teeth. By the time he got to the pavilion step he was erect again; beaten this time, sure, but already determined on his counter.

The old warrior showered quickly then, his head wrapped in a pale green towel, sat quietly in the corner of the dressing-room pondering not so much his humiliation (for that, precisely, is what it had seemed to everyone watching in awe of Holding's quite brilliant brutality), but his possible answer to it.

In the second innings, Boycott made a solitary single (a nick through the slips) before the rampantly sleek assassin, Holding, pranged him amidships again; this time, snaffled in the gully off another unplayable fizzer. It seemed really possible that the old boy who had first played for England almost twenty years before was through, *sans* eye, *sans* bottle.

Oh, us of little faith. What Boycott had made sure of was keeping a copy of the BBC tele-recording of that Holding over. Night after night, he had the BBC TV news reporter on the tour, a fellow Yorkie, Michael Blakey, play it through on the Steenbeck. I went with Geoff a couple of times to those late-night dark-room sessions. The loop was only four or five minutes long. He would watch it again and again and again, occasionally telling Blakey's operator to stop the machine so as to study the freeze-frame at a particular point in the over. He'd pore over the fuzzy monochrome, stop-start, rewind, or fast-forward to the last *coup de grâce*. Finally, just before the next Test began in Antigua two weeks later, Boycott seemed to announce himself satisfied that he'd seen enough.

In Antigua, on a broken pitch, Boycott saved the match and England's bacon with an unbeaten century. A smiling Holding shook the rum Yorkshire emperor's hand as he led the opposition's rueful applause at the pavilion gate at the end of the game.

That famous duck of Boycott's in Barbados had been so mercilessly and cruelly executed by Holding that I still reckon it contributed somehow to the utter tragedy that was to come that evening. The England team had been skittled out by close of play. The bus that took the team back to the hotel was full only of stunned silence: the feeling was that they had not only let themselves down but, even worse, their beloved coach, Ken Barrington, who had sat all afternoon at the pavilion window, chain-smoking and worrying as his grim-faced batsmen came regularly back and forth. Gatting 2,

Gower 17, Butcher 17, Botham 26, Willey 19, Bairstow 0, Emburey 0, Jackman 7, Dilley 0, Extras 8.

Only the press stayed up late that night. Ken and his wife Ann, who had arrived for a holiday a few days before, went out for an early supper. They were back about nine. In their bedroom, Ken flopped into an armchair and Ann pottered for a minute or two in the bathroom. When she came out, Ken didn't answer her. He was unconscious. Ann ran into the corridor to shout for their next-door neighbour, the team's physio, Bernard Thomas. He saw at once that Kenny was dead.

Next morning, the team unashamedly blubbed their eyes out as they stood to attention before play started for a minute's silence to their friend and coach and confessor. The death of Ken Barrington ruined the tour even more cataclysmically than being thrown out of Guyana at the end of the notorious 'Jackman Affair' ever did.

Only Graham Gooch, of that mortified band of young men, remains in the England colours this winter. If he had one, I always reckoned Gooch was Barrington's favourite: two of a kind, he admired hugely the deadpan stubbornness at the crease, the technical resolution, and the four-square honesty of the Essex man. Win or lose this series, I know Gooch will be invoking the spirit of his beloved mentor a great deal this next couple of months in the Caribbean.

And even grinning in affection as he tells tales of some of the onliest Barrington's endearing malapropisms when the chips were down.

Like the time there had been a minor riot during the first Test at Trinidad. Kenny had asked the local police to send some reinforcements to mingle in the crowd next day. 'That's it,' he said, 'we want a load more plain-clothes protectives!' Another time he praised Emburey for a caught-and-bowled off Richards – 'John, you really caught 'im in two-man's land!' When anything, like local practice wickets or generally scatty organisation, got his goat, he would say with cheery exasperation, 'I dunno, talk about Gymkhana's Army!' He meant of course, Fred Karno's. Opposition bowling, he would sometimes dismiss as 'pretty inosculous'; heavy rain would be coming down, not like stair-rods, but 'pea pods'; and if he slept well it would be 'yeah, like a baby lark'.

One of the last ever tasks of this good and kindly man was to chide his team of young bloods and yobs and ask them, please, to desist from referring rudely to the hordes of mostly retired, middle-class British holidaymakers (another army of them will be packing their khaki shorts and sunhats this week) out for a three-week package to watch the cricket. The team call them WINKS – as in 'Wankers Incorporated', and the game would be to send them up rotten whenever possible once they had emerged blinking (sorry, winking) from the tropical airport out of an English winter. Like, say, one is hobbling about the team's favourite bar on a walking-stick and cadging autographs. 'Ooh, look, a Wink on a stick!' and the team would be convulsed. Or another perhaps has been too readily introducing himself to the rum i.e., a 'tiddly Wink'. Another might look a bit camp in his beach shirt – nudge, nudge, 'a sod is as good as a Wink'.

One of the best was Dusty Miller's on that 1981 tour. An old boy and his wife, Penelope, had finally got the message that the team was more than slightly bored by his advice on how to stand firm against Holding, Roberts and co., and he had been led away from the bar by his wife for a stroll alongside the beach before supper. They looked, as they ambled, a perfect picture in the golden fiery sunset. What a lovely shot, said one of the players, romantically. 'More,' said Dusty, quick as a flash, 'like a pen and Wink drawing!'

Fair's fair, it really is about time the Winks had something to cheer about on their package hols. Wouldn't it be something if Gooch's lot could really bring home the bacon this time. I feel it in my bones. For Boycott's sake, for one thing, and for Kenny Barrington's blessed memory. It would, in his own words, 'be a brilliant performance in anyone's cup of tea!'

February 1990

Harry Secombe

GOON ON ANNUAL HOLIDAY

THERE is a pleasure boat which leaves Cala Bona for Cala Ratjada twice a day during the season and, as it nears a peninsula called Costa de los Pinos, a guide with a megaphone points out the various luxurious houses.

'This is da house of Jackie Kennedy. Over there is da villa from Franco. Dat one wid da red roof is belong to King Juan Carlos. And dis one wid da big pool and da white tower is da villa of 'Arry Secombee. All together English peoples shout 'Ello 'Arry.'

The passengers, loaded to the gunwales with fiery alcoholic concoctions, which they will subsequently lose over the side on the way back, raucously obey. Right on cue a short, stout man appears on his patio and waves a hand in greeting. The passengers wave back and the flamenco-damaged vessel ploughs on.

Now, I have a confession to make. That villa is not mine – I should be so lucky – and the short, stout chap is an extremely wealthy Spanish businessman who is awakened every day from his siesta by this unaccountable shouting; and he is not waving, he is shaking his fist. Meanwhile, tucked away in the pines I lie back on my rickety bamboo lounging chair and chuckle quietly to myself.

I am sorry to destroy this illusion of the glamorous film star life that British visitors to Majorca seem to think I lead, but at least I am able to preserve a certain amount of privacy in my own modest holiday home. After all, that is why I bought the place – for privacy. I am quite prepared to endure the good-natured banter of the fellow passengers on the flight out ... 'Sing us a song 'Arry boy,' they cry. ''Ere, ain't he gorn grey!' 'Got old Spike and Sellers with yer then?' 'Aren't you different in the flesh?' One large lady once held me firmly by the arm in the airport lounge, looked long and hard into my face, and then called back to her travelling companions, 'No, it's not him.' But when I arrive in Majorca I like to merge quietly into the background – a task comparable with that of Ian Paisley seeking an audience with the Pope. However, I do try, and it's easier out of season when the tourists are thin on the ground and only the spartan Germans stride bare-legged through the rain-swept lanes.

That is the time when the British residents come out from their summer hibernation, hurriedly check the position of the pound against the peseta in the *Majorca Daily Bulletin*, take the old blazers out of the mothballs and head for their favourite haunts. Invitations to 'drinks before dinner' drop into letter-boxes and over the next few months permutations of the same faces appear in permutations of the same houses. Fortunately, unlike English suburbia, there is no class distinction in these 'get-togethers'. We cling to each other because our 'foreignness' sets us aside from the locals, who regard us with a good-natured intolerance.

For example, if you had been in the main street of Cala Millor a few months ago, you would have witnessed a strange ceremony. A motley collection of British, Germans and Spanish gathered outside a brand new bar on the corner opposite the Banco de Credito Balear. A short, fat Welshman stood before the closed door, reading a speech.

'This is a corner of a foreign field which is forever Mayorkshire,' I declaimed, expecting a laugh and getting one. A stray dog had cocked its leg against my cream trousers. I cut short the proceedings. 'I hereby declare Andy's Fish and Chip Bar open and God bless all who sail in her.' I kicked the dog surreptitiously and opened the door with a flourish. Champagne flowed freely and Andy and Kathy, two lovely people from Bridlington, were launched into the battle against the domination of the paella.

Out of season is also the time for trying out new restaurants and once we took a chance on a café run by a German. I began talking to the proprietor in a friendly manner about my army experiences and discovered, a table away, an ex-German soldier with whom I had exchanged shots in North Africa during the war. When I say 'exchanged shots', I mean that the regiment of Artillery of which I was a small part had presumably fired upon his regiment of which he was a larger part – being a *Feldwebel* as opposed to my rank of Lance Bombadier. We had, however, won the battle in question because Hans had finished up in a prisoner of war camp in Canada. He said

that our unit had actually taken him prisoner. My remorse bought
him drink after drink until my wife led me away from the battlefield
under a flag of truce.

The next night I went along to the same bar to meet my new-found
friend, equipped with maps and books of the North African campaign. I discovered him in deep conversation with an English holi-
daymaker against whom he had apparently fought in the Battle of
Arnhem. It was only after I had bought the third round of drinks
that I realised that if Hans had been captured in 1942 he could not
possibly have been at Arnhem in 1944. There was nothing else to do
but join in the battle myself. Apparently, before my wife rescued me,
I was holding the north end of the Bridge single-handed, armed only
with a pocket knife. Old soldiers never die, their livers fade away.

I am ashamed to admit that after fifteen years of owning a holiday
home in Majorca I still have difficulty ordering goods in Spanish.
This causes much amusement in the village shops. A visit from El
Gordo, or the Fat One, as I am known locally, is the nearest thing to
entertainment that Son Servera can offer. At the butcher's a slap on
the leg accompanied by 'Baa-aa' means leg of lamb, a gesture
towards the small of the back and a 'moo' does service for steak,
although on one occasion I had a cold and got sweetbreads instead. I
daren't ask for sausages.

In spite of the language barrier, my family and I are beginning to
understand the working of the Majorcan mind. If you expect
promptness from tradesmen you're in for a big surprise. Shopkeepers will say yes out of politeness. We have had half an iron gate
for four years and our shutters are still held back with string. Every
six months the local blacksmith calls in for a sherry and looks at the
jobs he has left unfinished. He nods, promises, asks after the family,
then we ask after his and that's it for six months.

We had a hole in the ground for two years waiting to undergo its
metamorphosis into a swimming-pool. Strange-looking weeds grew
out of it, the kids kept falling into it, and every time we came out for a
holiday we went through the ritual of pleading and promising with
the builder. Then suddenly we arrived for an Easter break and it was
practically finished. It stayed practically finished until we came back
in August. Then there was a flurry of workmen and hey presto it was
completed – all except for the ladder, which was essential to aid my
getting in and out without scraping acres of skin off my belly. So I
had to sit high and dry like a stranded whale as the rest of the family

frolicked in the sparkling water. Then one evening the ladder arrived, unannounced, from Palma. The following morning the water in the pool had almost drained away owing to the loosening of several tiles. I now had a ladder and a pool, but no water. We managed to get all three elements together on the day we had to leave for home. I had a hasty dip and developed an eye infection from an overdose of chlorine.

Yet all these little pinpricks – the peccadillos of the tradesmen etc – are well worth enduring for the privilege of living part-time in Majorca. Beyond the concrete canyons of Can Pastilla, Arenal and Magaluf there are banks where the wild garlic grows, where honeysuckle blazes in roadside hedges and where you can still hear sheep bells and cocks crowing and the lowing of cattle; where you can buy bread hot from the baker's oven and find little village bars where for twenty-five pesetas you can buy a glass of locally-made liqueur which will blow your brain straight through the top of your sunburned skull. And if you think I am going to tell you where to find them, you must be crazy.

June 1978

HRH The Princess Anne
ONE'S TRAVELS

THE camel next door to me let off a series of the most revolting, flatulently bilious noises I have ever heard when asked to rise to its feet. He, she, or it was apparently not pleased about the position of its passenger, somewhere behind its second or stern hump. The noise only stopped after it was made to kneel down and the passenger moved to behind the forward hump. My camel was much more amenable and ambled off down the road on its well-worn path through the old town of Jaisalmer in Rajasthan. Just a little taste of the local form of transport on my way to visit a Save the Children Fund project in India. Next time I want to try a proper thoroughbred riding camel and not the equivalent of a tourist bus, but the beast is the only way to travel long distances in this part of the world.

Before I became President of the Save the Children Fund, I had done a little travelling of a fairly conventional kind – although with not very happy memories of my early experiences in the air or at sea – with my extraordinarily bad sea-keeping capabilities, it's a wonder I ever got further than the overnight train to Aberdeen! I do recall that when I was small the train was an adventure, and in those days you got an excellent breakfast as well.

However, a whole new dimension of my experience of travel really began the first time I went overseas to visit a Save the Children Fund project in Ethiopia, back in February 1973. As a result of a previous drought, the Fund had been asked to help in relief work and in setting up long-term mother and child care projects. Ethiopia is a large country with very poor roads and a few fairly basic airfields, and flying anywhere in Africa is uncomfortable if you cannot fly at dawn or dusk. The heat during the day causes tremendous thermals and one of my worst memories of any flight or landing was getting into an airstrip 8,000 feet up in the mountains but with much higher mountains rising all round so that the aircraft had to be flown in ever decreasing circles before it could land. If that was not bad enough, I then had to climb into a Land Rover (looking like a green being of average size from outer space and feeling worse) and drive 2,000 feet back up the mountain. But the trip was well worth it just to see the Coptic churches at Lalibala, carved down into solid rock. They are surely one of the less well known wonders of the world.

After an inspection of a Save the Children Fund clinic, I was allowed the luxury of three days in the Simien Mountains – the huge central plateau of Ethiopia, rising to some 14,000 feet in places. Fortunately, we started climbing from about 8,000 feet and had help from some local mules. They were nothing like the mules normally illustrated in the children's books of my youth or as used by the British Army or Gold Rush prospectors. They were barely the size of an English donkey and decidedly thinner, but their lungs were infinitely more efficient at that altitude than the lungs of those of us more accustomed to sea breezes. We spent two nights under canvas at about 12,000 feet and we walked to the edge of the plateau to look for *moufflons* which graze on what can only be described as precipices. I say 'walked' but wheezed and tottered would be a better description of our movements at that altitude. Also on that trip we passed several nomad settlements and it was already apparent that the demands being made on the limited resources of trees and soil were creating trouble for the future. However, a centuries-old way of

life is not easily changed by outside interference, especially when
there is no real alternative to the traditional form of agriculture. This
situation is found in many places and similar problems must be
appreciated by those who wish to make a genuine contribution to
developing countries.

It was a memorable trip for me in so many ways, not least because
of all the little 'friends' who shared my sleeping bag, and the amount
of weight I lost. So far, I have (regrettably) not managed to achieve a
similar reduction again!

Since then my travels have taken me to many other parts of Africa,
Asia, and briefly to the Middle East. The greatest distances were
covered in Andovers of The Queen's Flight, not fast, but very
practical, especially for some of the very rural areas that I need to
visit to catch up with our Save the Children Fund teams. In Africa
the most basic airstrip I have experienced was Goram Goram on the
edge of the Sahara in Burkina-Faso (or Upper Volta as it was when I
visited it). The strip was barely distinguishable from the desert
around it and certainly had no control tower, landing aids or services
such as fire extinguishers. However, a fire engine was found and
persuaded to drive all the way up there and fortunately was not
required.

In India I made the mistake of accepting the invitation of the
Captain to view the hills from the cockpit, but by the time I could see
the airstrip we were really quite close and it did not look long
enough. I reminded myself – not for the first time – that ignorance is
bliss and I would have been better off in the rear where you cannot
see what is about to happen to you and therefore don't worry about
it. Watching air shows, where they demonstrate how quickly a
particular aeroplane can stop, I have often wondered what it must be
like for the passengers within the aircraft. Now I know. As my
trainer used to say, 'Put it down to experience and don't do it again!'
The whole exercise was, of course, perfectly safe – or at any rate as
safe as or safer than, taking to the roads. The roads themselves vary
considerably from the recognisably tarmac variety to those indis-
tinguishable from the surrounding countryside. Again Burkina-
Faso comes to mind – this time for the slowest of road journeys
thanks to the ruts and bumps. In fact I abandoned the estate car
provided for me because of the rotten ride, and took to the Save the
Children's brand new Land Rover County, kindly donated by the
Worshipful Company of Carmen, since its rather more basic suspen-

sion ignored most of the bumps. But driving through the countryside really brought home the problems of these Sahel areas. Camels, sheep, goats, donkeys and even horses are all competing for much the same limited grazing. The acacia trees are few and far between, where once, I was told, there used to be an almost impenetrable forest. There were one or two small areas that had been fenced off where the vegetation, while not exactly lush, was considerably better than outside the fence, which just showed what could be done to improve the viability of the land. It was also on that drive that I came across a piece of international 'aid'. It was a bright, shiny and very large set of disc harrows that many farmers in the affluent West would have thought twice before buying – partly because of the size of the tractor required to pull it, never mind the cost. The harrows had been in the same place for six years, there being no tractors for hundreds of miles and certainly no diesel.

Running a car is difficult enough, but essential for the Save the Children Fund if its field workers are to reach the three clinics they run, each a minimum of 60 miles from the next. It was dry when I was there and the travelling was slow but possible. When it rains – if it rains – the roads simply disappear and, short of a hovercraft, no transport moves. In those conditions, the ubiquitous Land Rover is still the best bet (and I'm not even sponsored by them!).

In Bangladesh we had to abandon planes and cars and went by train, by boat and Shanks's pony. It is a very flat country: good news if you are walking, but bad news when the water level rises, as it does every year. Whether or not you get flooded is 'Inshallah' – 'The will of Allah'. That day we walked through three villages, visiting the locally trained Village Health Workers and Traditional Birth Attendants, who looked after the villagers' minor health problems and the vaccination programme. On foot you have time to see how well kept the houses are on the inside and the efforts the people have made to follow the example of their Health Visitor. The boats, some powered by outboard motor and some by manpower, are essential in a country which is basically a river delta. The river, and the sea into which it flows, control life completely and often very harshly.

Finally, I think I must mention one other form of 'transport' – although I did not use it on Save the Children business. It was as a result of a visit to Nepal in order to see the Fund's projects. I was allowed a couple of days in the Royal Chitawan National Park down on the Indian plain. We flew in to a grass strip and were met by our transport for the journey to the lodge, some way away into the jungle. We went down one set of aircraft steps and up another set, rather older and a bit wobbly, but really the only practical way to get a lot of tourists on to their first elephant! We climbed on to a reasonably well covered platform with a wooden running rail and four little uprights at the corners. The passengers sit at the corners with a leg each side of the upright and under the rail. At this point the elephant, which had been kneeling down, rose to its feet, a sensation that feels like I imagine a small earthquake would. Uplifting? It then marched majestically off towards the river. I will not describe any more because it would turn into a story of its own. Suffice to say that a young lady asked me the other day if I would rather drive a tank or ride a horse. The answer was a horse, but if she had asked me to choose between an elephant or a horse – well ... !

September 1985

Alexander Frater

TWO WEEKS BEFORE THE MAST

I FIRST heard about cruising during a childhood spent mostly in the South Pacific where the only way of getting about was by boat. Our waterborn equivalent of the family car was a tiny antique launch called *England Expects*. Only two people understood her foibles and eccentricities. One was my father and the other his sailor, a small, bent man named Hovis who had a scuttling gait, moist, lidless eyes and an oddly furtive look. Hovis was an expert at traditional Polynesian navigation, which involved jumping into the sea and floating motionless to get the measure of the currents and the steepness of the waves.

Over the years bits of him kept getting nibbled off by passing predators, and I recall him sitting there with only half a heel, chin resting on the good knuckle of his left hand and sniggering with disbelief as my father explained the principles of the compass and sextant.

The launch had been bought from a firm of sea-slug exporters on the mainland; the clerks had used it for taking documents and manifests out to the freighters moored in the harbour. The firm, many years earlier, had purchased the launch from a wild-eyed, London-born planter named Clench, and it was he who had given the craft its absurd name. It had a two-stroke engine, probably stolen from someone's Riley, which, even when running sweetly, laid down a smokescreen of such density that the flying fish whizzing in and out of the gloom landed in our swirling scuppers with eyes watering, while the patrolling hammerheads were racked by terrible barking coughs if they ventured too near. The hull, clinker-built, leaked steadily and from Hovis I learnt the art of fast two-handed bailing with coconut shells.

There were hard rainwood seats which could also be pressed into service as paddles and an awning that had once sheltered the entrance of the El Tropicano nightclub. Though torn and badly weathered, the phrase '... iptease by 12 Dusky Luvli ...' was still just discernible over the bows. In the bows also was a small storage locker which Hovis had turned into a tiny stateroom with sleeping mat, pillow and candle.

Despite all that, she wasn't a bad sea boat and we had some

pleasant times in her. When we landed at a new place my parents and I sought accommodation ashore, but Hovis preferred to sleep in his locker, usually rendered legless beforehand by a two-gallon bucket of palm toddy. My own duties included assisting him tidy up after a day at sea, coiling ropes, stowing cushions and so forth, and in the course of these hours together we grew quite close.

I still remember the island – Yip – and the circumstances attending his sudden confession that, more than anything else in life, he wanted to work as a ship's steward. At the time we were scrubbing the hull with giant sponges, removing evidence of a protest made apparently by disaffected bushmen upset by the policies then being pursued by Chamberlain and the British government 'No Apeezmunt!' said the phrase scrawled across our blistered paintwork in teak ash and honey, a mixture that was virtually indelible. 'A *what?*' I said.

'Steward blong big boat,' said Hovis. The westering sun glinted briefly on his bald head, reminding me that it had the shape and texture of a giant light bulb. 'Blong ocean liner, actually. But not one 'im blong North Atlantic run, allsame so-called Blew Ribbun boat, masta. They just trouble – big seas, big storms, night cold allsame buggery, brass monkey nights as they say.'

'Oh,' I said.

A lumbering, cod-like creature suddenly hauled itself from the water and lunged at a hovering mosquito, a young anopheles dozing on the wing; badly shaken, it took off in the direction of Australia, travelling so fast that it seemed to leave a tiny sonic boom behind it, no louder than the sound of a wavelet falling on shingle.

'What I really want,' said Hovis, 'is to go cruising.' A young nun walked along the beach collecting driftwood and he leered at her. 'Blessings blong bigfella Jissus be upon you, missus,' he called.

'And the same to you with knobs on, sport,' said the Little Sister of Mercy in the accents of South Sydney. Perhaps she had not heard him properly.

'*Cruising?*' I said.

'Yis. One friend blong me, old Po'ongo, work as steward on French Line cruise ship *Mavis Lotti* in charge of deck quoits. He say money good, hours short and women all over him. He say sea air make them allsame desperate, roaring for nooky nooky behind number two smoke-stack every bleeding hour of day and night.' He stood back and, with head tipped to one side, considered the planks he had been scrubbing. 'Po'ongo say women trip you up and beat you to the ground, dropping faster than marines hitting dirt when flak fly. And they tip good.'

I thought about this for a moment, assuming that Po'ongo's ladies kept throwing themselves to the deck because of rough seas. The lure of big money and short hours, though, I quite understood, and I knew also that these French cruise liners were very nice inside, their bulkheads lined with exotic woods like angelim, avodire, tiger oak, satinwood, sycamore and synara. The dining saloons were three decks high and longer than the Hall of Mirrors at Versailles, which they were supposed to resemble. There were Olympic-sized swimming-pools made from marble and, every morning at 11 sharp, stewards brought trays of ices around. Hovis confirmed that this was indeed so, and added that cold gin could be had for just threepence a glass.

I went off to join my parents for dinner, leaving him to his palm wine and stewed eel, with mangoes for afters. The months went by. War was declared and Hovis joined the merchant marine, working as a trainee stoker aboard a dumpy little coaster that did the general cargo run up to Wao.

Then came the news of Pearl Harbor and, amidst persistent rumours of invasion by the Japanese imperial fleet, arrangements were made to evacuate expatriate women and children to Australia. We were told to ready ourselves. On a certain day a steamer would call.

It turned out to be the French cruise liner *Calais*, 27,500 tons, a notably sybaritic ship with public rooms the size of skating rinks and walls of crystal. The sumptuous furnishings and fittings helped heal the hurt of parting from my father. We sailed and that evening, before dinner, heard a sudden shout. I looked around and there, approaching in a spotless white uniform, was Hovis. He beamed at us.

'Well, well, missus, bugger me, fancy this,' he said, seizing my mother's hand and shaking it warmly. I was delighted to see him and capered about a bit. There were gleaming epaulettes on his shoulders. He looked as grand as an admiral.

'What exactly do you do?' I asked him.

'I is chief bouillon steward,' he said, importantly. '*Fust cluss.*'

'Oh, smashing,' I said. 'Can I have an extra cup tomorrow?'

'You not fust cluss, masta. You evacuee, special cheap fare, no

fancy treatment, *no bouillon.*'

He was as good as his word. For the duration of the voyage he remained friendly but firm. Our roles had been reversed. He was now in charge and when I approached him for a chat I did so with a certain deference. I learnt that Hawaii and Florida were the best destinations for the cruise boats which, on those runs, carried legions of big tippers who were not overfond of bouillon and, consequently, made few demands on his time.

'Except for the women,' he said, darkly.

'Yes?'

'They can't keep their hands off me,' he said. 'Some days I so utterly exhausted that I got to have a lie-down. But you still too young to know much about this matter. Probly you still think babies come along in big birds blong Dutch fellas called allsame, um, corks.'

'Storks,' I said. His missing bits, I noted, had grown back again and he looked more or less complete.

'Okay. But I tell you this. Movie stars are worst. You know my limp? No? Well, I got to hobble about because all this famous international beauties kip sneaking up when I is unwrapping the Knorr cubes and kicking my feet from under me.'

I last saw him on the morning that we steamed into Sydney harbour. As we stood at the rail he approached with a jar of Beluga caviar and a pair of plucked geese that he had stolen from the ship's deep freeze. These he handed to my mother.

'For you, missus,' he said. 'No good food in Australia.' My mother demurred, but he was insistent. 'Souvenir of your first cruise,' he said, returning to his little kitchen behind the bridge.

What became of him later is not clear. According to one report he remained with the ship for ten or twelve years and then left abruptly

after an incident at Divine service one Sunday morning. My informant – who was not aboard – says Hovis threw his hymnbook at an
edible noddy bird as it flapped across the deck and brought it down,
squawking, within inches of the portable pulpit in which the captain
was preaching a sermon that took, as its text, the words, 'If Jesus had
been on the *Titanic*, would he have gone down with the ship or
walked away from it?'

January 1983

Patrick Barrington

SONGS OF A SUB-MAN

I'M NOT A VEGETARIAN

ALTHOUGH I never pandered
　　To cruelty or greed,
I set too high a standard
　　Entirely to succeed;
I'm not a vegetarian –
　　I never felt inclined
To so unhumanitarian
　　An attitude of mind.

I can't help feeling sorry for a radish;
　　I can't help feeling pity for a pea.
How a man can be so narrow with a vegetable-marrow
　　Has always been a mystery to me.
I look on it as cowardly and caddish
　　To massacre a pea-nut in its shell;
My views may be mistaken, but I keep to eggs and bacon;
　　And, after all, I manage very well.

I hate to see the life of a tomato
　　Inhumanly and mercilessly wrecked;
I look upon a beetroot as a sensitive and sweet root
　　Deserving admiration and respect.
I hate to see an apple in a tart, oh!
　　Imprisoned like a felon in a cell.
Humanity, awaken! Oh, return to eggs and bacon!
　　And, after all, you'll manage very well.

I weep for all the metres
Of asparagus they grow
For the vegetable-eaters
Of sinister Soho.
In some later generation,
Dare I hope will be revealed
Rather more consideration
For the lilies of the field.

My creed, which many look upon as crazy,
Was formulated many years ago.
I believe that souls of ours go to dwell in fruits and flowers
When their human life is finished here below.
A stockbroker may turn into a daisy,
A barrister become a heather-bell.
This faith of mine's unshaken; that is why I keep to bacon,
And, after all, I manage very well.

I like to think a plum may be a PLATO
For anything that anyone can know;
I like to think an onion may contain the soul of BUNYAN
Or a lettuce be the dwelling of DEFOE.
KING PTOLEMY may lurk in this potato;
This celery be SHAKESPEARE – who can tell?
Oh! leave its spears unshaken. Not on SHAKESPEARE but on bacon
I'll live. And I shall manage very well.

May 1933

Frank Muir

AUF WIEDERSEHEN, PETS

I MEAN, I've got nothing personal against the five assorted animals who live the life of Riley in our midst. Three cats and two dogs. Furry denizens of the furniture all day, when they're not tearing bits off it. And eating. Oh, my goodness, eating; tin after tin of the gourmet stuff as advertised and refusing even to look at commoner nourishment. Never mind. Only the best is good enough for our silent dependants. And then there are things like their flea-collars at about three quid each (most of my mind was on higher things when I first saw the notice 'Flea-collars' in the petshop window – I found

myself idly wondering how one buckled it round the neck of such a
small insect ...). But no begrudgement. Health before wealth.

It's just that, well, perhaps we should not allow ourselves to get
too soppy over our pets. There is another side to them which, as we
have no memory of pain, we tend to forget. Perhaps we should
reconsider this not-so-attractive side of domestic animals, if only to
remind ourselves that animals, however lovable, are only
pets, while we are – well, us.

The French poet Méry once rather impressively declared (and in
French, too) that a cat was God's way of allowing man to caress a
tiger. A piece of sentimental twaddle, I humbly submit, only to be
expected from a nineteenth-century Frenchman with a Christian
name like a pop group of three garçons and a fille – François-Joseph-
Pierre-Agnès. I have never, myself, personally, caressed a tiger – my
arm is about twenty feet too short – but years ago at the London Zoo
I once caressed a cheetah, a similar make of beast, and I can report
that caressing a cheetah is like stroking a wire flue-brush. It can draw
blood.

Blood is never far from the surface with cat owners. Our three cats,
two Burmese and an Abyssinian, sleep in the bed with us. They have
decided so to do and it is impossible to keep them out, so no moral or
hygienic judgments, please; let us just say that at least they keep the
foxes down. In the middle of the night cats need to stretch, so they

stretch, at the same time unsheathing their little scimitars and swiping out at the nearest soft surface. I caught sight of my back recently in the bathroom mirror and I look like a steel engraving from *Foxe's Book of Martyrs.*

It is my belief that your average mog is a mass of finely-tuned instincts and sophisticated reflexes but in the matter of intelligence is as thick as a Sumo wrestler's thigh. What sort of mighty hunter can't locate its food even when you've rammed its nose into the saucer?

When there is a bit of cold chicken left over in the fridge it becomes the sole objective of our three cats to get at it. Nestles (the greediest) is the stakeout man. He sits three feet away from the fridge door, *willing* it to swing open. He will wait there for days if necessary. Cinto, the Abyssinian, is an outdoor lad so he occasionally livens up Nestles's lonely vigil by dropping in and showing him bits of an ex-mouse. Gentle, middle-aged Kettering is the peterman. Once they have decided in their minuscule brains that the remains of the cold chicken carcass is not going to leap out and surrender, nor the fridge door melt, Kettering starts work on the bottom edge of the door with a gently probing claw. The fridge is often improperly closed due to something like a £1.08 litre-bottle of Turkish Chablis keeping the door slightly ajar, and Ketters often *can* open it. But then what happens? The three Great Thinkers tip the cold chick on to the floor and then haven't the faintest idea what to do with it. It is suddenly too big, or something. It looms over them, cold, alien, and the wrong colour, nothing like *real* food, like their beloved chunks of shiny, brown meat out of a familiar tin marked 'Carlton Pet Foods: 38p'. So they affect indifference to the mess on the floor, yawn, blink slowly several times and stroll off.

The dogs, too, have IQs difficult to discern with the naked eye. Our scrap of black mongrel, Battersea, named after the Dog's Home from whence we sprang her, is an ingratiator. Visitors get an all-over lick, and a liquid look which says: 'Take little me home with you; I am so badly looked-after here.' This is true. We don't even clean her ears out for her. The first time I tried she nearly had my leg off. We take her to the vet now; he's a 16-stone New Zealander and can just hold her down if she's under a general anaesthetic (£33.50).

And as for our pedigree standard poodle, Bognor Regis: aristocratic beauty ... 10/10 marks. Sense of fun ... 10/10. Affectionate nature ... 10/10. Canine instincts ... 10/10. Brains ... well, look at it this way. As I type these critical comments, Boggy is lying down under the desk keeping me company, as is her wont. She knows that I am saying nasty things about her and the other animals because I read aloud as I work. But will she do anything about it? Will she get her own back on me in some way? No, because that sort of thinking would require an understanding of cause and effect of which she, as a dog, is quite incapable.

No, she will just lie there on the carpet and continue playing innocently with the cable of my electric typewriter.

Now she has started giving the cable playful little bites, but I don't mind: to the world she may be an inferior creature of little intelligence but I will always th*ink of her as my friend*.

September 1986

Paul Jennings

LAST EXIT TO LUNACY

I WAS driving northwards to the ring road so that I could go south from Oxford, that baffling, elusive city so compatible for those who know that life is not obvious and predictable, so maddening to those who don't.

I had been speaking to some laughing booksellers (in itself an improbable term, you can't imagine a pub or even a novel called *The Laughing Bookseller*) in a room underneath another room where the Oxford University Press, which contains men who can set Greek and Chinese, were having their Christmas pantomime (*Oedipus and the Clog Dancers*, by the sound of it). Where but in Oxford would such a jolly audience have skipped a pantomime and come to hear *my* jokes (even though in the excitement of the evening I forgot my favourite current publishing one, which is about the Boydell Press of Ipswich; they recently brought out a book called *Modern Ferreting*, and printed a lot of car stickers advertising it as 'The Answer to *Watership Down*')?

Well, you know how it is driving out of anywhere, especially Oxford. You gain a couple of places in the queue by a bit of nimble (but of course perfectly legal and safe) lane-changing, and you can't bear to lose it all by pulling in to get the petrol you need at the one

garage on your side of the road (although it isn't only Oxford which
has failed to realise that people want petrol when they are leaving a
city, not when they are entering it). I'll get it at some nice big
many-pump station out in the country, you think ...

Ha. The next place you can get petrol on your side of the road (or
on *any* side once you've passed the next roundabout) is Greenford,
Middlesex. The A40, without a word of warning, becomes the M40,
you whizz through dark Chiltern heights and the unimaginable,
remote life of places like High Wycombe, asleep under unattainable
street lights. Woe betide you if you stop. Gaitered, menacing game-
keepers would appear from millionaire's granges, you would be set
upon by nomad chair-makers or the dreaded Executive Vigilantes.

The lights and laughter of Oxford seemed very far away as I
anxiously watched the needle drop down through all the red bit, and
kept the speed down to something idiotic like 43 mph (another part
of me always thinks this simply means it will be later still when I
finally run out).

But all the time I had the feeling that I was at the receiving end of
some very subtle, Oxford-tinged joke. Suddenly I realised that this
was only an intensification of the feeling all of us have, on any
motorway, even when the tank is full. Some huge, shadowy organisation is watching us, following us on maps, and slightly laughing at
us, as they undermine our sense of reality by subtle psychological
warfare. NO SERVICE FOR 53 MILES, they say, as soon as we get
on the M4, resisting, but only just, the temptation to add HA HA,
GOT YOU NOW!

The places where you can get service, some residual contact with
human life, all have patently made-up names. The first M4 one is
MEMBURY. A likely story. It is meant to disturb us, with its faint
overtones of *memory* and *remembrance* (what is our name, where are
we going, did we check the brake fluid?) Then they dip into women's
light fiction entirely made up with Wiltshire names for LEIGH
DELAMERE (*Mere*, secretary to gruff bachelor publisher *Littleton
Drew*, thinks she is in love with fine-boned, sardonic *Leigh Delamere*
whom she met on a ski-ing holiday, and against Littleton's advice
accepts a weekend invitation to Leigh's horse-ranch. It turns out to
be a sinister house, and when the butler, *Old Sodbury*, shows her to
her room and she hears the key softly turned, she gazes out over the
darkening Wiltshire landscape. 'Oh, Littleton,' she breathes ...)
Then they change the mood abruptly with ST AUST. Well, hands

up who ever heard of *him*? Some scowling Saxon hermit, originally
St Angst, the patron saint of neurotics ...

The M1 names are even more unconvincing. SCRATCHWOOD,
the first one out is called. A certain bleak significance there; it could
be a generic name for any of them, surrounded as they are by dismal
brush and saplings ('We'd been driving for three hours, so we pulled
in to a scratchwood'). Then they get more and more unlikely.
TODDINGTON (no such place, I'll be bound), WATFORD GAP
(*Watford?* Dammit, this is just outside Daventry, Warwicks),
LEICESTER FOREST (two football teams confused), WOOLLEY
EDGE (getting into Yorkshire, you see, fringe of wool-weaving
country, but also insinuating a vague disquiet, doubt, *woolly-
mindedness*) ...

I see it all. The motorways are run by one of those secret organi-
sations full of arts graduates who turn out to have brilliant practical
skills, in the best British amateur tradition, like all those people
deciphering the Enigma stuff at Bletchley during the war, or the
philosophy don, Oliver Franks, becoming one of our best ambassa-
dors to America.

Were not the first motorways, the *autobahnen*, built by Hitler for
strategic, military purposes? Well, if ever the Russians, or the
Chinese, or the Scots invade us, they'll be well advised to stick to B
roads. After their years of gentle practice on us civilian motorists,
this group, MI 50, will bring its full intellectual might to bear on
confusing the enemy. Already they are adept at reducing six lanes to
two, for long seven-mile stretches not remotely justifiable in civilian
road-mending terms. In war, long files of tanks would follow each
other blindly over the soft shoulder into special reservoirs, filled
overnight. Deep in some Oxford command-post there would be
donnish laughter as the débâcle was viewed on closed-circuit TV.

Yes, it must be Oxford; look at the M5 names, and you are really
into the country of Logical Positivism, the Oxford philosophy that
admits with a shrug we can never know anything about anything, all
definitions are circular (if I say *p* entails *q* and *q* entails *r*, so *p* entails *r*
– and that's the kind of thing you *have* to say to Logical Positivists – I
am not telling you anything new about *p*, or about *anything*. Lor,
how they go on). 'Frankly, I can't think of any new names, Alistair,'
one of them says. 'You've got it, Hugo, *what* a brilliant idea!' So the
first one out of Birmingham is called FRANKLY. Further down, as
a joke, they name one after MICHAEL WOOD, a lecturer special-

ising in Sienese Primitives who is the first head of MI 50. It was he who took a subtle pleasure in naming GORDANO not after the actual surrounding district, which *is* so named, but after the little known Sebastiano Gordano (1272–1340) whose delicious triptych of the *Vision of St Edna* now hangs in Metternich Cathedral ...

But naturally it is really on the M40 that these Oxford masters of the philosophical double-take really come into their own. 'If I say there is an invisible and intangible petrol station exactly a hundred yards before the Thame turn-off, Edwin, the words *petrol*, *station*, *yards*, and *Thame* are all derived from experience. The statement is therefore not nonsense in the same way that, say, *iggl woob frzink* is nonsense.'

'But James, you know very well you can have no *empirical* experience of an invisible petrol station. I rather doubt, with Wittgenstein and Russell, if you could have experience of a visible one, in any logically verifiable sense.'

'I say, an invisible petrol station! Lateral thinking at its best! Gordon, I think perhaps we should –'

Well, the hell with them. I did get to Greenford.

January 1978

Alan Coren

GYPSY ROSE COREN'S HOROSCOPE

CAPRICORN
(December 21 – January 19)

1979 looks like being a pretty good year for Capricorns. The laundry will find four of the shirts it lost during 1973, and while this represents only one shirt per million of you, it is nevertheless an encouraging sign. Around March, however, your knee will hurt. Try to avoid calling the doctor, the NHS is going to be harder pressed than usual this Spring (see *Gemini* below), and coming out in all hours to look at four million swollen knees is not going to make things any easier, especially if your GP is a Sagittarian. They do not get on with Capricorns at the best of times, and what with the conjunction of Saturn in a particularly moody phase and Sirius worried about black holes, a lot of furniture could get broken. Things look up, though, after June, when you get a reasonable quote for a chipboard room extension.

AQUARIUS
(January 20 – February 19)

With Venus on the cusp around early February, the Gulf Stream entering the Dog Days, and pigs flying over Joanna Southcott's box, you will undertake a long sea voyage. But book early: with four million of you going, dilatoriness could mean sharing a lifejacket with two dozen other Aquarians or travelling upright on the after-deck of an ice-breaker. In fact, given such hazards as crowded sea-lanes, stricken tankers, dock strikes, Russian naval movements in the eastern Mediterranean, work-to-rule at Lloyds, Indonesian unwillingness to disembark balsa rafts, and so on, it would be unwise to make any firm plans for the remainder of 1979. Aquarians who do manage to make it back home should be prepared for disappointment. Their shoes will still not be ready.

PISCES
(February 20 – March 20)

This is an ebullient year for Pisces! Coley will find itself growing ever more popular, cod remains bullish, and, around May, with Alpha Centauri entering the house of Mars, sprats could go through the roof. On the night of July 13, however, Jupiter and Neptune are trining Pisces, and the bottom could fall out of squid, with obvious ramifications for the more vulnerable shellfish. But whelks should recover in time for the Autumn Equinox, and an aura will hang over prawns until the end of the year. The Sun opposes Pisces for much of late November, though, and this will give oysters a sense of being at the crossroads; it is a period at which they should make no major decisions, particularly where business is concerned. The Winter Solstice could bring a false sense of security to hake.

 ARIES
(March 21 – April 20)

Major planets are in fire signs throughout the early part of the year, so romance becomes a question of grasping the nettle! Watch out for a tall dark stranger – and do watch rigorously, with four million of you on the lookout, there may well not be enough tall dark strangers to go round, and as Aries is a dignified sign it would be appalling if you were to engage in unseemly public brawls about who got to the tall dark stranger first. This brings me inevitably to a point in thousands of your letters; how tall, I am regularly asked, is a tall dark stranger? Well, these things are all relative, and if he/she is *very* dark then he/she need not be quite so tall. If he/she is fair, then, of course, he/she will have to be commensurately enormous. Then again, it need not matter overmuch if he/she is both short and fair, provided he/she is really very strange indeed.

 TAURUS
(April 21 – May 20)

An uncertain year, I'm afraid, in which Pluto is dominated by quasars and you could well have serious trouble with Uranus. It would thus be a great mistake if you were to engage upon new business enterprises; in fact, as regular readers of this column are well aware, I am *always* chary of recommending Taureans to engage upon new business enterprises. You are somewhat staid and un-imaginative folk, generally lacking a spirit of originality, and the last occasion upon which I suggested making a change in a business direction, four million of you opened tobacconists' shops, with the most appalling economic consequences. However, take heart! The clouds lift briefly on October 3, when Mercury stops moping about and pulls itself together, and it will be safe for you to walk to the pillar-box and back.

 GEMINI
(May 21 – June 20)

I have hinted at Gemini health problems (see *Capricorn* above), and the unfortunate fact of the matter is that in March, when none of your planets is in an air sign, you will go down with croup. Normally, this would present no major difficulty, provided doctors were able to lay their hands on four million bottles of useless brown linctus, but, as we have seen, the profession will simultaneously have to cope with four million Capricorn knees (or, indeed, if the moon still has a chip on its shoulder about Neptune's scepticism concerning the Second Coming of Prester John, eight million). In consequence of this, waiting-rooms will overflow with coughing Geminis and agonised Capricorns screaming at them to shut up, they don't know what real pain is, and as these signs are mutually inimical, anyway, nothing is boded but ill. The only advice I can offer is to find an Aquarian faith-healer, but as the vast majority of these (see *Aquarius* above) will be at sea, it is scant advice indeed. Perhaps it would be best just to turn your mind to something else; if you are tall, dark, or strange, try hanging around on street corners – Arians are going to be getting pretty desperate by March, and may well snap you up, croup or no croup.

 CANCER
(June 21 – July 20)

A relatively calm year. You will put the shelf up in the garage.

 LEO
(July 21 – August 21)

An extraordinary amount of activity among your stars this year! On March 20, the Sun (your ruler) makes a trine to Jupiter (ruler of your health), on March 29, Mercury (ruler of your hopes, wishes and money area) makes a good aspect to Saturn (ruler of your lunch arrangements, car repairs and soft furnishings), throughout April the planet Neptune (ruler of your central heating, library ticket and all gardening requisites) comes under the regular influence of Betelgeuse (ruler of your leisure wear), while during late Autumn, Pluto (ruler of your carport, funeral arrangements, hosiery and dentures) meets very favourably with Audax Minor (ruler of your personal effects to the value of not more than £100 unless specified on a separate sheet). Unfortunately, this leaves them with no time whatever to keep an eye on *you*, so watch out for manholes, lightning, tinned salmon, golf balls, falling masonry, high tide, police marksmen, and, indeed, anything else.

VIRGO
(August 22 – September 22)

Fortunately, the position of Saturn in Virgo throughout the year is very encouraging, since Virgo is one of the earth trinity signs and Saturn is an earth planet, so there is considerable basic harmony there which would not be the case were Virgo, say, the sign for an unmanned level crossing. This harmony means that 1979 is your friendship year, and Virgos should actively go out and seek new contacts. This will not always be easy, of course, since there are only a limited number of new friends to go round: even limiting your-selves to two new friends each, this means eight million people, and as four million Aquarians will be on the high seas, and eight million Capricorns and Geminis suffering from either sore knees or hacking coughs which will have put them in a foul and unresponsive mood, you Virgos are looking at nothing more nor less than about half the population, many of whom may not be friendly types! So be on the *qui vive* – smiling incautiously on the Tube may well bring you a belt in the mouth, extending the hand of friendship in a public place could result in six months without the option, and if you happen to be tall, dark or strange, you could end up lumbered with an Arian who refused to go away.

LIBRA
(September 23 – October 22)

The Sun dips on your graph for most of this year, and the Black Cat lines are unnervingly erratic. While Pluto, which is your sign, can bring money to you, when it is in conjunction with Uranus it becomes unstable, and for much of this year Pluto is also moving through unfavourable financial aspects. These would be enhanced, were Venus not at an ill phase with the Moon, which still has a chip on its shoulder about 1964. All of this means that your financial aura is unprecedently poor: your only chance to make money is between 11.14 and 11.18 pm on May 28. As this is the Spring Bank Holiday, Librans seem to be in for a somewhat lean year.

SCORPIO
(October 23 – November 22)

A truly remarkable 1979 reaches its apogee in early September, when

Mars and Venus combine with Pluto and Saturn to bring you forty of Eve Boswell's biggest hits for only £1.99!

 SAGITTARIUS
(November 23 – December 20)

Throughout 1979, Sagittarians will get gradually fatter. There is nothing you can do about this, since Mars conjoins with Mercury in your house, Saturn is still not speaking to Pluto, and the Moon, with his usual selfishness, is having an early holiday to take advantage of off-peak rates. For those Sagittarians who start the year thin, of course, this need not be too calamitous a forecast, involving your life in little more than letting out a seam or two or wearing vertical stripes to minimise the effect. Heavier Sagittarians will have to resign themselves, however, to strengthening joists, selling the Mini, bulk-buying Ambre Solaire, and visiting marriage guidance counsellors, particularly if Sagittarians have been unwise enough (and against my advice, I might say, over the years) to wed one another. *Very* heavy Sagittarians, mind, may just weather the storm: if they become strange enough, Arian ectomorphs could well become interested. But not before November, at the earliest.

December 1978

After-dinner speaking

Norman Birkett

ON SAYING A FEW WORDS
AFTER DINNER

'Why streams the life-blood from that female throat?
She sprinkled gravy on a guest's new coat.'

THE unknown author of these moving lines was clearly a regular
after-dinner speaker who had lived to see waitresses flitting about the
tables in city banqueting halls and places where they speak. Mr D.B.
Wyndham Lewis has preserved the author's fame in the pages of *The
Stuffed Owl*, and the writer, who seeks to record some of the pains
and pleasures of saying 'a few words after dinner' (as the invitations
go), must feel thankful that his lines provide at least a colourful start.

The good lady who found the lost piece of silver followed tradition
by calling her friends and neighbours together and saying 'Rejoice
with me,' but it does not appear that she made any further speech
when they accepted the invitation. Nowadays when men and women
meet together at a public dinner, whatever the occasion may be, it
seems an almost invariable rule that some speeches should be made,
though there are excellent precedents to the contrary. The Benchers
of the Honourable Society of the Inner Temple when they issue their
invitations to dinner on Grand Night always add the comforting
words – NO SPEECHES. It is said that when Palmerston went to the
Whitebait dinner at Greenwich, at a time when his colleagues were a
little at variance with him, he looked round upon their somewhat
gloomy faces and said with great animation – 'Gentlemen, do you not

think that we ourselves would be
wise to emulate the example of
these wise little fishes and to
drink a great deal but say
nothing.'

Of course it may not have been
Palmerston, for anybody who
attends public dinners with any
regularity, and listens to the
speeches, will be quite accustomed to the confidence or carelessness with which quite famous
sayings are attributed to the
most unlikely people, and how
ancient stories are passed off as
new with some such phrase as –

... has its own ...

'A friend of mine had a curious experience the other day.' Abraham
Lincoln has thus become the reputed author of more amusing
sayings than he could ever have had time to utter in his lifetime, and
F.E. Smith appears to have spent his days in court making devastat-
ing retorts to angry judges and most scathing replies to his opponents, simply to provide some after-dinner speaker with an amusing
and apposite touch with which to adorn his speech.

The sad truth is that there are very few new stories to be told,
though there are many revised versions, and at any public dinner
when a story is revised and revived almost everybody present makes
a note of it for his own future use. This is done quite openly and
without shame, and the pencils race over the menu cards; for there is
a kind of mutual free trade in after-dinner stories based on the belief,
in which there is much truth, that the storyteller of the moment
certainly got it from somebody else. Indeed the very age of the story
can itself form a quite amusing part of an after-dinner speech. For
example, one of the oldest stories known to lawyers is a rather silly
story which runs like this:

> 'There was once a deaf judge, a deaf plaintiff and a deaf
> defendant. When they were all assembled the deaf judge
> said to the plaintiff "You begin." The deaf plaintiff who
> heard nothing but saw that the judge's lips had stopped
> moving thereupon said "My Lord, my claim is a claim for

rent." The judge who heard nothing but saw that the
plaintiff's lips had stopped moving then said to the
defendant "What do you say to that?" The defendant who
had heard nothing at all but saw that the judge's lips had
stopped moving thereupon said "My Lord, how can that
be when I grind my corn at night?" The judge who had
heard nothing at all of all this thereupon said "This is a
most difficult case, but I have come to the conclusion that
she is your mother, and you will both maintain her.'''

In J.W. Mackail's *Select Epigrams from the Greek Anthology* it will be
seen that Nicarchus told that self-same story nineteen hundred years
ago, yet it can still be heard in an after-dinner speech in Chancery
Lane or wherenot. When the diners have gone home with their
scribbled menu cards, it is quite astonishing how quickly the stories
told at one dinner are repeated at another. When the American Bar
Association held its meetings in London in 1957 the Chairman of the
Court of the University of London gave a small private dinner to the
Chief Justice of the United States and other leading legal personalities. Towards the end of dinner the Chairman leaned across the table
and said to Chief Justice Warren 'There will be no speeches, but I
will present the toast of the American Bar Association in a sentence
and you can acknowledge it in the same way.' The Chief Justice
replied 'That suits me very well, for I have always remembered the
saying that "the whale is in no danger of being harpooned except

... rules ...

when he comes up to the surface
to spout".' The Chairman, who
heard the saying for the first time
and liked it, obtained the Chief
Justice's permission to use it,
with acknowledgments, in presenting the toast. Although the
dinner was a private one, the
saying of the Chief Justice
appeared in a surprising number
of after-dinner speeches in the
next few weeks, sometimes with
acknowledgment but more often
without.

But nobody complains, except

when the saying or story is so garbled or distorted that the true effect
is lost. The most popular story for after-dinner would still seem to be
the old and famous story of Daniel in the lion's den, but it is a very
rare thing to hear it told as well as when it was first delivered. In that
magnificent book of legal reminiscences *Pie Powder*, by J.A. Foote,
KC (now long out of print, alas!), the author tells of the occasion when
the story was first told, and it may be well to set the exact language
down on paper. Mr Foote says:

> 'Of Lord Bowen's after-dinner stories the best is prob-
> ably that which I heard him deliver when Mr Justice
> Charles was entertained by the Western Circuit on his
> elevation to the Bench. Every post-prandial orator has
> borrowed it since; but in its original form and delivered
> with Bowen's characteristic voice and manner it was
> inimitable.
>
> '"One of the ancient Rabbinical writers – I have forgot-
> ten his name, but I have no doubt that it can easily be
> ascertained – was engaged in compiling a history of the
> minor prophets; and in due course it became his duty to
> record the history of the prophet Daniel. In speaking of
> the most striking incident in that great man's career – I
> refer to his critical position in the den of lions – he made a
> remark which has always seemed to me to be replete with
> judgment and observation. He said that notwithstanding
> the trying circumstances in which he had been placed, the
> prophet had one consolation which has sometimes been
> forgotten. He had the consolation of knowing that, when
> the dreadful banquet was over, at any rate it was not he
> who would be called upon to return thanks."'

That particular passage reads very well, but as a general rule it is in
after-dinner speaking that the difference between the written and the
spoken word is most marked. Hazlitt has said the last word on this
subject, but it should always be remembered that a speech after
dinner is spoken for that moment only, and the occasion on which
the thing is said with 'the wine and the festal glow', is an essential
part of the performance.

A City dinner in one of the great Livery Companies' halls can be a
very great occasion, possessing that peculiar charm that belongs to
old and cherished institutions. It is here that the great after-dinner

speakers of the past have found their most congenial atmosphere, and high upon the list of masters of the art of after-dinner speaking must come the name of the late Lord Hewart, formerly Lord Chief Justice of England. Many of his best performances are still repeated as examples of wit or humour or grace and lucidity of speech. Observe the subtlety and skill with which, on an occasion when he was replying to the toast of The Guests, he created the atmosphere he needed for his purpose. He began by saying that no after-dinner speaker should reply to the toast of The Guests without doing three things. He must speak of the importance of the occasion. This done, he should then speak of the weakness of the chosen vessel; and then, if time should permit, he should say a few words about the toast itself. In speaking of the weakness of the chosen vessel he said that he was sorry that he had nothing new to say in replying to a toast that was so esteemed by all the City companies, and recalled with great envy the happy state of a speaker he had heard perform the duty at an earlier dinner. This gentleman had protested in none too steady a voice that the hospitality of the Company had been so lavish and he had partaken of it so freely that he could not now remember the name of the Company that had invited him. He had then shaded his eyes and peered across the room, and seeing on the wall a picture of Venus, had said with sudden firmness 'But, Master, it would appear that it is not the Drapers' Company – though perhaps it may be the Skinners.'

Perhaps Lord Hewart's greatest triumph was at the Mansion House at the Lord Mayor's dinner to Her Majesty's Judges when his speech consisted of a very few words indeed. To be called on at a very late hour when many speeches have been made is perhaps the most difficult situation any after-dinner speaker can have to face. Many of

... and they must be observed.

the diners are hurrying from the hall before the speaker rises so that they can catch the last train home, and there is a general air of having-had-enough-speaking-for-one-night abroad. This was the situation when Hewart rose to reply for Her Majesty's Judges. To a rather weary audience he opened by saying that he had feared this situation might come about and that he would be called on at a late hour, and he had therefore prepared two speeches to be ready to meet the situation whatever it might be. One speech was a short speech, the other one was a little longer. He had been considering what he should do. (Here the audience settled down for a moment in the expectation that he would say that he proposed to give the short speech.) He then announced that he had decided to deliver them both. (Here the audience uttered a long, loud collective sigh.) Lord Hewart then went on – 'I will begin with the short one which was "Thank you," and I will also give the longer one which was "Thank you very much."' He then sat down to the loudest applause of the evening.

But it is not only the great and practised speakers who win after-dinner triumphs. It has fallen to my lot to hear most of the speakers in London at almost every kind of gathering. Cricket dinners have a special charm of their own, and a speaker like Patsy Hendren can make a fascinating speech full of interest and bubbling over with humour. By his natural manner he has the power to capture his audience in the first few minutes, the ideal to which all after-dinner speakers aspire. He once had to speak after some very accomplished performers had taken up a great part of the evening and opened with these words: 'You can't expect me to stand comparison with these professionals you've just heard – after all I've only been two terms at Harrow.' Patsy Hendren had, of course, at that time recently taken up his duties as coach at Harrow School.

In England the scarlet-coated toastmaster confines himself as a rule to a general prayer for silence for each successive speaker. The toastmaster in the United States is apt to take charge of the whole proceedings. His duties are best illustrated by the familiar story of the chairman who, in introducing the guest speaker of the evening, made what was, even as such speeches go, an oration of exceptional length and tedium. The distinguished guest began to nod and the toastmaster, to keep him awake, tapped him gently with his gavel. But the speaker still went relentlessly on until the guest really fell asleep. The toastmaster then tapped him quite sharply on the head, and the distinguished guest awoke and said in a loud clear voice 'Hit me again, I can still hear him.'

After-dinner speaking has its own rules, and they must be observed. The diners are gathered for amusement and pleasure. They are happily relaxed, usually in the company of old friends, and the speeches that are most welcome are those that are light and bright and entertaining. Very few people can maintain this standard for more than ten minutes. The ideal speech, as well as being short, gives the impression of absolute spontaneity, an effect that is usually achieved by the speaker's toiling throughout the previous night. Preparation there *must* be, for, as Lord Hewart observed in one of his famous speeches, 'Extempore speeches are rarely worth the paper they are written on.'

November 1959

George Grossmith

THE DIARY OF A NOBODY

Sunday, November 4. – CARRIE and I troubled about that mere boy LUPIN getting engaged to be married without consulting us or anything. After dinner he told us all about it. He said the lady's name was DAISY MUTLAR, and she was the nicest, prettiest, and most accomplished girl he ever met. He loved her the moment he saw her, and if he had to wait fifty years he would wait, and he knew she would wait for him. LUPIN further said, with much warmth, that the world was a different world to him now, – it was a world worth living in. He lived with an object now, and that was to make DAISY MUTLAR – DAISY POOTER, and he would guarantee she would not disgrace the family of the POOTERS. CARRIE here burst out crying, and threw her arms round his neck, and in doing so, upset the glass of port he held in his hands all over his new light trousers. I said I had no doubt we should like Miss MUTLAR when we saw her, but CARRIE said she loved her already. I thought this rather premature, but held my tongue. DAISY MUTLAR was the sole topic of conversation for the remainder of the day. I asked LUPIN who her people were, and he replied, 'Oh, you know MUTLAR, WILLIAMS AND WATTS.' I did not know, but refrained from asking further questions, at present, for fear of irritating LUPIN.

November 5. – LUPIN went with me to the office, and had a long conversation with Mr PERKUPP, our principal, the result of which was that he accepted a clerkship in the firm of JOB CLEANANDS AND Co., Stock and Sharebrokers. LUPIN told me, privately, it was an advertising firm, and he did not think much of it. I replied, 'Beggars should not be choosers;' and I will do LUPIN the justice to say, he looked rather ashamed of himself. In the evening we went round to the CUMMINGS', to have a few fireworks. It began to rain, and I thought it rather dull. One of my squibs would not go off, and GOWING said, 'Hit it on your boot, boy; it will go off then.' I gave it a few knocks on the end of my boot, and it went off with one loud explosion, and burnt my fingers rather badly. I gave the rest of my squibs to the little CUMMINGS boy, to let off. Another unfortunate thing happened, which brought a heap of abuse on my head. CUMMINGS fastened a large wheel set-piece on a stake in the ground by way of a grand finale. He made a great fuss about it; said it cost seven shillings. There was a little difficulty in getting it alight. At last it went off, but, after a couple of slow revolutions, it stopped. I had my stick with me, so I gave it a tap to send it round, and, unfortunately, it fell off the stake on to the grass. Anybody would have thought I had set the house on fire from the way in which they stormed at me. I will never join in any more firework parties. It is a ridiculous waste of time and money.

November 6. – LUPIN asked CARRIE to call on Mrs MUTLAR, but CARRIE said she thought Mrs MUTLAR ought to call on her first. I agreed with CARRIE, and this led to an argument. However, the matter was settled by CARRIE saying she could not find any visiting-cards, and we must get some more printed, and when they were finished would be quite time enough to discuss the etiquette of calling.

November 7. – I ordered some of our cards at BLACK's, the Stationers. I ordered twenty-five of each, which will last us for a good long time. In the evening, LUPIN brought in HARRY MUTLAR, Miss MUTLAR's brother. He was rather a gawky youth, and LUPIN said he was the most popular and best amateur in the Club, referring to the 'Holloway Comedians'. LUPIN whispered to us that if we could only 'draw out' HARRY a bit, he would make us roar with laughter. At supper, young MUTLAR did several amusing things. He took up a

knife, and with the flat part of it, played a tune on his cheek in a
wonderful manner. He also gave an imitation of an old man with no
teeth, smoking a big cigar. The way he kept dropping the cigar sent
CARRIE into fits. In the course of conversation, DAISY's name
cropped up, and young MUTLAR said he would bring his sister round
to us one evening – his parents being rather old-fashioned, and not
going out much. CARRIE said we would get up a little special party.
As young MUTLAR showed no inclination to go, and it was approaching eleven o'clock, as a hint I reminded LUPIN that he had to be up
early tomorrow. Instead of taking the hint, MUTLAR began a series of
comic imitations. He went on for an hour without cessation. Poor
CARRIE could scarcely keep her eyes open. At last she made an
excuse, and said 'Good-night.' MUTLAR then left, and I heard him
and LUPIN whispering in the hall, something about the 'Holloway
Comedians', and to my disgust, although it was past midnight,
LUPIN put on his hat and coat, and went out with his new companion.

November 1888

Susan Jeffreys

FLAMENCO

WHEN I got to the *Instituto* I was sweating like *un puerco*. It was hot
that summer and I had run with the buses. That thing with the buses
when you run for one and do not catch it so you run to the next stop
and do not catch another bus until in the end you have saved yourself
the fare.

'The courses started last week,' said the official one behind the
desk. 'If you wish to do Cake Maintenance, Smocking for Weight
Control or English as a Second Helping, you are too late. These
classes are all full.'

'I do not want such classes, *camarada*. I wish to learn the flamenco.'

'Do you reap the bitter harvest of *los giros* or are you on *el regular
earner*?'

'A bit of this, a bit of that,' I answered.

'Then you must pay the full fee.'

'Take it,' I said and threw the money at him, 'but I will do only the summer course.'

'That is what they all say,' he replied as he swept the money into a drawer and locked it. 'But you will become like the others. Obsessed.'

I went to the hall where they did the flamenco, it was empty. From the room above came the urgent, rhythmic hammerings of the upholstery class. Terrible gaspings came from the courtyard below where unfit men played five-a-side football. The evening sun streamed in through the windows, blood red across the sand in the *balde de fuego*, the fire bucket.

An *inglés* came into the hall, he was pale and wore glasses. He unbuttoned his shirt so that his string vest showed. He took out a handkerchief and tied a knot in each corner. He put the handkerchief on his head.

'*¡Madre de Dios!*' I said. 'Is this how you dress for the flamenco?'

'Well, I get sweaty,' he said and rolled down his socks.

Two more *ingleses* came into the hall. They carried plastic bags from Waitrose.

'*Salud*,' said the one in the string vest.

'*Salud*,' they replied and took out shoes from the bags. The woman's shoes had steel on the heels and toes. The soles of the man's were studded with small silver nails.

'Do you practise much?' I asked.

'*¡Nah! ¡*Leave off!' they said. 'We live in a maisonette.'

More people came into the room; they greeted each other and were friendly and pleasant.

My heart sank. I was hoping for blood feuds, card reading and perhaps a knife fight. I had hoped for hooped ear-rings, tight trousers and yards of black lace but these people shopped at Marks and Spencer. They were *gente bastante regular*, ordinary people.

I got up to leave; as I did so, three *hombres* came into the hall. They carried guitars and reeked of garlic. Their cheek-bones were sharp as blades and their sideburns met under their chins. My heart rose and I sat down again.

They began to tune the strings of their guitars. One of them took a thin *cigarito* from the corner of his mouth and parked it on the neck of his guitar. He leaned towards the others and hissed, 'I see that Arsenal have signed Charlie Nicholas.'

'*¡Mierda!*' I thought. 'I will learn *nada* here, I have thrown away

my money for nothing. I obscenity on your Adult Education.' In
disgust I turned to look down into the courtyard where the unfit men
were playing five-a-side football. One of them seemed to be dying,
with little dignity and no priest.

When I turned my head again the *profesor de flamenco* had arrived.
He wore flared trousers and plimsolls. He looked Welsh. Again I got
up to leave. If I had left the room then I would still be *una mujer libre*,
a free woman. But the way was blocked, I was trapped in the room
and now am trapped in an obsession.

What happened next was like that thing with Clark Kent and the
telephone booth. The class barred the doorway, very straight and
still. The *profesor* clapped
his hands, the guitarists
struck a chord and the *gente
bastante regular* were trans-
formed. Smouldering fire
burnt in the eyes of women
who had entered the hall
respectable matrons. *Macho*
arrogance oozed from every
pore of men who had seem-
ed mild-mannered. The
man and the woman with
the steel-bottomed shoes
looked as if they slept in the
cold, open field and had
never been in a maisonette
in their lives.

As for the *hombre* in the
string vest, he was like a
tiger. Every movement he
made seemed fierce yet
graceful, he looked lithe
and dangerous. Even his
string vest looked virile.

With a rhythmic
zapaedo the class
swept across the
floor past the fire
buckets, drowning

out the noise of the upholstery class and the five-a-side football. Their fingers snapped and their eyes flashed. They clapped their hands and slapped their thighs. They were not the *gente bastante regular* who had first come into the hall.

I stood on my chair and shouted '*¡Ole!* ¡Triff and brill! ¡Keep it up, chaps!' as the dance reached its climax.

When it was finished I went up to the *profesor de flamenco*. I approached with great respect, he was no *hombre regular*.

'Can you teach me to do that?' I asked.

'Well, it's a bit tricky, see,' he said, 'but we'll have a bash. You need to practise, mind.'

And he was right. You must practise often if you wish to clap with the dry, sharp sound of the *palmada* and at the same time stamp out the rhythm with the feet. I practise much, usually in bus queues. I keep warm and soon get the stop to myself.

I am not good at the *pito*, the finger-snapping. All the fingers on both hands must make a loud sound if it is to be done well. With the right hand it is not too bad but the left has the resonance of a bunch of bananas. I practise all the time even in bed and now live a life of great solitude.

For me the *caida* is nothing. It is that moment in the dance when the rhythm is at its most furious and the dancer falls flat on the face. For me this is easy, but I have much work to do on the *getting up again in the same breath-taking moment*.

I like to do the hammerstep. For this you must jump forward on to your left toe and slam the right heel down behind it. It is a powerful step and banned above ground level in all Adult Education *Institutos*. It pulls the floor away from the walls. A team of flamenco anarchists could destroy every bridge in London. I practise it wherever I find a parquet floor.

But there is one thing I can never master however much I practise: *el haughty look*. For this you must stand very straight and look over the cheek-bones to the proud swell of the bosom. I practise all the time but all I can ever see is my feet.

Why do I do this thing? Why spend all my spare time stamping and twitching and my spare cash at the shoe menders? Why do the rest of the class do it?

There is a printer who started so that he could keep his back from stooping and some nurses who find it gets rid of the tension that comes from being nice all day. There is a man joined because he could not get into the photography class and some more who joined either because they saw *Carmen* or take their holidays in Spain. But these excuses are not the real reason.

I pretend I learn the flamenco for that time when I am an old one and take the Senior Citizens Winter Break to Spain. In those times I will wear tweeds, thick stockings and sensible shoes. The flamenco dancer who will be brought in to entertain the old *inglesa* will see me and choose me to be his partner to make a fool of me. But I will be magnificent. I will whip out my false teeth and as they chatter out the rhythm, my stout brogues will stamp out the *taconeo*.

But this is also an excuse. It is not the truth. For the truth is that the flamenco is a drug and once you have spent an evening sweating, stamping and oléing you wish to spend all your evenings doing it. Every time you master a step you have an appetite for a harder step. Each dance you learn makes you all the hungrier to learn a new one. It serves no purpose. It is an obsession.

But at least it got me off jigsaw puzzles.

January 1985

Paul Dehn

SCHOTTO BOTTLED

ADVERTISING in a recent issue of the *New Yorker*, Messrs Barton and Guestier (Wine Merchants Inc.) have undertaken the enlightened task of introducing their clientèle to certain European wines which many an American has either never heard of or (if we may credit rumour) is too frightened to order on the telephone for fear of mispronouncing. The advertisement contains the following list:

So tairn.	Shah blee.
May dock.	Mah kon.
Bow Joe lay.	Mawn rah shay.
Poo yee Fweesay.	Poe mahr.
Schotto Neff du Pop.	Grahv.

Sant Ay mee lee on.

Literate Europeans and Orientals will, of course, recognize at once the titles of eleven comparatively well-known national Drinking

Songs. But I wonder how many Americans will know the words (or, indeed, the meaning) of these 'ditties' that Messrs Barton and Guestier are obviously recommending their clients to sing, while the unfamiliar bottle goes round the table. It is for their benefit that I take the liberty of adding an explanatory 'gloss' on some of the better-known songs.

So tairn became popular in Scotland about 1796:

> *So tairn frae yon stuir,*
> *An' glauer me the tassie.*
> *Wha helpit the puir*
> *Nae gowaned a lassie!*
>
> *Nae gowaned a mither*
> *Wha whelpit a bairn!*
> *We'll quecht it thegither, –*
> *So tairn, lassie, tairn!*

[*stuir:* mess. *glaur:* toss. *tassie:* utensil. *gowaned:* solicited (*sc.* for advice). *quecht: turpitudinem alicui per vim inferre.*]

The ladies (or 'lassies') should courteously *turn* as each man drinks the wine from his individual utensil. The piece has been translated into Lallans by Sidney Goodsir Smith, but the original is the simpler version.

May Dock is a fourteenth-century English wassail song. The words of these often had very little relevance to the act of drinking, until they resolved into the rollicking chorus that was wassail's happiest convention:

> *Sith May dock blowe,*
> *We schal hav snowe*
> *When bulluc lowe*
> *Wid windes snell.*
>
> *Ac fadeth May dock*
> *In fold and padock,*
> *Ne holt ne hadock*
> *Moun swete smell.*
>
> *Then troll the boll, boteler ... etc.*

[*snell:* painful. *hadock:* haycock; not (as Quiller-Couch in *The*

Oxford Book of English Verse) haddock.]
  Bow Joe Lay is a straight eighteenth-century drinking shanty:

> *'Twere nor' nor' west from Port o' Brest*
>   *(Yare, yare and away!)*
> *That hard abaft the scupper-tholes*
>   *Bow Joe lay.*
>
>> *With a ho, Joe! Blow, Joe!*
>>   *Row me round the bay.*
>> *Fill us a tot and wet the spot*
>>   *Where Bow Joe lay.*

Bow Joe has never been satisfactorily identified. Some hold that
'bow' refers to the shape of his limbs and is an *ellipsis* for 'bow-legged
Joe'; others, that it is a corruption of Fr. *beau* and that, for a naval
man, he was singularly beautiful.

Poo-yee Fweesay is a Chinese *haiku* (circ. 5080 B.C.) and should
strictly be sung only when drinking wine that has been distilled from
rice.

> *Poo-yee fweesay,*
> *Ori-tamac!*
> *Nao, nao, hou han shi.*
> *Shan-kuci fweesay, ho tsai yü.*
>
> *Princess Poo-yee,*
> *Come down!*
> *Nao, nao, blows the autumn wind.*
> *I long for a royal lady, but dare not speak.*

(*tr.* Arthur Waley)

The author Po, is said to have died of drink.
  Schotto Neff, Du, Pop? is a traditional Yiddish lament still sung,
over a glass of *klatsch* on the Sabbath, by the descendants of those
Jews who were driven from the Great Ghetto of Neff by edict of Czar
Nicholas at the turn of the nineteenth century.

> *'Schotto Neff, du, Pop?*
> *Schotto Neff, du, Pop?'*
> *'Weh, weh, bontsche schnee!*
> *Schot' woh' Neff dein Pop.'*

> *'Dost remember Neff, thou, mine father?*
> *Dost remember Neff, thou, mine father?'*
> *'Woe, woe! Silent snow!*
> *Remembers well Neff thine father.'*

With the words of the remaining songs I am unfamiliar, though any reasonably experienced folklorist will recognize the titles.

Sant Ay, Mee Lee On was first sung in French by a group of seventeenth-century Catholic missionaries far from their home village ('St Ay, white-roofed, still calls ...') and translated by their Hawaiian converts, whose descendants sing it to this very day – though its regional significance has long been forgotten and it is sung chiefly during beach-banquets arranged at moderate cost for the tourist trade. I am indebted to the *Guide Michelin* for a comprehensive note on modern St Ay:

> **ST-AY** Loiret. ●-① - 620 h. Alt. 100 - ⚓🏨⚐. -
> 🚗 Bouguereau. 🅝 🅿⚓

Shah Blee is a loyal toast from the fourth-century Persian; *Mah Kon*, a popular Siamese love-song; *Mawn Ray Shay*, a ritualistic Hindu invocation to Rah Shay (King Breath), which is not really a drinking song at all, unless Messrs Barton and Guestier have actually bottled the waters of the Ganges; *Poe Mahr* (more correctly *Po Mahr*: 'A little more!'), a *skjemtsang* (joke-song) in which second-year students of Upsala University induct freshmen into the joys of Aquavit; and *Grahv*, a Latvian dirge.

A good list, on the whole, though there are notable omissions. What of the Tibetan *Ahman Yak*? Or that festive group of Italo-Yugoslav *canzonette della frontiera* compositely called *Romanay Contee* (Tales of the Gypsies)? Or the bitter little Trinidad calypso, *Ma, go!*? Or the evergreen *Arnjew*:

> *Arnjew de kutiest*
> *Butiest frutiest*
> *Beibi –*
> *Arnjew?*

But this, on second thoughts, is still in current usage among certain irredentist minorities all over America. The Vanderbilts are said to sing it in family conclave once yearly. New York (one so easily forgets) used to be Nieuw Amsterdam.

March 1955

Mark Bevan

HOLD
MY
COAT ...!

FEW
Articles of attire
Arouse my ire,
Get my goat
Or generally ruffle
Me
To the same degree
As the duffle
Coat.
True,
Should one cower

On the poop
Of some sloop
Or on a conning-tower
Caked with ice,
To draw a cowl
Round one's stubbly
Jowl
Must be doubly
Nice.
Moreover, whatever
    prejudice lingers,
One must succumb
To the view
That numb
Fingers
In a mitten
Would soon be frost-bitten
As mutton
Unless spared
Being bared
To seek the conventional
    button.
While I do not care for,
I must, therefore,
Accept those toggles ...
But one's sense of life's fitnesses
Boggles

When one witnesses
Such raiment
On strollers
Wearing bowlers
(Above pale faces
And tanned dispatch cases)
Hesitating
On the pavement,
Umbrella in hand,
Prior to navigating
The Strand.

February 1982

George Mikes

HOW TO BE IMPORTANT

THE Importance of Being Important is one of the great, new sciences
of this scientific age of ours. It is not to be mixed up (as, regrettably,
it often is) with Snobology (the science of How to be a Snob) or
Braggology (the Art of Showing Off) or Pompology (How to be a
Pompous Ass). Each of these studies has its well deserved and
honourable place in the World of Science. But Fussology (as the
Importance of Being Important is sometimes referred to briefly and
somewhat casually in the Science Report of *The Times*) is a novel and
fast-growing science in its own right. Professor Pilkerton-Stockdale-
Winn, the greatest living Fussologist, told me of a simple but most
effective importance-test: 'Would the British Government send a
destroyer to rescue you?'

The Professor has, in fact, touched on a very sore point. I had been
in trouble in Hungary a few months before but in vain did I scan the
horizon, no British destroyers were sailing down the Danube. I
found this even more galling because the most notorious incident in
Palmerston's career – when the crew of a British gunboat was sent to
whip a recalcitrant African chieftain – occurred to avenge some
minor impertinence committed against a *naturalised* British subject.
A Portuguese, not even a Hungarian. Be that as it may, my colleague's question started a train of thought. 'Is it possible that
naturalised British subjects have declined in importance? Or is it
possible that Britain herself has declined in importance and that I
missed my boat, or rather my gunboat, by a century?'

It would be impossible to sum up the result of vast researches on
these pages, so some indications must suffice. In the academic world
it is decisively important to be invited as a Research Fellow to

(preferably) an American University and receive a staggeringly high salary. Luckily, it is not too difficult. 'Research' in nine cases out of ten is another word for doing nothing but how much more cultured and academic a word it is. The longer you bask in the Californian sun at somebody else's expense, the greater a scholar you will be deemed to be.

A writer must be *quoted*. To write and address your readership directly is nothing, after all that's a writer's job. But to be quoted by others makes you important. I have been quoted dozens of times as having said this: 'A Hungarian is a man who is behind you in a revolving door but gets out in front of you,' a saying I have never said. But that's beside the point. To have something *attributed* to you, reflects even more glory (Prof. P.-S.-W. told me) and is incomparably better than to be quoted on something you have actually said.

A union leader is really important if he can call large, long and disastrous strikes. Strikes which do not really damage the national economy are not much good. On the other end of the economic scale, an executive has really made it as soon as he has got his own private lavatory. Not just to have the *key* to the executive loo – that's nothing. He must have his own private and exclusive loo. To be able to invite the president of a rival (or even larger) company, visiting him, a president who may not have thought yet of installing his own accommodation for a truly private ... what I mean to use his private loo, is not far short of heaven.

It is, and remains forever, essential to be known and revered by headwaiters and top-hatted hotel-porters. I often feel that the sole function of these top-hatted liveried porters is to make others feel important – thus they themselves rank among the most important members of humanity.

I knew a headwaiter in Vaucluse, France, who, whenever a middle-aged man appeared with a young woman, asked for his permission to taste the wine for him. He did so and shook his head in slight disapproval. The man, having tasted it himself in the meantime, said modestly that it was quite good, really. 'Very good indeed, Sir, for everybody else; but not for *you*.' The headwaiter took out the offending bottle, sealed it again with a new cork, returned to the table, took out Cork No. 2 from Bottle No. 1, tasted it again, smacked his lips with delight and said: 'Yes. That's the wine for *you*, Sir.' At the age of forty-two he retired with a fortune. He was a great headwaiter; and even a greater student of the human psyche.

Rules like that have remained unchanged throughout the ages. But the actual importance of people – the pecking order – keeps changing. I find that to be the *friend of a lord* still amounts to something; to be a lord is nothing. If it is a title, it must be Duke. One of the few members of the aristocracy I know well, told me: 'I was born a lord; later I was a marquess; now I am a Duke. I laboured under the mistaken impression that I have always been the one and the same person. Not at all. As a lord and a marquess I was nobody; as a Duke I'm semi-divine.'

A modern Captain of Koepenick would be arrested, worse, laughed out of existence in no time, not only in Britain but even more in Germany. To be an army officer carries no prestige. The glory of the film-star has declined and the film-caesar's place has been taken by the faceless banker. Artists, painters, writers, etc., lost no prestige because they had no prestige to lose. To be an 'executive' meant something for a few years (under strong American influence, here it goes against the grain) but since everyone in business is an executive nowadays, people find it difficult – and utterly boring and pointless – to distinguish between the executive who sells bananas from a stall in Clapham and the executive who runs ICI.

So how do we stand today? How to be important in 1971?

(1) Money is still good (although after the Rolls-Royce case, bankruptcy, too, has a certain snob appeal). It does not stink any more as it did in the distant past. A truly rich manufacturer of plastic mugs or deodorants ranks high above a medium-rich squire in a manor-house. But the rich man must be rich; we have accepted the Texan ideas of rich millionaires and poor millionaires. A poor millionaire – an impecunious chap with just a million or two – doesn't cut much of a figure.

(2) Criminals are in but once again they must be top of their class. A con-man who has cheated poor people out of millions or a train-robber on the run is a highly esteemed member of our society.

(3) A new power-group is emerging slowly, almost unnoticed: interior decorators, stage-designers and – above all – fashion designers who dictate to us, have power to form our lives and decide whether we are allowed to see women's knees. And things like that.

(4) Television shows no sign of declining. To show your face on the telly ennobles you. Television news-readers (nice enough chaps,

to be sure, usually without any particular skill, let alone talent), are more highly esteemed and much better known than the Speaker of the House of Commons. And when the Prime Minister faces an ill-mannered and arrogant television-interviewer, a journalist of average skill and intelligence, there is little doubt who is the master and who is on the carpet. I heartily approve of all that. Whenever I am given a chance of showing my face on television for a fleeting moment, I become the King of Fulham for twenty-four hours. I am treated with awe by the greengrocer and revered by the butcher. Luckily (I really mean unfortunately) there are too many faces shown on television and my glory passes in a day or two.

Look important, that's the trick. I saw once a most magnificent, impressive, arrogant, exalted figure completely deflated in the lobby of Claridges when a man walked up to him and asked: 'Excuse me, Sir, but are you anybody in particular?' It was all his fault, of course, because the question made him collapse. Had he smiled benevolently and mysteriously, making the enquirer understand, without actually uttering one single word, that he might be the Shah of Persia, the Dalai Lama or even Engelbert Humperdinck himself, he would have gloriously weathered the storm.

Many years ago, before my first book was published in English, and before any English person could possibly have heard of my existence, I gave a talk to Hungarians in Hungarian in a Club, near Piccadilly Circus. As soon as the talk was over, I had to dash away. One man, who, for mysterious reasons, wanted my autograph, ran for me, caught me in the street and placed a piece of paper on the bonnet of my car where I signed it. Two or three others who had listened to the talk followed suit. I signed my name obediently and was completely taken aback by this attention paid to me. When I looked up there was an endless queue of passers-by all clamouring for my autograph. I heard one or two ask who I was. No one knew. But even when one or two of them were told my name by some Hungarians, they persisted. Others wanted my autograph and, God knows, the opportunity to get it might never recur. Alas, the police soon charged and dispersed the crowd in order to reopen Windmill Street to traffic. It was my finest hour. Well, my finest ten minutes.

February 1971

Patrick Barrington

SONGS OF A SUB-MAN

I HAD A HIPPOPOTAMUS

I HAD a hippopotamus; I kept him in a shed
And fed him upon vitamins and vegetable bread;
I made him my companion on many cheery walks
And had his portrait done by a celebrity in chalks.

His charming eccentricities were known on every side,
The creature's popularity was wonderfully wide;
He frolicked with the Rector in a dozen friendly tussles,
Who could not but remark upon his hippopotamuscles.

If he should be afflicted by depression or the dumps,
By hippopotameasles or the hippopotamumps,
I never knew a particle of peace till it was plain
He was hippopotamasticating properly again.

I had a hippopotamus; I loved him as a friend;
But beautiful relationships are bound to have an end.
Time takes, alas! our joys from us and robs us of our blisses;
My hippopotamus turned out a hippopotamissis.

My housekeeper regarded him with jaundice in her eye;
She did not want a colony of hippopotami;
She borrowed a machine-gun from her soldier-nephew, Percy,
And showed my hippopotamus no hippopotamercy.

My house now lacks the glamour that the charming creature gave,
The garage where I kept him is as silent as the grave;
No longer he displays among the motor-tyres and spanners
His hippopotamastery of hippopotamanners.

No longer now he gambols in the orchard in the Spring;
No longer do I lead him through the village on a string;
No longer in the mornings does the neighbourhood rejoice
To his hippopotamusically-modulated voice.

I had a hippopotamus; but nothing upon earth
Is constant in its happiness or lasting in its mirth.
No joy that life can give me can be strong enough to smother
My sorrow for that might-have-been-a-hippopotamother.

June 1933

Stanley Reynolds

SOUTH
OF THE
BORDER

JEEVES was always going to something called 'subscription dances' in Camberwell. That was between the wars. Much earlier than that, in the 1880s, George Bernard Shaw, for some extraordinary reason, got quite cross when someone suggested that Camberwell was in the suburbs. This was not true at all, the great man said. Camberwell was, he said, Bloomsbury transported across the river. Not the suburbs but 'a genteel slum', said GBS.

I often think of Jeeves and GBS as I pick my way across Camberwell Green, carefully stepping over the chaps who seem to gather there each day of fine weather for sherry parties. But most of the time I think of the Editor of the *Guardian* who is a neighbour of mine and who suggested, when I moved down to London from Liverpool four years ago, that I set up in Camberwell. Misery, I have often thought since then, truly does love company.

But Shaw was right. Camberwell is both genteel and a slum. But should a man who managed to spend twenty years in Liverpool complain about South London? Well, just as folk in the metropolis do not understand the provinces, we of the Smoky North do not understand London. For most of my years in Liverpool I lived in a house that had been built as a bishop's palace, set in the middle of a park where hardly ever a word of Scouse was heard and where, even though we shared an MP with Toxteth, one could go for months without setting eyes upon the angry lumpenproletariat, white or dusky.

I had no idea that nowhere in South London is free from blight. Step from the unequalled charm of South London's Cleaver Square and there it is, all around you, hideous, appalling, crumbling houses and stunted people; a crime against architecture and a sin against humanity. You remember how it was when you first came up or down to London, looking for a place to live, staggering about in a daze, the compass broken, with no bearings, how easily you were seduced by the pleasant street full of trees or the one house, like the one good tooth in a mouth full of decay. You see the one good house and turn a blind eye to the rest; like the husband of a loved but wayward wife.

The house I bought belonged to no less a grand and beautiful couple than Albert Finney and Diana Quick, Lady Julia out of *Brideshead Revisited*. Neville Chamberlain once lived in the street. Boris Karloff was born there, in 1887, as William Pratt. We have something called the Camberwell Society which sells Christmas cards and postcards of scenic old Camberwell, which we send to one another. So far I haven't been to a subscription dance, but Christ knows how many times I've been to the police station. Five break-ins last year alone.

The last one was a real beauty, a real Camberwell Beauty. The car wasn't in its usual place so my friendly neighbourhood burglars thought I was out when I was upstairs in bed, turning into a pacifist as I read a book about the horrors of nuclear war. But allow me to set the scene.

I was in bed wearing my major-general's greatcoat, an American Civil War Union Army greatcoat which has been in the family ever since great-great-grandad, for some reason best known to himself, went out and freed the slaves – and which I use as a dressing-gown. Suddenly I heard footsteps on the stairs. Thinking this was merely my baby coming home to me, I continued reading the pacifist tract. Then I heard what sounded like more footsteps. But I thought it was merely my baby coming in on all fours, again. Then I counted them. There was no way my baby had six feet.

How quickly one acts in a situation like that! They had come in before. God knows how many times. But I was never in. You wonder what you'd do if they came when you were there. I heard of a man who opened his wardrobe door to find a six-foot-three-inch West Indian standing there. Quick as a flash the man asked, 'Would you like a cup of tea?' 'No, man,' the West Indian said, 'I gotta be runnin' a-long.'

I like to think that I shouted 'Charge!' or maybe even 'Banzai!' I rather suspect it came out more as 'Arrggggh!' as I grabbed the baseball bat and had at them, chasing them down the stairs, thinking all the time, 'This is why you left America all those years ago! This is the reason you are not living in New York!'

And the bandits? What fear a military figure like mine must have struck into them! They thought it was hilarious. They turned to see how close I was in pursuit, saw the major-general's greatcoat and they started to laugh. Not even laugh. They were giggling, all the way into the garage, which is built into the house, and where I had them trapped while I dialled 999.

Of course I didn't have them trapped at all. That was the way they had come in. They managed to break right through a steel garage door.

'They'll get through anything, sir,' one of the coppers said as we all stood round in the cold, looking at the smashed door. At least *I* was looking at the door. The cops were looking at me, in the general's coat, with these ridiculous pyjama-legs coming out of it, and out of the pyjama-bottoms my ridiculous, big, white bare feet. The police were giggling, too. 'Hey, Bill,' I heard one of them say in a stage whisper, 'come on in and see this.'

They were black that night but they could have just as easily been white. Ever since I moved to Camberwell I've been swotting up on the social history of South London and it has always been a den of thieves. In Victorian times it was even worse than now. Lambeth was particularly bad, full of slums and gangs and prostitution. Lambeth has been cleaned up; we go to Lambeth to wine bars and restaurants, and soon we'll be going to the Old Vic again.

Brixton, just round the corner from my place in Camberwell, has that jolly market along Electric Avenue – famous now in a pop song – and we go there because it has the best fishmonger in South London and a lot of local colour and good times, really, unless something sudden happens or it gets dark.

You cannot walk the streets of Brixton from, say 10 P.M. to 3 A.M. without getting mugged. It doesn't matter what colour you are, you'll get mugged. Lambeth has been restored to civilised life. But Brixton, once full of music halls, a place of lovely, tucked-away, little squares with prim Victorian houses, where theatricals loved to live in

order to be close to the West End and on the road to Brighton, is lost
to civilisation once the street lights go on.

No place in South London is safe from burglars or the muggers
suddenly leaping out at you. The poor, innocent Camberwell Society
fought an heroic but, thank God, vain battle recently to have South-
wark council put replica Victorian lamplights in my street. How
much light would they have shed on the muggers?

And what of those beautiful trees that line the street and which
first won my heart over to it that snowy day in February, just four
years ago this week, on Valentine's Day, in fact, when I first set eyes
upon the Grove and fell in love at first sight, thinking, 'How like a
Christmas card it looks!' and 'Won't it be lovely in the spring?'

In a horrible vision of a future South London I see these trees
being cut down because of the hiding place they offer the muggers,
waiting to spring on you as they did on a dear old lady neighbour of
mine, who might possibly walk out of the house again, some day.

One fine day, in the height of summer, I came home from work to
find they had been in again. But nothing was taken. Then I went to
close the back door and the door was gone. Obviously someone had
smashed their own door and they needed another. They eke out a
modest living in South London robbing each other. A girl I know in
Brixton, who says she has been broken into so many times she could
not possibly add them all up, came home and saw they had got in
once more but they hadn't taken anything. Then she went to put a
record on the hi-fi and nothing happened. They had come to get a
new needle.

Another girl was walking home alone at night in South London
when three of them were suddenly surrounding her. She was a
Guardian woman. 'Why don't you piss off and join the police where
you belong?' she said. They stood there, sort of puzzled, and let her
past. Which leads me to the police. They never seem to catch any of
the burglars, but they always manage to seem interested when they
come round after a bit of banditry. What I'm more worried about are
my neighbours. When you've been done enough times you realise
they know your every move. You realise that the neighbours do not
dial 999 when the bandits are breaking into your house in broad
daylight because it is the neighbours who are breaking in.

This fact would seem to undermine any hopes for the Home
Secretary's new neighbourhood police-support scheme in South

London. The neighbourhood scheme, announced in Parliament two weeks ago, is not, Sir Kenneth Newman, the Metropolitan Police Commissioner, is quick to say, the setting up of vigilantes. What he and the Home Secretary have in mind is a neighbourhood committee composed of a local copper, a councillor, traders and simple ratepayers to 'help in the fight against rising crime.'

Just how they would do this nobody has said. Somehow I don't see them getting my door back. And the sort of committee you'd get out of my street is rather terrifying to imagine. My local, which I suppose gives you the best idea of what a neighbourhood is like, is composed in equal parts of the National Front and loud, jovial South Londoners with their mouths full of Cockney, who suddenly get all quiet and confidential and attempt to sell you all sorts of things which have just fallen off the backs of lorries.

'Stan, you're in the writing lark, Stan,' one of them said to me the other Sunday lunchtime. 'How'd you be interested in four new electric typewriters, golf ball style? £150 each.' Sunday lunchtime is the day for such bargains. (Fellow in there the other day selling a back door.) The only thing I ever bought in the pub was a dozen bottles of Thousand Island Salad Dressing. £1.50 the dozen. Off the back of a lorry. They had absolute cases of the stuff going that day.

Oddly enough, the Home Secretary's neighbourhood committees did not actually spring from people being worried about the robbers. It comes, we are told, in answer to 'the demands of some Left-wing groups for more control of the Metropolitan Police'. So the whole thing is a notion to watch the cops rather than the robbers.

In the end, what the South London householder does is barricade himself in with all manner of special locks and alarms. The drain-pipes at my place in Camberwell are covered in grease and the downstairs windows are barred. None of this enhances the beauty of a house when you are attempting to sell it. Neither does the presence of the locksmith and chippy when, after the house had been more than a year on the market, a live one finally came to call the other day.

There is something highly distracting about a man hammering and chiselling away, putting in a special lock and attempting to shore up the garage door, while you are showing the prospective home-buyer around.

'There,' the locksmith and carpenter said, 'that ought to keep the bastards out.'

'For Gawd's sake,' I thought. 'How am I supposed ever to sell this place?' When all at once the man who came to see the house laughed.

'Do you have break-ins?' he asked.

No, I said to myself, I'm a crazy man, I'm trying to lock myself in. It's a harmless eccentricity.

'Well, you know how it is,' I said, 'it's something you have to put up with everywhere in the world today, the way the world is today, what the world is coming to today I don't know. Have you seen the box room? You know, that could easily be used as another bedroom. Why, the people who lived here before did. There was a girl living in there, six foot four, twenty stone if she were a day. Said she loved it.'

'I'm in electronics,' the prospective buyer said. 'I won't bother with locks. I'll electrify the place. That'll give them a shock.' Then *he* giggled, a dirty, evil sort of giggle like a crocodile deciding he'd lie very still and pretend to be a log.

I sold the house. I am turning back the clock, moving back to the original genteel slum of Bloomsbury. Found a wonderful little place.

'Get many break-ins?' I asked as he went through the motions of unlocking a front door which had so many locks and chains on it that it could have doubled for Marley's Ghost.

'No,' he said, 'I honestly don't know why I bother. I just happened to get these cheap. From a fellow at the local. Apparently they fell off the back of a lorry. You in the literary game? Well, sometimes Virginia Woolf's ghost manages to break in but ...'

Actually I did check with the cops at Theobalds Road station. In Bloomsbury the villains don't bother with petty stuff like the Literary Editor of *Punch*'s pathetic little flat upstairs, they're busy dynamiting the safe in the jeweller's shop on the ground floor. I can hardly wait.

February 1983

A.P. Herbert
INDUSTRIAL NOTES

TROUBLE is brewing, it is feared, in the Bottle-Washing Trade. Opinion in the Lobbies last night showed no tendency to minimise the gravity of the situation. Indeed, many well-informed persons did

not conceal their view that if the position does not improve within
the forthcoming week it may grow worse in the next seven days. The
possibility that the *status quo* will be preserved is not seriously
entertained by anyone.

The situation is complicated by the fact that on Monday week the
Amalgamated Society of the Bottle-Washers and Cork-Drawers of
Great Britain is to hold their Annual Conference at Llandrindod
Wells. There is little doubt that the main struggle will rage about the
Resolution which stands in the name of Mr T. Pipp of Lowestoft, the
well-known irreconcilable, and the terms of the Resolution are a
guarantee that the discussion will be lively:

> 'That this Conference of the Amalgamated Bottle-
> Washers and Cork-Drawers of Great Britain records its
> emphatic determination to at all times and by every legiti-
> mate use of the industrial sledgehammer prosecute the
> cause of World Peace, and which the present capitalist
> Government by its habitual failure to ratify the mass
> instructions of the last Conference in regard to the estab-
> lishment of an International Bottle-Washing Convention,
> the Nationalisation of Glass Bottles and the Abolition of
> Cork-Tins in British Dependencies has jeopardised, and,
> with a view to further registering the proletarian solidarity
> of the bottle-washers in the direction of economic emanci-
> pation we hereby order His Majesty's Government to
> adopt the Walsall Programme of the 26th May ult. and so
> without delay hand over the bottles to the people.'

The terms of this Resolution are clear enough, but for a proper
understanding of the situation they should perhaps be read with
some recent utterances of some of the more responsible leaders. Mr
George Bott said on Monday at Southend:

'There must be a *medium quo*. The Walsall Programme is one
thing, but the Government policy of standardised serfdom is
another. They may bring their soldiers and their bayonets, but they
cannot draw the corks. At the same time I am prepared for any
settlement that is consistent with a non-deterioration of the international cork-level as desiderated in the York Amendment. Give us
the standard minimum plus two-fifths of the minimum addendum
calculated on the basis of the Three-Bottle Hour, abolish cork-time
and consolidate the 1917 scale for slingers and huffkins, and the men

will be back in the pantries tomorrow.'

This has been interpreted in many quarters as an olive-branch, but on the same day, at Hoxton, Mr Bott said:

'There must be a *status ante*. The Prime Minister has sabotaged the 1920 Bottle-Datum. We ask him for our babies' bread and he flings us a stone. I stand where I stood.'

And on Tuesday at Rottingdean Mr K. Tinker, a powerful member of the International Union of the Bottle-Washers of the Left, speaking at a delegate Conference of the District Executives convened by the Solidarity Committee of the Anglo-Russian Bottle and Cork Nucleal Association, said:

'The President of the Board of Trade is an assassin.'

At the same gathering Mr Watt-Shrimp (Millwall) said:

'The Foreign Secretary is a burglar.'

And Mr R.Q. Flapp (Southend) said:

'The Parliamentary Secretary to the Secretary of State for Home Affairs is a Thug.'

In the face of these utterances few responsible observers affect an exaggerated optimism as to the outcome of the present imbroglio. On the other hand certain passages in an article in *The Bottle*, by Sir Frederic Bung, Chairman of the United Union of Master-Bottle-Washers, has lent colour to the view entertained in certain influential quarters that an issue not wholly unsatisfactory may be looked for with reasonable confidence before the year is out:

'We cannot recede from the position which we have taken up. *Per contra*, however, it is fair to say that this plain statement of our position is not incompatible with the assumption that were we, by some extraneous means of which perhaps it would be indiscreet to say too much at present – (Laughter and "Hear, Hear") – to be transported to a position obliquely but not, in the geographical sense, directly to the rear, we should then be in a position in which we might fairly say that that was a position so definitely behind the position in which we were before we were transferred to that position that anyone could reasonably say that we had receded from the position which, as I say, we have taken up. And on these lines there is no doubt that, given goodwill on all sides, the whole situation might be finalised tomorrow.'

Sir Patrick Spens, on the other hand, at the Annual Meeting of the Central Federation of Bottle-Masters and General Drinkers, said, 'Curse them! We stand where we stood, only more so.'

That, then, roughly, is the situation as between two of the seventeen parties to the dispute. The position of the Government may perhaps best be deduced from the somewhat ambiguous observations of the Chancellor of the Duchy of Lancaster at the opening of the Quinquennial Bazaar at Mundesley two years ago: 'His Majesty's Government,' he said, 'are wedded inextricably to the *ne plus ultra*. It is monstrous of the employers to protest against political interference. On the other hand it is outrageous of the employees to demand political intervention. We shall preserve unswervingly the *equilibrium plus*. The finances of the country do not admit of the spending of a single public penny. Up till 11.35 A.M. tomorrow we offer £20,000,000 in subvention of all pantries not excluded by the Washington Clause. After that date we cannot afford a bean. (Laughter.) The position of the Government is perfectly clear. What we might have done yesterday we could do tomorrow but for what has happened today, and in view of the developments of yesterday it is idle to expect the same policy to eventuate tomorrow as if that which did not occur today had taken place in the sense that was expected in the ante-penultimate periods of the day before yesterday.'

A note upon the practical conditions of the trade may not perhaps be out of place. Some confusion seems still to exist in the public mind as to the exact relation between huffkins, slingers and rag-holders. Even the Special Committee was unfortunately indefinite upon this point, and it cannot be too often repeated that it is the huffkins who hold the bottle, while the slinger, as his title indicates, turns on the tap, and the rag-holder, in the technical phrase, 'holds the rag'. Of these three the huffkin is a skilled labourer; the slinger is paid at the rate of 3s. 6d. a month plus the Baddely Award and 79·8 per cent less three-fifths of a doughnut and two Royal Commissions, while the rag-holder is generally a vegetarian and is not paid at all, except sideways under the Davison Judgment. It is widely held that had these simple distinctions been brought home to the public at an earlier date the issue would have emerged much previously.

Four bottles were broken by non-union labour at Rugeley yesterday. The basket-workers have struck in sympathy. Sir Thomas Flogg said, 'Moscow corked those bottles'. Huddersfield is quiet.

July 1926

Archibald Marshall

SIMPLE STORIES

I – THE ROBBER

ONE day Milly Fairbrother was going for a walk with her nurse
Gladys Conk when they met a robber in the wood.

The robber said give me some money and Gladys Conk said how
much money?

He said a shilling, and she said I haven't got a shilling, and he said
yes you have.

She said well at any rate I shan't give it to you, and he said if you
don't I shall kill you.

Milly was frightened at that but Gladys Conk was not frightened.
She said you can't do that, and he said why not? And she said because
I shall kill you first.

The robber laughed at that and said oh you will will you? and she
said yes I will will I.

The robber laughed again and said that's good, what with? and she
said with my umbrella.

Now Milly's mother
had given Gladys Conk
a new umbrella for a
Christmas present. It
had a duck's head on the
handle made of imitation
silver and she always
took it for walks with her,
and it was a good thing
she did because of the
robber.

The robber's face as-
sumed a ghastly hue and
he said I never thought
of that, and Gladys Conk
said well you can think
of it now.

'I shall kill you with my umbrella.'

So Gladys Conk killed the robber and he had a lovely funeral with arum lilies and Milly was allowed to go to it.

Well the next day a policeman came to the back-door and asked for Gladys Conk.

The cook opened the door because she was just going out to get a chicken to make some chicken-broth for Milly. Milly was in bed with a sore throat that morning, but she was better the next day and got up, and her friend Jean Hale came to tea with her and they played with the animals in her Noah's Ark.

So the cook said do come in and sit down, and he came in and sat down, and she gave him some beefsteak-and-kidney pie which she had made for lunch upstairs, but she said they can have some cold meat, it won't do them any harm. And she gave him some stout which she had paid for out of her wages.

When he had eaten half the pie and drunk all the stout he said where is Gladys Conk?

The cook said what do you want with Gladys Conk? and he said ah you may well ask.

The cook said she is busy ironing and she doesn't want to have anything to do with policemen she is too young.

And he said she is not too young for me and the judge wants to see her about having a trial.

She said what for? and he said for killing the robber.

The cook said oh, and he said ah you may well say oh.

So she said well I'll go and fetch her.

So they had a trial and the judge was a very kind man and he liked Gladys Conk because he had had a little girl of his own called Gladys, but she was grown up now and *she* had a little girl called Gladys Mary. And the judge had sent her a book of poetry for her birthday and she had learnt three pieces in it. And two of her aunts had given her two fountain-pens one for black ink and one for red, and one of the mistresses of the school she went to had borrowed the one for red ink to correct exercises with.

So the judge said to Gladys Conk don't be frightened, and she said no I won't.

And he said that's right why did you kill the robber?

She said well wouldn't you? and he said yes I would.

So the judge gave Gladys Conk a watch which he paid for out of his own money, and afterwards she married the policeman and had several wedding presents. She loved him rather but he was aggravating, and the cook said of course everybody could please themselves but she wouldn't have married him herself not if he had been the only man in the world.

They had six children, five girls and one little policeman, and when Milly went to tea with her she had brown bread and butter with apricot jam and macaroons and was allowed to bath the baby.

August 1926

Rose Fyleman

FAIRIES

THERE are fairies at the bottom of our garden!
  It's not so very, very far away;
You pass the gardener's shed and you just keep straight ahead;
  I do so hope they've really come to stay.
There's a little wood, with moss in it and beetles,
  And a little stream that quietly runs through;
You wouldn't think they'd dare to come merrymaking there –
        Well, they do.

There are fairies at the bottom of our garden!
  They often have a dance on summer nights;
The butterflies and bees make a lovely little breeze,
  And the rabbits stand about and hold the lights.
Did you know that they could sit upon the moonbeams
  And pick a little star to make a fan,
And dance away up there in the middle of the air?
        Well, they can.

There are fairies at the bottom of our garden!
  You cannot think how beautiful they are;
They all stand up and sing when the Fairy Queen and King
  Come gently floating down upon their car.
The King is very proud and *very* handsome;
  The Queen – now can you guess who that could be
(She's a little girl all day, but at night she steals away)? –
        Well – it's ME!

May 1917

Robert Graves

FRIDAY NIGHT

LOVE, the sole Goddess fit for swearing by,
Concedes us graciously the little lie:
The white lie, the half-lie, the lie corrective
Without which love's exchange might prove defective,
Confirming hazardous relationships
By kindly *maquillage* of Truth's pale lips.

This little lie was first told, so they say,
On the sixth day (Love's planetary day)
When, meeting her full-bosomed and half dressed,
Jove roared out suddenly: 'Hell take the rest!
Six hard days of Creation are enough' –
And clasped her to him, meeting no rebuff.

Next day he rested, and she rested too.
The busy little lie between them flew:
'If this be not perfection,' Love would sigh,
'Perfection is a great, black, thumping lie ...'
Endearments, kisses, grunts, and whispered oaths;
But were her thoughts on breakfast or on clothes?

November 1957

Jeffrey Bernard

SOHO

I CAN'T help feeling about Soho as I might about a woman. Forgive
the metaphors and the odious comparisons but there it is. I met and
fell in love with her when I was sixteen. We had a mad and passionate
affair for a few years until Lord Wolfenden ruined her by putting her
on the straight and narrow. The honeymoon has long since been over
and we're quietly settled down. When I look at her now – and I see
her nearly every day – I don't get the same throb of excitement but I

still love her and with great fondness. Her mascara is smudged and she's what Charlie in Berwick Street market would call an 'old scrubber' but she's been good to me in spite of having led me astray day in and day out for years.

Twice I've been unfaithful to her, once with a flighty but pretty village in Suffolk and once with a real tart of a village in Berkshire. But Soho has always taken me back. She is very forgiving and her arms are always open. I just wish she could be more discriminating but I suppose one shouldn't expect that of a whore. Take a last look at her before the property developers and pornographers make her unrecognisable with dreadful transplants.

It was by accident that I first went into Soho. My brother was a student at St Martin's School of Art and he one day suggested I meet him there in a café by Foyles where the students went in their coffee breaks. It was instant magic for a repressed schoolboy brought up under the severest discipline. Here was everything that I had been led to believe to be wicked. There were poets, layabouts, bums, thieves, eccentrics, and, above all, girls. Masses of them. I thought I was in some sort of Aladdin's Cave. There was a mad, debarred solicitor called Redvers Gray who had taken to invention and had recently tried to patent a submarine made out of blotting-paper – surfacing was the chief stumbling-block – and there was 'Ironfoot' Jack, so called because he made up for a short leg with an iron frame. He wore a cloak and looked like Dr Caligari.

The students who had grants or who lived at home with parents fared well enough but the rest kipped and dossed on other people's floors and sofas and survived on the freemasonry that existed between would-be painters, failed poets, novelists without pens or paper, and Charing Cross Road bookshop thieves. And what thrilled this teenage school-leaver was the fact that all of these people believed in 'free love' and some of them even lived 'in sin'. It was very heady stuff for a boy who told his mother that he spent most days in the Science Museum or National Gallery. Surely such occupations couldn't have accounted for the pallor and the nicotine-stained fingers?

But apart from this chiaroscuro of humanity, the state of mind of Soho, there was the physical Soho. There is now barely a single dirty bookshop, strip club or amusement arcade that wasn't then a bistro, delicatessen, restaurant or café. And money seemed less important, not simply because we were younger but because we could nurse a cup of tea for hours. Being broke was acceptable and expected. None of us had then entered for the rat race. You could spot a rat easily in those days. He was the man who could order chicken or veal escalope, both of which were 3/6d – 1/6d more than you could earn in an hour washing dishes – and I did just that for Victor Sasse when he had a café called the Budapest, years before the Gay Hussar.

All this and that was the first half of the game and affair with Soho.

After the interval in National Service we embarked on the second half, which was the transition from café society to pub-going. Now, into the 1950s, Soho blossomed for me with the change of friends and companions that I met in the pubs and clubs and who seemed to accept me as being part of the furniture and fittings. It was like *The Boyhood of Sir Walter Raleigh*. I listened spellbound at the feet of painters like John Minton, Robert Colquhoun, Robert McBryde, Francis Bacon and Lucian Freud. Poets like George Barker, Dylan Thomas, Louis MacNeice and Sidney Graham and the composers Alan Rawsthorne and Malcolm Arnold. This is not an exercise in name dropping. I mention such people merely in an attempt to convey the quality of the people who lurched and staggered in and out of the Gargoyle Club, the Mandrake Club, the Club des Caves de France and the Colony Room Club. Six of those people are now dead and their replacements are a pretty disappointing bunch.

I feel a particular nostalgia for mornings in the French pub. At opening time the first arrivals were local shopkeepers and the French girls of the street who were a charming bunch and who did no one any harm in spite of what Lord Wolfenden was later to report. Aperitifs were swapped and Soho village life was discussed. It was all so civilised. There was no such thing as a denim-suited advertising executive. At the other end of our rainbow even the crooks and ne'er-do-wells had a sort of style if not class. They were nearer to Damon Runyon than they were to the *News of the World*, although they frequently featured in the latter. There was Sid the Swimmer, Handbag Johnny, Italian Albert Dimes, French Albert and No Knickers Joyce. You didn't interfere with them and they weren't interested in drawing you into their little web. You had a drink with them and passed the time of day. Frank Norman and I regarded our morning appearance in the French pub as arriving for work. And Soho was Cinderella. Hampstead and Chelsea were and are the ugly sisters.

Well, as I say, Cinderella has lost her looks and a bit of her charm but I am still obsessed with her. Soho still makes me feel safe. Wherever I have had the good luck to travel to in recent times, the return journey is enhanced by the feeling I have that I'm going *home*. It does, after all, still make you feel welcome when you know it. The other day a bunch of us in the Coach and Horses got chatting to a salesman from Glasgow who was paying his first visit to Soho as he passed through London. He obviously enjoyed it. He came in for one drink and stayed until closing time and missed his train. He did the same thing the following day and the day after that. Eventually he did get back to his wife and his home. We got a card from him in which he wrote, 'You have ruined my life. Will you all be there next week?' Admittedly he was Glaswegian and so more likely to be led astray, but I doubt whether, say, Notting Hill Gate or Islington could get such a golden seal of approval.

Although the wheels may be at last falling off my village, I can after all these years savour some of its defects. I'd be lost without Norman's rudeness in the Coach and Horses. If he hands me a menu instead of throwing it at me, if he serves me promptly without swearing at me, then I know he has most likely just suffered a deeply tragic and personal loss. In this event we regulars make solicitous enquiries. I myself suffered a sense of loss recently when I spent an entire hour in the Colony Room without spotting a single cockroach. Can this be what they mean by cleaning up Soho?

And now, as both Soho and I are passing peacefully away to our rest, I have taken up the role of teacher. In recent months we have been inundated by young men who all think they are 'Jack the Lad' and who desperately want to become what they call 'Soho Characters'. Not that they will ever have the presence of a Maurice Richardson or be able to conduct a conversation standing on their head as Robert Newton could, but I think they should have the equal opportunity to be able to do so. At any rate I feel it my duty to pass on my obsession with Soho if I can. At least it would keep them off the streets and in the pubs.

March 1985

Miles Kington

THE FRANGLAIS LIEUTENANT'S WOMAN

UN NOVEL COMPLET CONDENSÉ ET TRADUIT DE L'ORIGINAL DE JEAN FOWLES

LYME Regis est un typical village de fishing sur le South Coast d'Angleterre, une de ces petites villes qui, sur la route à nowhere, n'ont pas été totalement ruinées par le progrès et les juggernauts. Pittoresque, mais business-like, Lyme Regis est toujours un beau petit spot, par exemple, comme une refuge pour un auteur comme moi. Depuis 1867 elle n'a pas beaucoup changée. Si un habitant de Lyme en 1867 fut transporté soudain par time travel en 1986, il dirait: 'Pouf! Lyme n'a pas beaucoup changée! Un peu de growth suburbain, peut-être, et ces choses curieuses qu'on appelle saloon cars, mais otherwise c'est pretty much la même.'

C'est ici que j'ai écrit mon novel classique, 'The Franglais Lieutenant's Woman', et c'est aussi ici que les gens de Hollywood ont choisi pour le filming du major movie du même nom. Vous avez jamais vu les gens de Hollywood en action? C'est fantastique. Ils disent: 'Hmmm – away avec les pôles de telegraph! Away avec les double lignes jaunes, et les parking meters! Up avec les pseudo-façades Victoriennes! Bring on les stage-coaches et les yokels en smock!' Dans le twinkling d'un oeil, vous avez un fake Lyme Regis. J'aime bien cela. Le mingling de l'illusion et la réalité, c'est mon stock en trade.

Et si vous transporterez l'habitant de 1867 en 1986, il serait quite unaware qu'il était dans un film set. Parce qu'en 1867, il n'y avait pas de film sets. Vous ne savez pas? Eh bien, vous savez maintenant. Parce que mes novels sont pleins de knowledge incidental comme ça. Stick avec moi, et vous allez recevoir quite une éducation.

Où étais-je? Ah, oui. En 1867, à Lyme Regis, Charles et Ernestina prenaient un petit stroll, totalement unaware qu'ils étaient dans un major novel. Charles étaient un des ces Victorian gents qui ont plenty d'argent et plenty de leisure time. Jeune, prepossessing, un bachelor, avec un joli petit sparkle, il n'avait pas précisément un job. Un job pour un gentleman, ce n'était pas nécessaire en 1867. Mainte-nant, si vous dites: 'Je n'ai pas un job,' on dit: 'Ah, pauvre petit, vous formez partie de l'army des unemployed, personellement je blâme Mrs Thatcher, je vais avoir un petit mot avec Uncle Fred, peut-être a-t-il un opening dans Allied Drinks, etc.' Mais en 1867, on disait: 'Il n'a pas un job. Il est un gentleman.' Intéressant, eh?

Charles était un fanatique des fossils. Oui, avec son petit hammer et son petit fossilbag, il parcourait le landscape de Lyme Regis et les environs pour chercher les relics jurassiques et dévoniens. Un waste de time? Peut-être. Mais il faut se souvenir qu'en 1867 Charles Darwin était hot news. L'évolution, oui ou non? C'était une burning question. Donc, Charles cherchait les fossils, dans l'espoir de dire:

'Oui! Darwin est sur le ball*! Ce petit fossil est le proof!' Ou bien: 'Darwin est un charlatan, et le Livre de Genesis est le gospel truth.'

Charles était aussi good-looking, pas hunky exactement, mais attractif. Un peu comme Robert Redford, peut-être. Of course, dans le film il était joué par Jeremy Irons qui n'est pas truthfully mon exacte idée de Charles, mais je n'avais pas total control sur le casting. Some vous gagnez, some vous perdez ...

Et Ernestina était un produit typical de l'epoque de Victoria (1837–1901). Sa fiancée Ernestina était jolie, pert, indépendente, bien eduquée, et quite a catch pour un gentleman comme Charles. Elle tolérait la passion de Charles pour les fossils, et pourquoi pas? Être jaloux des fossils, c'est stupide. Je ne vais pas donner une pleine description d'Ernestina parce que, si vous voulez vraiment savoir, je ne suis pas un dab hand avec l'analysis des femmes. Elles sont un mystery breed pour moi. Fascinant, mais un mystère. Never mind.

So, Charles et Ernestina prenaient un stroll dans Lyme Regis, en 1867. Vous avez la picture? Up le High Street, down le High Street, et puis along a plage, un stroll ordinaire, quoi. Et ils parlaient des choses dont parlent les fiancés.

'Quand nous nous sommes mariés, il faut que j'aie une chambre spéciale pour mes fossils,' dit Charles.

'D'accord. Et aussi une chambre spéciale pour les enfants.'

'Enfants? Quels enfants? Nous n'avons pas d'enfants ...'

'Pas encore, Charles. Mais by et by ...'

'Ça sera chic!' s'écria Charles. 'Des petits enfants, qui vont m'accompagner sur le fossil-hunt! Oui, beaucoup de petits enfants, pour continuer le good work de fossil-hunting.'

Ernestina avait un petit frown sur sa pretty face. Hmm. Fossil-hunting était OK comme un hobby, mais il était un peu obsessionel. La palaeontologie n'est pas nécessairement héréditaire, elle pensa. En quoi, elle était wide du mark, parce que le Leakey family d'East Africa a changé la palaeontologie en un family business. Mais, en 1867, c'était difficile à anticiper.

Meanwhile, Charles et Ernestina continuaient leur stroll jusqu'au Cobb. Vous avez vu le film de 'The Franglais Lieutenant's Woman'? Le Cobb était un landmark dans ce film. C'est un grand breakwater, ou plutôt un quai, ou peut-être un sea-wall – anyway, c'est une

---

* Of course, Charles n'aurait pas dit: 'Sur le ball'. C'est une expression moderne, une phrase de soccer, datant de 1953.

grande construction de rocks et boulders qui est un landmark de
Lyme Regis, espécialement après le movie. Je ne sais pas pourquoi il
s'appelle le Cobb. Je ne peux pas faire le research de tout, vous savez.
Je ne suis pas omniscient.

'Regarde!' dit Charles. 'Qui est la femme au bout du Cobb?'

Dans la drizzle, ils pouvaient voir une lone figure, dans un cloak,
en position au tip du Cobb. Un peu comme la Statue de Liberté,
quoi, ou peut-être comme Jean la Baptiste – solitaire, melancholique,
triste, enveloppée dans ce grand cloak.

Ernestina donna un petit shiver. 'C'est the Franglais Lieutenant's
Woman.'

'Come again?' dit Charles.

'C'est une triste histoire,' dit Ernestina. 'Elle est une countrywoman qui est tombée amoureuse d'un matelot franglais. Last year,
il y avait un shipwreck. Le lieutenant a été rescué. Il a eu une affair
avec une pauvre, simple countrywoman. Puis le lieutenant est rentré
en France, en disant: "Attends-moi, honey, je vais revenir avec un
ring et une wedding date." Et maintenant, chaque jour, elle est sur le
Cobb, avec les yeux fixés sur le coast-line de France.'

En silence, Charles et Ernestina marchaient le long du Cobb. Il
était très windy, not to say stormy, not to say tempestueux. La lone
figure se tenait là, comme un light-house, ou bien un figure-head,
avec le cloak whipping dans le vent. Vous avez vu le film? C'est très
dramatique dans le film.

Au bout du Cobb, Charles donna un petit cough. Il ne voulait pas
donner un shock à la Franglais Lieutenant's woman. Heuh, heuh,
heuh, fit-il. La lone figure ne se tourna pas.

Heugh, heugh, heugh, fit Charles. Même réaction.

'I say!' dit Charles. 'Etes-vous OK?'

La lone figure se tourna. Consternation! Ce n'était pas une jeune
femme. C'était un homme, bearded, avec sun-glasses.

'Mon Dieu!' dit Charles. 'Vous êtes un homme, bearded, avec
sun-glasses. Où est Meryl Streep?'

'En California,' dit l'homme. 'Je fais le stand-in pour cette scène.
Dans un cloak, from behind, qui sait la différence?'

Charles donna un gasp. L'homme était handsome. 'Qui êtes-
vous?'

'Je suis Chuck Yerbonski, 3ème assistant producteur sur le film. Je
suis de la même physique que Meryl Streep, donc un naturel pour le
stand-in.' Charles donna un second gasp. Chuck Yerbonski était *très*

handsome. Sur le spot, il tomba amoureux de ce chunky 3ème assistant producteur du film.

'Charles!' dit Ernestina. 'Charles? Charles! CHARLES!'

Il était trop tard. Charles, un jeune gentleman de 1867, était madly in love avec Chuck, un assistant producteur de 1980, avec beaucoup de complications sociales. Mais Charles était blind aux implications. Une belle petite histoire, non?

Venant bientôt à votre neighbourhood screen: 'The Franglais Lieutenant's Assistant Producer!' Mind-boggling, hein? Un blending de réalité et illusion? Well, why not?

'Beats *The French Lieutenant's Woman* dans un cocked hat' (*Barry Norman*). Nominé pour 11 Oscars. Don't miss it.

April 1986

Alex Atkinson

THE NEW MAYHEW – A NOBLEMAN IN REDUCED CIRCUMSTANCES

ORE of these are to be met with now than formerly; and my researches show that their number seems likely to increase. I was unable to arrive at any precise figure, but the man from whom I received the account which follows assured me that he was personally acquainted with two others in comparable circumstances, one being related to the Duke of —— and at present engaged in the underwear trade in a selling capacity.

My informant was a man in his late forties, with recognizably aristocratic features, a stutter, and a fondness for chilled white wine. Despite his straitened circumstances he was at first reluctant to regard himself as a member of the teeming army of London's poor; indeed he conducted himself through the interview in a manner so patrician that at last I felt he had done me an honour by arranging for

me to pay the bill for our refreshment. Yet the truth is that, bur-
dened with a title, as well as a castle in a remote county, he is hard
put to it to make ends meet.

He had, he said, studied the great philosophers and had therefore
come to expect very little in this life, and rather less in the next. But
he confessed himself bewildered that hard times should befall one
who had 'always tried to play the g-game'. He also acknowledged a
sense of fear at having no point of contact with the world of today,
into which he found himself suddenly tossed. His feeling was
strengthened when he found that he could no longer even *purchase*
the comfort of servile obedience, congenial companions, or the love
of grateful peasants.

Upon my asking what single factor had, in his opinion, contributed most to his downfall, he exclaimed with great vehemence
'D-death duties, by G-d!'

His grandfather had died, at a great age, causing a distress among
his dependents which was later deepened by their realization that
after the requirements of the Inland Revenue Department had been

met the value of the estate
was reduced, by about
half, to something less
than a quarter of a million
pounds.

'This was bad enough,
in all conscience, and
many members of the
family began seriously to
discuss the possibility of
entering commerce. But
worse was to follow. A
bare twelve months later
my poor f-father died in
an accident. D-death
duties again! The result
was, when all was settled
up, that there remained
l-less than a hundred
thousand pounds all told,
and little of that in actual
money!'

To keep the castle staffed and in repair was obviously impossible. Moreover, my informant now found himself obliged to provide for his mother and a number of other relatives, several of whom had, until that time, been merely names to him. 'One, I found, had been cheerfully destitute in one of the c-colonies for the better part of half a century!'

The upkeep of the castle soon proving unendurable he moved, with his mother and the less marriageable of his sisters, to a small flat in London, at a monthly rental of eighty pounds. This now constitutes so heavy a drain on his resources that he contemplates the purchase of a terrace house at —— Common, where he hopes to set up in business, under an assumed name, as a bookmaker. 'Naturally enough,' he told me, 'I have always l-loved horses.'

He can find no buyer for the castle, which is situated in a bleak and inaccessible moor, with cramped, cold rooms and none but the most dubious sanitation. Nor is it suitable for exploitation as a *stately home*: for it has no features, either architectural or historical, likely to interest even the most rabid of sightseers; and to levy a charge of half a crown for the privilege of exploring its draughty estate would be something not far short of sharp practice – to any form of which, up to the present, he has been loath to resort.

'No, we could not have stayed on up there, even using three rooms. Our circle was composed of people of substance: c-company directors, heads of advertising agencies, wholesale g-grocers. They affected not to sneer at our second-hand station-wagon and threadbare hunting-kit; but one soon grows sensitive to slights, however disguised. Also, the villagers themselves had latterly tended to patronize us, and even show us k-kindness. This my mother could not bear; for, as she said, she dreaded the time when they might begin to leave bowls of soup and bundles of cast-off clothing for us on the d-drawbridge at dead of night.

'Yes, my capital is rapidly diminishing. I have had no training in shorthand and typewriting, or the composing of essays for the Sunday newspapers. And yet now I must seek some m-means of supporting myself. No, I cannot believe that I have deserved to reach such straits, since I have lived my life on what I conceive to be Christian principles, so far as they have seemed appropriate. What harm have I done, that I should now be thrown unprepared into an alien way of life, my family possessions daily disappearing, the long and honourable record of my ancestors c-counting for nothing?'

Indeed, this man's position is harsh and unenviable; and yet under prevailing conditions it is not easy to see how it may be alleviated. Moreover, his character appears to have suffered in the process of partial readjustment: where once he was pleased to patronize such arts as came within his ken, he now subscribes to popular Philistinism; where once his charitable works were widespread and anonymous, he will now openly elbow aside a street musician with a curse; and although from the age of sixteen his outlook and inclinations were, as he puts it, 'foolishly liberal and enlightened', he now embraces his own personal species of stubbornly reactionary Toryism.

Surely our country, which has always found room for pleasant anachronisms, will not allow such unfortunates to suffer indefinitely?

January 1958

Keith Waterhouse

UNDER PLAIN COVER

The Central Intelligence Agency has come out of the cold
and into the warm glow of Madison Avenue prose.
In strikingly unspooklike language, the Agency, whose
thirty-year history has been cloaked in secrecy, has begun
advertising campaigns in twelve large newspapers, seeking
people who want a 'spirit of adventure' and can make
'on-the-spot decisions'.

Guardian

IN response to your advt in the Sits Vac Column for spies no exp. needed, I am wondering whether you are contemplating opening a branch of the CIA in Croydon. If so, would like to apply for position. Can claim to have requisite managerial qualifications for running a sub-office, and am quite used to making 'on-the-spot decisions' as required. I possess a spirit of adventure.

I note that renumeration offered is $14,414–$19,263 per annum, no mention of annual increments, company car or index-linked pension, but can always take these up with your personal mgr or at staff association level, if granted favour of interview.

Aged 45, married with two kiddies, I possess GCE certificates in English and Maths, and am at present employed in an under-managerial capacity at the Croydon branch of the Eyeglass & General Assurance Co. Whilst I have no professional experience of espionage, I have the onerous responsibility of weeding out 'dodgy' insurance claims and reporting same to my superior, Mr Yarmby. This involves 'relying on one's wits' as specified in your advt. Case in point: a certain client who shall be nameless recently claimed £24.75 in respect of shag hearthrug supposedly burned by flying cinders. Shaky handwriting, plus fact that my sister lives in same block of flats so I happen to know they are centrally-heated by gas radiator, suggested to me that subject was lying. Such was case. Investigation by Eyeglass & General 'plumbers' (i.e., fraud investigators) proved that he had tapped out pipe on hearthrug while in middle of heavy drinking bout (vodka & lime), thus enabling us to deny liability under Act of God clause. Saving to company: £24.75p.

With Bay of Pigs etc to your credit, above incident will seem small beer to you, but take it from me it is only the tip of the iceberg as regards Croydon, as any secret agent opening a branch office in said borough would quickly discover. We have communists and sub-versives without number, as well as sexual deviates if these interest you at all. Appreciate that your advt specifies 'overseas assignments', but assume this means overseas as regards 'our colonial cousins' as we call you Americans on this side of pond. I would definitely not wish to move out of Croydon, where I have strong family ties. I mention this only so that we do not get in farcical situation of your man in Moscow being posted to Croydon, while at same time I am being posted to Moscow. In any case, I do not speak any foreign languages, including Russian.

Should you wish to consider my suggestion of opening a CIA Croydon branch, there are excellent shop-fronted premises available on Begonia Avenue Parade, between Dibbs the Estate Agent's and the Eyeglass & General district office. If successful in my application to become CIA branch manager, I assume I would be authorised to wear false beard and dark glasses as otherwise would be recognised by Mr Yarmby and other erstwhile colleagues next door. Before interview with your personnel mgr I will give some thought as to what the CIA's 'front' should be in Croydon. Besides Dibbs and the Eyeglass & General, there are already a fishmonger's, chemist's and heel bar, plus the Tolpuddle Building Society, so it could not be any of these. The parade does not have a sub post-office – we have petitioned for one for many years – but I imagine this would mean taking the Brit. govt. into your confidence. Whether you wish to do this or not is for you to decide when you have consulted your files on Mrs Thatcher (I think she is quite reliable for what it is worth), but should you reject the sub-post office subterfuge for any reason, the businessmen and secretaries in this area are crying out for a really good take-away sandwich bar. This is assuming that the CIA would provide funds for stocking up same, as well as facilities for sending me on sandwich-making course, either to your training school in Washington or to the Croydon Tech. I think this would be a justifiable expense as it would be pity to 'blow my cover' by inexpertly slicing liver sausage or not having faintest idea what to charge for potato salad.

(NB: Would I be expected to re-order bread & sandwich fillings through Head Office, or should I use my initiative and make own arrangements with local tradesmen, receipts of course to be provided? If latter course, there is an excellent delicatessen-cum-baker not far away, but the owner hails from Poland I believe. Would he have to be 'screened'?)

One further point on assumption we go ahead with sandwich bar idea. It would NOT be advisable to store poison capsules, typhoid-infected darts and similar toxic materials on the premises, as our local health inspector is a stickler for 'going by the book' so far as food-handling is concerned. I have a high shelf in my bathroom at home which would be admirable for the purpose, provided I am able to inform my wife why they are there and who issued them (otherwise they will finish up in dustbin as she has a horror of hoarding anything in the pill line in case the kiddies think they are sweeties). For present, however, I have told my wife nothing, so should your personnel mgr ring up for an appointment and she answers, I would appreciate it if he would not say that he is the United States Central Intelligence Agency. If he wants a 'cover' he could pretend to be telephoning me in regard to a with-profits endowment insurance policy, and I could reply that I will prepare a proposal form for his perusal and signature and meet him under some mutually convenient tree.

Referring once again to your advt, I note that it states, 'In these times of meaningless jobs, here's a career where you can make a difference.' If I may say so, above sentiment, together with previously-mentioned qualification of making 'on-the-spot decisions', is why I finally decided to make this application after carefully weighing up the many pros and cons of changing employment at an age when most people are looking forward to retirement in twenty years' time.

For some years I have felt that I am getting nowhere in my meaningless job. Mr Yarmby, my so-called 'superior' mentioned earlier in this letter, has no better qualifications than I, yet he is district manager at age 41. My belief is that it is because he is a Freemason. I think Croydon Lodge of the Order of Water Bison, of which Yarmby is leading light, is certainly worthy of investigation by CIA. It should be easy to infiltrate by using false beard mentioned earlier. Also, Mrs Bleekman, Yarmby's 'secretary' as she has cheek to call herself (cannot even type), is almost certainly a Communist agent. She certainly has Labour leanings, which is why she got job instead of my wife, who can type 65 wpm. I will not trouble you with list of sex perverts at present but my sister has these. Owner of burned shag hearthrug is No. 1 on her list.

As to my new career 'making a difference', I am enclosing estate agents' circulars showing how following up my suggestion of taking shop on Begonia Avenue Parade would save £2 per foot over conventional office space in 'downtown Croydon' as you would call our main shopping centre. I would effect other economies by employing wife and sister as 'sidekicks', provided there are establishment vacancies for part-time spies.

Finally, it has always been understood that my two kiddies Melvin (10) and Stephanie (8) would follow me into insurance business as clerk and typist respectively. As Yarmby and Mrs Bleekman will have to believe I have died from heart attack so that I can keep them under surveillance in false beard without arousing suspicion, this will mean I no longer have 'contacts' in insurance world. Is there any opening for kiddies in espionage? If so, please send leaflets re training schemes, number of 'O' and 'A' levels required etc. The boy is particularly excited at idea of becoming spy, provided there are adequate pension provisions and luncheon voucher allowance.

August 1979

A.A. Milne

WHEN WE WERE VERY YOUNG

IX – TEDDY BEAR

A BEAR, however hard he tries,
Grows tubby without exercise.
Our Teddy Bear is short and fat,
Which is not to be wondered at;
He gets what exercise he can
By falling off the ottoman.
But generally seems to lack
The energy to clamber back.

Now tubbiness is just the thing
Which gets a fellow wondering;
And Teddy worried lots about
The fact that he was rather stout,
He thought: 'If only I were thin!
But how does anyone begin?'
He thought: 'It really isn't fair
To grudge me exercise and air.'

For many weeks he pressed in vain
His nose against the window-pane,
And envied those who walked about
Reducing their unwanted stout.
None of the people he could see
'Is quite' (he said) 'as fat as me!'
Then, with a still more moving sigh,
'I mean' (he said), 'as fat as I!'

Now Teddy, as was only right,
Slept in the ottoman at night,
And with him crowded in as well
More animals than I can tell;
Not only these, but books and things,
Such as a kind relation brings,
Old tales of 'Once upon a time,'
And history re-told in rhyme.

One night it happened that he took
A peep at an old picture-book,
Wherein he came across by chance
The picture of a King of France
(A stoutish man), and, down below,
These words: 'King Louis So-and-So,
Nicknamed "The Handsome."' There he sat,
And (think of it!) the man was fat!

Our bear rejoiced like anything
To read about this famous King,
Nicknamed 'The Handsome.' There he sat,
And certainly the man was fat.
Nicknamed 'The Handsome.' Not a doubt
The man was definitely stout.
Why then a bear (for all his tub)
Might yet be named 'The Handsome Cub!'

'Might yet be named.' Or did he mean
That years ago he 'might have been'?
For now he felt a slight misgiving:
'Is Louis So-and-So still living?
Fashions in beauty have a way
Of altering from day to day;
Is "Handsome Louis" with us yet?
Unfortunately I forget.'

Next morning (nose to window-pane)
The doubt occurred to him again.
One question hammered in his head:
'Is he alive or is he dead?'
Thus nose to pane he pondered; but
The lattice-window, loosely shut,
Swung open. With one startled 'Oh!'
Our Teddy disappeared below.

There happened to be passing by
A plump man with a twinkling eye,
Who, seeing Teddy in the street,
Raised him politely to his feet,
And murmured kindly in his ear
Soft words of comfort and of cheer:
'Well, well!' 'Allow me!' 'Not at all.'
'Tut-tut! A very nasty fall.'

Our Teddy answered not a word;
It's doubtful if he even heard.
Our bear could only look and look:
The stout man in the picture-book!

That 'handsome' King – could this be he,
This man of adiposity?
'Impossible,' he thought; 'but still,
No harm in asking. Yes, I will!'

'Are you,' he said, 'by any chance
His Majesty the King of France?'
The other answered, 'I am that,'
Bowed stiffly and removed his hat;
Then said, 'Excuse me,' with an air,
'But is it Mr Edward Bear?'
And Teddy, bending very low,
Replied politely, 'Even so.'

They stood beneath the window there,
The King and Mr Edward Bear,
And, handsome, if a trifle fat,
Talked carelessly of this and that ...
Then said His Majesty, 'Well, well,
I must get on,' and rang the bell.
'Your bear, I think,' he smiled. 'Good-day!'
And turned and went upon his way.

A bear, however hard he tries,
Grows tubby without exercise;
Our Teddy Bear is short and fat,
Which is not to be wondered at.
But do you think it worries him
To know that he is far from slim?
No, just the other way about –
He's *proud* of being short and stout.

Ernest H. Shepard

February 1924

Miles Kington
LET'S PARLER FRANGLAIS!

OÙ EST LA PLUME DE MA TANTE?

Lui: Où est la plume de ma tante?

Elle: C'est un joke, ou quoi?

Lui: Non, c'est for real. Tante Betty, qui vient manger notre TV dinner ce soir, m'a donné une plume à Noël. Un superslim exécutive fountain pen avec bleep.

Elle: Et ça marche?

Lui: Non. C'est un ornamental fountain pen. Mais si Tante Betty vient nous voir, reste assurée qu'elle vient aussi voir sa plume. Donc, je demande: où est la plume de ma tante?

Elle: Je parie que c'est la première fois dans l'histoire du monde que cette question ait été sérieusement posée.

Lui: Ah, non! Vous vous souvenez de Tante Beryl? Tante Beryl était dans showbiz. En 1950 elle était une Bluebell girl.

Elle: Vraiment? J'adore les chemins de fer miniatures.

Lui: Non, c'était à Paris. Elle était une danseuse très glam, très leggy, très ooh-la-la.

Elle: Une strippeuse, en effet.

Lui: Oui. Elle avait cet acte sensationnel avec un ostrich feather.

Elle: Comme Rod Hull et Emu, quoi?

Lui: Oui, mais moins intellectuel. Anyway, mon holiday job à Paris en 1950 était comme dresseur de Tante Beryl. C'était facile; elle portait *seulement* cette queue d'ostrich. Pendant le jour je soignais le feather: je lui donnais du grooming, du dry cleaning, de la maintenance, des running repairs, etc. Et puis, un jour affreux, le feather était missing! Un stage-door Johnny l'avait volé comme souvenir! Ma tante allait être *nue*!

Elle: Et tu as crié partout dans le théâtre: 'Où est la plume de ma tante?'!

Lui: Ah. Vous connaissez cette histoire déjà?

Elle: Non, pas du tout. Dis-moi, c'est vrai?

Lui: Non, pas du tout. Une fabrication totale.

Elle: Ah! Un moment! Ta plume! Maintenant je me souviens. A la weekend, chez Oncle Richard, j'admirais ses roses, et il m'a donné l'adresse de son nurseryman ...

Lui: Oui?

Elle: ... et je t'ai dit: 'Donne-moi ta plume et je vais l'écrire ...' Je l'ai laissée derrière l'oreille de son gnome.

Lui: C'est à dire: la plume de ma tante est dans le jardin de mon oncle.

Elle: Je parie que c'est la première fois dans l'histoire de l'univers que cette remarque ait été faite.

Lui: Mais non! Vous vous souvenez de mon oncle Benjamin? Qui est retiré à Kendal pour fabriquer un Kendal mint cake liqueur, 90% proof? Eh bien, en 1948 il était à Damascus ...

August 1979

Robert Chalmers

PUTTING OFF THE RITZ

'A MAN of sense,' Lord Chesterfield wrote to his son, 'carefully avoids any particular character in his dress; he dresses as well, and in the same manner as the people of sense and fashion of the place where he is.'

Anyone who has attempted the long walk from Tottenham Hotspur's stadium to the Seven Sisters underground station whilst wearing a red and white scarf will know what Lord Chesterfield was getting at. The idea of public propriety in dress depends less on fashion *per se* than on the style favoured by one's immediate neighbours. Some establishments still feel the need to encourage or formalise our natural tendency to conform; though the punishment for disobedience, admittedly, usually falls short of the kind of penalties imposed on the Tottenham High Road.

The strictest dress codes tend to be 'enforced' with the consent of members of private clubs: White's Gentlemen's Club in St James's, for instance, still requires a dress suit, collar and tie. Blazer and trousers 'may occasionally be admitted'. (Blazer and trousers do better than women in this respect. Ladies have been allowed in, White's told me, 'about twice this century'.)

The extension of a dress code to business premises with public access, like restaurants and hotels, is more bemusing in that it breaks the eleventh business commandment – the one relating to the wilful turning away, while being of sound mind, of a would-be paying customer. I visited some establishments in London and Manchester, to try to discover what on earth possesses them to enforce their arcane complex set of dress requirements.

THE JACKET AND TIE

Where formal dress requirements for men are concerned, certainly in the more traditional establishment, all outfits aspire to the condition of black tie. These days, however, few British hotels or restaurants insist on dinner dress, except for special functions (though some, like The Savoy, encourage it on Saturdays). A jacket and tie, however, is still *de rigueur* in most of the public areas of the more exclusive hotels. I found this out during my two abortive attempts to gain admission to **Claridge's Tea Room** (*Jacket and Tie for Men; No Jeans*), finally I was allowed in with a three-piece suit.

Most male guests in the room were also wearing the modern 'sack suit', which remains, in many ways, the ideal leveller. Its rectangular shape and limited colour range offer the anonymity of a military uniform; at the same time the sack suit conceals sagging middle-aged flesh and is highly unflattering to the figure of a 'bronze Adonis'. I was reflecting on this when the combinations of the heat and the *Eau de Nile* decor became too much. I slipped off my tie.

Taking your tie off in Claridge's has the effect of removing a more intimate garment in another place. The hotel tearoom has maintained its dress code since 1814, but the embarrassment, even in 1989, is acute and immediate, though it *is* a good way of getting a waiter quickly. I had mine by my side in eighteen seconds, giving me the kind of look you see on the faces of regulars at the local in Dracula films when travellers stop and ask for a lift to the castle. The last of the three waiters who spoke to me argued precedent. 'It's always been that way in Claridge's. It's been that way for – I don't know for how long – a hundred years or so.' Finally, after heroic tact on his part, I got the red card, which in Claridge's takes the form of having your table cleared against your will. The classier establishments' desire to avoid an unseemly fracas has given rise to a 'hidden etiquette' of genteel alternatives to the Hollywood 'heave-ho' into the gutter. I found an interesting variation at Brown's Hotel (*Jacket and Tie; No Jeans*) where my 'expulsion' took the form of being asked to remove myself to the writing-room, taking, as Oliver Hardy once said when playing a butler, 'Yer eats with you'.

Terry Holmes of **The Ritz** (*Jacket and Tie; No Jeans*) told me that the rule is imposed 'so that nobody will be embarrassed by turning up incorrectly dressed', though whether being cold-shouldered in the busy foyer is less embarrassing than getting outside of a Ritz tea *sans cravate* was, my companion pointed out, a matter of opinion. The idea of taking an informal tea would probably not have distressed the man from Birmingham whom I passed on my premature exit from the Ritz. 'That,' he told his friends in a stage whisper, 'is the most expensive cup of tea I've ever had.'

I rejoined my companion, who had bolted during the closing stages of play at the Ritz, and we set off for the **Savoy American Bar** (*Jacket and Tie; No Jeans*). Again I went in a suit and took my jacket off. After a couple of public warnings the senior waiter, a man of saint-like patience, opened the window for me, and stood by it. Seeing no reaction, he adopted the posture favoured by bathers on nineteenth-century posters advertising northern coastal towns, inhaling deeply and smiling to demonstrate the beneficial effect of the ozone ('Can you feel the fresh air coming?'). On the way out I asked him what his next move would have been if I hadn't left ('A punch'). Peter Crome of the Savoy group, which also owns Claridge's, put in a 'time and motion' plea: 'If you went to The Savoy specially dressed and saw people in T-shirts, you would ask yourself why you had gone to all that trouble. It should,' he added, 'be the experience of a lifetime.' (It certainly was for me ...)

Fearful of boosting my already considerable expenses beyond the tolerance of my commissioning editor, I decided on an early exit from **Maxim's de Paris** (*Upstairs restaurant: Jacket and Tie; No Jeans*). I was a little surprised to be served at the bar, but then the waiter made his move: 'Once you go into the restaurant you have to put your jacket and tie on.' Following Alex Higgins, patron saint of the tieless, I pleaded fear of constriction around the throat during activities where huge amounts of cash were at stake. 'In that case, sir, I am obliged ...' – familiar by now with the valetudinal tone, I reached for my bag – 'to make an exception in your case.' The waiter looked genuinely confused by the contrast between my look of horror as I fumbled for a credit card and the expression of undisguised glee on the face of my companion, who told me that the level of humiliation by association was making her feel a little like Lord Godiva.

Maxim's dress restriction is typical for a restaurant of its type. Most of the 'top' London establishments require jacket and tie for men, at least for dinner, and may dither over whether or not to serve ladies in jeans. Silvano Giraldin of **La Gavroche** argued exclusivity as his rationale. 'La Gavroche is not a restaurant on the corner. We don't want or expect people to come every day. It's an occasion to remember. And we ask them to dress up.'

NO JEANS

Jeans were in their heyday as code-breakers in the late Sixties and early Seventies, when events like the Isle of Wight pop festival inspired 'No Hippies' and 'No Denim' notices all over the country. Seventies football fans, too, got denim a bad name by viewing it as an acceptable 'second strip' when their Oxford bags were in the wash. Presumably they were attracted by the handy riveted pockets ('Ideal,' says Sharon Rosenberg, in her book, *Denim*, 'for carrying heavy ore samples'). Thirty-five years after *The Wild One*, I expected, as I set out in full denim rig-out, to have a relatively trouble-free evening.

I had not expected to be *persona grata* in **Annabel's** (*Smart Dress; Dark Suit or Black Tie for Men*), or **Stringfellows** (*Smart Casual; No Jeans or Training Shoes*); but I also got the thumbs-down at a number of mainstream clubs including **The Hippodrome** (*No Jeans; No Training Shoes*). One or two pubs felt that they could do without me; notably **The Ship** in Lime Street, EC3, which continues to display a rather quaint 'No Jeans' sign.

Things started hotting up once I went outside London. On a Saturday night in Manchester I was turned away from most of the bars and clubs in the Piccadilly area, including **Yates's Wine Lodge** (*No Jeans Saturday Night*) in High Street. Yates's has rocketed up market over the last few years and has, like many pubs I visited, adopted a 'tight' door policy at the weekend. A lady from the company explained that 'denim is associated with the kind of trade we would not want.' This, she told me, meant 'people likely to be undesirable in some way'. Later that evening, when I returned to Yates's in a jacket and tie, I was rather taken aback to see one of my fellow revellers (not, admittedly, wearing jeans), comatose and spread-eagled in a pool of vomit in the Gents (the wall of which was decorated with the slogan 'Burnley Suicide Squad kick to kill'). But then it all depends, as Lord Chesterfield would no doubt have reflected, on what you mean by 'undesirable'.

Denim, being the only unambiguous uniform to have maintained its challenge to the sack suit, has become a kind of shorthand for the proscribable. The 'No Jeans' regulation is especially handy in places with no established practice and little faith in the ability of their door staff to judge character. With the most ferocious football supporters now wearing tweeds, and a Liberty denim jacket and standard designer jeans together costing well over £100, the received attitude towards denim has clearly been overtaken by events. But as Terry Holmes had told me at the Ritz: 'You can't tell people that they can wear jeans as long as they're designer jeans.'

NO WORKING CLOTHES

The restriction of 'No Working Clothes' is probably the most puzzling of all to the philosophically-minded punter, who might argue that 'working clothes' could range – depending on your occupation – from top hat and tails to no clothes at all. (In the establishments where I tried to develop the argument, this train of thought turned out to be an express route to the exit.)

I 'teamed' a brand new boiler suit – laundered and pressed so that I would not be ejected on a 'bum rap' of soiled clothing – with a blue woolly hat, tool bag and polished army boots, and headed for the City. The area has a healthy mixture of construction workers and stockbrokers (so healthy that one pub, **The Viaduct** near Bart's

Hospital, was displaying – with scant respect for the hands that made it – a 'No Builders' sign). I was served here, and at nine other of the fifteen pubs I visited. Interestingly, intimidating signs referring to working clothes seemed to offer little clue as to the establishment's attitude. Several of the places which refused me (like the **Three Compasses** in Cowcross Street) displayed no warning.

At **The City Pipe** (*Only Those Customers Respectably Attired will be Served*), near St Paul's, I got past the doorman easily enough. Combined with a purposeful look, overalls – especially with a name stencilled on the back – command as much authority as any other dark blue uniform. Here I was turned away for being, as Peter might have put it, in the 'condition' of boiler suit. The barman, who refused to serve me, told me that the sign meant 'suit and tie'; the doorman dutifully explained that 'it means no jeans'.

After a chat with a spokesman for Davy's, who own the pub, I was able to establish that my entry for the establishment should read: The City Pipe (*No Jeans, Boiler Suits Or Training Shoes. Jacket and Tie Essential Unless You Go In With a Group Who Are Appropriately Dressed and Keep Your Head Down*).

NO SOILED CLOTHES

For my visits to City pubs displaying a 'No Soiled Clothes' sign, I chose a suit and tie with tomato ketchup and half a can of vegetable soup emptied down the front. As I'd had some difficulty in persuading a taxi-driver to take me, I was surprised to be served in all the places I visited, including **The Jamaica Wine House** (*No Soiled Clothes or Dirty Footwear*). It was service with a smile this time at The Three Compasses. Even The City Pipe served me, after an old-fashioned look from the barman.

In desperation I set out for **El Vino's**. The Fleet Street bar/ restaurant has long been in the van – or, depending on your point of view, the rear – guard of sartorial restriction. Here again I was served at the bar; I had lasted less than a minute in my denim outfit. It is as hard to be ejected from establishments like El Vino's 'suitably' attired as it is impossible to get in if you are not wearing a jacket and tie. *Any* jacket and tie. (On another occasion I tried a pair of 28-inch flared Terylene check trousers, an ill-fitting Seventies disco jacket with a floral shirt and kipper tie. I had only gone twenty yards on the way to the taxi in Crouch End before I was being loudly mocked by a group of teenage girls. El Vino's, however, was happy to serve me, though as I was leaving the barman called out 'let me know when it comes back into fashion'.

Mr Mitchell, director of El Vino's, explained the rationale behind the code at his establishment. 'For gentlemen, we require jacket and tie. For ladies, a skirt or dress. Trousers are *not* suitable attire. In our humble opinion. If you do allow trousers,' Mr Mitchell continued, 'then you get awful scruffy old women in jeans and God knows what else and it's just not good enough.' Mr Mitchell did, however, tell me that the bar would try to supply a spare tie 'if a gentleman comes in with some chap from up north who hasn't got one'; news which should be of some comfort to the Burnley Suicide Squad.

SMART CASUAL

Dress codes are especially bewildering when experienced in rapid succession. You cannot get into most bars at The Savoy without a tie, but until recently at The Intrepid Fox in Wardour Street (now *No Restrictions*) they wouldn't serve you if you did have one. Older night people in suits reported difficulties in gaining admission to trendier clubs like The Hacienda in Manchester, established by pop entrepreneur Tony Wilson (thirty-nine). Claridge's grudgingly allowed me to wear my 'Waialae Country Club' Hawaian baseball hat in their tea-room, The Chicago Pizza Pie Factory wouldn't have any item of headgear at all. Leather outfits won't get past the doorman in many West End clubs, but at Skin Two (at Zeeta's in Putney) they won't let you in without one.

Restrictions are overwhelmingly aimed at male guests. Silvano Giraldin at La Gavroche cracked a joke that I heard several times during my research, explaining that the code at his restaurant was 'Men – jacket and tie; women naked'. ('If a woman goes out with a man in a nice suit she knows very well that she cannot wear jeans.')

Apart from fretting about the soft furnishings, explanations of dress codes boiled down to three: The School Uniform (everybody does it, it stops people feeling embarrassed); Weddings and Funerals (it's a special occasion, you dress up); and Tradition (it's been like this since 1814). I found this last more convincing in the case of Claridge's than at the Manchester hotel/club **Sacha's** ('We've done it ever since we opened – last December.') Sacha's is a temple to roaring kitsch. The decor includes a model of a hammerhead shark, a stuffed polar bear and a teal. The effect is the more horrific when you realise that you are sitting in what used to be the children's shoe department at C&A.

I asked Mr Mitchell whether El Vino's would ever relax its code to admit what Sir Richard Maitland called 'newfangleness of geir'. 'Relax? Never. We might even get tourists.'

June 1989

H.F. Ellis

FOR MEN IN APRONS

OF the disappointingly few letters I have received in response to my offer, made a month ago in this paper, to help you with your household problems, perhaps the most interesting is one which deals with the vexed question of getting cold porridge out of the crevices of saucepans. But before I answer this point in detail, may I permit myself the luxury of a general reflection on saucepans?

In the old pre-war days, it will be remembered, when in some sudden emergency we offered our assistance at the sink, it was always clearly understood that we men did not concern ourselves with saucepans – nor indeed with any cooking utensil likely to have dried foodstuffs adhering tenaciously to its sides and bottom. We did the plates and cutlery and we held the glasses momentarily under the tap. But the rest was women's work; somebody would do it in the morning. Those spacious days are over. Nothing, literally nothing, is nowadays considered too revolting for a man to touch. When I say that men have been known to tackle those brown earthenware jars used for Lancashire hot-pot, from the rims of which (for this is not the place to speak of their unimaginable interiors) the jagged ridges of caked and blackened gravy must be chipped off with a chisel, when I mention this simple fact returning husbands will, I think, gain some notion of the pass to which we have come.

Very well, then. Now to my correspondent, whose name I decipher as Brandsop or (more improbably) Brushoff. He writes:

'I can get most of the porridge out all right with the scratcher, but it won't do the corners or the part where the handle joins the top of the saucepan. Poking about with a skewer is fatiguing work and makes me late with the fireplaces, nor does it really do the job properly. I am at my wits' end and would give up porridge altogether, if we could get any eggs, bacon, kidneys or fish.'

Well, this is a problem that has puzzled most of us in our time. Nor is it to be solved by any such drastic expedient as dropping porridge off the menu, because (apart from any other considerations) exactly the same difficulty crops up with boiled milk. So let's face it boldly, shall we?

When Mr Brandsop speaks of the 'scratcher' he is referring undoubtedly to that bundle of twisted wire which is usually kept in a soap-dish on the draining-board or under the plate-rack, and he is absolutely right to use it for the main interior surfaces of the pan. Used fearlessly, with a brisk rotatory movement, the scratcher will clear up the most stubborn situation in no time. But it is not designed to penetrate nooks and crannies. For such pockets of resistance as the corners of a saucepan and (as Mr Brandsop well says) the junction of the handle with the main framework, a special instrument has been devised and is to be found in any well-appointed scullery. If Mr Brandsop will look round he may find a piece of apparatus resembling a bundle of twigs bound about the middle with a metal clasp. It is often balanced behind the kitchen taps, where these are close enough together to afford a lodgment, and may have escaped his observation. The correct name for this thing is not known to me; it is referred to in this house as the 'scritcher', and the name, which conveys with some fidelity the greater precision and delicacy with which it scratches, will serve as well as another. Now, having possessed yourself of scratcher *and* scritcher, here is the way to go to work. First scour out with the scratcher, rinse and pour away. Most of the porridge will now be embedded in the scratcher, but that need not concern you. Bad as things are, the time has not yet come when we men are expected to clean the scratcher. Next take the scritcher and scritch lightly but firmly in all the crevices. Rinse again. Finish by whisking round the rim of the saucepan in such a way that half the bristles of the scritcher are inside and half out. Give it a final rinse, mop out and hang up or hurl under the dresser according to local custom.

Before I leave Mr Brandsop's or (as seen from some angles) **Mr Brushoff's** letter, I must just sound one rather serious note. He talks of being made 'late with the fire-places' by his difficulties with the porridge saucepan! If this means, as I fear it does, Mr Brandsop, that you are leaving the fireplaces until after breakfast, I can only say that you are starting the day under a hopeless handicap. Do get the sitting-room at least tidied up and the fire laid *first thing* in the morning. We were not allowed to be slovenly in the Army. Don't let us be content with a lower standard in the privacy of our own homes.

I have spent so long over this very important problem of saucepans that I have only time now to deal very briefly with a point raised by Mr Joseph Twill, of Mole's End, Gloucestershire. He wants to know whether it is possible to stop milk boiling over, and suggests that a really deep saucepan might conceivably be a solution.

I propose to answer Mr Twill's question by enunciating a number of rules for milk-boilers. They are based on common sense and a wide experience of mopping up milk both on gas and electric stoves.

1. *Never* boil milk. Heat it till turgid and remove.

2. It is impossible to combine the heating of milk with any other pursuit whatsoever. (The same rule applies to the toasting of bread under a grill. Thus to attempt to heat milk and toast bread at the same time – a very common fault – is the height of insanity. The only thing to be said for it is that the milk in boiling over puts the toast out.)

3. An unwatched pot boils *immediately*.

4. Half a pint of milk brought to a temperature of 100° Centigrade rises to a height greater than the walls of the saucepan, *irrespective of the dimensions of the saucepan*. To take an extreme case, if a jug of milk were poured into the crater of Vesuvius, Pompeii would inevitably be engulfed a second time.

5. The speed at which boiling milk rises from the bottom of the pan to any point beyond the top is greater than the speed at which the human brain and hand can combine to snatch the confounded thing off.

Follow these rules, Mr Twill, and you will be all right. But keep a dish-cloth handy.

February 1946

E.V. Lucas

THE MURDER AT THE TOWERS

The Most Marvellous Mystery Story in the World

NB No clues will give you the slightest assistance in unravelling this weird mystery.

CHAPTER I
DEATH

Mr Ponderby-Wilkins was a man so rich, so ugly, so cross, and so old that even the stupidest reader could not expect him to survive any longer than Chapter I. Vulpine in his secretiveness, he was porcine in his habits, saturnine in his appearance, and ovine in his unconsciousness of doom. He was the kind of man who might easily perish as early as paragraph two.

Little surprise, therefore, was shown by Police-Inspector Blowhard of Nettleby Parva when a message reached him on the telephone:

'*You are wanted immediately at The Towers. Mr Ponderby-Wilkins has been found dead.*'

The inspector was met at the gate by the deceased's secretary, whom he knew and suspected on the spot.

'Where did it happen, Mr Porlock?' he asked. 'In the shrubbery?'

The stout officer's face was like a mask, but paler at the point of the nose.

'In the shrubbery,' answered Porlock quietly and led the way to the scene.

Mr Ponderby-Wilkins was sus-

The Inspector was met at the gate by the deceased's secretary

pended by means of an enormous woollen muffler from the bough of a tree which the police-officer's swift eye noticed at once to be a sycamore.

'How long has that sycamore tree been in the shrubbery?' he inquired suspiciously.

'I don't know,' answered Porlock, 'and I don't care.'

'Tell me precisely what happened,' went on the inspector.

'Four of us were playing tennis under the ordinary rules when a ball was hit out into the bushes. On going to look for it at the end of the set, I found Mr Wilkins dangling as you see him, and called the attention of the other players to the circumstances at once. Here they all are.'

And pushing aside the boughs of a laurel, he showed the police-officer two young women and a young man. They were standing reverently in the middle of the tennis-court, holding their tennis-racquets sombrely in their hands.

'Do you corroborate Mr Porlock's account of the affair?' inquired Blowhard.

'We do,' they answered quietly in one breath.

'Give me one of those tennis-balls,' said Blowhard.

Porlock gave him one. He threw it on the ground. It bounced.

'Hum!' mused the inspector, stroking his chin. 'By the way', he continued, 'I wonder whether life is extinct?'

He went and looked at the body. It was.

'A glance showed us that life was extinct when we found it,' said the four, speaking together, 'and we thought it better to go on playing tennis as funereally as possible until you arrived.'

'Quite right,' said Blowhard. 'I shall now examine the whole household *viva voce*. Kindly summon them to the drawing-room.'

They went together into the large white-fronted mansion, and soon the notes of a gong, reverberating through the house and all over the grounds, had summoned the whole house-party, including the servants, to the Louis-Seize

The gathering consisted of the usual types involved in a country-house murder

salon overlooking the tennis lawn. The gathering consisted, as the inspector had foreseen, of the usual types involved in a country-house murder; namely, a frightened step-sister of the deceased, a young and beautiful niece, a major, a KC, a chaperon, a friend, Mr Porlock himself, an old butler with a beard, a middle-aged gardener with whiskers, an Irish cook, and two servants who had only come to the place the week before. Every one of them had a bitter grudge against the deceased. He had been about to dismiss his secretary, had threatened to disinherit his niece, sworn repeatedly at his step-sister, thrown a port decanter at the butler's head, insulted the guests by leaving *Bradshaws* in their bedrooms, pulled up the gardener's anti-rrhinùms, called the cook a good-for-nothing, and terrified the housemaids by making noises at them on the stairs. In addition, he had twice informed the major that his regiment had run away at Balaclava, and had put a toad in the KC's bed.

Blowhard felt instinctively that this was a case for Bletherby Marge, the famous amateur, and sent him a telegram at once. Then he ordered the body to be removed, walked round the grounds, ate a few strawberries and went home.

CHAPTER II
BEWILDERMENT!

Bletherby Marge was a man of wide culture and sympathy. In appearance he was fat, red-faced, smiling, and had untidy hair. He looked stupid, and wore spats. In fact, whatever the inexperienced reader supposes to be the ordinary appearance of a detective was exactly the reverse of Bletherby Marge. He was sometimes mistaken for a businessman or a bimetallist, more often for a billiard-marker or a baboon. But whenever Scotland Yard was unable to deal with a murder case – that is to say, whenever a murder case happened at a country house – Bletherby Marge was called in. The death of an old, rich, and disagreeable man was like a clarion call to him. He packed his pyjamas, his tooth-brush and a volume of *Who's Who* and took the earliest train.

As soon as he had seen the familiar news-bill –

'ANOTHER COUNTRY-HOUSE OWNER INEXPLICABLY
SLAIN'

he had expected his summons to The Towers. Telegraphing to the coroner's jury to return an open verdict at Nettleby Parva, he

finished off the case of the Duke of St Neots, fragments of whom had
mysteriously been discovered in a chaff-cutting machine, and made
all haste to the scene of the new affair. He had now dealt with
forty-nine mysteries, and in every single case he had triumphantly
killed his man. A small silver gallows had been presented to him by
Scotland Yard as a token of esteem.

'We are in deep waters, Blowhard, very deep,' he said as he closely
scrutinised the comforter which had been wrapped round Mr
Ponderby-Wilkins's throat. 'Just tell me once more about these
alibis.'

'Every one of them is perfect,' answered the police inspector, 'so
far as I can see. The butler, the cook and the two housemaids were all
together playing poker in the pantry. Miss Brown, the deceased's
step-sister, was giving instructions to the gardener, and the KC was
with her, carrying her trowel and her pruning-scissors. The chaperon and the friend were playing tennis with Mr Porlock and the
major, and the niece was rowing herself about on the lake, picking
water-lilies.'

A gleam came into Bletherby Marge's eyes. 'Alone?' he queried.

'Alone. But you forget that the lake is in full view of the tennis-
court. It almost seems as if it must have been constructed that way on
purpose,' added the inspector rather crossly. 'This girl was seen the
whole time during which the murder must have occurred, either by
one pair of players or the other.'

'Tut, tut,' said Bletherby Marge. 'By the way,' he went on, with a
slight hoisting of the eyebrows, 'I suppose you have been into the
pigeon-loft?'

'No', replied Blowhard, with a slight drooping of his moustache.
'The holes were too small.'

'Have you walked about in the lake?'

'Not yet,' answered Blowhard. 'It is too full of mud.'

'Excellent,' said Bletherby Marge. 'Now take me to the scene of
the crime.'

Arrived at the sycamore tree, he studied the bark with a micro-
scope, and the ground underneath. This was covered with dead
leaves. There was no sign of a struggle.

'Show me exactly how the body was hanging,' he said to Blowhard.

Police-Inspector Blowhard tied the two ends of the comforter to
the bough and wrapped the loop several times round Bletherby
Marge's neck, supporting him, as he did so, by the feet.

'Don't let go,' said Bletherby Marge.

'I won't,' said Blowhard, who was used to the great detective's methods in reconstructing crime.

'Have you photographed the tree from every angle?' went on Bletherby.

'Yes.'

'Were there any finger-prints on it?'

'No,' replied Blowhard. 'Nothing but leaves.'

Then together they wandered round the grounds, eating fruit and discussing possible motives for the murder. No will had been discovered.

'Don't let go,' said Bletherby Marge

From time to time one or other of the house-party would flit by them, humming a song, intent on a game of tennis or a bathe in the lake. Now and then a face would look haggard or strained, at other times the same face would be merry and wreathed with smiles. Once Bletherby picked up a large stone under a bush. It had an earwig on it, and he put it down again.

'Do you feel baffled?' asked Blowhard.

Bletherby Marge made no reply.

CHAPTER III
SUSPENSE!

The house-party were having a motor picnic at Dead Man's Wood, ten miles from The Towers. The festivity had been proposed by Bletherby Marge, who was more and more endearing himself, by his jokes and wide knowledge of the world, to his fellow guests. Many of them had already begun to feel that a house-party without a detective in it must be regarded as a literary failure.

'Bless my soul!' said Marge suddenly, when the revelry was at its height, turning to Blowhard, who was out of breath, for he had been carrying the champagne across a ploughed field; 'I ask you all to excuse me for a moment. I have forgotten my pipe.'

They saw him disappear in a two-seater towards The Towers. In little more than an hour he appeared again and delighted the company by singing one or two popular revue-songs in a fruity baritone. But as the line of cars went homeward in the dusk Bletherby Marge said to Blowhard seated beside him, 'I want to see you again in the shrubbery tomorrow at 10.30 prompt. Don't begin playing clock-golf.'

Inspector Blowhard made a note of the time in his pocket-book.

CHAPTER IV
DISCOVERY!

'Perhaps you wonder why I went away in the middle of our little outing?' questioned Marge as they stood together under the fatal sycamore tree.

'I suspected,' answered Blowhard, not moving a muscle of his face except the ones he used for speaking, 'that it was a ruse.'

'It was,' replied Marge.

Without another word he took a small folding broom from his pocket and brushed aside the dead leaves which strewed the ground of the shrubbery.

The dark mould was covered with footprints large and small.

'What do you deduce from this?' cried Blowhard, his eyes bulging from his head.

'When I returned from the picnic,' explained the great detective, 'I first swept the ground clear as you see it now. I then hastily collected all the outdoor shoes in the house.'

'All?'

'Every one. I brought them to the shrubbery on a wheelbarrow. I locked the servants, as though by accident, in the kitchen and the gardener in the tool-shed. I then compared the shoes with these imprints, and found that every one of them was a fit.'

'Which means?'

One or two popular revue-songs in a fruity baritone

'That every one of them was here when the murder took place. I have reconstructed the scene exactly. The marks of the shoes stretch in a long line, as you will observe, from a point close to the tree almost to the edge of the tennis-lawn. The heels are very deeply imprinted, the mark of the toes is very light indeed.'

He paused and looked at Blowhard.

'I suppose you see now how the murder was done?' he barked loudly.

'No,' mewed the inspector quietly.

'I then collected all the outdoor shoes'

'Ponderby-Wilkins,' said Marge, 'had the comforter twisted once round his neck, and one end was tied to the tree. Then – at a signal, I imagine – the whole house-party, including the servants, pulled together on the other end of the comforter until he expired. You see here the imprints of the butler's feet. As the heaviest man he was at the end of the rope. Porlock was in front with the second housemaid immediately behind him. Porlock, I fancy, gave the word to pull. Afterwards they tied him up to the tree as you found him when you arrived.'

'But the alibis?'

'All false. They were all sworn to by members of the household, by servants or by guests. That was what put me on the scent.'

'But how is it there were no finger-prints?'

'The whole party,' answered Bletherby, 'wore gloves. I collected all the gloves in the house and examined them carefully. Many of them had hairs from the comforter still adhering to them. Having concluded my investigations, I rapidly replaced the boots and gloves, put the leaves back in their original position, unlocked the kitchen and the tool-house, and came back to the picnic again.'

'And sang comic songs!' said Blowhard.

'Yes,' replied Marge. 'A great load had been taken off my mind by the discovery of the truth. And I felt it necessary to put the murderers off their guard.'

'Wonderful!' exclaimed Blowhard, examining the footprints minutely. 'There is now only one difficulty, Mr Marge, so far as I can see.'

'And that is?'

'How am I going to convey all these people to the police-station?'

'How many pairs of manacles have you about you?'

'Only two,' confessed Blowhard, feeling in his pocket.

'You had better telephone,' said Bletherby, 'for a motor-omnibus.'

CHAPTER V
HA! HA!!

The simultaneous trial of twelve prisoners on a capital charge, followed by their joint condemnation and execution, thrilled England as no sensation had thrilled it since the death of WILLIAM II. The Sunday papers were never tired of discussing the psychology of the murderers, and publishing details of their early life and school careers. Never before, it seemed, had a secretary, a step-sister, a niece, an eminent KC, a major, a chaperon, a friend, a butler, a cook, two housemaids and a gardener gone to the gallows on the same day for the murder of a disagreeable old man.

On a morning not long after the excitement had died away Bletherby Marge made his way up the drive of The Towers, which, owing to the recent tragedy, was still 'To Let'. Avoiding the main building, Bletherby Marge went to the stables and fetched a ladder. Propping this against the pigeon-loft he ascended. He put his hand into one of the compartments and drew out an egg. Stifling an exclamation of annoyance he tried again, and found a dusty bundle of papers tied together with a bootlace.

It was Ponderby-Wilkins's will. On the first page was written –

> '*Nobody loves me, and I am about to commit suicide by hanging myself in the shrubbery. If Bletherby Marge can make it a murder I bequeath him all my possessions, which are lying in jam-jars at the bottom of the lake.*'

'My fiftieth!' murmured the great detective as he came down the ladder with a smile.

May 1929

Alan Coren

AN EXCLUSIVE INTERVIEW WITH IDI AMIN

Coren: President Amin, I'd first of all like …

Amin: And Managing-Director.

Coren: I'm sorry?

Amin: President And Managing-Director Amin.

Coren: I see. Well, then.

Amin: And Chairman. President And Managing-Director And Chairman Amin. We getting the door done today. Also where it says holder of the Victoria Cross, KBE, SRN, and Commissioner For Oaths.

Coren: That's going to be some door, Mr President, ha-ha-ha!

Amin: You wipe that grin off of your face, whitey, if you don't want the Papal Guard comin' round and nailing your head to the skirting!

Coren: I'm sorry. I didn't realise you were a holder of the Victoria Cross. What did you get it for?

Amin: For the brown worsted.

Coren: I beg your pardon?

Amin: That's the kind of talk I like to hear!

Coren: What I meant was, I don't understand about your getting the Victoria Cross for the Brown Worsted. This was some glorious defeat of a native regiment, I imagine? Worsted by the Germans, no doubt?

Amin: What this crap you giving me here? I got the Victoria Cross for the brown worsted on account of the bronze is setting off the material a treat. It go with the Old Wykehamist tie, also. For the charcoal grey, I got the Iron Cross.

Coren: I see.

Amin: With the crossed oak-leaves and palms.

Coren: Ah, well, sir …

Amin: Wow! Hit me with that again, whitey.

Coren: What?

Amin: That sir stuff. That the real thing!

Coren: Yes. What I wanted to talk about first of all is your telegram to the Secretary-General of the UN saying, and I quote, 'Germany is the right place where, when Hitler was the Prime Minister and Supreme Commander, he burnt over six million Jews'.

Amin: He done pretty good for a white man. Must be on account he was coal-black first time around.

Coren: I'm sorry?

Amin: I had Buddha on the phone this morning. He come straight through, no messing about with the 'This are Buddha's secretary on the line' routine, like Rippon. You tell Rippon, next time he come here, he gonna get ate. Anyway, Buddha says 'Is this President And Managing-Director And Chairman Amin what I got the honour of speaking to?' and I said 'You damn right, by Jove' and he said 'Hum, I had no idea you was an Oxford man' and I told him about being Bee Ay and Pee Aitch Dee and now working for the famous O Level, and he said 'A man can't get too much education, I got Adolf Hitler up here and he right beside me and he nodding away and he also want to point out where he was black first time aroun' and no hard feelings over the Jesse Owen business, just his bad luck coming back all white, had to take what he could get' and I said 'That's all right, Buddha, it don't matter whether you is black or white, so long as your heart is in the right place, but I gonna fix the Jews, anyhow, and they had an easy ride since poor old Adolf got his.'

Coren: I see. You also said in that same telegram that all the Israelis should be kicked out and sent to Britain. I don't follow you.

Amin: You watch your language, pig. Anyone don't follow me likely to wind up as hamburger.

Coren: I meant I didn't understand why the Israelis should go to Britain.

Amin: That called a firm grasp of history. You don't want to try understanding that unless you can read them books with all the syllables joined together. I got a man does it for me. And while we're on the subject, I'm telling you all the Chinese better get back to Gerrard Street pretty damn quick, else me and God going to want to know the reason why. What I'm talking about is where all these yellow bastards is sitting on this top-class real estate in the Far East what rightfully belong to the black man, according to Isaiah xiv, 23. After that, we gonna give Wales back to the Sioux.

Coren: What I was really trying to discover, Mr ...

Amin: Hold on, it time for my levitation.

Coren: Levitation?

Amin: Every morning at eleven, I float around the office for a bit. It are working wonders for dyspepsia, also give me gleaming coat. There we go.

Coren: I can't actually see ...

Amin: Wow, the world look totally different from up here, by Jove! We chucking out all people with the lousy eyesight by the way, also cutting off their ears at the airport. How'm I doing?

Coren: Absolutely amazing. Mr President! Do mind the chandelier.

Amin: This sure as hell beat walking on the water, baby! I think I'll chuck all the Christians out next. If it good enough for Attila the Nun, it good enough for me.

Coren: Attila the Hun.

Amin: And him. Now we got the Russians and the Asians and the Brits chucked out, we got a bit of room to see. There too many damn Christians about this place, also having some very nice property; I gonna get me a cathedral, man in my position he got to have a decent spire, got to be able to see all these Jews and Pakis coming up the road. I think I'll put a twelve-pounder in the belfry, teach 'em not to start messing around with God. Whoops, here come another vision!

Coren: Can you describe it?

Amin: It a rainbow with Colonel Gadhafi on the end of it. He carrying a suitcase full of used notes. Boy, it good being a Muslim these days! Did I tell you we got plans to get all the tsetse flies out of Uganda? Disgusting, hanging around here knocking off cattle and hoarding foreign currency! It Britain's responsibility. You got to take 'em back.

Coren: President Amin, I wonder if ...

Amin: No good lookin' up there, boy. I back down here now. Under this halo.

Coren: Forgive me ...

Amin: Oh, pour that stuff on! You really know your place, son. Okay, just this once, ego absolvo te, and that'll be ten aves, ten paternosters, and fifty quid to the Distressed Ugandan President's Fighting Fund, no cheques. You lucky I a Muslim, you gettin' off pretty damn light there. Hum, it just come to me that being of the West Nile tribe, it about time I chucked out all them other black creeps what are cluttering up this great country. It gonna be called West Nile from now on. It gonna be me and God runnin' these eighty thousand West Nile fellahs, there gonna be plenty goin' round for everyone.

Coren: But what about the Baganda, what about the Tutsi, what about the Sudani?

Amin: Hm, I see you been readin' the famous Whitaker's Almanac, I warning you, son, God and me got plans to wipe out anyone not stickin' to *A Is For Apple* like they been told. There's too many clever bastards knocking about this country. As far as them tribes go, they going, and bloody sharp, too. They polluting the pure West Nile blood stock, also eatin' too much gross national product, also their women got thin legs. Just gonna be me and the West Nile people and God. And I tellin' you, if the West Nile people start gettin' any funny ideas, pretty soon it gonna be just me and God.

Coren: There's one more thing, Mr President. I wonder if you have any idea why I'm making you sound like the white racist stereotype of a minstrel-show illiterate who can't tie his own shoelace without getting a white man in to do it for him?

Amin: You just go on talking there for a bit, son, I'm gettin' another big thought coming through.

Coren: Don't you think it might be because what infuriates me more than anything is that you've done more than anyone this century to give the white supremacists an argument for claiming that *every* African black man is a minstrel-show illiterate who can't tie his own shoelace without getting a white man to do it for him?

Amin: Here come that big thought, son. You remember me telling you about how if the people get any funny ideas, it just gonna be me and God left in this place?

Coren: Yes.

Amin: It just occurring to me that God better not start getting no ideas above his station, neither.

September 1972

Ann Leslie

THE FIRST TWO WEEKS ARE THE WORST

I'M told that along the rainswept pierheads of English summer-seasons, the damp souls of comics are still sprouting honeymoon stories, knowing that a joke about newly-weds has the effect of instantly galvanising old ladies in deckchairs – like hitting them on the knee with a hammer. 'No, see, eh?, no, don't laugh, there was this honeymoon couple see ... ooooh, *naughty*, I can see you darlin', put 'im *down* ... anyway, this honeymoon couple ...' Nudge, nudge, ho, ho. Maeve and Else cackle joyously through their toffomints remembering how Fred's mates at the bottle-works put frogs in Alice's wedding bed and gave her such a turn. In those days, honeymoons were epic events in one's life, something worthy of being laughed at ...

Mind you, it was always working-class honeymoons which were supposed to be ipso facto screamingly funny: never upper-class ones. Working-class honeymoons were spent in boarding houses with noisy bed-springs which rang out like tocsins across the prom. Upper-class ones were apparently always Romantic, spent by limp-wristed young things called Charles and Amanda at Cap d'Antibes, surrounded by champagne buckets and portly Hungarians playing passionate fiddles under the tree. Curiously, sex didn't seem to come in to the latter sort of honeymoon at all, whereas in the first type, it was the only thing that did.

But on the whole it looks as if the honeymoon joke is gradually losing its place in the joke-book pantheon, along with all those other sure-fire rib-ticklers, Scotsmen, sporrans, mother-in-law and public loos. Permissiveness has probably killed it off.

After all, the whole point of the honeymoon joke was that it was the First Time they'd Had It. Now, by all accounts, everyone's Had It almost as soon as they've cut their milk teeth.

I remember being told by one world-weary little thirteen-year-old in California how much she deplored the declining moral standards of today's eight-year-olds. 'Sex, sex, sex, that's all they ever think of. Why, when I was their age I was still playing with dolls,' she said, as she popped Tuesday's pill out of its easy-dial packet and set off for another hair-bleaching session at the beauty salon.

Now *I* was brought up – ah, what innocent aeons ago – by nuns who told their spotty little charges that a man who Truly Loved you would Respect you until the wedding night, whereupon, apparently, appalling disrespect would take place, which was unfortunately the price you had to pay for the privilege of frying his fish-fingers and soaking his smalls for the rest of your days.

We heard a great deal about woman's Finer Feelings and man's

Lower Instincts but never had a chance to put the theories to the test
since the only males for miles around our convent were Ron, the
scrofulous gardener's boy, and gloomy Father Flaherty, the parish
priest, fresh from the bog, with a face like a fist, a hot line in hellfire,
and a habit of tying his gloves to his wrists in case he lost them, so
that during his passionate sermons on Fleshy Lust, they bobbed and
weaved hysterically about his body like giant bees ...

But nowadays of course it's all different and the whole sexual
initiation part of a honeymoon has gone. Now the honeymoon is
meant to be nothing less than a divine, star-spun interlude for you
both before you get down to the real nitty-gritty of life among the
Squezy mops in Spanland.

Of course, you're still supposed to spend most of it joyously
tumbling about in bed together, only none of that beginner's stuff:
it's got to be a really jazzy production number these days, real
high-wire acrobatics. The whole thing imposes an intolerable strain
on a couple who've only just managed to pull through the horrors of
the wedding reception.

Most of my married friends swear they all came nearest to divorce
during their honeymoons.

Like a girl-friend of mine who spent her wedding night tramping
about Dawlish and district in the rain with a husband who said he
swore he remembered the hotel they'd booked into was called
Seaview, and for Christsake, stop moaning, there couldn't be more
than twenty Seaviews in Dawlish, *could* there ... Well, there could,
and actually it was called Seacliffe, and by the time they got there
Mrs Potter said she was ever so sorry but she'd disposed of the Bridal
Suite to a commercial traveller, and some hours later the bride
barked coldly at her spouse as she boarded the coach home to mother
'I'm having THIS annulled for a start!'

Surviving the honeymoon is probably the first great hurdle in a
marriage. I was once despatched to Canada on a ship which, my
editor was erroneously informed, was a Honeymoon Special, groaning at the gunwales with 1,500 emigrating newly-weds.

In fact there were four. The first couple had inadvertently been
booked into separate cabins by the steamship company: she sharing
with three Jehovah's Witnesses, and he with four members of a
construction gang heading for Saskatchewan.

The other couple, who'd won their 'dream' honeymoon in a
cornflake contest, were together, but only just, as she spent most of

the time being sick in the cabin while he glumly downed Guinnesses and played shove ha'penny in the bar. Beneath us the wintry Atlantic heaved like a peptic whale. After a honeymoon like that, married life in Moose Jaw or Calgary could only be blissful improvement.

Of course, the over-selling of honeymoons has even begun to worry social workers. One of them, the secretary of the Fulham and Hammersmith Citizens Advice Bureau, no less, recently quoted by the *News of the World* as blaming 'honeymoon blues' for the break-up of so many young marriages. 'The proceedings', she said, 'aren't as romantic as they would like them to be.'

Well of course not. Honeymoons are a time for the destruction of illusions, particularly those appertaining to the naturally dewy-fresh beauty of the bride. Before marriage you could maintain your beauty was a gift from God and didn't come expensively bottled by Max Factor.

Many's the young husband who must have suffered a cold frisson of fright on first glimpsing his wife minus eyebrows and eyelashes and all greased up like a Channel swimmer in Orange Skin Food. Of course, in America they've already thought of that, and the bride can buy sex-prufe lipstick, eyelashes and wigs, and in case you've got the sort of droopy boobs which hit your knees with a thud when you shed your bra, you can buy nightdresses with built-in foundation garments: 'So soft, so subtle, He'll never Guess!'

To keep the illusion going, you can also book into that ultimate sexual depressant, the Honeymoon hotel, complete with heart-shaped bed, heart-shaped bath, heart-shaped swimming pool, heart-shaped skating rink, and heart-shaped jokes pinned over the dining room exits saying 'We know where you're going!' Over the beds, there's a heart-shaped mirror so you can watch yourself in action, if, that is, you've got the heart for it any more ...

The only honeymoon I've had so far doesn't encourage me to try another. Ever. We were married in Compton and squabbled furiously all the way down to our hotel in Midhurst.

On arrival, my husband, who puts his all into rows and consequently finds them very debilitating, sank exhausted with rage onto the fourposter and fell asleep, while I went downstairs and watched James Mason in 'Five Fingers' on the hotel telly. Actually this was rather appropriate as I'd been in love with Mason for years and had always dreamt, while doodling on my Latin Primer, of spending my wedding night with James anyway. I once wrote him a poem in which I described his voice as 'soft footfalls in the dark' which I thought amazingly good, but which inexplicably failed to bring him panting to my side. My husband had always felt the same way about Anne Bancroft, but well, there you are. James and Anne always seemed to be otherwise occupied, so we'd had to settle for each other instead.

The next day we flew to Switzerland to ski, where I promptly broke my leg, due to being hit by a tree which sprang out of the ski-slope, narrowly missing my husband but pole-axeing me. It probably knew I was on honeymoon. By then suffering from honeymooners' paranoia, I felt sure I heard it rattling its cones with sadistic glee as I passed out in a red haze at its feet.

I spent the rest of our honeymoon – all ten days of it – in a plaster-cast lying on a playdeck half way up an Alp wedged between motionless rows of old ladies wrapped in blankets mummifying in the sun, with plastic 'beaks' sprouting from their sunglasses to save their noses from peeling. They resembled a lot of up-ended owls and none of them were great conversationalists – except for the lady who told me every day that she could forecast avalanches by the excruciating twinges she got in her lower intestine, and her friend, who apparently owned three-quarters of Peru and had an understandable thing about Communists.

After three days of this, the sight of my husband, bronzed, merry, magnificent, shussing down the mountainside surrounded by gaily carolling girls made me long to shove him down a crevasse, hobble home and collect on the life insurance.

Things are improving now, but the honeymoon scars took some time to heal and I can't say I've ever quite forgiven him yet ...

April 1971

E.S. Turner

DOG, SPARE THAT POSTMAN

IF asked by a quizmaster 'In what sphere of human endeavour should you *keep your head and heart up and your hands and feet down?*' the average citizen might guess 'rock-climbing' or even 'watching a dull film'. In fact, this advice was given by Mr Ephraim Martin, postmaster of Boston, Massachusetts, to his postmen at the opening of the dog-biting season (May to August).

Mr Martin wants his hard-bitten staff to show 'more respect for every dog'. He offers the usual tips which dog-lovers have offered to dog-loathers from time immemorial: 'Don't antagonise dogs or strike them ... make no sudden movement ... don't run ... stand still and speak to them in a soothing tone ... give them time to get used to your friendship'. Unexceptionable advice. The only thing wrong with it is that it frequently fails to work.

Similar instructions were given to the postmen of Switzerland in 1953, with important additions. If the dog was a French-speaking one it was to be addressed as '*chien*' (many French dogs have no other name). For difficult animals a distribution of bones or sausage was recommended, at the postman's own expense. In emergencies, the postman was advised to crouch like a prize-fighter, take partial cover behind his bag, look his foe in the eye and sharply exclaim 'Scram!' (a word evidently understood by all Swiss dogs).

To return to Boston. Mr Martin said his department was tired of trying to protect its men with chemical dog repellents. It was true that a reasonably effective substance had been sprayed on the bottoms of trouser-legs, but it had caused the treated portions to disintegrate and fall off. Fortunately it was never tried on trouser seats.

Six years ago American postmen were being bitten at the rate of 5,880 a year. Of these, 500 took to their beds for two days or more and nearly seventy-five per cent required medical aid. Seventy-two per cent of bites were below the knee, thirteen per cent on hand or arm, and three per cent in regions delicately listed as 'elsewhere'.

It was disclosed then that many postmen had taken to carrying water pistols filled with a weak solution of ammonia. Dogs did not show any special resentment but their owners did and the idea was abandoned on the ground that it was bad for public relations. The public image of the American postman has always been that of a friendly, if garrulous, philosopher, not of a man skulking about with his finger on the trigger.

Other proposals were that postmen should wear pantaloons reinforced with metal corset stiffeners, or with wire mesh; but trials showed that armoured pantaloons were disagreeable to wear. From California came a suggestion that a postman should take a big dog

round with him, but this was thought likely to start more fights than
it would prevent.

At that time the American postal authorities were really worried;
and they announced that householders who refused to restrain their
dogs would have to fetch their own letters. To some, this seemed
hardly in keeping with the spirit of the Postal Pledge, as laid down by
Herodotus: 'Neither snow, nor rain, nor heat, nor gloom of night
stays these couriers from the swift completion of their appointed
rounds.' But Herodotus would have listed dogs if he had thought it a
postman's duty to fight them off; evidently he had not.

What may have further agitated the authorities was the filing of a
claim by a postman of Great Neck, New York, for £35,000 damages
in respect of eighteen bites received over a period of eleven years.
This ex-Marine who had come through the war unscarred complained that his first assault (by a poodle) had deprived him of the
ability to employ the postman's best defence against dogs: a well-
aimed swipe with the letter-bag. His figure of £35,000 would have
seemed on the high side to the Malayan Postal and Telecommuni-
cations Uniformed Staff Union, whose members in 1959 presented a
demand for a flat sum of £5 17s. per bite (they also urged that
dog-owners should install letter-boxes on the periphery of their
property).

Whether American postmen are more susceptible to dog-bites
than those of other lands is hard to say, since no proper international
statistics are kept. In Britain postmen face about two-and-a-half
million dogs at least once a day and they keep their heads and hearts
up without any official exhortation to do so. The Postmaster-
General disclaims all responsibility when a postman is bitten on
duty, but he will offer advice if an injured postman decides to sue a
dog-owner (in Malaya the Government contributes towards the cost
of advocacy in approved cases). Postmen are warned that there is
little hope of a successful prosecution unless a dog is known to be
ferocious.

Reluctantly a number of postmen do bring actions against householders. Sometimes the chairman of the bench says 'Postmen must
and will be protected,' and orders that, if the animal offends again, it
must be destroyed. Sometimes the owner, after a caution, is given an
absolute discharge. Sometimes the bench takes no action and it is the
postman who leaves the court with his tail between his legs.

These prosecutions show the enormous forbearance of Her Majesty's couriers. 'I don't blame the dog,' said a postman at Guildford, 'I was a stranger to him.' At Winchester a postman went voluntarily into the box to give evidence of character on behalf of an elkhound accused of biting a child. 'In the course of my job,' he said, 'I have met a good many dogs and I think this dog is as docile as a dog can be.' A Hornsey postman said he was on excellent terms with almost all the two hundred dogs on his delivery. Very probably he delivered Christmas cards to the more privileged of them.

Dog-owners emerge from the courts less creditably. They hold it right and reasonable that a civil servant should have to ingratiate himself with two hundred dogs in the course of a day's work; if a man is pinned to the railings by a Boxer it is obviously due to a defect in the fellow's character. They say that if a dog bites a postman it must have been kicked by a postman in infancy. They blame the postman for 'not standing firm' or 'showing the white feather'. They blame him for going about in a uniform. They say their dogs never attack meter-readers, milkmen or dustmen. They are indignant at being brought to court and, if they apologise, the fact is never reported.

The postman's view is likely to be that 'a dog that will bite a postman will bite anybody'. If pressed, he will probably list the most aggressive dogs as fox terriers, Scotties and Cairns. Scotties, it seems, have a habit of presenting a friendly face and then attacking from the rear.

It is a tradition that 'the mail must go through', but tradition does not insist that it must go through a barrage of sharp yellow teeth. If a British postman is confronted by a hostile dog he is entitled to withdraw and write on the letter 'Dog at large – delivery delayed' or words to that effect. If his next two attempts to deliver are rebuffed, the householder is informed – by whatever means are available – that if he wants his mail he must call and collect it.

Meter-readers do not always escape canine attention. At Doncaster in 1955 an official of the RSPCA gave advice on dog-befriending to employees of the Yorkshire Electricity Board. 'Dogs must be understood,' said the spokesman, whose name might well have been Ephraim Martin. 'The right approach is to treat a dog as a human being.' A by no means despicable body of opinion holds that the right approach is to treat a dog as a dog.

Two years ago the Medical Officer of Health for Hendon expressed the view that dustmen received fewer bites than postmen because they saved food scraps to buy off potential aggressors.

Municipal officials in Camberwell concurred. A Post Office spokesman replied that a postman may carry titbits with him if he wishes,
but these are not a departmental issue or expense.

It remains to say that postwomen are also bitten from time to time.
At Swindon an indignant postwoman called on a householder to
show him a group of toothmarks on her leg. The Alsatian responsible
thought he was being offered another opportunity and bit her again;
a very natural misunderstanding, as any dog-lover will testify. The
records reveal that householders have bought pairs of stockings and
even underslips for postwomen; which only goes to show how little
we know what our neighbours are up to.

May 1962

Jonathan Sale

THE DOGS OF WAR

SNOB the Dog was certainly old enough to fight for his country. In
fact he fought for two countries, first on the Russian side in the
Crimea and then, sensing that his owner's corpse would not be much
good at providing walkies, for the British. There haven't been many
animals 'turned' le-Carré-style (Tinker, Taylor, Soldier, Snob the
Dog) but this one served the Queen loyally until death, when a full
military funeral was provided by the mourning regiment, complete
with pall-bearers and three rounds of ammunition fired over the
grave.

Don't take my word for that, check the stuffed hound in the
exhibition *Animals in War* at the Imperial War Museum near
Lambeth North Tube. Perhaps you will be able to answer something
on my mind: if the dog was given a Christian burial, how come its
carcass is Exhibit No. Eighteen in the third case on the left? If this is
another Hitler's diaries scandal, Lord Dacre should be called in to
verify it isn't a fur and skin forgery. (And then we consult an expert.)

There is no doubt about Judy the Pointer, the only animal ever
officially registered as a POW, who was sentenced by a Japanese
camp commandant to be placed on the menu but who escaped to
have her photograph taken for the exhibition, yet never starred in a

remake entitled 'The Bitch on the River Kwai'. Air Dog Prince No. 6073 is represented by a certificate commemorating his posthumous Silver Medal for Gallantry awarded by the People's Dispensary for Sick Animals, won in Libya in 1964.

The highest award for dumb friends (and some of them have been very dumb, like Wojket the Bear, who followed the Polish Army and was on twenty fags a day, which he preferred to eat, a practice doubtless picked up from his captors) is the Dickin Medal, the 'animal's VC', which has gone to thirty-one pigeons, eighteen dogs, three horses and a cat.

The cat's contribution to the war effort escapes me but the pigeons certainly deserved their gongs, to judge by the tiny parachute behind glass, and, dangling from it, the stuffed but still embarrassed pigeon, clearly feeling as uncomfortable as a fish with a snorkel or a giraffe on high heels. This was a WW1 wheeze that involved dropping trussed birds into occupied France with a note asking passing peasants to fill in the attached form with details of any troop movements they happened to know about and release at once, *merci beaucoup*.

Jacob the Goose is a hard act to follow. Saved by a sentry from a fox near Quebec in 1838, he repaid the compliment by chasing off a band of marauders too timid to say boo to him. Tirpitz the Pig was another honourable defector, this time from the rapidly submerging *Dresden* (the first example of pigs leaving the sinking ship); he joined up with *Glasgow* and later transferred to the Whale Isle Gunnery School, though not, we hope, as a target.

The exhibition, which was opened by Sefton the Hyde Park horse, a pelican from RAF Central Flying School, and Barbara Woodhouse, should have taught us that we have inflicted quite enough damage on conscripts from the animal kingdom. But the last room of *Animals in War* reminds us that some dolphins and bedbugs are being drafted for military purposes, heaven help us, and indeed heaven help them.

The only consolation for bedbugs is that they are not listed in the latest in a series known as the IUCN Red Data Books, devoted entirely to species with the skids under them. The volume *Invertebrates* (£14, World Wildlife Fund) is a list of creatures involved in a war not with humans but against them. Or rather, the humans are, one way or another, stamping them out. They are all perfectly ghastly, the insects, that is, not the humans.

Take the Dusty-headed Tailless Whip Scorpion (but only with a

pair of stout gloves). This creature was once common in the outside
lavatories of the state of Florida. Alas, now that the houses there have
been poshed up, outside loos are a thing of the past and the scorpion
has not evolved a brain capable of getting inside.

Worse, it has also forgotten how it survived in the days before
there were dwellings, and outside lavs, in Florida, so it is going into a
decline, not to say dying out. Its only consolation is that its fellow
Dusky-headed Tailless Whip Scorpions in Mexico are going from
strength to strength, so watch yourself when using the smallest, or
any other, room South of the Border.

The words 'endangered species' summon up something spectacular like the whale or the big cats. No one is going to walk around in a
T-shirt proclaiming 'Save the Earwig' (except perhaps an earwig)
but we should add that garment to our wardrobes, particularly in
view of the state of play as regards the world's largest specimen, eight
nasty centimetres long. This is found in the Mid-Atlantic island of
St Helena. At least, it was found there in 1798 but was lost again
until discovered in 1965. Since then, a man has been looking for it
again but with no joy so far.

The World Wildlife Fund has, you will recall, for its symbol the
cuddly panda, hence the Godalming HQ's name, Panda House. It
does not refer to its premises as 'No-eyed Big-eyed Wolf Spider
House' – but that thing too has its problems. The spider in question
is blind, leaps on its prey without bothering to spin webs and is
suffering from tourists who drop cigarette ends all over its Hawaiian
caves. It could join the millions of species that become extinct – some
of them so obscure they've never been scientifically catalogued or
had a date with David Attenborough.

Scientists are worried about this and so is the Zuiderzee Sea Slug,
whose reaction to the Dutch damming programme can be described
as both sluggish and damning. We are all sorry about the whole
process, none more than the Penitent Mussel of Alabama, which has
never been the same since they started messing around with the
drainage system.

At first sight, the Pygmy Hog Sucking Louse has a fine time of it,
being a parasite for whom the object on which it lays its head is also
breakfast, lunch and supper. It is riding high on the hog, you might
say, until you learn that the Pygmy Hog itself has survival problems,
threatening both the premises and meal-ticket of the louse.

We are all conservationists now, but, even so, few of us lose sleep over the (very) Boring Clam, scandalously over-fished by the Taiwanese, or its relative, the Small Giant Clam, which tends to be recycled as Philippino birdbaths. The Giant Small Clam, if such there be, seems to have kept its shell down when the fisherman sail past.

Sources close to the Scarce Large Blue Butterfly report that it is soon to become the Very Scarce Large Blue Butterfly. If it becomes the Ex-Large Blue Butterfly, it will never be conscripted for military service and hence never featured in exhibitions in the Imperial War Museum. Still, it would never manage to take off with all those Dickin medals clanking round its neck.

June 1983

Jeremy Taylor

TOLLER APPLIES

To Hamlet B. Smith, Theatrical Agent

SIR, – I would ask you to put me down on your lists for employment on conclusion of hostilities. I understand that parts and contracts are normally negotiated by interview, but this for me, as you will appreciate, is at the moment impossible except perhaps through the medium of an artist known to you at present serving on the French front with Ensa.

In this connection you may know an artist called Miss Faery Swansdown, who does a type of semi-ballet number – unfortunately influenced by the wind when she appeared on this sector recently, this artist leaping high, being caught in a flurry of gusty rain and falling into the arms of 2/Lt Stookley, who has since refused an introduction.

Should the exigencies of the service allow, I would be willing during a rest period (for which we are shortly due) to contact this artist and render selected passages from Shakespeare on which she could submit a confidential report to yourselves. Perhaps you will like to write to Miss Swansdown on this subject, at the same time letting me know her address, as I understand she has changed concert parties and 2/Lt Stookley refuses to help in the matter.

Prior to entering the services and maintaining my position for four years as an Army officer, I had considerable experience of acting, taking part in a Greek play while at school when I discovered a faculty for tiding over awkward moments with gagging, such as the moment when a boy playing with a frog accidentally caused a written crib of my part to fall down the inside of my trousers and I was compelled to conjugate a verb in lieu of a dramatic soliloquy.

The ability to overcome stage-fright and keep my head was also proved in an open-air Shakespearean play, performed by moonlight on a grassy sward surrounded by bushes, since in the character of Demetrius I was in pursuit of Lysander with a sword through the bushes, calling, to the best of my recollection, 'Where art thou, vile Lysander?' when this actor became entangled in a slight thicket so that unintentionally I ran the sword, which was of a Malay variety borrowed from the owner of the house, sharply into his rear, at the same time myself tripping on a root and spraining my ankle so that the stage was left vacant. This called for a considerable amount of gagging OFF during which I attempted to sustain the situation by crying out expressions such as 'Vile Lysander', 'Base fellow for stealing fair Hermia', 'Roguish varlet', 'Avaunt, you lily-livered boy,' until unfortunately I was hit over the head by a small branch, Lysander not realizing the conversation as part of the play.

Although my preference is for playing Shakespeare I should be willing to take other parts, and have in fact portrayed Joseph Surface in amateur theatricals in aid of a church fund, the only difficulty being in regard to stockings, the suspension part of a belt I had borrowed snapping suddenly in a love scene; but this would doubtless be overcome in a professional production.

Should there be no vacancies in straight plays I am prepared to try vaudeville and musical shows, and in this connection would suggest some act recalling the audience to their soldiering days, such as a property armoured car driving on the stage and the commander in the turret asking a French peasant in English how far it is to the Belgian frontier and the peasant replying in Polish, since he is in fact escaping from conscription with the German forces. Considerable further amusement could be caused by the commander talking in code on the wireless to another vehicle, which turns out to be only the other side of the hedge – this would be part of the scenery – and finally the act would end by a pretty farm girl running out from a farm with a bouquet of roses which she throws at the commander, hitting him on the ear.

I am specially qualified to present vaudeville acts from experience of organizing military training demonstrations, while generally Army work has contributed to my theatrical value, as on the recent occasion when 2/Lt Stookley and I were called on to make impromptu speeches of liberation to a French village; while, on the question of travelling long distances with touring companies, I am accustomed to the gypsy mode of life from four years in the field, in special from our existence of the past few days, when we might equally have travelled from the Bristol Hippodrome to an engagement at the Old Vic bearing a full load of props.

For the portrayal of character studies, I have met all types of male characters during the war years, although not having had altogether the desired facility for understanding feminine natures, opportunity for which, however, it is hoped will recur in better quantity on release from the service, a desire shared by 2/Lt Stookley who has unfortunately lost the companionship of an American nurse with whom he planned to grow cotton in South Carolina and is now involved in a pathetic one-sided idyll with Miss Faery Swansdown as mentioned above.

In the matter of make-up, I recently took part in a foot patrol at night when patrol members made up to the exact replicas of pirates, down to blackened faces, cap comforters worn as piratical nightcaps, knives and soft shoes. I can also make up successfully as a Fifth Column peasant, performed on exercises in England (although these have not materialized in the present campaign), when I tied string round the knees of an old pair of flannel trousers, carried a pitchfork, said 'Ur', and unfortunately got attached to a farm where I overstayed the end of the exercise stacking hay.

From this you will gather I am a theatrical type with promise of making good in the profession. Perhaps you will not address any reply c/o the Commanding Officer, as from a military point of view this application strictly is premature, and a recent communication from a detective agency anxious to secure my services after the war has caused some complication and embarrassment.

Yours faithfully,

J. TOLLER, *Lt.*

October 1944

Mary Dunn

LADY ADDLE ON THE TURF

Bengers, Herts, 1946

MY dear, dear readers, – Nothing in my life-time has changed so greatly, I think, as racing, which is brought to my mind by the running of the Grand National last week. Once the sport of kings – most of whom had dandled me, and all of whom had had Mipsie, on their knee – the pastime of the nobility and gentry – and of course the common people, in their proper place. Today – one is hard put to it to tell one side of the course from the other. The most peculiar people are seen, I am told, even in the Royal Enclosure at Ascot, while a cousin of mine by marriage, Lady 'Dopey' Twynge (she should know better, for she was a Leek), was seen by Humpo just before the war in a picnic party on the downs at Epsom. 'Don't say anything,' she whispered. 'It's to please my cook.' Sad straits indeed for an earl's sister and a duke's daughter-in-law.

I remember many famous racing personalities, chief amongst them being dear old Lord Bathwater, who lost three wives' fortunes on the turf. He was one of the grand old school and a familiar figure at every meeting, as he always wore a pale blue top-hat, pale blue spats and a pale blue carnation. It is said that the last cost him thousands yearly to produce in his gardens, and in the end, when his whole estate was beggared, it was discovered that Lord Bathwater was completely colour-blind. His son then gave orders that pink carnations were to be given to his father in future, but to be called blue. It was a touching sight, I believe, seeing the old man walk on to the course, proudly fingering his buttonhole, while the crowd loyally preserved a nobleman's secret to the end.

Another great character in the racing world was the Duchess of Drambuie, who was one of the first women to own racehorses, and knew as much about them as any trainer. They were certainly her whole life, and she identified herself with their interests to such an extent that she invariably used a curry-comb on her own hair and employed a nosebag for a hot-water-bottle cover. She also made a practice, the night before a big race, of dining with her horses, partaking of exactly the same fare, as she would trust no one, and even accused the duke of tampering with a horse's diet because he once went to the stables after dinner to try to persuade his wife to drink a glass of port. Next day one of the horses, who had been second favourite, was not even placed in the Thousand Guineas, and to her dying day the duchess maintained that her husband gave the port to the animal, mistaking it in the half-light for her. Nevertheless, he was completely devoted to his duchess and when she died, of an overdose of bran, he put up the most beautiful monument to her memory, in the form of a loose box in white marble, bearing the words 'She is past the post now'.

Mention of diet reminds me of Mipsie's unfortunate experience the only time she essayed to drown her sorrows in racehorse owning. 'Men have disappointed me so deeply, Blanchie,' she said to me at the time. 'Let us try what a horse can do.' Alas, four legs proved no more use than two to my poor sister. She was given a beautiful bay gelding called Top Price by the Nawab of Hotgong, in gratitude for some small service she had done him, I know not what. The horse had been running so well that he was considered a probable winner of the National in 1906, the only serious competitor being the favourite, the famous French horse Petillant. As the day drew near excitement ran high, big money being placed on both horses. Mipsie stayed with my grandparents, the Duke and Duchess of Droitwich, at Great Goutings, which is of course near Aintree, and is also, it happens, near the racing stables where Petillant was being housed before the great event. That night Mipsie could not sleep. She tossed and turned, and was just about to take a sleeping draught when suddenly she thought of the poor favourite, less than a mile away, lonely perhaps in a strange country, unable to understand the language, nervous and highly strung possibly, through that Latin temperament which Mipsie understood so well. All her sympathy was aroused at the thought of her poor suffering dumb friend, and rising quickly, she slipped a sable wrap over her silken nightdress, donned fur gloves and fur boots, and thus lightly clad made her way out into the night to the neighbouring stables. There, in the winning way she knew so well, she soon persuaded a stable-boy to administer the sleeping draught to the favourite and then sped back, conscious of a good deed done. What was her consternation the following day to hear that Petillant was not fit to run? An inquiry followed, in which harsh and cruel things were said of my sister – things no man should ever say to a woman, only a woman to a man, Mipsie said. As a result she was warned off the course, and has never patronized a race, except as a spectator, since that day. Small wonder that she finds her memories too bitter to send me a contribution to this article. However, I am delighted to say that I have persuaded my dear Addle, who is so much more qualified to write on the subject than I, to pen a few words on 'Grand Nationals I Have Known'.

'I have seen a good few horses over the sticks in my time and a good many Nationals run. Dashed good race, the National. Shows up a good man. I remember a good many good National riders in my time. "Stumpy" Jackson now. I forget which year he rode the winner and I forget what won that year. But he was a dashed good rider. Also "Jingo" Matheson. Weighed only 6 st. 10 lb. and once won a race carrying 14 st. Dashed good performance. Trouble with him he was too successful. Couldn't take his corn. Pity. Jolly good rider though. He rode Bell Bottom II – or it may have been Bell Bottom III – when the horse came a cropper at the first fence and still won the National in '06, or '07, I forget which.

Finest National horse I ever saw was Settee – by Chesterfield out of Sofa – always ridden by Lord Hugh Baulk – Huggins to his friends – who was the wittiest chap I ever struck. Kept us all in a roar. He had a famous story about a parrot or an ostrich or some bird. I forget what it was but I know we all roared. Another fine horse was Lemon Curd or was it Lemon Cheese-Cake …'

Addle had dozed off when I had to take the copy to send to the printers. But I know my dear readers will appreciate this fragment from his fine spirited pen.

April 1946

Joanna Lumley

JUMBLE

IT started with swapping: my set of jacks, one missing, for a tennis ball which was still impressively hairy but bounced like an apple; three crayons in yellow, pink and a reluctant burnt umber for a little wooden donkey on a pedestal, whose base, when depressed, caused the donkey's legs to give way, only some of the elastic had perished; a bra, all cotton, size 32A, for *Bamalama Bamaloo* by Little Richard (hellish hard, that last one, but the bra was a status symbol I couldn't be without).

Particularly strapped for cash one summer term, Mary Steele and I emptied out our desks and top drawers and arranged the – well, frankly – the detritus, the gubbins on to a tray, priced it, and trotted round the corridors selling the stuff. We displayed half-eaten erasers, broken pencils, lids off lost jars, bottles with no tops, Italian stamps, elastic bands, three sheets of crumpled airmail paper – nothing was too shabby or dingy for our sales push. In an hour we had sold every last gew-gaw and were the richer by £1 0s. 2d. As our whole term's pocket money was one pound, we were in a frenzy of wealth and excitement. We particularly congratulated ourselves on the sale of half a pair of scissors, which we told a junior girl 'would be useful for something' (she was a jumble addict if ever I've seen one). From my share, I paid 2/6d for a Parian ware figure of a boy picking something out of his toe at the school fête, but that takes me down a different track of serious collecting which doesn't concern us here. However, I have never forgotten the feeling of mild disappointment at the end of the tray sale: we had money, certainly, but our desks gaped too tidily, our blazer pockets were strangely uncluttered. I never want to know again that kind of gnawing emptiness (and indeed I never have). I decided to change sides: vendor into emptor.

I should like to introduce my parents at this stage. As with many married couples, one is a Normal and one a Jumblie. Brought up to see into both camps, my sister and I have worked out a kind of compromise: throw away regularly the real rubbish we have accumulated to make room for the next influx of life-enhancing bargains. It would not be true to say that the Jumblie in us has been handed down through the female side. Indeed, my mother has developed a spectacular new approach which involves 'feeling sorry' for things and 'giving them a kind home'. This theme has emerged since the 'bound to come in useful' or 'almost the same colour' myth has been exploded. We now know, from her untiring example, that the jumble cup matcheth not any saucer neither shall the button ye purchase for a snip ever find a fellow. She plays a kind of cosmic Kim's Game, trawling in destitute knick-knacks, and no item is too

large to escape her friendly compassion. Thus we have managed to
train our own families to recognise the delights of differently patterned plates and the unparalleled thrill of wearing secondhand
clothes. What is a whole Rockingham tea-set compared with one
exquisite Rockingham milk-jug? Simply this: the second is easier to
store, easier to admire (excess can glaze the eyes of appreciation;
think of a roomful of Mona Lisas and you get the picture) and very
much easier to buy.

My first chance for self-expression came when four of us shared a
flat in Earl's Court in the first half of the Sixties. Since I was salaried
at £8 a week before tax, there was not much boodle over to make the
home Ideal. I shared with three other open-handed clutter addicts,
however, and in no time we had chambers fascinating enough to rival
the British Museum. Our skilfully exhibited possessions included an
ostrich egg, tin advertising signs, an old-fashioned camera, peacock
feathers, long patterned pieces of cloth and a set of brass scales.

Readers growing restless will want to know our contacts, our
sources. Nothing fell off the back of a lorry, although some things
looked as though they had, and as though the lorry had been travelling at some speed when they did. We visited junk shops and street
markets, of course, but the sight to raise blood pressure (be still, my
beating heart) was a hand-drawn notice reading 'Jumble Sale
Church Room Today'.

You see, in a street market the laser-eyed dealers are about; they
will have snapped up the aces before you have stumbled from your
bed, and re-priced them and put them into ritzy curio boutiques (but
I once won a Tiffany lampshade in oyster-coloured glass, some beads
missing, for £4 in Brick Lane). In a jumble sale you have only the
organisers to outwit; if they don't know their onions they will sell
them to you for peanuts.

Example given: a straining grey November afternoon near
Chelmsford, a charity jumble sale, jolly few people about; my fingers
sifting in the old cardboard box full of broken jewellery; suddenly I
am holding a dirty pink and black brooch marked 3p ('It's only
plastic, dear'); my eyelids slam down over my eyes in case she sees
the pound sign pinging up like a cash register; I give her 10p (it *is* a
charity) and I own a perfect eighty-year-old cameo, palest cream and
shell pink, set in solid silver. In the same sale, an excellent dinner
jacket and trousers for £2. It was only when I got them home that I
saw that they must have belonged to Fat Daniel Lambert, as they

would have hung loosely on Cyril Smith. So it's swings and round-abouts and which gambler could resist it?

At a good jumble sale, there will be a trestle table groaning with home-made cakes and pots of elderberry and rhubarb jelly, cheese straws and shortcake and stoneground, husk-whiskered, underfelt biscuits. There will usually be a fruit cake of immense proportions whose leaden weight you are invited to guess. This stall empties the quickest so many people visit it first. Then there is a Soft counter selling peg-bags, small cushions, shoe-bags, cloth dolls, knitting-bags, aprons and bags. These, as they are all clean and new, are good Christmas presents as they can be received, kept in a drawer and sent off to another sale next year. Some bags have been doing the rounds for many years and have forgotten their original purpose. There is a Bottle stall where you will fix your eyes on a bottle of whisky and win some tomato ketchup or a dandruff shampoo. There is a Tombola, where you will win nothing. Then, on table after table, rack upon rail, the jumble itself.

There are several views on how it should be displayed. Some feel happiest when it is all thrown together, like a Russian salad: I prefer books here, records there, bric-à-brac further along, but I have a suspicion that if it is too well-sorted laser-vision will have had a look-in. Taken from their natural surroundings, each object assumes an incandescent desirability. Decide swiftly: don't ponder and wander on, for it will be gone when you return. Have as many arms as the goddess Kali and remember that the good-natured punters are in fact grasping fanatics, as untrustworthy as a short spit. Only when the fever is dying and the pocket is empty can you afford to be magnanimous ('Oh, that's lovely, well done, what a find, pity about the stain'). Drained, you take a cup of tea in a thick china mug. Such a feeling of achievement swarms over as you have never felt before (since the last time). Later, you will pore and gloat over your booty, polishing and washing and boasting.

I am sometimes asked to officiate at charity jumble sales or fêtes, or Fayres as they're occasionally called. I warn them with quiet insistence that I will not be making a speech, no, cannot be per-suaded. Two reasons (which I do not give) are these: first, I am awful at public speaking; and second, and far more important, once when I did attempt a few words ('Great pleasure ... worthy cause ... blah ... do spend ...'), I saw at the far end of the hall a stout, tweed-coated woman had jumped the gun and was negotiating in whispers over the price of a Coalport tureen. So now, barely pausing by the microphone to shout, 'Good afternoon, it's open', I hurl myself, elbows out, into the crowd of human locusts.

December 1984

A.P. Herbert

LITTLE TALKS

THE BARGAIN COUNTER

THANK you, Madam; pay at the desk, please. Good morning, Madam – My dear, what a crush! Like flies, aren't they? Well, my dear, I wanted to tell you, it's all up, Arthur and me, I mean. We had a scene last night, such a scene; well, scene's not the word – Cami-bockers? No, Madam; straight through and on the right – Don't hurry me, dear, I'm in such a state I can't hardly think. Well, Arthur came in last night, you see, and I could tell at once there was something in the wind because he was wearing his bowler, you see, and I told him long ago I didn't like him in his bowler, and he's never worn it since, not till last night, so I said 'The bowler, eh? I suppose your passion's burnt itself out?' – joking, you see – Boys' pants? No, Madam, in the Juveniles, the next department – Well, he looked sheepish at that, like when you tell a man he's got no soul for music and he hasn't, and after a bit he said he was sorry, but the fact was, he'd come to say Good-bye, because if the truth was told he was going to be married. So I said 'Married, eh? Congratulations, I'm sure, and what may her name be?' Because I wasn't going to show anything, you see. 'Well, if you want to know,' he said, 'her name's Sylvia Wilkins.' And then he told me all about her, from her blasted eyes to her blasted address, which is Addison Road, if you please. Well, we were sitting in the front-room, you see, because it was raining, and just then Father comes along the passage, and Father's always said he'd horsewhip anybody if their intentions wasn't honourable – Father's very old-fashioned, you see – so when I saw Father I said – No, Mr Arundale, I wasn't gossiping, I was just saying to Miss Williams, these Windsor night-gowns have all gone but six and it seems to me we're throwing them away at the price – Nasty little rat! I'd be ashamed to

be a shop-walker if I was a man! – So I said to Father, 'Congratulate
Arthur, Father, he's going to be married.' 'To you, my dear?' says
Father, all of a radio. 'No,' I said, 'to Sylvia Wilkins.' Well, you see,
I've always let on to Father that me and Arthur were more or less
engaged, because if I hadn't done that he'd have put his hoof down
long ago – Girls' Outfits? the next department, Madam – So when
Father heard about Sylvia Wilkins, he saw scarlet you see – well, I
think he'd had one or two, and he said to Arthur: 'Look here, young
scum-of-the-earth, you've betrayed my daughter, and I'm goin' to
horsewhip you, see?' So I said Arthur hadn't betrayed me, and
Arthur said he wasn't going to be horsewhipped – Ribbons, Madam,
yes, Madam, straight through to the Fancy and Specialities – That
young woman's buying half the shop, my dear, getting her trousseau
I shouldn't wonder. I can't stand those sunflower shingles, can you?
– well, so Father went into the kitchen to look for the horsewhip –
Pyjamas? Yes, Madam. Would it be for your personal wear? Certainly. We are selling a great many of the Paris Pyjama – for camp
and yacht-wear. Yes, Madam, they are very much worn. The helio-
trope are very fetching, Madam. Or would you prefer the Cambridge
blue? One-three-ten, Madam, reduced from thirty-five shillings. We
are practically giving them away, Madam. Two pairs of the Cambridge? Very well, Madam. Cash, Madam, or on account? Wonderful weather, Madam, quite a treat. A little fresher today, I think.
Thank you, Madam. Will you pay at the desk, please? Good
morning, Madam – Well, my dear, Father couldn't find the horsewhip, because Mother hid it the moment she heard him on the
rampage, you see, but that only made him the madder, and he came
back waving the coal-hatchet and shouting and swearing something
terrible, and he said to Arthur 'Will you come out in the yard and be
horsewhipped, young man?' And Arthur said 'Not with a hatchet,
Sir,' very polite, you see. Well, Father was mad at that, you see, and
really I think he thought the hatchet was a horsewhip, so he lifted up
the horsewhip, the hatchet, I mean – Yes, Mr Arundale? Miss
Farrow, forward, bust-bodices, please – Well, Arthur never turned a
hair, but I thought it was all up with him, but just then Mother came
in, and she gave Father one of her suffering looks and she said
'Where did you put the aspirins, Tom, my head's splitting?' Well,
that seemed to sober Father, because he always says that Mother's
headaches knock the stuffing out of him, so he put down the hatchet
and Mother said 'What's the argument about?' – Boys' under-

clothes? Straight through to the Juveniles, Madam – You wouldn't
think there were so many boys in the world, would you? Where was
I? Oh yes. Well, Arthur spoke up and he said he'd been gone on this
Sylvia Wilkins for years, only she wouldn't have him, but she'd gone
and changed her mind, you see; and he said he and me were very
good friends but that was all. So I said 'That's right'. Well, I'd have
said anything to save a scene. So Father flared up and he said
'Friends my eye! Then what's all the kissing and cuddling for, tell
me that!' My *dear*, wasn't it awful? Well, Mother said 'Don't be
vulgar, Tom!' And there's no getting away from it. Father *is* vulgar
when he's worked up. So he said 'Vulgar, am I? Well, will this young
feller-me-lad answer a straight question – has there been kissing and
cuddling or has there not?' So Arthur said there might have been a
little kissing and cuddling, but only Platonic, you see. Well, then the
fat was in the fire. 'Platonic!' shouts Father, 'you dare to try those
games with my daughter!' And he picks up the hatchet and he makes
for Arthur. Well, Mother caught hold of him and I caught hold of
him, and there was a regular dog-fight, and the next thing I knew,
there was Arthur lying on the ground with the blood all over his face.
My *dear*, the blood! You never saw anything like it – Are you being
attended to, Madam? We have a very cheap line in silk bed-socks
today. Pardon? Cheese, Madam? That will be in the Provisions,
through the Livestock. Thank you – 'Well,' says Father, 'is he dead?'
'Looks like it,' Mother said. 'Well,' says Father, 'the first thing is to
get rid of the body, I won't have a scandal in this house,' because
Father reads a lot of these murder stories, you see. Well, Mother and
me bathed Arthur's face, while Father walked up and down thinking
how to get rid of the body. And really I did think Arthur was done
for, he lay so still. But presently he sits up, and it was only a
flesh-wound, so Father apologised and we all had supper – Boys'
pants? Straight through to the Juveniles, Madam – Well, that's the
end of *my* little *romance* – Night-gowns? Yes, Madam. The Windsor
style is very attractive. All silk, hand-lace, as worn by the Queen of
Serbia. We have them in the three shades, Madam, Rose du Barri,
Cerise and Flesh. There has been a great run on this style, Madam.
These are the last half-dozen, Madam. We are selling them at a very
considerable reduction, Madam, twenty-six shillings, Madam,
marked at two guineas. I will inquire, Madam – Mr Arundale! – Yes,
Madam, for that number we would let them go at half-price,
Madam. Shall I send them? Certainly, Madam. The weather is

wonderful, is it not, Madam? Quite a treat. A little fresher today, I think. And the name, please? Miss Sylvia Wilkins. Miss Sylvia *Wilkins*, did you say, Madam? And the address? 410, Addison Road. Thank you, Madam, I will have them sent by the next delivery. Will you pay at the desk, please? *Good* morning, Madam – Well, my dear, what d'you think of that? That's the little fairy that's ruined my life – and I've sold her six nighties for half-price!

July 1927

Jeremy Lewis
AUNTS

DESPITE the best endeavours of stuffies and fogeys of all ages, a good many much-loved ingredients of English life have been removed from the communal store cupboard over the past thirty years or so, from half-a-crowns and bowler hats to bottle-nosed ex-majors eking out a living as prep-school masters, hobbling across games pitches on their gammy legs and lashing out clips to left and right.

Foremost among our Endangered Species – on a par, perhaps, with Distressed Gentlefolk in South Kensington, crouching over gas fires in Drayton Gardens in well-worn tweeds and sipping sherry out of tooth mugs – is that finest example of womanhood, the English maiden aunt. In the days of my youth the country positively pulsated with maiden aunts – running WIs, waving walking sticks, transfixing small boys with looks of thunder, rescuing underprivileged Spanish donkeys, arguing with greengrocers, knocking up sponge· cakes, keeping nephews and nieces supplied with 10/- postal orders, showing visitors round the local church ('The stained glass windows are at least a hundred years old,' explained a scholarly aunt, referring to Fairford's famous fourteenth-century glass, 'and they were taken down and hidden during the Civil War'), agreeing with every word in the *Daily Express*, and displaying symptoms of alarm at the goings-on of that foaming revolutionary, Clement Attlee. Even more plentiful were great-aunts, of the kind that terrorised Bertie Wooster: their numbers were accounted for, we were told, by the slaughter on the Western Front, which had left these ladies with no one to marry and energy to spare.

Like many children of my generation, I grew up hemmed in by maiden aunts, mostly of the 'great' variety. My favourite great-aunt was Auntie Annie. A wizened, bent figure, with an enormous curved nose like a Brazil nut and big, round eyes like prunes (the family claimed – or at least my mother claimed on their behalf – a sizeable dash of gypsy blood), she lived alone in a tiny flat up in Onslow Gardens. Annie had spent most of her life as a nurse in the East End: winter or summer, she wore an aged fox fur slung round her neck and a green felt hat, held firmly in place by one of those enormous, pearl-headed hat pins that featured so largely in mystery stories between the wars. She had legs like broomsticks in stockings, on the bottom of which could be found a highly polished pair of brown 'sensible' shoes.

A keen amateur carpenter and electrician, she frequently fused the lights in the entire block of flats, and liked nothing better than to engage my father in technical debate about lathes and chisels. Though hospitable to a degree, she lived off diminutive chops or the occasional kipper cooked over an ancient Baby Belling (the culinary equivalent of the Austin Seven, perhaps): the walls of her midget-sized bathroom were covered with useful and cautionary notices designed to assist the unwary visitor ('Pull chain down STRAIGHT' by the lavatory chain). Despite her proper demeanour, she was game for anything, tossing down the sherry at the least provocation and more than once – when far too old for such antics – joining my parents in various wild sprees, her fox fur and green felt hat remaining firmly in place as she scaled a six-foot wall or was lowered down a drainpipe into the garden of some unsuspecting party-giver. She must have been well over eighty when she eventually deserted Onslow Gardens and moved down to Eastbourne to join two of her sisters. Away from her beloved London, from the peeling stucco and the sulphurous winter smogs, she seemed a shadow of her sparrow-like self, and within a year she was dead.

Though tirelessly good and generous, her Eastbourne sisters were altogether less magical to a child. Auntie Mary, the forceful one, was a short, stout woman, with bristly grey hair and pendulous jowls of the kind unflatteringly referred to as dewlaps. She was, I suspect, a kind old thing, but her gruff voice, ferocious gaze and more than a touch of the regimental sergeant-major made her a force to be

reckoned with. Before moving to Eastbourne, she and her sister Ada had lived
in Blatchington, a genteel part of
Seaford with a golf course to hand, a
large number of hydrangea bushes con-
cealing spacious Edwardian houses, and
an engagingly upper-middle-class population of retired tea planters, prep-
school masters, solicitors in lovat green
tweeds and rival teams of maiden aunts.

Seaford in those days was much
favoured by stern-looking ladies in
demob suits, trilby hats and string ties
who moved about the town with enormous strides and (I liked to
think) smoked huge cigars in the privacy of their suburban gardens:
Auntie Mary looked, at first sight, as though she might have been a
member of this curious sorority, though in fact she cherished a
melancholy, unrequited and lifelong passion for a major over the
road. As a motorist she was a public menace – which was hardly
surprising since once she had lowered her enormous frame into the
bucket seat of her Vauxhall, little could be seen above the windscreen
but the top of her head and her hands, firmly gripping the wheel in
the approved 'ten-to-two' position. On the day of her funeral, as we
were walking away from the church, my Auntie Annie turned to her
surviving sister, tapped her watch and said in sepulchral tones, 'Ada,
I think she must be nearly there by now.' If Mary's motoring was
anything to go by, she must have spent a great deal of time mounting
the kerb and mowing down innocent pedestrians *en route* for the
Pearly Gates but like most of my family, she was a stickler for
punctuality, so Annie's prognosis may not have been so far out after
all.

Auntie Ada, who outlived them all, was the only remotely rich
relation we had, and far and away the saddest. Even as a young and –
judging by the photographs – very fine-looking girl in the early
1920s, she had a wistful, haunted look about her. She had spent a
good deal of time in China, and her houses were crammed with
pop-eyed turquoise porcelain pekes, lacquered gold and black
wardrobes with impenetrable Oriental locks, jade Buddhas on circular black stands, and glass cabinets in which tiny, colourful figures
enacted forever the elaborate rituals of an Imperial Chinese pro-

cession; and over them all there hung a curious musty smell that remains for me – quite wrongly, no doubt – the quintessential whiff of the Orient. While out in the East the sad-seeming Ada met and married an amiable, well-heeled Yorkshire businessman, a good many years older than her: within only a few months of their wedding he was dead.

Ada returned home to England, where she moved into a large, red-brick, tile-hung, mullion-windowed Edwardian house, along with her sister Mary. With its rhododendron bushes, tennis court, clipped hedges, tradesmen's entrance, vegetable gardens, crunching gravel drive and bell-push discreetly positioned under the dining-room table within reach of the proprietorial toe, it was exactly the kind of house Richmal Crompton's William Brown must have lived in: unlike William, Ginger and Henry, those great-nephews and great-nieces who occasionally paid a visit were very much on their best behaviour, politely picking at neatly trimmed cucumber sandwiches and speaking only when spoken to, and exhaling sighs of relief as polite farewells were said, and the benign but somewhat daunting elderly aunts disappeared from view in the back window of the car. For all her kindness and the protective affection she inspired, poor Ada remained an unhappy, nervous, dissatisfied figure: the only one of those particular aunts to have married and yet, perhaps, the one that most embodied all those wearisome, condescending clichés about the sadness and the frustration of the maiden aunt.

Maiden aunts are a dying breed, and are likely to become ever scarcer as the years roll by. Smaller families, the notion that women – whether married or not – have the 'right' to a child, sexual permissiveness, the oppressive and patronising stigma attached to those who, often for perfectly good reasons of their own, choose to remain single or even (shame upon them!) chaste: faced with such pressures as these, the classic English maiden aunt – eccentric, forceful, devoted to good causes and curious branches of knowledge, source of solace, anecdote, family lore and endless jars of pickle and home-made jam – seems doomed to follow cane-swishing schoolmasters in mortar-boards and gowns and scholarly, absent-minded vicars into the Elysium reserved for those whose time is past.

January 1985

Robert Buckman

WHICH DOCTORS?

You all know me.
I have never lacked the courage boldly to address
controversial issues that have not been boldly addressed
before. Not by me, anyway. Yet there is one such issue that
I must boldly confess I have been boldly ducking out of – the
controversy over alternative medicine. A recent report has
examined this in detail and so many people have asked me to
let them have the official and authoritative Punch *medical*
correspondent's view on alternative medicine that I have, at
last, been forced to speak out.
I had no alternative.

WHY ALTERNATIVE MEDICINE?

CURRENTLY, a lot of people believe that while modern doctors have improved their skills and prowess in treating diseases, they have lost their ability to care and to relate to their patients as human beings.

Now obviously this criticism does not apply to me, because, as a caring and humane medical practitioner, I recognise the merit in this viewpoint and I fully empathise with the motivations behind it – even though the published evidence suggests that alternative medicine is a load of horse-crap, packaged by a crew of sycophantic, glib cowboys who could sell ice to the Eskimos, particularly if they could call it holistic ice.

No no no, I didn't mean that, just kidding, ahahahaha.

Anyway, the people who are most attracted to alternative medicine are usually people who suffer from troublesome, but not life-threatening conditions, e.g. living in Islington. No, that's not true either. Sorry.

Now lots of perfectly nice people have a recurring medical condition for which conventional medicine cannot offer a cure or do anything about, e.g. low back-ache, compulsive nose-picking, working in advertising, not wanting an independent deterrent etc. So the idea is that you go to an alternative medical practitoner, who cannot offer a cure or do anything about it either, but says so in a nice way and takes longer about it. Seriously, though, what alternative medical practitioners are good at is treating their patients as human beings in the context of their community and all its complex inter-relationships.

Of course, a few conventional doctors are pretty nifty at that sort of approach, too, e.g. in California, although on this side of the Atlantic we call it something different, e.g. wife-swapping. However, the main point is absolutely undeniable – which is that we conventional doctors, as a group, are not all that good at certain high-tech complex medical doctor-patient interactions such as smiling, looking interested, remembering names, staying awake.

What is happening now is that, in response to our customers voting with their feet, we conventional doctors are re-learning all that stuff in postgraduate courses. I myself have a PhD in nodding sympathetically and I presented a dissertation on fifty different ways of saying 'good morning' nicely (except I nearly failed in my oral when my examiner said 'good afternoon' and I didn't know what to reply. I mean, I'm a specialist, aren't I? Yes).

So, there is clearly a valuable lesson for us conventional chappies to learn from our alternative colleagues, crawl crawl slime slime slime, and it can only help all of us in doing what we really want, i.e. helping our patients in the best way possible and maybe getting famous as well.

In addition to the humane aspects, alternative medicine has some pretty powerful proponents and patrons. One of them is a person whose name I will not mention but whose identity I will hint at by saying that when his mum stops doing what she's doing, he'll be King of England. It is unclear precisely why this person is such a strong fan of alternative medicine, but I feel that this kind of broad commonsense view of health issues is precisely what this country needs – and PS my CBE hasn't arrived yet, though I sent in all the box tops last February.

However, despite all the obvious psycho-social advantages of alternative medicine, does it cure diseases? In other words, *does it actually work*?

Well, there's no point in asking me, is there? I mean, I'm The Enemy, aren't I? I mean, it's like asking the President of Coca-Cola whether Pepsi-Cola is actually nicer-tasting, isn't it?

Anyway, it doesn't matter because I shall now consider many of the alternative medicine techniques individually and let you judge for yourselves.

Please consult your own doctor before reading any further.

PHRENOLOGY

This is not actually a form of alternative medicine at all, but I thought we might start off on a fairly non-controversial note, otherwise there'll be tears before bedtime, you mark my words.

Phrenology was the science (if such it could be called) of diagnosing a person's talents and peculiarities by the shape and the bumps of their skull, or cranium, or, as we conventional doctors call it, head. The idea was that your personality inside your brain sort of pushed up from within and shaped the skull over it. Well, of course nowadays we know that in a few cases a personality with certain strong characteristics *can* alter the shape of your skull, e.g. a psychopath with an axe in Central Park after dark, but your own personality won't shift it a smidgen. No sirree.

What phrenologists were good at was psychotherapy. They would place their hands on their customers' heads and make intelligent guesses about their lifestyle and personality by subtle clues – an expensive hairdo, a tiara, a Nazi helmet, things like that. And they would proceed by making exploratory statements which were bound to be true, e.g. 'there are two women in your life', 'you care too much about things', 'this'll cost you a florin' etc. And the interview would proceed depending on what the client replied, such as 'no, three' or 'no, I don't, I'm going to annex Austria' and so on.

So really phrenology was a pseudo-science, a lot of hocus-pocus and mumbo-jumbo based on a minimal amount of slightly intelligent guesswork – the CIA is another example. Only when those guys feel your bumps, your bumps stay felt. Yes sirree.

PSYCHIC SURGERY

Psychic surgery is a fascinating form of therapy which has been categorised in the language of the transactional-phenomenological school of psychology as 'crap'. What happens in psychic surgery is that you go along to a psychic surgeon and he or she moves his or her hands over your body or, if you're too busy to attend yourself, over your photo or X-ray or wig or credit card or last school report. Using

their special psychic powers they then 'divine' where the trouble is
and what is causing it.

Now I have seen similar techniques used by other disciplines, e.g.
plumbers and television repairmen, but I suppose the big difference
was that they had dirtier overalls and charged more. Anyway, once
the psychic surgeon has divined what is wrong, he organises the
procedure known as psychic surgery. I don't know a lot about it
myself, but I believe it's a pretty respectable sort of business with a
proper psychic waiting-list and the option of going in a psychic
side-room with private phone etc.

I'm told that one of the main advantages of psychic surgery is that
you don't need to be anaesthetised (by a psychic anaesthetist) and it
doesn't hurt ten days later when they take the psychic stitches out –
though for the same money, why can't they use soluble ones?

Another advantage is that while the operation is being performed
you (the patient) don't need to be there at all. Now think how helpful
that could be for the NHS. I mean, all year round poor surgeons get
hassled by executives who want their haemorrhoids fixed in August
so they don't miss work – if we had psychic surgeons in the NHS we
could do these guys' piles while they're actually working, so they
don't even have to miss lunch. The only snag is that I don't know
whether psychic surgeons ever do haemorrhoids, although I think I
might be able to divine the answer if I just close my eyes and
concentrate.

HOMOEOPATHY

Homoeopathy is not like phrenology at all. Really it isn't. But the
true scientific basis of the homoeopathic principle is not yet fully
established, although it might be proven any decade now, and no
thanks, I'm perfectly comfortable, I'm just shifting from foot to foot
because there's a stone in my shoe and I always wring my hands like
this when I'm talking about something complex and difficult to sort
of, well, talk about.

What they do in homoeopathy is use very small doses of medicines. This is actually a very smart idea indeed since it has been
shown that 10–30% of 'conventional' hospital patients suffer side-
effects from drugs. If you use tiny doses of drugs, you'll have tiny
side-effects.

What they also do is individualise each drug administration. This is also a very good idea. They look at you as a real person, your eye colour, your skin, your build, your credit-rating etc and pick the type and schedule of homoeopathic medicine accordingly. So it's not like conventional medicine, where you get ampicillin, £2.20, that's your lot, complete the course and who's next? In homoeopathy, you get ElizabethJonesicillin, it matches the colour of your eyes especially for you, with all our love and best wishes for a speedy recovery. £4.75 and call again soon.

There's something to be said for giving people less but giving it with more care and more heart.

Like this column, really. I mean a small dose'll probably do you just as much good as a big one.

Please call again next week, I wrote this only for you and I love you so much.

HIGH COLONIC IRRIGATION

For many years when I was young I used to see adverts on the back of the *New Statesman*, which was a kind of newspaper in those days, advertising High Colonic Irrigation. I must say that I visualised something like the Tennessee Valley Authority – or maybe Mesopotamia – bringing needed water to the parched valley of High Colon etc.

The truth is more bizarre, but less picturesque. It is based on the idea that – oh you know what it's based on, you just want to see me get embarrassed and coy, don't you? Anyway, for every Keynesian who believes that a good throughput is the mark of a good economy, there are two sceptics who uphold the law of diminishing returns and five opportunists who know that where there's muck there's brass. The defence rests.

ROLFING

Rolfing is actually a serious alternative practitioner's discipline, and is all based on the belief that many diseases are caused by bad posture exaggerated by the effects of gravity, which I suppose might be true in certain circumstances, e.g. if you're drunk or shot. Anyway, practitioners who practise rolfing (known as 'rolfing contractors') do a sort of deep massage 'to loosen certain muscles and fascia and free the emotions and the mind'.

Actually, I had a cousin from out of town who used to do that sort of thing and she got eighteen months, but then she didn't know she was rolfing, did she? Anyway, rolfing can be performed on a part-time or full-time basis and there are annual displays and exhibitions (e.g. the ProAm Rolf Championships). You have to be careful not to confuse ordinary rolfing with 'rolfharrissing', which is Australian and much less tasteful, although in some bizarre way I suppose you could think of it as an alternative to health.

SHIATSU

Shiatsu, like acupuncture, is based on traditional Oriental medicine and is fervently supported by many people who can relate to something mysterious and totally unintelligible, provided it's Oriental. These are the same people who are ready to believe in ginseng but not Horlicks, in Rabindrinath Tagore but not Desmond Morris, in bad karma but not bad moods, and in yin and yang but not Marks and Spencer.

Well, shiatsu scores heavily on the mysterious Oriental scale, let me tell you. It's all based on the technique of applying pressure to one part of the body in order to produce an effect in another part (similar techniques are in use in the Western world, e.g. strangling). Thus, if you have a pain in your gall-bladder, the shiatsu doctor will apply pressure to 'the outside of your leg from the pelvis to the knee'. Though my manual doesn't say which leg – I suppose it depends on whether you dress with your gall-bladder to the left or right. In shiatsu teaching, the stomach is 'just to the outside of the front ridge of the shinbone from the knee to the ankle', which sounds odd to non-orientals, but is actually the exact place where my stomach happens to migrate to on certain occasions, e.g. dentist's appointments or the morning after drinking half-a-bottle of sake.

Funnily enough, the shiatsu method doesn't say what to do to cure pain in the head – perhaps you're meant to apply shiatsu pressure to another part of the body entirely, e.g. your family doctor. More research is clearly needed here.

BOGUS DOCTORS

I must admit that bogus doctors are not exactly recognised by anybody as genuine alternative practitioners, but that's an issue in itself. I mean if Alternative Practitioners grumble that *they're* not properly recognised by the regular Non-Alternative Practitioners (e.g. me and the Big Boys up the BMA), they can hardly complain if someone who isn't recognised as an Alternative Practitioner by *them* goes ahead and practises (in a fairly alternative way), without being recognised by any practitioners whatsoever. It's like being thrown out of the Association of Non-Conformists for not conforming to Association rules. And in real life, these bogus doctors often practise for ages without being recognised. Or caught. And what happens when they are caught? The moment they haul off some poor ex-invoice-clerk-who-always-wanted-to-be-a-doctor to court for having handled thirty-five women and tried to perform a few toe-nail removals, all his patients say how nice he was, and gentle, doctorly, authoritative and human.

We shouldn't put these guys in prison – we should employ them in the Health Service. For a start, they could teach medical students how to be nice and gentle, yet firm, authoritative and human (I'd teach those skills myself except I'm too busy using them to sell double-glazing in the evenings). Secondly, we could use them in Out-Patients. I mean, recent surveys have shown that 30% of all patients seeking medical advice haven't got a defined organic medical condition – which means, to one way of looking at things, that they're Bogus Patients. And we all know that doctors are absolutely awful at dealing with psycho-social problems (i.e. being nice to people who earn less than them), so why not employ a whole lot of proper Bogus Doctors to look after the Bogus Patients?

We could start a whole new Bogus College of Physicians which would issue proper 100% Bogus Diplomas (which have to be properly forged by accredited counterfeiters) and doctors, patients and Health Service would all benefit. We could probably pay them with genuine Monopoly money, which would not only solve a lot of funding problems but would also mean that they could get annual Monopoly pay increases as recommended by the Review Board – that would put them streets ahead of the rest of us ordinary doctors for starters. I believe that this suggestion of mine would bring alternative holistic humane medicine once more into the domain of the NHS, and would drastically reduce waiting-lists, patients' complaints, drugs' bills and unemployment in one bold and brilliant stroke.

August 1986

Walter De La Mare

THE CORNER

GOOD News to tell!
Friends, mark it well!
Old Mister Jones –
Once all but bones –
There never was
A sight forlorner –
At last, at last,
All danger past,
Has been and gone and
Turned the corner;
  And every hour
    Is growing younger.

A week ago
By almanac
His long white beard
Went jetty black,
The red into his cheeks
Came back.
His teeth were sharp
And thirty-two,
His faded eyes
A bright bird-blue.
When two more days
Were scarcely run
He slips from forty
To twenty-one;
He skips and dances
Heel and toe;
He couldn't downwards
Quicker grow.
All that he's learned
  Begins to go;
    His memory's melting
      Just like snow.
        At plump four foot
          He burst his stitches,
            His trousers dwindled
              Back to breeches;
                The breeches gone,
                  There came short clothes

Two dumpling cheeks,
   A button nose,
      A mop of curls,
         Ten crinkled toes.
            And now as fast
               As he is able
                  He's nestling down
                     Into his cradle.

            Old Mrs Jones
               With piping eye –
                  She rocks and croons
                     Him *Hush-a-by*.
                        Last Sunday gone
                           He turned the corner
                              And still grows
                                 Younger, younger,
                                    younger …
                                       Old Mister Jones.

June 1941

William Makepeace Thackeray
MR JEAMES AGAIN

'DEAR MR PUNCH,

'As newmarus inquiries have been maid both at my privit ressd-dence, The Wheel of Fortune Otel, and at your Hoffis, regarding the fate of that dear babby, JAMES HANGELO, whose primmiture dissap-pearnts caused such hagnies to his distracted parents, I must begg, dear Sir, the permission to ockupy a part of your valuble collams once more, and hease the public mind about my blessid boy.

'Wictims of that nashnal cuss, the Broken Gage, me and MRS PLUSH was left in the train to Cheltenham, soughring from that most disagreeble of complaints, a halmost *broken Art*. The skreems of MRS JEAMES might be said almost to out-Y the squeel of the dying, as we rusht into that fashnable Spaw, and my pore MARY HANN found it was not Baby, but Bundles I had in my lapp.

'When the old Dowidger, LADY BAREACRES, who was waiting heagerly at the train, that owing to that abawminable brake of Gage, the luggitch, her Ladyship's Cherrybrandy box, the cradle for LADY HANGELINA's baby, the lace, crockary and chany, was rejuiced to one immortial smash; the old cat howld at me and pore dear MARY HANN, as if it was huss, and not the infunnle Brake of Gage, was to blame; and as if we ad no misfortns of our hown to deplaw. She bust out about my stupid imparence; called MARY HANN a good for nothink creecher, and wep and abewsd and took on about her broken Chayny Bowl, a great deal mor than she did about a dear little Christian child. "Don't talk to me abowt your bratt of a babby," (seshe); "where's my bowl? – where's my medsan? – where's my bewtiffle Pint lace? – All in rewins through your stupiddaty, you brute you!"

'"Bring your haction against the Great Western, Maam, says I," quite riled by this crewel and unfealing hold wixen. "Ask the pawters at Gloster, why your goods is spiled – it's not the fust time they've been asked the question. Git the gage haltered aginst the nex time you send for *medsan* – and meanwild buy some at the Plow – they keep it very good and strong there, I'll be bound. Has for us, *we're* a going back to the cussid station at Gloster, in such of our blessid child."

'"You don't mean to say, young woman," seshee, "that you're not going to LADY HANGELINA: what's her dear boy to do? who's to nuss it?'

"'*You* nuss it, Maam,' says I. 'Me and MARY HANN return this momint by the Fly." And so (whishing her a suckastic ajew) MRS JEAMES and I lep into a one oss weakle, and told the driver to go like mad back to Gloster.

'I can't describe my pore gals hagny juring our ride. She sat in the carridge as silent as a milestone, and as madd as a march Air. When we got to Gloster she sprang hout of it as wild as a Tigris, and rusht to the station, up to the fatle Bench.

"'My child, my child," shrecx she, in a hoss, hot voice. "Where's my infant? a little bewtifle child, with blue eyes, – dear MR POLICE-MAN, give it me – a thousand guineas for it."

"'Faix, Mam," says the man, a Hirishman, "and the divvle a babby have I seen this day except thirteen of my own – and you're welcome to any one of *them*, and kindly."

'As if *his* babby was equal to ours, as my darling MARY HANN said, afterwards. All the station was scrouging round us by this time – pawters & clarx and refreshmint people and all. "What's this year row about that there babby?" at last says the Inspector, stepping hup. I thought my wife was going to jump into his harms. "Have you got him?" says she.

"'Was it a child in a blue cloak?" says he.

"'And blue eyes!" says my wife.

"'I put a label on him and sent him on to Bristol; he's there by this time. The Guard of the Mail took him and put him in a letterbox," says he; "he went 20 minutes ago. We found him on the broad gauge line, and sent him on by it, in course," says he. "And it'll be a caution to you, young woman, for the future, to label your children along with the rest of your luggage."

"If my piguniary means had been such as *once* they was, you may emadgine I'd have ad a speshle train and been hoff like smoak. As it was, we was obliged to wait 4 mortial hours for the next train (4 ears they seemed to us), and then away we went.

"'My boy! my little boy!" says poor, choking MARY HANN, when we got there. "A parcel in a blue cloak," says the man? "No body claimed him here, and so we sent him back by the mail. An Irish nurse here gave him some supper, and he's at Paddington by this time. Yes," says he, looking at the clock, "he's been there these ten minutes."

'"But seeing my poor wife's distracted histarricle state, this good-naturd man says, "I think, my dear, there's a way to ease your mind. We'll know in five minutes how he is."

'"Sir," says she, "don't make sport of me."

'"No, my dear, we'll *telegraph* him."

'And he began hopparating on that singular and ingenus elektricle inwention, which aniliates time, and carries intellagence in the twinkling of a peg-post.

'"I'll ask," says he, "for child marked G.W.273."

'Back comes the telegraph with the sign "All right".

'"Ask what he's doing, sir," says my wife, quite amazed. Back comes the answer in a Jiffy –

'"C.R.Y.I.N.G."

'This caused all the bystanders to laugh excep my pore MARY HANN, who pull'd a very sad face.

'The good-naterd feller presently said, "he'd have another trile", and what d'ye think was the answer? I'm blest if it wasn't –

'"P.A.P."

'He was eating pap! There's for you – there's a rogue for you – there's a March of Intaleck! MARY HANN smiled now for the fust time. "He'll sleep now," says she. And she sat down with a full hart.

* * * * * * *

'If hever that good-natered Shooperin-tendent comes to London, *he* need never ask for his skore at the Wheel of Fortune Hotel, I promise you – where me and my wife and JAMES HANGELO now is; and where only yesterday, a gent came in and drew this pictur of us in our bar.

'And if they go on breaking gages; and if the child, the most precious luggidge of the Henglishman, is to be bundled about in this year way, why it won't be for want of warning, both from PROFESSOR HARRIS, the Commission, and from

'My dear *Mr Punch's* obeajent servant, 'JEAMES PLUSH.'

June 1846

Libby Purves
THREE WOMEN IN A BOAT

WE took a paperback Jerome K. Jerome with us, for inspiration. To give us some sort of alternative view of the whole sordid adventure ...

It was a glorious morning, late spring or early summer, as you care to take it, when the dainty sheen of grass and leaf is blushing to a deeper green; and the year seems like a fair young maid, trembling with strange, wakening pulses on the brink of womanhood ...

It was, as a matter of fact, a cold, grey, inglorious Saturday which saw three travellers – all well over the brink of womanhood and down the other side – assemble doggedly beside the River Thames. The legend of *Three Men In A Boat* has long haunted the English summer; young men, periodically, set out three-at-a-time in double-sculling skiffs to retrace the innocently rollicking path of George and Harris and J.K.J. Sometimes they do it for television, making much of their big manly blazers, deep laughs, sweaty backs and fancy feathering of the oars (to prove they were at Trinity, not the LSE), sometimes they do it for private satisfaction. Yet another trio of wistful neo-Victorians shot under Cookham bridge even as we watched, their bodies between their knees. Women were deemed suitable in 1889 only to shriek and giggle and tangle up the tow-lines in their frilly skirts; an undemanding brief. But, in one of those moments of inspiration which come to editors in between taking the big cigar out of their mouths and putting it back in again, the idea had sprung full-fledged to Coren's master brain. 'Put three *women* in a boat! Terrific!'

So he was standing now, with a look of shifty alarm, watching the fragile boat unloaded from a trolley. My George and my Harris were beside him: Merrily Harpur, an artistic game-fisherwoman with wild, pale eyes and a brisk motherly way with wildlife ('Mayfly, dearest, *do* move over. I need that seat now') and Mandy Rice-Davies. The latter, at that moment, was gazing wryly downstream towards Cliveden House, former home of sundry Astors and the scene, two decades ago, of those entertainments which led John Profumo to the obscurity of Good Works and Mandy to lasting fame for cheeking the judge from the witness-box. 'An *unlikely* trio,' typed someone up at the *Daily Mail*, ruefully pushing aside his Thesaurus and his *Big Boy's Book of Libel Law*; but we saw nothing unlikely about it. When you are planning to sit in a small, tippy, roofless boat and tow thirteen miles upstream, pursued by a boatful of grinning oafs from *Breakfast Time*, you do well to choose your companions carefully. And Mandy, on one previous meeting, had struck me forcibly as a girl to go up the Amazon with. She combines the serpentine wisdom of forty years' ritzy survival with the effortless, unpretending charm of the Worst Girl In The School. And she has been out East of Suez and seen a thing or two, founded an Israeli glossy magazine, run fashion shows in the desert during the Yom Kippur War, written one-and-three-quarter books, toured to wide acclaim in a Stoppard, and is currently bringing the house down as Helga the Wronged Wife in another touring farce. My faith in the girl was confirmed by the way she turned now from her reverie politely, to answer some query on her present occupation. 'Oh,' she said casually, 'I'll be in *A Bedful Of Foreigners* in Wolverhampton on Monday.' Not a smirk, not a scowl. 'By gum,' breathed Coren in the background. 'Now that's a girl who'll pull a good oar!'

The *Breakfast Time* crew, rushed out expensively to Cookham on the promise of a story consisting entirely of monosyllables (like 'three' and 'boat') which would not give their latest autocuties too much trouble to introduce, began filming Mandy's blonde curls, frilly blouse, and designer-faded jeans with enthusiasm. Harpur and I hovered in thankful anonymity behind, she darkly sinister in black shades and a Pembroke College blazer four sizes too big, I solid and reliably boaty in a quilted jacket and mouldy sun-hat. A dreadful apparition in a pastel-striped blazer and BBC Wardrobe boater appeared, and began chirruping into his microphone. Grey clouds thickened overhead, and a keen chill wind whistled over the troubled waters. A headwind to us. 'Sure you can row uptide?' asked a yard man. 'Fastest current I seen for a bit, running now.' Grimly, we stuffed sleeping-bags into dustbin liners and tried to stow Mandy's Gucci hold-all. The boat – a long, thin, delicate varnished shell – shuddered, tipped, and took aboard a gallon of icy water as Harpur landed heavily in the bow. 'Christ,' muttered the boatyard man, shielding his eyes. 'All ready, girls?' beamed Mister Breakfast Time, as the stuffed Alsatian fell off its cute perch on the camping-hoops and struck me in the eye (one small improvement womankind made on Jerome K. was a pee-free dog). Mandy descended, catlike, into the stern, and drew up her white golfing shoes in resigned horror at the slopping of water around the picnic-hamper. Drops of rain began to fall, and the empty river swirled grimly beneath us, hell-bent for Cookham weir. I took both oars, determined to sell my life dearly; Mandy looked curiously at the steering-lines, with the air of a girl who had pulled herself out of tight corners by frailer strings than these. 'I didn't mean it to be like this,' muttered Coren. 'I meant there to be crowds, and sunshine, and all the river life ... people ... blazers ...' He opened a bottle of our champagne with an air of desperate festivity, and drank from it.

> *'Right it is,' we answered; and with Harris at the sculls and I*
> *at the tiller-lines, and Montmorency, unhappy and deeply*
> *suspicious, in the prow, out we shot onto the waters which, for*
> *a fortnight, were to be our home.*

Well, not a fortnight. Couple of days, more like; just as far as Henley. We shot onto the waters all right, though. Eighty-year-old skiffs are made to shoot along like varnished glittering fishes, for a tenth of the effort that moves a great white slab of motorboat. With a rather eccentric motion, caused by my having learned rowing in rubber dinghies on the sea (short, deep strokes) and Merrily Harpur

having learned her technique by standing under a big hat at Henley (long, languorous river-strokes), we nonetheless made impressive speed. And gleams of sunshine began to appear, and our surroundings to seem more benevolent. And, 'Oh, darling coot!' cried Harpur ecstatically, missing a stroke. On this dull, forbidding Bank Holiday the river life was all feathered; and none the worse for that. 'Dear ducks, look at them. Having a gang-bang.'

Jerome, gentle man, had an uncharacteristically savage view of the selfish riverside landowners who placed forbidding notice-boards on their land. The feeling returned, as fresh as he had known it, to haunt us in turn. NO MOORING ... NO LANDING ... STRICTLY PRIVATE decorated the banks; huge slavering Rottweilers ran down to the waterside as we slipped inoffensively under the bank to keep out of the tide. We received a cold glance from a middle-aged woman apparently gardening in a Judge's full-bottomed wig. Merrily thought it might have been curlers, but Mandy and I were pretty sure. Thames Valley richies may have their little quirks, surely; if the wife of some unerotic arms-dealer chooses to boost her thrill-quotient by putting on the black cap every time she throttles a slug, who are we to condemn?

We rowed on, Mandy displaying an unexpected neatness of stroke on no experience. Faint pains began to shoot along forgotten ligaments, but rowing is not a bad life: no responsibilities for steering, no need to look out, just keep the oar moving. Extraordinary follies reared on the bank: gigantic thatched cottages, half-timbered bungalows. As the sun warmed, a few boats began to move; bottle-nosed persons in small cruise liners puttered past, their foredecks festooned with illicit women. After two hours, stiffening, we stopped for lunch. 'It's a good thing we're English,' said Mandy, sitting in a goose-turd,

"So this is hay fever!"

and critically extracting a lump of chèvre and a digestive biscuit from the damp hamper. We opened another bottle of pink champagne, and gazed hopefully along the meagrely-forested bank for a convenience. Not very hopefully.

Did you know that if you are a woman, and you squat discreetly behind a bush, at the critical moment there will be a burst of wild laughter from some passing boat? Wild laughter unconnected, of course, with any gap in the vegetation, for what Briton would dream of guffawing at such a discovery? But still ...

'What – only borscht, cream, chives, lobster and chicken mayonnaise, chocolate mousse, and absolutely nothing to propitiate swans?'

It helps if you are slightly drunk. We stepped smartly back into the good ship *Jezebel*, and proceeded at a steady 2 mph over the rushing tide. Gradually we became Left-wing; moving along at water-level between towering white gin-palaces; propelling yourself by the sweat of your back past the monstrous follies of wealth, has a radicalising effect. Mandy's chic waterproof ski-top (the only short-sleeved raincoat on the Thames) took a raffish, *sans culotte* aspect, and Harpur's red-and-white spotted neckerchief and misshapen roll-up cigarettes gave an authentic air of jacquerie. For who says that Britain has no Disneyland? The Thames banks, running down from Marlow lock, are Disneyland absolute. We sweated past concrete castles, past giant Venetian palazzos made of half-logs, past Islamic minarets and pink thatch and – perched on a steep bank – an actual half-timbered swimming-pool. As the heat grew, the stream against us increased, and the sweat ran into our eyes, it was like rowing through someone's disordered fantasy. The cooling bottle was passed from hand to hand. 'Motorboats!' cried Harpur, waving a disintegrating fag. 'What do they know of Life?' We had been bidden to tea at 3.30 at the Compleat Angler. We rowed with silver teapots hovering in front of us, like a mirage.

With beginners' luck, we shot into Marlow lock to fill the last long, thin space beside the motorboats. Unimpressed, the lock-keeper looked down half-a-mile at our dishevelled shapes. 'Got a current licence?' he snarled, as if suspecting it of having elapsed in 1949. We rose unsteadily on the tide, muttering about civil liberties. Seeing us closer, at his feet, he relented. 'You picked a fine day to try and row upstream, anyway,' he said, walking back to his machinery. 'Lot o'current. Mind the weir.' We edged out.

'The WEIR!' shrieked Harpur, suddenly noticing it. Marlow weir is a vast, curving, sluicing Niagara: a hole in the world. The Com-

pleat Angler is just next to it. To bring a skiff alongside you have to
ship your cumbrous inside oar, by taking it completely out of the
rowlock. To put it in again for propulsion takes a moment or two;
should the official bank-grabber fail to make contact, or end up with
a handful of grass as the bow bounces off, you have rather less than
two moments before the weir gets you. One go at this was enough.
We escaped, and circled under the bridge for a moment, undecided.
The man at Marlow Rowing Club, his moustache a-quiver, gave a
welcoming hail: 'YOU CAN'T MOOR 'ERE, IT'S PRIVATE.'
'You'd think' said Merrily, quivering, 'that they'd have more chiv-
alry at a *rowing club* when they see women in trouble.' Sudden female
machismo gripped me, rowing wildly: 'WE ARE NOT IN
TROUBLE,' I shrieked. 'WE ARE PERFECTLY ALL RIGHT!'
'We have had a Brush With Death,' said Mandy, firmly. Finally, we
tied up to Marlow Rowing Club after all. Moustache even took our
rope, drawn by curiosity, 'Yer own boat, is it?' No, we said evasively,
'just delivering it to Henley.' 'Ah, sort of freelance boat-deliverers,
are you? Move a few eights upriver for us, would you?' Yes, yes,
anything. We tottered damply across to the hotel ('once frequented
by famous *Punch* Artist Phil May' – Merrily was moderately thrilled)
and squelched thankfully up to the tasteful pink marblette powder-
room.

In the end, we were so early that the *Mail* photographer, who
alone had caught up with us, had to pay £24 for our plateful of scones
and strawberry tarts. We ate it, in temporary truce with capitalism.

Then two bin-bags, suspiciously stuffed, floated by. 'Is that our sleeping-bags?' asked Mandy rather quietly. 'Oh God.' We watched fascinated. Suddenly the church bells opposite pealed out triumphantly. Revolutionary paranoia set in again. 'They wouldn't', I said shakily, 'ring the church bells just because our sleeping-bags had gone over the weir, would they? They don't hate us that much, even in Marlow, do they?'

It was, in the event, a wedding, and someone else's bundles adrift; but we felt a pressing need to row clear of the place. We did a bit of fancy feathering, to impress Moustache. Easy.

We had intended to capture a nice young man off some passing boat, and ask him to share our al fresco dinner, and sit afterwards under the stars, discoursing of life and philosophy until:

> ... *Night, like some great loving mother, gently lays her hand upon our fevered head, and turns our little tear-stained face up to hers and smiles, and though she does not speak, we know what she would say, and lay our hot flushed cheek against her bosom* ...

But the only likely-looking boat we passed had a man on board reading *Exchange and Mart*, in the company of a caged canary; and though he did not speak, we knew what he would say, and thought better of it.

It was agreed, regrettably, that since Jerome K. had slept in the boat, under the rotting canvas and wobbling hoops, I should do likewise; leaving Mandy and Merrily to occupy the pup-tent on the bank. Two dozen large heifers jostled and butted and trod in the supper as we erected this edifice by a secluded grove of young oaks opposite Medmenham Abbey; they plopped dung attractively next to our box of Prue Leith Chicken 'n' Lobster mayonnaise, trod on the chives for the bortsch, and urinated copiously and with pleasure around the bivouac. 'I always knew,' said Mandy thoughtfully, 'that I wouldn't like camping. I have this innate instinct not to be unhappy.' Harpur strove to spread a more positive attitude ('Oh look, we're moored to a rose-bush') while I baled a few more gallons of water from my bedroom-designate. The *Mail* photographer, a remarkable sleuth, loomed among the heifers and hopefully, we invited him to dinner. But after a quick look at the dripping oaks, the steaming cow-pats, the sullen, watchful band of Canada Geese and the wild fluttering of Merrily's vast blazer-sleeves as she hurled rice salad to some darling ducks, he followed the immemorial example of his kind, made his excuses, and left.

Even Harpur, as dusk fell, grew tart and morose. 'Did you know that she-ducks often drown because of the weight of males on top of them trying to mate? Nature is an absolute washout, in my view.' '*Rousseau*,' said Mandy, 'used to send his laundry home to his Mum.'

As to the succeeding night, let other pens dwell on guilt and misery. What thoughts passed through my head about Coren, about his narrow bloody sleeping-bag, about Jerome and English sentimentality and permeable canvas roofs, I will not enumerate. I will only observe that when, with aching and horribly pinioned arms, you have lain for two hours sleepless between plank and plank, you are actually quite glad of the diversion of a couple of vast Canada Geese bursting into your dim canvas tunnel, all wet skinny feet and hysterical wings. It is, at least, company.

At 3.30 the storm came. Claps of apocalyptic thunder; then lightning illumined the sodden green tunnel, etching the stark ribs of the ancient skiff. Some girlish giggling was heard from the tent, and the low comforting monotone of Merrily telling Mandy that oak groves were always the first to be hit by lightning.

We must all have slept, then. On waking, we had between us aged some forty-five years. Merrily began stiffly to operate her Patent Volcano Kettle with an old *Guardian*. Mandy commenced her toilette with an Evian vaporiser and a pot of cream, while I poured Perrier water on my hat and scrubbed briefly at my ruined features.

'Could you atomise enough into the kettle for us to have tea?'

It was, however, a beautiful day. And we saw a kingfisher as we drifted up to Hambleden Lock, and drank another bottle of the pink and bubbly in it, toasting the curious spectators as the swirling water threatened our scalloped, varnished, impossibly elegant Edwardian flanks. Life was good, at such moments.

So it would seem unnecessary to dwell too much on the later spectacle of Mandy Rice-Davies, urbane *femme du monde*, pathetically cadging cigarettes from strangers on the towpath while the rain ran in rivers down her slender neck; uncharitable to remark on the feeling which arose when Harpur decided on some fancy steering during a second monsoon downpour on the approach to Henley Bridge ('I wanted to see if we could *fit* through there'). I would prefer to think more of the high times than of the slow, sodden collapse of the ill-tied canvas as we lurched up to Hobbs's boat pontoons.

We half-ran up the soaking street towards the Angel for sustenance, Mandy dragging on her first cigarette since dawn.

'I have *never*', she said in mild outrage, 'smoked in the street in my life. Never.' And I felt a small pang of guilt at having reduced her to this.

But when the last morsel of food was shovelled in by six eager, blistered hands, and six sodden feet began to steam gratefully in the hotel's heat, Mandy stretched, and smiled contentedly, and flicked a lock of wet blonde hair from her eyes. 'I feel,' she announced, 'very well indeed.'

Well, she would, wouldn't she?

June 1985

A.A. Milne

WHEN WE WERE VERY YOUNG

XXV – HAPPINESS

JOHN had
Great Big
Waterproof
Boots on;
John had a
Great Big
Waterproof
Hat;
John had a
Great Big
Waterproof
Macintosh –
And that
(Said John)
Is
, That.

Ernest H. Shepard

June 1924